MOUNTAIN BIKE!
The Canadian Rockies

A GUIDE TO THE CLASSIC TRAILS

2ND EDITION

WARD CAMERON

Menasha
Ridge
Press

Cataloging-in-Publication data available from the Library of Congress.

ISBN 1-55068-098-6

Photos by the author unless otherwise credited
Maps by Ink Spot, a design company™
Production by Manuscript Ink™
Cover photo by Dennis Coello
Cover and text design by Suzanne Holt

Menasha Ridge Press
P.O. Box 43673
Birmingham, Alabama 35243
USA
Distributed by The Globe Pequot Press

Vanwell Publishing
1 Northrup Crescent
St. Catharines, Ontario L2R 7S2
Canada
(800) 661-6136

All trails described in this book are legal for mountain bikes. But rules can change—especially for off-road bicycles, the new kid on the outdoor recreation block. Land-access issues and conflicts between cyclists, hikers, equestrians, and other users can cause the rewriting of recreation regulations on public lands, sometimes resulting in a ban of mountain bike use on specific trails. That's why it's the responsibility of each rider to check and make sure that he or she rides only on trails where mountain biking is permitted.

CAUTION

Outdoor recreational activities are by their very nature potentially hazardous. All participants in such activities must assume the responsibility for their own actions and safety. The information contained in this guidebook cannot replace sound judgment and good decision-making skills, which help reduce risk exposure, nor does the scope of this book allow for disclosure of all the potential hazards and risks involved in such activities.

Learn as much as possible about the outdoor recreational activities in which you participate, prepare for the unexpected, and be cautious. The reward will be a safer and more enjoyable experience.

CONTENTS

CONTENTS

iv CONTENTS

BANFF NATIONAL PARK AND AREA

MOUNTAIN BIKE! · Map Legend

Ride trailhead

| Primary bike trail | Direction of travel | Optional bike trail and trailhead | Other trail | Hiking-only trail |

| Trans Canada Highway (with exit no.) | US Interstate | State or provincial routes | Other paved roads | Unpaved, gravel, or dirt roads (may be 4WD only) |

| Scale | True north | Cities and towns | Forest Service roads | Provincial or state border |

Vancouver ◉
Mt. Vernon ◉

| Public lands* | Ski trails | Ski lift | River or stream |

✈ Airport

♥ Archaeological or historical site

Boat ramp

▲ Campground (CG)

≡ Cattle guard

⚰ Cemetery or gravesite

♠ Church

Cliff, escarpment, or outcropping

🚰 Drinking water

Fire tower or lookout

Falls or rapids

Ⓟ Parking

Gate

♠ House or cabin

Lodging

Mountain or butte

Mountain pass

△ Mountain summit
3312 (elevation in feet)

✗ Mine or quarry

Observatory

Park office or ranger station

ᴛ Picnic area

Power line or pipeline

Rest rooms

Spring

Stable, corral, or ranch

Swimming area

Transmission towers

Tunnel or bridge

* Remember, private property exists in and around our national forests.

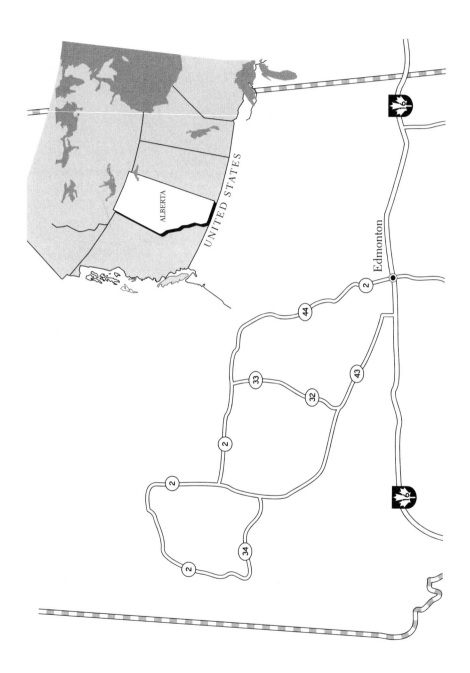

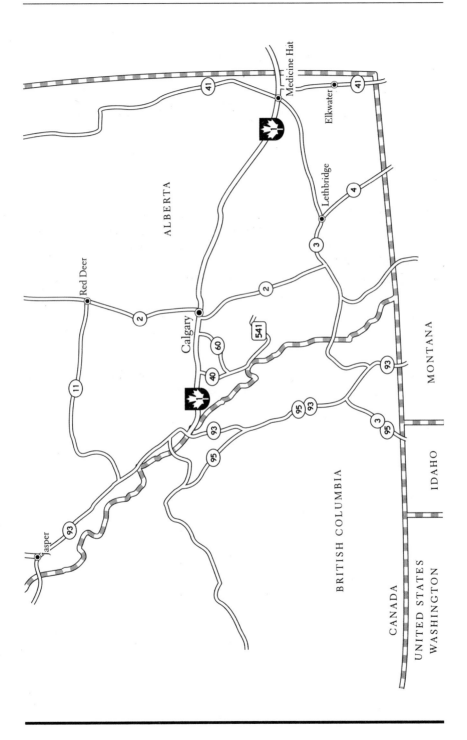

ACKNOWLEDGMENTS

This book could not have been accomplished without the support of bike shops throughout Alberta. Many locals revealed their favourite trails at the risk of the rides becoming more popular through publication of this book. I also want to thank the staff of the Alberta Forest Service office in Blairmore, Alberta, for its help in locating some of the well-hidden rides of the southern Rockies.

Sue Baker deserves a special thank you for standing by me during the two years it took to research this guide. She rode some of the trails with me and picked me up after some of the ordeals. Her encouragement helped keep me going when my mind said "quit."

Finally, I want to thank my parents, Bruce and Shirley Cameron, for teaching me the value of perseverance, a lesson repeatedly tested during this project. I hope I have picked up a little of their strength.

FOREWORD

Welcome to *North America by Mountain Bike*, a series of more than 20 books designed to provide all-terrain bikers with the information they need to find and ride the very best trails everywhere. Whether you're new to the sport and don't know where to pedal, or an experienced mountain biker who wants to learn the classic trails in another region, this series is for you. Drop a few bucks for the book, spend an hour with the detailed maps and route descriptions, and you're prepared for the finest in off-road cycling.

My role as editor of this series was simple: First, find a mountain biker who knows the area and loves to ride. Second, ask that person to spend a year researching the most popular and very best rides around. And third, have that rider describe each trail in terms of difficulty, scenery, condition, elevation change, and all other categories of information that are important to trail riders. "Pretend you've just completed a ride and met up with fellow mountain bikers at the trailhead," I told each author. "Imagine their questions, be clear in your answers."

But the overwhelming majority of trails are discovered and pedaled by our authors themselves, then compared with dozens of other routes to determine if they qualify as "classic"—that area's best in scenery and cycling fun. If you've ever had the experience of pioneering a route from outdated topographic maps, or entering a bike shop to request information from local riders who would much prefer to keep their favorite trails secret, or know how it is to double- and triple-check data to be positive your trail information is correct, then you have an idea of how each of our authors has labored to bring about these books. You and I, and all mountain bikers, are the richer for their efforts.

You'll get more out of this book if you take a moment to read the Introduction explaining how to read the trail listings. The "Topographic Maps" section will help you understand how useful topos will be on a ride, and will also tell you where to get them. Those of you who have not traveled the backcountry might find "Hitting the Trail" of particular value.

In addition to the material above, newcomers to mountain biking might want to spend a minute with the glossary (see page 349) so that terms like hardpack, single-track, and waterbars won't confuse you when you come across them .

Dennis Coello, St. Louis

PREFACE

The Canadian Rockies offer a wide range of landscapes and a sense of the un-explored. These qualities attract millions of people to challenge this wilderness each year. It's a wide-open area with few people, but lots of places to disappear into and explore. For the mountain biker, it's a place that begs for exploration.

The Canadian Rockies straddle the Continental Divide and the boundary between Alberta and British Columbia. This alpine landscape provides endless challenges. The trails are often long with difficult gradients. Riding straight up or straight down, it's a rare pleasure to find a trail without dramatic changes. It takes time to acclimate to the altitude, and a trail's steep character will test the fittest set of lungs. Once you get hooked on the Rockies, you'll find yourself re-turning time and again for the challenge of the high country.

As an additional treat, this book describes one wonderful area providing a mixture of plains with a bit of the foothills—Cypress Hills Provincial Park. It's also about as far from the mountains as possible, while remaining in Alberta. The Cypress Hills, like the Rockies, rise high above the surrounding prairies.

As I set out to write this guide, I had little understanding of the magnitude of the task I had so casually undertaken. As someone who makes quick decisions and then has to figure out how to accomplish them, I buried myself in trail maps and regional guidebooks. I began reacquainting myself with old friends—those trails I return to over and over—and followed that by exploring unknown areas. I found myself riding the ridges and retracing the footsteps of early pioneers. Many of the trails we now ride were originally designed to provide access to re-mote areas in case of forest fire. Since the helicopter has made that access ob-solete, these former fire roads offer exciting cycle routes today.

With the wide variety of trail options in this area, it's easy to understand why mountain biking tends to be an all-consuming activity. I hope you'll spend some time exploring the Canadian Rockies and become as hooked on this area as I am.

THE WEATHER

The weather can be anything and everything. We like to say: "If you don't like the weather, wait five minutes!" This is a land where the winter temperatures can vary from –51°C to +15°C (–60°F to +50°F). Not only is the variation huge, but the rapidity of the change is incredible. In January 1983, temperatures in Calgary, Alberta, rose from –17°C to 13°C (1.4°F to 55°F) in just four hours. During the summer months, temperatures can drop equally fast. Midafternoon storms appear from nowhere and disappear just as quickly. Snow in July is normal.

Many things affect the climate of western Canada and result in rapidly changeable weather. With our northern latitude, generally 50° and north, the sun's rays reach a maximum angle of 65°. We never get true overhead light in the north.

The altitude also creates havoc in our climate. Thin air not only contains less oxygen but also holds less heat, leading to temperature drops of 0.6°C for every 100 m (1°F for every 300 ft.) of elevation gain. This means that at 3,000 m (10,000 ft.), the air temperature will be 16°C (33°F) colder than at sea level at the same latitude. Stated another way, a rise of 300 m (1,000 ft.) will provide the same change in temperature as driving 480 km (280 mi.) north. A seemingly innocent rise of 30 m (100 ft.) delays spring by one day.

To complicate things further, temperature doesn't always drop with elevation. The mountains have a way of turning the weather upside down, occasionally creating a rise in temperature as you climb. Often, cold air, which is heavier, will settle into the valleys, displacing warmer air. This phenomenon, which causes the temperature to rise as you climb, may be accompanied by a layer of clouds indicating the condensation level.

Mountains also influence the wind. In the Rockies, less than ten days a year are completely calm due to the influence of the mountains on the prevailing winds. These same, predominantly western winds affect the weather. Heading inland from the Pacific Coast, they begin as moisture-laden clouds that cool rapidly as they climb uphill to traverse the Rockies. This drop in temperature forces them to release much of their moisture as snow and rain long before they reach the eastern side of the Continental Divide, creating a wetter, lusher ecosystem on the western side of the mountains compared to the opposite reality on the eastern slopes. To illustrate, Vancouver receives 1,113 mm (43.8 in.) of annual precipitation, while Revelstoke, still in the interior of British Columbia, gets 1,064 mm (41.2 in.). On the other side of the Rockies, the rain shadow produced by this loss of moisture as the weather climbs eastward causes Banff to receive only 400–600 mm (15.8–23.6 in.).

Not to be outdone, the prairies also influence our weather. Despite normally western winds, the eastern slopes often feel the sting of easterlies during early summers or cold winters. In this case, the normally westerly flowing weather patterns reverse. With the weather patterns moving eastward, the clouds are still moisture-laden when they reach the mountains. As they move west, they cool, and we find ourselves digging out the rain gear. This "upslope weather," as it is known, can sit on us for days at a time. The story has a bright side, however, and it's a west side story. This pattern is easily identified by the presence of clear weather on the western side of the Continental Divide. Thus, traveling west may help you escape the grasp of an upslope storm.

Upward movement of weather can also occur on a much more local basis. Orographic lifting causes water droplets to evaporate during the day, then rise and rapidly cool. This localized pattern often results in clouds around the summits of certain mountains on otherwise cloudless days. Since the patterns vary with local geography, if you move from one side of a valley to another, you may encounter huge variations in weather. Orographic lifting can also lead to orographic weather. As the warm air condenses around the mountaintops, it accumulates. By mid- to late afternoon, enough moisture has condensed to cause a sudden, torrential downpour. This type of storm is usually short-lived and localized, but it can be extremely violent and prone to lightning. When you're mountain biking on hot summer days, it's important to be on the lookout for these sudden storms. Although this weather pattern is closely connected to the mountains, the Cypress Hills, as a high point surrounded by much lower plains, experiences similar weather disturbances. Since the weather systems must rise rapidly to climb over the hills, they drop moisture as they rise.

When riding in the mountains, barometric pressure decreases about one-thirtieth for every 300 m (1,000 ft.) climbed. Since the atmosphere is thinner, it's less effective in deflecting incoming solar radiation than is the case with an area at sea level. In fact, at around 3,658 m (12,000 ft.), the radiation can be as much as 280 percent higher than at sea level. This condition is accompanied by an increase in the intensity of violet and ultraviolet radiation. I don't need to mention the higher potential for sunburns and other maladies caused by too much sun. Don't forget your sunscreen!

This increased solar radiation, along with increases in altitude, has a significant effect on air and ground temperatures. Since those surfaces exposed to sunlight heat rapidly, and those not exposed stay cool, the difference between sun and shade is drastic. This difference can be as great as 22–28°C (40–50°F), a major factor in allowing some of our remnant glaciers to survive today. By sticking to the north-facing slopes, glaciers receive significantly less sunlight and melt at a much slower rate.

For the same reason, mountain locations heat up rapidly during the day and cool just as rapidly in the evening. As a result, daily temperature variations in alpine areas are much higher than those at lower elevations.

For humans, one danger of high-altitude travel is mountain sickness. Caused by low air pressure, the symptoms include nausea and headaches accompanied by weakness. This low pressure makes it difficult for our bodies to extract the oxygen we need to survive. Some people begin to show the symptoms as they head above 2,500–3,000 m (8,200–9,800 ft.). The effect on individuals varies; some people may not feel the effects at all, while others may rapidly begin to suffer as they ascend. The secret is to acclimatize and to listen to your body. If it says head down, listen to it.

THE LAND

When we look at the Canadian Rockies today, we see a land of contrasts. We usually focus on the western mountains, as they attract the majority of our tourism. Ironically, without those mountains we wouldn't have the prairies. The predominant weather patterns move east over the mountains and lose most of their moisture before they reach Alberta. Wrung dry before they depart the high country, they leave a rain shadow behind the mountains—we know this area as the prairies. The true prairies are very limited in area and are directly in the shadow of these rocky sentinels. Most of what we call the plains today was forested at one time and part of the Aspen Parkland. These lands eventually fell under the plow, and the park land disappeared from almost 90 percent of its original range. This area is now our most productive farmland. The true prairies are incredibly dry and arid, but with the assistance of irrigation, they also produce excellent crops.

When most people think of the Rocky Mountains, they think of the entire chain of mountains along the western part of this continent. However, within this larger definition of the Rockies lie dozens of localized ranges with different characteristics. The true Rocky Mountains comprise only one of these ranges, and this book describes only the northern section of these true Rockies. Of Canada's western mountains, the Rockies comprise the most easterly range of cordillera. They stretch approximately 150 km (93 mi.), from slightly west of Calgary, to Golden, along the Trans Canada Highway (Highway 1). In the north, along the Yellowhead Highway (Highway 16), the Rocky Mountains comprise the area between Hinton, Alberta, and Valemount, British Columbia. To the south, along the Crowsnest Highway (Highway 3), their reach includes the area to the east of the Crowsnest Pass in Alberta to Cranbrook, British Columbia.

Using this definition, the Canadian Rockies are a narrow band of mountains trending in a southeast-northwest direction. Narrow but not insignificant, this slender belt of rock includes all of the highest peaks in this country.

These mountains provide some of the most rugged and challenging riding in Canada. Because of the limitations of landscape and elevation, many of the trails are out-and-back, with limited loop options. When possible, I have tried to provide a circular option, even if it requires some roadside riding.

The Canadian Rockies are the result of a series of collisions between two continental plates, the North American Plate, on which we sit, and the Pacific Plate. During the first collision, which occurred on the West Coast approximately 175 million years ago, the Pacific Plate was forced beneath the North American Plate, sending huge compressional forces inland. This set off the first period of mountain building, or orogeny as these events are technically labeled. During the Columbia Orogeny (it formed British Columbia's Columbia Mountains, made up of the Caribous, Selkirks, Purcells, and Monashees), the shock wave moved eastward and forced huge masses of rock to crack and slide up over their neighbours. This thrust faulting was instrumental in the formation of the western mountains. The shock wave began piling up the western ranges of the Canadian Rockies, and then the main ranges, around 120 million years ago.

The second collision occurred about 85 million years ago and set off a new series of shock waves that began the Laramide Orogeny. The force behind this second collision provided the energy to form the front ranges and foothills of the Canadian Rockies. The wave died out as it approached Calgary, so the prairies were left undisturbed.

The mountains were originally much larger than they are today. Once they were exposed, the agents of water, wind, and ice began wearing them down and washing them into the oceans. In time they may completely disappear—that is, if another period of mountain building doesn't interrupt the process.

Compared to the mountains, glaciers are a recent occurrence. Arriving on the scene around 100,000 years ago, they have had a dramatic impact on the landscape. Glaciers are a very special type of ice. Unlike the brittle ice we know and love, glacial ice acts more like an extremely thick liquid. As ice accumulates into huge masses, immense pressure is imposed on the lower layers. This pressure allows the ice to flow very slowly under the force of gravity. On the glacier surface, the ice isn't under pressure, so it remains brittle and forms huge crevices, or cracks, as it moves over obstacles.

Contrary to popular belief, glaciers are always moving—even during the hottest days of summer. Sometimes they simply melt back from the toe faster than they move forward. If a glacier moves forward about 18 m (60 ft.) in a year, but melts backward 23 m (75 ft.) during the summer, then the net movement is 5 m (16 ft.) up the valley. We call this a receding glacier, and it is the condition of most glaciers in the area today.

Glaciers deserve a lot of the credit for the many roads and trails through the Rockies. Before the last Ice Age, most of the valleys had been carved by the action of streams, which left extremely deep, sharp, V-shaped valleys. As glaciers came onto the scene, they inherited the streams' drainage patterns and slowly sculpted the land into wide, U-shaped valleys. This action made later exploration and development in this area much easier (although some of the old-timers who built the Banff/Jasper and other highways in the area would dispute that fact).

A glacier picks up rocks and debris along its margins and carries this material as it moves down a valley. As these rocks become incorporated into the ice, they form a powerful abrasive, slowly scraping and scouring the valley bottom. As you might imagine, the rocks are quickly ground into a fine powder, known as rock flour, which then makes its way into streams and lakes. Incredibly fine, this powder stays suspended in our mountain lakes for several days. As light hits the surface of these lakes, the rock flour reflects only the blue and green wavelengths of light. This process gives the lakes the incredible colours that are known the world over.

THE PLANTS AND ANIMALS

The area described here has a diverse plant life, which is a reflection of its varied landscape. Each landscape manifests itself in the plant life that it supports. The mountain summits, with their steep relief, hold little plant life, while lower down, lush forests of lodgepole pine and white spruce dominate. Each region creates a unique interrelationship between its plants and its animals.

The plains of Alberta are relatively arid and contain few trees. At one time the wide expanses of grasslands were maintained by a combination of fire, lack of moisture, and grazing (i.e., bison). The plant life reflected this open, dry character and contained many grasses and sun-loving wildflowers.

Originally, the Aspen Parkland was much more extensive than the true prairie. A collection of trembling aspen groves intermittently covering an arid fescue grassland, it provides some of the province's most productive farmland.

Today, almost 90 percent of the Aspen Parkland has fallen under the plow, yet it still covers 11 percent of the province, making it Alberta's second largest ecoregion. Within the parkland, south-facing slopes are often devoid of tree life, but the cool river valleys see more diverse growth.

The plains and parkland provide a wonderfully productive habitat for wildlife. Small ponds come alive with waterfowl. Cattle churn up insects, which attract insect-eating birds, such as the cowbird. The fences along the roadways often provide a perch for hawks waiting for one of the province's endless supply of ground squirrels. Coyotes also wander the fields, looking for squirrels or even smaller morsels (mice and voles). Large grazing animals like the white-tailed deer and, farther east, the pronghorn take advantage of the open grazing. Sheltered areas provide cover for forest-dwelling birds like the great horned owl and cedar waxwing.

Moving west, rising altitudes bring about changes in the plant and animal communities. Three main ecosystems, the Montane, Boreal Foothills, and Boreal Uplands, combine at low elevation to create a diverse forest system typical of the foothills and lower eastern slopes. Wind-blasted valleys often show tough stands of Douglas fir and limber pine. They thrive in areas with extensive chinook activity, including the Bow Valley and Crowsnest Pass areas. Further upslope, we begin to see stands of lodgepole pine and white spruce providing a solid wall of evergreen. The understory depends on the penetration of sun beneath the trees. Bearberry, buffaloberry, and juniper provide much of the ground cover. Beneath the tall lodgepole pines, the delicate calypso orchid may show its head during June. Sunny slopes explode with wildflowers, while moist areas show a lush growth of cow parsnip and bog birch.

Wildlife abound in these low-elevation forests. The white-tailed deer and mule deer, along with elk, moose, and, in a few areas, mountain caribou, can be seen constantly browsing. Black bear are more commonly encountered than grizzlies, as grizzlies prefer higher elevations. Wolves and coyotes, along with the occasional cougar, may also be seen.

A climb in altitude brings a change in the plant and animal communities. The subalpine region begins at approximately 1,675 m (5,500 ft.). White spruce gives way to Engelmann spruce, and lodgepole pine disappears. Subalpine fir becomes common, and its sticky resin blisters will cover anyone who mistakenly leans against them. As you climb, the trees begin to exhibit a stunted nature—the effects of altitude become evident. In the upper extent of the subalpine region, the trees, some of which may be hundreds of years old, have been reduced to low clumps of shrublike vegetation. Avalanche slopes keep trees cleared, allowing a lush growth of sun-loving plants like hedysarum, glacier lily, and cow parsnip to thrive.

In the subalpine zone, diverse vegetation attracts a variety of wildlife. Many animals associated with the higher alpine area actually spend more time in the subalpine. These include bighorn sheep, mountain goat, grizzly bear, and cougar. Even elk and moose feed in the extensive subalpine meadows. Bird life includes the flicker, pileated woodpecker, and red-breasted nuthatch. The pine marten and flying squirrel also call the subalpine home. During the winter, heavy snow cover makes it difficult for animals to stay in this area. Some migrate to the valley bottoms, while others head upslope to the windswept summits. Ptarmigan are one of the few creatures capable of toughing out the winter in the heavy snows of this region.

The alpine zone is easily identified by a total lack of trees and begins between 2,200 and 2,500 m (7,218–8,200 ft.). This landscape is difficult, with endless challenges for plants looking to get a roothold. The growing season may be only a few months long, and the climate is similar to that of the arctic tundra. Flowers like the paintbrush, western anemone, and alpine forget-me-not add a splash of colour to this rugged landscape.

A variety of survival strategies allows alpine wildflowers to thrive. Some have specifically adapted to this climate and aren't found in the lower elevations, where the competition is much greater. Since the growing season is often too short to allow seeds to germinate, many wildflowers spread out vegetatively by using long, horizontal shoots. This allows the flowers to colonize the alpine faster than if they depended on those rare seeds that managed to put down roots.

The open nature of the alpine region provides plenty of forage for bighorn sheep and mountain goat. In the winter, high winds help keep the ridges clear of snow, allowing the animals to find sufficient food. Occasionally, deer, elk, or moose may wander upslope during warm summer weather. Pika and marmot call the rocky scree slopes home, and ptarmigan eat the soft buds of the willows.

The ruggedness of the alpine country is also what makes this area so fragile. It has taken hundreds—if not thousands—of years to develop. A single mis-placed footstep or bike tread can erase many years' worth of colonization—not to mention some very special plants. When you travel through the alpine zone, try to stay on the trail. This precaution will minimize the impact and ensure the flowers' return for a recurring engagement.

BEARS

Bears are a concern when you're traveling in the mountains. Although your chances of encountering bears during your wilderness forays are rare, you still need to understand something about these hefty hunters. Mountain biking, with its borderline out-of-control nature, is a natural recipe for disaster. I know one rider who hit a black bear while riding full tilt. Screaming down a steep hill, he rounded a corner too quickly for either to react. Luckily, he chose one direction to exit, the bear chose another. This collision could have had a very different ending. It's important to keep in mind that we are not the only users of trail sys-tems and that other human, and nonhuman, users also take advantage of these convenient travel corridors.

How do you tell the difference between a black bear and a grizzly? Some would advise you to climb a tree. If it climbs up after you, it's a black bear; if it pushes the tree down, it's a grizzly. Of course, there are easier ways to distinguish one bruin from another. Black bears may be any colour, from black to white. Cinnamon- and blond-coloured black bears are very common in the west. The black bear's absence of a grizzly-like shoulder hump is one of its most distinctive features. Also, the face of a grizzly is slightly dished in: it almost looks as if someone took a club to its face. Black bears are similar to dogs in appearance, with a straight line from the forehead to the tip of the nose.

Vegetation accounts for more than 75 percent of the diet of both black bears and grizzlies. Early in the season, they look for various members of the pea family, like hedysarum and sweet vetch. You may see them digging for roots or munching down dandelions. Later in the season, as berries ripen, the buffaloberry becomes a staple of the bears' diet. They supplement these with other berries, carrion, and, in some cases, garbage.

Grizzlies do more digging than black bears. As a result, they have longer claws and a huge muscular shoulder hump. Black bears and grizzlies not only excavate roots and tubers, they also try to dig up marmot and ground squirrel nests, often tearing up large areas. It takes a lot of work to get one ground squirrel, but ground squirrels are high in fat, and bears need a lot of fat to get them through the next winter.

Bears are well adapted to their alpine environment and help add an air of mystery to life in the mountains. When in bear country, you need to add caution to your outdoor excursions. Have a great ride, but keep those eyes open!

THE PEOPLE

Throughout the West, local natives have hunted and fished for more than 12,000 years. That may not seem so long, until you realize that 12,000 years ago the glaciers were still the predominant landform in the mountains. Archaeologists believe that during the Ice Age a land bridge joined Siberia to Alaska. Around 12,000 years ago, the ancestors of all the native Indians on this continent traveled across this bridge, wandered along an ice-free corridor between the mountain glaciers and the huge continental glacier (basically between Banff and Calgary, Alberta), and spread out from the southern margins of the ice sheets. Some of the oldest archaeological sites on the entire continent are located between Banff and Calgary. Basically, the ancestors of all of North America's Indians traveled through this area before heading south. Later, as the ice retreated, these natives advanced north and resettled the area now known as western Canada.

Many groups of native Indians reside within Alberta. The Blackfoot ruled the plains, raiding as far south as California. They were the most warlike of the province's natives and were widely feared. The Blackfoot nation was made up of the Blackfoot, Blood, and Piegan Indians. They were the first to acquire horses and guns, and they took pains to keep their enemies from becoming similarly equipped. The Sarcee were distinct from the Blackfoot but culturally related.

Another band, the Stoneys (related to the eastern Sioux), preferred the isolated valleys of the foothills and mountains. This preference insulated them from the brunt of smallpox epidemics in the 1830s and 1860s. These plagues decimated the western Indians; in some cases, pox killed 60–80 percent of their population in less than a year. A peaceful people, the Stoneys could be incredibly fierce when the situation demanded it; even the mighty Blackfoot knew not to arouse their anger. Stoney guides facilitated many of the white explorers' discoveries in the Rockies.

Native culture has left its mark on the West in the names of many of its geological features, and native folklore has added much to the richness of western Canada. Today, with a resurgence of native culture, we can see a bit of the past creeping into the present, and we're all the better for it.

One of the things that has always excited me about this area is the way our history, albeit short, reads like a good adventure novel. The early European history belongs to the Hudson Bay Company. As the oldest corporation on earth, it has operated consistently since its inception in 1670. As the competition for furs increased, the Hudson Bay men moved farther afield and eventually set up trading posts throughout the West. For generations, the Hudson Bay Company traded with the Indians of Alberta, and their posts became a vital part of life on the plains.

The Hudson Bay Company discouraged settlement in the West, believing that an influx of settlers would harm the fur trade. They kept all information on the fertile lands of Alberta tightly locked in their vaults, and it wasn't until 1858 that the riches of the West were finally discovered by the rest of Canada. John Palliser was commissioned to lead an expedition to do the first surveys of western Canada, and his subsequent report did much to pave the way for western expansion.

In 1869 the Hudson Bay Company relinquished its claim on its western holdings, and suddenly the West was left without any formal government representation. Without the stabilizing force of the Bay men, whiskey traders flooded north from Montana and began selling rotgut whiskey to the local natives. Within a few years, whiskey had decimated the character of the plains Indians, and it became clear that something had to be done. Finally, in 1873, the Northwest Mounted Police, the forerunners of today's Royal Canadian Mounted Police, were formed. They rode westward and quickly forced the whiskey traders south of the 49th parallel.

Alberta remained quiet until the railroad arrived in 1885. Suddenly the West was open for business. That same year a tiny preserve in the mountains became the precursor of Banff National Park, Canada's first national park. As trainload after trainload of settlers arrived on the plains, the fertile land of Alberta quickly filled up. Along the foothills, cattle ranchers set up shop. The former police outpost of Fort Calgary quickly grew in size. Fort Edmonton, a Hudson Bay outpost, grew at a slower pace, but later gained its own railroad.

Despite all this activity, Alberta remained part of the vast Northwest Territories and did not become a province until 1905. The province was built on agriculture, and since 1912 the Calgary Stampede has helped celebrate that heritage.

In 1914, the province's first oil well was opened in Turner Valley, southwest of Calgary. Suddenly the boom was on, and it continues today. Calgary alone hosts over 600 oil and gas companies. Much of today's oil comes from areas farther north, near Leduc, Alberta, but Calgary remains the oil industry headquarters.

In 1988, Calgary hosted the Winter Olympics, and suddenly a billion people were introduced to Alberta. Since this hugely successful event, tourism in the province has skyrocketed. Busload after busload of tourists flock to the mountains to take in the scenery, and the province looks to tourism to increase dramatically over the next ten years.

MOUNTAIN HEALTH AND SAFETY

Wood Ticks   Wood ticks are common in the Rockies, as they are in many other locations. But don't panic. We don't have the tiny deer ticks that are a problem in many areas of the United States. The wood tick looks like a small spider at 5 mm (0.2 in.) long. They are larger than deer ticks and easily seen and removed.

Spring is the main season to check for these eight-legged cling-ons. They climb to the top of grasses and other ground-based vegetation and wait for a potential host (i.e., you) to pass by. They grab you as you pass—they don't jump on you from trees—and then begin the search for a site to feed. If they don't find a suitable site, they drop off and wait for the next victim. Pants tucked into socks can discourage ticks from sticking around.

If they do find a nice dark, moist spot, they embed their mouthparts—only their mouthparts—and begin drawing blood. The females can swell to many times their original size, while males take only a small donation. Since they tend to search for a while before finding just the right feeding spot, a check immediately after your ride can often discover them before they embed. If they have already begun feeding, simply grab them and pull firmly until they come off. Make sure their mouthparts don't break off and stay in the wound, since such remnants can cause infections. Be sure to remove them with a pair of tweezers and disinfect the wound.

Lyme disease has not been recorded in this area yet. Wood ticks occasionally transmit Rocky Mountain spotted fever, a disease that, if left untreated, can be fatal. I have never heard of anyone contracting the disease, but it must be considered a possibility. The best defense is to make sure you check for ticks before they embed.

Ticks are a reality in the mountains. However, they are a small problem here compared to other areas, and it's uncommon to find more than a few in a season.

Beaver Fever   People once believed that the mountains were a place where you could dip your water bottle into a crystal-clear stream and taste some of the cleanest water in the world. This used to be true. Unfortunately, parasites can live in even the cleanest water. One such parasite is called *Giardia* ("gee-ARD-ee-uh") *lamblia*. So tiny that more than 15,000 can fit on the head of a pin, it takes only a dozen or so to bring on an unpleasant malady known as giardiasis. This is the most common gastrointestinal parasite in the world, and it seems to follow humans into the wilderness. The parasite is spread through feces, and poor backcountry hygiene has been instrumental in spreading it to even more remote areas. Giardiasis is often blamed on beavers—hence, the nickname "beaver fever." It can be transmitted by any warm-blooded animal, and all water sources must be considered suspect.

Symptoms include diarrhea, loss of appetite, abdominal cramps, nausea, weight loss, bloating, and excessive gas. Treatment includes large doses of the drug Flagyl, which kills *Giardia.*

Always fill your water bottle at home. Chemical treatments with tetraglycine hydroperiodide (sold under various brand names) will kill *Giardia,* but not

Cryptosporidium, the new protozoan on the block, so options include boiling or filtering and using iodine or chlorine to kill viruses. Filters must have an "absolute pore size" of four microns or smaller for *Giardia* and of one to two microns for *Crypto.*

Life with Layers This area is famous for more than just its mountains—it's also notorious for its changeable weather. Proper clothing is critical in the West. All too often, visitors head out onto the trails with just a light day pack, only to find themselves in trouble as temperatures suddenly drop. As rapidly as the weather can change, and with the potential for bikers to cover vast amounts of territory in a single day, the possibility of disaster is always near. Break a chain in the backcountry, and you could be in trouble if you don't have extra layers with you as evening—or an afternoon storm—sets in.

The secret to comfortable travel always involves carrying a pack with extra clothing. Since the climate can change from hot and sunny to cold and wet in a matter of minutes, various types of clothing are essential. Rather than carry a heavy coat for chilly weather, carry a series of thin layers that can be added to and removed as the weather changes. Thin layers help avoid sweating as you warm up during activity. Sweating may be a way of life in warmer climates, but it can be downright dangerous in cold weather. Wet clothing quickly draws heat away from the body and leads to a dangerous drop in body temperature. Layers allow you to regulate your body temperature as the weather, and your activity, dictates.

Don't forget to leave the cotton behind when you head west. When it gets wet, cotton can act like a giant sponge, remaining wet for long periods and drawing away body heat. Synthetics, like polypropylene, don't absorb moisture, so they retain their insulating ability regardless of the weather. They also help keep you dry by wicking moisture away from the body.

Hypothermia Hypothermia is characterized by a drop in the body's core temperature. It is caused by exposure to the cold and is a constant danger in the mountains. Watch for symptoms like slurred speech, loss of coordination, and drowsiness. As the condition worsens, the body actually stops shivering, and the patient may feel a sense of well-being—he just wants to stop for a nap.

This situation should be taken very seriously. Once the body enters a state of hypothermia, it loses the ability to warm itself. Wrapping the patient in blankets only serves to keep him cold; an external heat source is needed. Many books will tell you to remove your clothing and snuggle up with the patient in a sleeping bag, but acting on this advice doesn't work. The human body is well designed; as soon as we expose it to the cold skin of a hypothermia sufferer, our surface blood vessels shut down. Within a few minutes, our skin feels as cold as that of the cotton wearer. In situations where I've been required to perform this noble task, I found that an assembly line of warm bodies was required. As I became cold, I tagged the next person to take my place. This sounds silly, but it really does work.

In addition to human sources of warmth, other external heat sources can help greatly. If the patient is not nauseated, you can administer warm fluids. This can aid greatly in quick recovery.

Frostbite   Along with hypothermia, frostbite is another concern. Mountain bikers spend most of their time in contact with potentially frigid metal. Although we pad our handlebars, the brakes are usually very cold. Warm gloves are an important accessory, particularly for early-morning rides. Even a hot summer day can begin as an icy, frosty morning. Taping some neoprene onto your brake levers can help prevent the cold metal from freezing exposed fingers. Watch for numbness, and take the time to warm your hands and ears when they begin to get cold. Don't wait until numbness sets in.

Earaches   One malady that many visitors to the mountains don't expect is earache. However, riding against frigid winds with the cold in your ear canal can quickly cause a painful earache. I've found that in the morning I need to wear earplugs, or at least some cotton, to prevent this painful inconvenience. You might also try wearing a headband under your helmet.

Sunny Solutions   On the other end of the spectrum lie those days where the sun beats down with an intensity that surpasses the heat of areas hundreds of miles south. Because of the altitude, the sun's rays are many times more intense than in areas nearer sea level. Remember, at an altitude of 3,658 m (12,000 ft.), the sun's rays are 2.8 times as intense as in a coastal area. The danger of sunburn is always a reality in the mountains. Riders from milder climates often scoff at the possibility of burning in the cool climates of the mountains, but I guarantee that on a sunny day without proper sunscreen, you will burn. Make sure you include some powerful screen whenever you ride in the mountains.

I have included these weather-related considerations for your safety. They are not here to scare you. With a little caution and planning, you can avoid these minor inconveniences and enjoy some of the most exciting riding anywhere.

OBTAINING MAPS

In Canada, topographic series maps provide the basic guide for route-finding. Produced as part of the National Topographic Series (NTS), they are available in a variety of scales. The most useful is the 1:50,000 scale, which provides enough detail to locate most natural features and trails. With these maps, 1 km is represented as 2 cm on the map (1.25 in = 1 mi.). This scale is not as detailed as the maps available in the United States, but for most trails it is adequate. Unfortunately, many maps are badly out of date. Some are based on information from the 1970s, which means that the information presented on the maps is equally dated. As a minimum, they provide a reliable guide to traditional routes and natural features. They are available from local information centres and map dealers, or they can be ordered directly from Map Town Ltd., 640 6th Avenue SW, Calgary, Alberta, T2P-0S4. Map Town's phone number is (403) 266-2241.

Gem Trek Publishing has produced some more up-to-date topographic maps for some of the areas described in this book. The NTS maps have been updated to reflect current facilities and trails. Most are available in retail stores and information centres near the riding areas. You may wish to contact Gem Trek directly to order the maps in advance. The address is Gem Trek Publishing, Box 1618, #6, 245 2nd Avenue East, Cochrane, Alberta, T0L-0W0. The phone number is (403) 932-4208 and the Web address is www.gemtrek.com.

Parks Canada has undertaken its own publishing venture and has created a series of park maps. Most of these maps are too large in scale to be of use for actual route finding, but they are excellent for route planning as you have an overview of a much larger area. The Waterton Lakes National Park Map is one exception, and it follows the standard 1:50,000 scale generally used for trail maps. Each of these maps is available at information centres within the park and can be ordered directly from the relevant park. Addresses are listed in the introductions to each section.

Other parks, like Cypress Hill Provincial Park and Kananaskis Country, have maps produced internally to show the many trails within their boundaries. These are available on site or by contacting the parks directly. Their addresses are listed in each section's introduction.

Ward Cameron

Family

1 Canmore Townsite Trails
6 Canmore Canalside
13 Evan-Thomas Bike Path
38 Spray Loop
39 Goat Creek Trail
44 Fenland Trail
45 Vermillion Lakes Road
46 Sundance Canyon
54 1A Highway—Lake Louise to
    Continental Divide
69 Celestine Lake Road
108 Shoreline Trail

Novice and Beginner (short)

1 Canmore Townsite Trails
6 Canmore Canalside
13 Evan-Thomas Bike Path
15 Whiskey Jack–Pocaterra Loop
17 Burstall Pass
38 Spray Loop
44 Fenland Trail
45 Vermillion Lakes Road
46 Sundance Canyon
49 Tunnel Mountain (Hoodoos)
    Trail
50 Water Tower Trail
55 Lake Louise Tramline Trail
60 Saskatchewan Trail
62 Siffleur Falls
63 Athabasca River Trail
64 Valley of Five Lakes and
    Wabasso Lake
72 Kicking Horse Fire Road
104 Streamside Trail
105 Mitchell Trail
106 Beaver Creek–Nichol Springs
    Campground Trail
107 Horseshoe Canyon Trail
108 Shoreline Trail

Novice and Beginner (long)

19 Mount Shark to Spray Lake
    Westside Road
21 Odlum Creek
38 Spray Loop
39 Goat Creek Trail
40 Spray Fire road

53 Redearth Creek
54 1A Highway—Lake Louise to
    Continental Divide
57 Pipestone River Trail
58 Lake Louise Ski Hill—Temple
    Chalet
59 Lake Louise Ski Hill
    Whitehorn Lodge
61 Saskatchewan River Excursion
69 Celestine Lake Road
70 Snake Indian Falls
71 Ottertail Road
72 Kicking Horse Fire Road
73 Otterhead Fire Road
75 Glenogle Creek
74 Moose Creek Road
79 Gorman Creek
80 Hospital Creek
81 Blaeberry River
82 Collie Creek
83 Ensign Creek (Amiskwi Pass)
84 West Kootenay Fire Road
86 Crandell Mountain Circuit
87 Wishbone Trail
88 Snowshoe Trail
89 Lille Coal Mine Trail
94 McGillivray Creek
101 Hartley Pass
102 Morrissey Ridge

Intermediate and Advanced (short)

2 Canmore Nordic Centre
3 CNC World Cup Route
4 CNC Canada Cup Route
5 CNC Georgetown Trail
7 Benchlands Trail Network
12 Terrace Trail
18 Sawmill Trails
23 Plateau Mountain
24 Cataract Creek to Upper Falls
25 Powderface Creek Trail
26 Prairie Creek Trail
31 McLean Creek Off-Highway
    Vehicle Zone
42 Banff Springs to Gondola Trail
43 Stoney Squaw
47 Healy Creek
65 Overlander Trail

66 Saturday Night Loop
67 Signal Mountain Fire Lookout

Intermediate and Advanced (cont.)
68 Palisades Lookout
77 Moonraker Trail System
99 Fernie Alpine Resort
100 Coal Creek Trails

Intermediate and Advanced (long)
8 Baldy Pass
9 Stoney Trail
10 Prairie View Trail
11 Jewel Pass
14 Skogan Pass
16 Whiskey Jack–Lookout Loop
20 Loomis Lake
22 Rye Ridge
27 Cox Hill Ridge
28 Jumpingpound Ridge Trail
29 Tom Snow Trail
30 Telephone Trail
32 Quirk Creek–Wildhorse Loop
33 Moose Mountain Fire Road
34 Forgetmenot Rounder
35 Big Elbow–Little Elbow Loop
36 Elbow-Sheep Trail
37 Junction Mountain Fire
    Lookout
41 Rundle Riverside Trail
48 Allenby Pass
51 Cascade Fire Road
52 Lake Minnewanka
56 Moraine Lake Trail
66 Saturday Night Loop
67 Signal Mountain Fire Lookout
68 Palisades Lookout
76 Canyon Creek Canyon
78 Mount Seven Summit Road
85 Paradise Mines
88 Snowshoe Trail
90 Hastings Ridge Rider
91 Ironstone Lookout
92 Racehorse Pass–Deadman's Pass
93 Sunkist Ridge
95 Ptolemy Pass
96 Tent Mountain Pass
97 South Drywood Creek
98 South Castle River
103 Spruce Coulee Trail

Loops
1 Canmore Townsite Trails
2 Canmore Nordic Centre
3 CNC World Cup Route
4 CNC Canada Cup Route
5 CNC Georgetown Trail
7 Benchlands Trail Network
10 Prairie View Trail
15 Whiskey Jack–Pocaterra Loop
16 Whiskey Jack–Lookout Loop
18 Sawmill Trails
22 Rye Ridge
30 Telephone Trail
31 McLean Creek Off-Highway
    Vehicle Zone
32 Quirk Creek–Wildhorse Loop
34 Forgetmenot Rounder
35 Big Elbow–Little Elbow Loop
38 Spray Loop
44 Fenland Trail
63 Athabasca River Trail
64 Valley of Five Lakes and
    Wabasso Lake
65 Overlander Trail
66 Saturday Night Loop
76 Canyon Creek Canyon
77 Moonraker Trail System
86 Crandell Mountain Circuit
90 Hastings Ridge Rider
92 Racehorse Pass–Deadman's Pass
99 Fernie Alpine Resort
100 Coal Creek Trails
103 Spruce Coulee Trail
104 Streamside Trail
105 Mitchell Trail
107 Horseshoe Canyon Trail

Out-and-Backs
17 Burstall Pass
20 Loomis Lake
21 Odlum Creek
23 Plateau Mountain
24 Cataract Creek to Upper Falls
33 Moose Mountain Fire Road
37 Junction Mountain Fire
    Lookout
43 Stoney Squaw
45 Vermillion Lakes Road
46 Sundance Canyon
48 Allenby Pass

51 Cascade Fire Road
52 Lake Minnewanka
53 Redearth Creek
54 1A Highway—Lake Louise to
    Continental Divide
57 Pipestone River Trail
58 Lake Louise Ski Hill—Temple
    Chalet
59 Lake Louise Ski Hill
    Whitehorn Lodge
60 Saskatchewan Trail
61 Saskatchewan River Excursion
62 Siffleur Falls
67 Signal Mountain Fire Lookout
68 Palisades Lookout
69 Celestine Lake Road
70 Snake Indian Falls
71 Ottertail Road
72 Kicking Horse Fire Road
73 Otterhead Fire Road
75 Glenogle Creek
74 Moose Creek Road
78 Mount Seven Summit Road
79 Gorman Creek
80 Hospital Creek
81 Blaeberry River
82 Collie Creek
83 Ensign Creek (Amiskwi Pass)
87 Wishbone Trail
88 Snowshoe Trail
89 Lille Coal Mine Trail
91 Ironstone Lookout
93 Sunkist Ridge
94 McGillivray Creek
97 South Drywood Creek
98 South Castle River
101 Hartley Pass
102 Morrissey Ridge

Point-to-Points

6 Canmore Canalside
7 Benchlands Trail Network
8 Baldy Pass
9 Stoney Trail
11 Jewel Pass
12 Terrace Trail
13 Evan-Thomas Bike Path
14 Skogan Pass
19 Mount Shark to Spray Lake
    Westside Road

25 Powderface Creek Trail
26 Prairie Creek Trail
27 Cox Hill Ridge
28 Jumpingpound Ridge Trail
29 Tom Snow Trail
33 Moose Mountain Fire road
36 Elbow-Sheep Trail
37 Junction Mountain Fire
    Lookout
39 Goat Creek Trail
40 Spray Fire road
41 Rundle Riverside Trail
42 Banff Springs to Gondola Trail
47 Healy Creek
49 Tunnel Mountain (Hoodoos)
    Trail
50 Water Tower Trail
54 1A Highway—Lake Louise to
    Continental Divide
55 Lake Louise Tramline Trail
56 Moraine Lake Trail
65 Overlander Trail
69 Celestine Lake Road
84 West Kootenay Fire road
85 Paradise Mines
95 Ptolemy Pass
96 Tent Mountain Pass
99 Fernie Alpine Resort
103 Spruce Coulee Trail
106 Beaver Creek–Nichol Springs
    Campground Trail
107 Horseshoe Canyon Trail
108 Shoreline Trail

Technical Heaven

2 Canmore Nordic Centre
3 CNC World Cup Route
4 CNC Canada Cup Route
7 Benchlands Trail Network
8 Baldy Pass
11 Jewel Pass
12 Terrace Trail
16 Whiskey Jack–Lookout Loop
32 Quirk Creek–Wildhorse Loop
34 Forgetmenot Rounder
35 Big Elbow–Little Elbow Loop
41 Rundle Riverside Trail
43 Stoney Squaw
52 Lake Minnewanka
56 Moraine Lake Trail

65 Overlander Trail
66 Saturday Night Loop
76 Canyon Creek Canyon
77 Moonraker Trail System

Technical Heaven (cont.)
85 Paradise Mines
99 Fernie Alpine Resort
100 Coal Creek Trails
103 Spruce Coulee Trail
104 Streamside Trail
107 Horseshoe Canyon Trail

High-Speed Cruising
2 Canmore Nordic Centre
3 CNC World Cup Route
4 CNC Canada Cup Route
5 CNC Georgetown Trail
9 Stoney Trail
11 Jewel Pass
12 Terrace Trail
13 Evan-Thomas Bike Path
15 Whiskey Jack–Pocaterra Loop
19 Mount Shark to Spray Lake
  Westside Road
21 Odlum Creek
30 Telephone Trail
31 McLean Creek Off-Highway
  Vehicle Zone
32 Quirk Creek–Wildhorse Loop
33 Moose Mountain Fire Road
35 Big Elbow–Little Elbow Loop
36 Elbow-Sheep Trail
38 Spray Loop
39 Goat Creek Trail
40 Spray Fire Road
41 Rundle Riverside Trail
45 Vermillion Lakes Road
46 Sundance Canyon
47 Healy Creek
51 Cascade Fire Road
53 Redearth Creek
54 1A Highway—Lake Louise to
  Continental Divide
57 Pipestone River Trail
61 Saskatchewan River Excursion
63 Athabasca River Trail
64 Valley of Five Lakes and
  Wabasso Lake
66 Saturday Night Loop
69 Celestine Lake Road

70 Snake Indian Falls
71 Ottertail Road
72 Kicking Horse Fire Road
73 Otterhead Fire Road
75 Glenogle Creek
74 Moose Creek Road
79 Gorman Creek
80 Hospital Creek
84 West Kootenay Fire Road
86 Crandell Mountain Circuit
87 Wishbone Trail
88 Snowshoe Trail
97 South Drywood Creek
98 South Castle River
101 Hartley Pass
102 Morrissey Ridge
107 Horseshoe Canyon Trail
108 Shoreline Trail

Wildlife Viewing
6 Canmore Canalside
44 Fenland Trail
45 Vermillion Lakes Road
49 Tunnel Mountain (Hoodoos)
  Trail
52 Lake Minnewanka
54 1A Highway—Lake Louise to
  Continental Divide
56 Moraine Lake Trail
67 Signal Mountain Fire Lookout
107 Horseshoe Canyon Trail
108 Shoreline Trail

Great Scenery
1 Canmore Townsite Trails
6 Canmore Canalside
7 Benchlands Trail Network
8 Baldy Pass
10 Prairie View Trail
12 Terrace Trail
14 Skogan Pass
16 Whiskey Jack–Lookout Loop
17 Burstall Pass
20 Loomis Lake
22 Rye Ridge
24 Cataract Creek to Upper Falls
25 Powderface Creek Trail
27 Cox Hill Ridge
28 Jumpingpound Ridge Trail
33 Moose Mountain Fire road
34 Forgetmenot Rounder

INTRODUCTION

TRAIL DESCRIPTION OUTLINE

Each trail in this book begins with key information that includes length, configuration, aerobic and technical difficulty, trail conditions, scenery, and special comments. Additional description is contained in 11 individual categories. The following will help you understand all of the information provided.

Trail name: Trail names are as designated on National Topographic Series (NTS) or other maps and/or by local custom.

At a Glance Information

Length/configuration: The overall length of a trail is described in kilometres and miles, unless stated otherwise. The configuration is a description of the shape of each trail—whether the trail is a loop, out-and-back (that is, along the same route), figure eight, trapezoid, isosceles triangle, decahedron . . . (just kidding), or if it connects with another trail described in the book. See the Glossary for definitions of *point-to-point* and *combination*.

Aerobic difficulty: This provides a description of the degree of physical exertion required to complete the ride.

Technical difficulty: This provides a description of the technical skill required to pedal a ride. Trails are often described here in terms of being paved, unpaved, sandy, hard-packed, washboarded, two- or four-wheel-drive, single-track or double-track. All terms that might be unfamiliar to the first-time mountain biker are defined in the Glossary.

Note: For both the aerobic and technical difficulty categories, authors were asked to keep in mind the fact that all riders are not equal, and thus, to gauge the trail in terms of how the middle-of-the-road rider—someone between the newcomer and Alison Sydor—could handle the route. Comments about the trail's length, condition, and elevation change will also assist you in determining the difficulty of any trail relative to your own abilities.

Scenery: Here you will find a general description of the natural surroundings during the seasons when most riders pedal the trail and a suggestion of what is to be found at special times (like great fall foliage or wildflowers in bloom).

Special comments: Unique elements of the ride are mentioned.

Category Information

General location: This category describes where the trail is located in reference to a nearby town or other landmark.

Elevation change: Unless stated otherwise, the figure provided is the total gain and loss of elevation along the trail. In regions where the elevation variation is not extreme, the route is simply described as flat, rolling, or possessing short, steep climbs or descents.

Season: The best time of year to pedal the route, taking into account trail conditions (for example, when it will not be muddy), riding comfort (when the weather is too hot, cold, or wet), and local hunting seasons.

Note: Because the exact opening and closing dates of deer, elk, and moose seasons change from year to year, riders should check with the local fish and wildlife department or call a sporting goods store (or any place that sells hunting licenses) in a nearby town before heading out. Wear bright clothes during autumn, and don't wear suede jackets while in the saddle. Hunter's-orange tape on the helmet is also a good idea.

Services: This category is of primary importance in guides for paved-road tourers, but it is far less crucial to most mountain bike trail descriptions because there are usually no services whatsoever to be found. Authors have noted when water is available on long mountain routes and have listed the availability of food, lodging, campgrounds, and bike shops. If all these services are present, you will find only the words "All services available in . . ."

Hazards: Special hazards like steep cliffs, great amounts of deadfall, or barbed-wire fences very close to the trail are noted here.

Rescue index: Determining how far one is from help on any particular trail can be difficult due to the backcountry nature of most mountain bike rides. Authors therefore state the proximity of homes or nearby roads where one might hitch a ride, or the likelihood of other bikers being encountered on the trail. Phone numbers of local police departments or hospitals are hardly ever provided because phones are usually not available. If you are able to reach a phone, the local operator will connect you with emergency services.

Land status: This category provides information regarding whether the trail crosses land operated by the provincial or national parks or logging companies; or land owned by the Canadian government, called Crown land; or private land whose owner (at the time the author did the research) has allowed mountain bikers right of passage; and so on.

Note: Authors have been extremely careful to offer only those routes that are open to bikers and are legal to ride. However, because land ownership changes over time, and because the land-use controversy created by mountain bikes still has not completely subsided, it is the duty of each cyclist to look for and to heed signs warning against trail use. Don't expect this book to get you off the hook when you're facing some small-town judge for pedaling past a Biking Prohibited sign erected the day before you arrived. Look for these signs, read them, and heed the advice. And remember: There's always another trail.

Maps: The maps in this book have been produced with great care and, in conjunction with the trail-following suggestions, will help you stay on course. But it is strongly suggested that you obtain even more detailed maps of the area you plan to ride.

In Canada, topographic series maps provide the basic guide for route finding. Produced as part of the National Topographic Series (NTS), they are available in a variety of scales. The most useful is the 1:50,000 scale, which provides enough detail to locate most natural features and trails. With these maps, 1 km is represented as 2 cm on the map (1.25 in = 1 mi.). These maps are not as detailed as the maps available in the United States, but for most trails they're sufficient. Unfortunately, many of the maps are badly out of date. Some are based on information from the 1970s. As a minimum, they provide a reliable guide to traditional routes and natural features. They are available from local information centres and map dealers, or they can be ordered directly from the Canada Map Office (see "Topographic Maps" below).

Finding the trail: Detailed information on how to reach the trailhead and where to park your car is provided here.

Sources of additional information: Here you will find the address and/or phone number of a bike shop, governmental agency, or other source from which trail information can be obtained.

Notes on the trail: This is where you are guided carefully through any portions of the trail that are particularly difficult to follow. The author also may add information about the route that does not fit easily in the other categories. This category will not be present for those rides where the route is easy to follow.

RIDE CONFIGURATIONS

Combination: This type of route may combine two or more configurations. For example, a point-to-point route may integrate a scenic loop or an out-and-back spur midway through the ride. Likewise, an out-and-back may have a loop at its farthest point (this configuration looks like a cherry with a stem attached; the stem is the out-and-back, the fruit is the terminus loop). Or a loop route may have multiple out-and-back spurs and/or loops to the side. Mileage for a combination route is for the total distance to complete the ride.

Loop: This route configuration is characterized by riding from the designated trailhead to a distant point, then returning to the trailhead via a different route (or simply continuing on the same in a circle route) without doubling back. You always move forward across new terrain but return to the starting point when finished. Mileage is for the entire loop from the trailhead back to trailhead.

Out-and-back: A ride where you will return on the same trail you pedaled out. While this might sound far more boring than a loop route, many trails look very different when pedaled in the opposite direction.

Point-to-point: A vehicle shuttle (or similar assistance) is required for this type of route, which is ridden from the designated trailhead to a distant location, or endpoint, where the route ends. Total mileage is for the one-way trip from the trailhead to endpoint.

Spur: A road or trail that intersects the main trail you're following.

Ride Configurations contributed by Gregg Bromka

TOPOGRAPHIC MAPS

The maps in this book, when used in conjunction with the route directions presented in each chapter, in most instances will be sufficient to get you to the trail and keep you on it. However, you will find superior detail and valuable information in the 1:50,000 scale National Topographic Series (NTS) topographic maps. Recognizing how indispensable these are to bikers and hikers alike, many bike shops and sporting goods stores now carry topos of the local area.

But if you're brand-new to mountain biking, you might be wondering, "What's a topographic map?" In short, these differ from standard "flat" maps in that they indicate not only linear distances but elevations as well. One glance at a topo will show you the difference, for "contour lines" are spread across the map like dozens of intricate spider webs. Each contour line represents a particular elevation, and at the base of each topo a particular "contour interval" designation is given. Yes, it sounds confusing if you're new to the lingo, but it truly is a simple and wonderfully helpful system. Keep reading.

Let's assume that the 1:50,000 series topo before us says "Contour Interval 20 m," that the short trail we'll be pedaling is two centimetres in length on the map, and that it crosses five contour lines from its beginning to end. What do we know? Well, because the linear scale of this series is 1 km to the centimetre (roughly 1.25 in. representing 1 mi.), we know our trail is approximately 2 km long (2 cm = 1 km). But we also know we'll be climbing or descending 100 vertical metres (5 contour lines = 20 m each) over that distance. And the elevation designations written on occasional contour lines will tell us if we're heading up or down.

The authors of this series warn their readers of upcoming terrain, but only a detailed topo gives you the information you need to pinpoint your position exactly on a map, steer yourself toward optional trails and roads nearby, plus let you know at a glance if you'll be pedaling hard to take them. It's a lot of information for a very low cost. In fact, the only drawback with topos is their size — several feet square. I've tried rolling them into tubes, folding them carefully, even cutting them into blocks and photocopying the pieces. Any of these systems is a pain, but no matter how you pack the maps, you'll be happy they're along. And you'll be even happier if you pack a compass as well.

In addition to local bike shops and sporting goods stores, you'll find topos at major universities and some public libraries where you might try photocopying the ones you need to avoid the cost of buying them. But if you want your own and can't find them locally, contact:

Canada Map Office
615 Booth Street
Ottawa, ON K1A-OE9
(613) 952-7000

TRAIL ETIQUETTE

Pick up almost any mountain bike magazine these days and you'll find articles and letters to the editor about trail conflict. For example, you'll find hikers' tales of being blindsided by speeding mountain bikers, complaints from mountain bikers about being blamed for trail damage that was really caused by horse or cattle traffic, and cries from bikers about those "kamikaze" riders who through their antics threaten to close even more trails to all of us.

The authors of this series have been very careful to guide you to only those trails that are open to mountain biking (or at least were open at the time of their research), and without exception have warned of the damage done to our sport through injudicious riding. We can all benefit from glancing over the following International Mountain Bicycling Association (IMBA) Rules of the Trail before saddling up.

1. *Ride on open trails only.* Respect trail and road closures (ask if not sure), avoid possible trespass on private land, obtain permits and authorization as may be required. Federal and state wilderness areas are closed to cycling.

2. *Leave no trace.* Be sensitive to the dirt beneath you. Even on open trails, you should not ride under conditions where you will leave evidence of your passing, such as on certain soils shortly after rain. Observe the different types of soils and trail construction; practice low-impact cycling. This also means staying on the trail and not creating any new ones. Be sure to pack out at least as much as you pack in.

3. *Control your bicycle!* Inattention for even a second can cause disaster. Excessive speed can maim and threaten people; there is no excuse for it!

4. *Always yield the trail.* Make known your approach well in advance. A friendly greeting (or a bell) is considerate and works well; startling someone may cause loss of trail access. Show your respect when passing others by slowing to a walk or even stopping. Anticipate that other trail users may be around corners or in blind spots.

5. *Never spook animals.* All animals are startled by an unannounced approach, a sudden movement, or a loud noise. This can be dangerous for you, for others, and for the animals. Give animals extra room and time to adjust to you. In passing, use special care and follow the directions of horseback riders (ask if uncertain). Running cattle and disturbing wild animals is a serious offense. Leave gates as you found them or as marked.

6. *Plan ahead.* Know your equipment, your ability, and the area in which you are riding—and prepare accordingly. Be self-sufficient at all times. Wear a helmet, keep your machine in good condition, and carry necessary supplies for changes in weather or other conditions. A well-executed trip is a satisfaction to you and not a burden or offense to others.

For more information, contact IMBA, P.O. Box 7578, Boulder, CO 80306, (303) 545-9011.

HITTING THE TRAIL

Once again, because this is a "where-to," not a "how-to" guide, the following will be brief. If you're a veteran trail rider, these suggestions might serve to remind you of something you've forgotten to pack. If you're a newcomer, they might convince you to think twice before hitting the backcountry unprepared.

Water: I've heard the questions dozens of times: "How much is enough? One bottle? Two? Three?! But think of all that extra weight!" Well, one simple physiological fact should convince you to err on the side of excess when it comes to deciding how much water to pack: a human working hard in 32°C (90°F) temperature needs over nine litres (ten quarts) of fluids every day. Nine litres. That's two and a half gallons—12 large water bottles, or 16 small ones. And, with water weighing in at approximately 1 kilogram per litre, a one-day supply comes to a whopping 9 kilograms (20 pounds).

In other words, pack along two or three bottles even for short rides. And make sure you can purify the water found along the trail on longer routes. When writing of those routes where this could be of critical importance, each author has provided information on where water can be found near the trail—if it can be found at all. But drink it untreated and you run the risk of disease. (See *Giardia* in the Glossary.)

Tools: Ever since my first cross-country tour in 1965 I've been kidded about the number of tools I pack on the trail. And so I will exit entirely from this discussion by providing a list compiled by two mechanic (and mountain biker) friends of mine. After all, since they make their livings fixing bikes, and get their kicks by riding them, who could be a better source?

These two suggest the following as an absolute minimum:

tire levers
spare tube and patch kit
air pump

Allen wrenches (3, 4, 5, and 6 mm)
six-inch crescent (adjustable-end

But, while they're on the trail, their personal tool pouches contain these additional items:

channel locks (small)
air gauge
tire valve cap (the metal kind, with a valve-stem remover)
baling wire (ten or so inches, for temporary repairs)
duct tape (small roll for temporary repairs or tire boot)
boot material (small piece of old tire or a large tube patch)
spare chain link
rear derailleur pulley
spare nuts and bolts
paper towel and tube of waterless hand cleaner

First-aid kit: My personal kit contains the following, sealed inside double Ziploc bags:

sunscreen
aspirin
butterfly-closure bandages
Band-Aids
gauze compress pads (a half-dozen 4" by 4")
gauze (one roll)
Ace bandages or Spenco joint wraps
Benadryl (an antihistamine, in case of allergic reactions)
water purification tablets or water filter (on long rides)
moleskin Spenco "Second Skin"
hydrogen peroxide, iodine, or Mercurochrome (some kind of antiseptic)
snakebite kit

Final considerations: The authors of this series have done a good job suggesting that specific items be packed for certain trails—rain gear in particular seasons, a hat and gloves for mountain passes, or shades for desert jaunts. Heed their warnings, and think ahead. Good luck.

Dennis Coello

AND NOW, A WORD ABOUT CELLULAR PHONES . . .

Thinking of bringing the Flip-Fone along on your next off-road ride? Before you do, ask yourself the following questions:

- Do I know where I'm going? Do I have an adequate map? Can I use a compass effectively? Do I know the shortest way to civilization if I need to bail out early and find some help?

- If I'm on the trail for longer than planned, am I ready for it? Do I have adequate water? Have I packed something to eat? Will I be warm enough if I'm still out there after dark?

- Am I prepared for possible injuries? Do I have a first-aid kit? Do I know what to do in case of a cut, fracture, snakebite, or heat exhaustion?

- Is my tool kit adequate for likely mechanical problems? Can I fix a flat? Can I untangle a chain? Am I prepared to walk out if the bike is unridable?

If you answered "yes" to *every* question above, you may pack the phone, but consider a good whistle instead. It's lighter, cheaper, and nearly as effective.

If you answered "no" to any of these questions, be aware that your cellular phone does little to reduce your risks in the wilderness. Sure, being able to dial 911 in the farthest corner of the White Mountains sounds like a great idea, but this ain't downtown, friend. If disaster strikes, and your call is routed to some emergency operator in Manchester or Bangor, and it takes awhile to figure out which ranger, sheriff, or search-and-rescue crew to connect you with, and you can't tell the authorities where you are because you're really not sure, and the closest they can come to pinpointing your location is a cellular tower that serves 160 square kilometres (60 square miles) of dense woods, and they start searching for you but dusk is only two hours away, and you have no signaling device and your throat is too dry to shout, and meanwhile you can't get the bleeding stopped, you are out of luck. I mean *really* out of luck.

And when the battery goes dead, you're on your own again. Enough said.

Jeff Faust
Author of Mountain Bike! New Hampshire

MOUNTAIN BIKE!
The Canadian Rockies

CANMORE/KANANASKIS COUNTRY

Never heard of Kananaskis Country? You're not alone. Next to the 100-year history of Banff National Park, Kananaskis is a virtual newborn. In 1977, the premier of Alberta at the time, Peter Lougheed, set aside 4,250 square kilometres (1,641 square miles) of Alberta's eastern slopes as Kananaskis Country Provincial Recreation Area. Geographically, the area lies west of Calgary, Alberta, and borders with Banff National Park and the Continental Divide on its western margin.

This area is managed under a multiple-use concept, which allows it to support a wide variety of activities. For mountain bikers, this area finally provides a place that not only allows us access but actually embraces backcountry cycling as a viable activity.

The area's zoning has been based on the types of impact that can be sustained. Sensitive areas are classified as "prime protection," while other areas are zoned to allow development. Also, six provincial parks lie within this large area; the most impressive is Peter Lougheed Provincial Park.

Kananaskis Country straddles the transition from foothill to Rocky Mountain. For the biker, the foothills offer a wider variety of routes with gradients more closely matched to backcountry biking. Also, within the eastern portion of Kananaskis, the widest variety of rides in the Rockies provides an undeniable attraction to cyclists of all abilities.

The Kananaskis Country has been traveled by the Stoney Indians for generations. Long before the coming of the Europeans, they hunted and trapped in its isolated valleys. The first white man entered the valley in 1854, when James Sinclair brought a group of settlers through it on their way to the newly opened Oregon Territory. Later, John Palliser traveled this rugged route during his 1858 surveys of the area. He named it *Kananaskis*, after a legend of an Indian who survived a blow to the head by a battle ax.

Loggers entered the valley in the late 1880s and used the Kananaskis River to drive the logs to distant sawmills. During the Great Depression, a camp for unemployed workers was developed, and the workers built some of the valley's early recreational facilities as well as a rough road down the valley. Later, the camp was converted to house German prisoners of war during World War II.

After the war, the valley remained the quiet retreat of adventurous souls willing to bounce their way down its poorly maintained road. The Kananaskis Lakes were raised to provide hydroelectricity, and the Kananaskis River was dammed to make another reservoir, today known as Barrier Lake.

With the area's official designation in 1977, development began in earnest, and the facilities today rival those of its much older neighbour, Banff National Park. When Calgary hosted the 1988 Winter Olympics, Kananaskis Country held both the downhill and cross-country events. This public exposure introduced the world to the Kananaskis; since then, it has become an international tourist destination.

Kananaskis Country provides some of the best mountain biking in the province. The trails are well maintained, with only moderate restrictions placed on riders. This area has a mandate to accommodate diverse users, and it accomplishes this task with aplomb.

For further information, contact:

Kananaskis Country
Box 280
Canmore, Alberta
T0L-0M0
(403) 678-5508

RIDE 1 · Canmore Townsite Trails

AT A GLANCE

Length/configuration: Variable, with ranges up to 10 km.

Aerobic difficulty: These trails are flat, focusing on the river valley.

Technical difficulty: Nil.

Scenery: Along the route there are fabulous views of the entire range of mountains lining the Bow Valley.

Special comments: This is a pleasant, rolling ride, making it perfect for the whole family.

The town of Canmore began as a simple coal-mining community in the 1880s. For almost a hundred years, miners worked the tunnels to bring black gold to the surface. The mines finally closed in 1979, but sections of this trail follow some of the original rail lines that were integral in the making of this long tradition. Canmore sits in an incredible mountain valley along the banks of the Bow River. To the west, the long range of Mount Rundle, the rolling summit of Ha Ling Peak (formerly Chinaman's Peak), and the triple summit of Three Sisters dominate the horizon. To the east, the summits of the Fairholme Range glisten in the evening sunlight. Throughout this route, the open views showcase this glorious country. While the trail is flat and level, the surrounding landscape is anything but. You also pass by the Rundle Power Plant, constructed in 1951 to harness another energy source—gravity. This hydro-generating station can provide sufficient electricity for a city of 35,000 people, a far cry from the present population of 10,000.

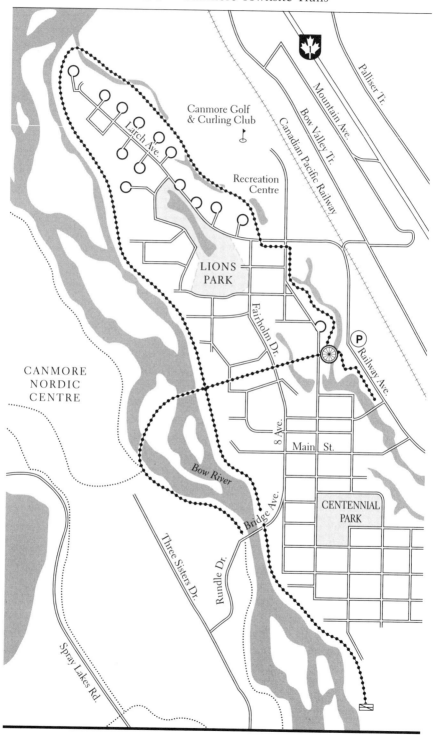

The trails around the town of Canmore offer a great way to experience the landscape around this fast-growing mountain town. The distance can be varied according to your tastes and levels of ambition. The route, as described here, makes an 8.56-km (5.14-mi.) figure-eight circuit that showcases the most popular sections of these trails.

General location: Within the town of Canmore.

Elevation change: Nil.

Season: May to October.

Services: All services are available in the town of Canmore.

Hazards: Keep in mind that cyclists, joggers, dog walkers, and all manner of wayward wanderers use this trail. Be sure to share the trail with others. There are a few sharp corners, but few other challenges.

Rescue index: This trail is urban, so you're never far from help. If no other trail users can offer assistance, simply knock on the door of one of the many residences en route, or call 911 from any phone. A good cellular signal is available within the town site.

Land status: Municipal land.

Maps: The NTS 1:50,000 Series topographic map for this trail is 82 O/3 Canmore; however, this route is not marked on it. A better option is the Canmore Alberta Recreation Map produced by TerraPro Recmaps, P.O. Box 1016, Whistler, British Columbia, V0N-1B0. Another good map, produced by *Where* magazine, is called "Canmore and Kananaskis Map" and is available at most gas stations and small retail shops.

Finding the trail: There are access points throughout town, but the trail as described begins at the corner of Railway Avenue and 10th Street. Park in the IGA Parking lot and cross Railway Avenue to begin driving down 10th Street. As you approach the bridge over the creek, a trail leaves the road on the right side. Take this trail.

Sources of additional information: Contact Tourism Canmore/Kananaskis at 801 8th Street, Canmore, AB, T1W-2B3, or call (403) 678-1295.

Notes on the trail: The route rolls along a wide trail passing behind gray condominiums on your right and Policeman's Creek to your left. At km 0.31 (0.19 mi.), there are several small houses to your left, along the riverbank. Beyond the houses, there is a brown fence with an opening. Go through that opening and the trail continues. Just beyond the fence, the trail forks. There is a bridge to the left, which takes you toward the Bow River. For this route, go right for a few metres, and then turn left to continue the ride on the same side of Policeman's Creek. This section of trail continues to wind behind condos on the right and the creek on your left. Cross a bridge over Policeman's Creek at km 0.73 (0.44 mi.), and meet the road at the corner of 17th Street and 8th Ave.

To continue on the trail, turn left onto 17th Street and roll along for 0.16 km (0.1 mi.), where the trail will leave the road on your right. Almost immediately, the trail winds right and crosses the creek on a high-quality bridge. Cross the bridge and turn left to follow the creek bed. The wide trail brings you to a junction at km 1.35 (0.81 mi.). To the left is a bridge—don't cross it. This is merely another access point for the trail. Stay straight, continuing on the same side of the creek. The trail winds along the creek, making a nice slalom-like course through the aspen trees, and at km 1.7 (1.02 mi.) it begins to parallel the chain-link fence of the Canmore Golf and Curling Club. The ride crosses a small bridge and continues to roll past the residential backyards on the left and the golf course on the right. After leaving the chain-link fence behind, the trail winds along a marshy creek channel before meeting a T intersection at km 2.41 (1.45 mi.). The trail to the right, after a short distance, simply dead-ends at the Bow River, so you want to go left at this junction.

This section of ride rolls along the east bank of the Bow River, with numerous access points coming in from the left. At km 3.46 (2.08 mi.), a hiking trail forks off to the right toward an area known as the Larch Islands. This trail is closed to bikes, but it is worth getting off and walking through this unique area. Once you've finished exploring the Larch Islands, continue along the wide pathway. The next major junction is at km 4.15 (2.49 mi.). Here, a trail crosses from the left to span the river over a large bridge to your right. Do not take this trail yet; we will return on that route near the end of the ride. Rather, cross this trail and continue on the same side of the river. Stay on this wide trail as it approaches a small picnic area with benches aplenty. Cross the pavement of Bridge Road at km 4.85 (2.91 mi.), just to the left of the main bridge over the Bow River. Continue riding along the river, with homes to your left and the river to the right. This trail meets a gate at km 5.54 (3.32 mi.). Beyond it are many informal trails worth exploring. However, in our description of this trip, we will backtrack to the pavement of Bridge Road.

After retracing your route back to Bridge Road, turn left on the pavement and cross over the Bow River. Just beyond the bridge, a trail goes to the right as a chain-link fence ends at km 6.34 (3.8 mi.). Turn right onto this trail and go past a brown metal gate as you rejoin the river (now on the west bank). This wide trail rolls along the shores of the Bow River with stunning panoramas. You'll go through two green metal gates at km 6.75 (4.05 mi.) as you approach the powerhouse of the Rundle Power Plant. Beyond these gates a high staircase climbs to the left. These stairs provide access to the Georgetown Trail, another popular local ride. However, for this ride, go through another gate and cross on the bridge directly above the powerhouse. This route will take you over the first of two bridges across the Bow River, one at km 7.09 and the second at 7.5 km (4.25 and 4.5 mi.). The second bridge brings you back to the point at which you earlier crossed this trail. Stay straight and leave the river behind.

The trail takes on a more urban feel now as it quickly runs down a wide alley-like road. It crosses Fairholme Drive at km 7.94 (4.76 mi.), then becomes a wide trail again. Cross 7th Avenue at km 8.16 (4.9 mi.) and a final bridge at km 8.24 (4.94 mi.). Turn right after the bridge and emerge at the trailhead at km 8.56 (5.14 mi.).

RIDE 2 · Canmore Nordic Centre

AT A GLANCE

Length/configuration: Variable, with loop options of 1.0 km (0.6 mi.) to as much as 50 km (30 mi.).

Aerobic difficulty: Varies from tender to lung-blasting, depending on the route.

Technical difficulty: Equally variable. While the signed trails are generally smooth and rolling, many hidden single-track lines can be extremely steep and loaded with natural obstacles.

Scenery: Many of the trails are in the trees, but some of the higher lines offer striking views of the Fairholme Range to the north, Three Sisters to the east, and the long range of Mount Rundle to the south.

Special comments: This is a premier location for mountain bikers of all abilities. New riders will find the smooth cross-country trails perfect for honing their skills, while expert riders will seek out the hard-core single-track lines that attract world-class riders to this network.

If you're a competitive rider looking for challenge, this is the place for you. As the former host of the cross-country and biathlon events during the 1988 Winter Olympics, it provides an endless collection of trails. Since the trails were designed for cross-country skiers, the level of difficulty varies from beginner to expert. Cross-country skiers need a mixture of uphill, downhill, and level terrain, so these trails are naturally rolling.

Beginning at the day lodge, you have options that vary from 2.5 km (1.6 mi.) to 50 km (31 mi.) or more. Since the trails are designed to provide loops of differing lengths, you can create almost endless diversity by linking up the various options. The trails' Nordic connection also provides the added benefit of a one-way designation for part of the system. Such designations provide suitable options for riders who simply must ride on the edge of control.

Many competitive events have been hosted at this site over the past few years, and it is becoming increasingly popular for mountain biking. The trails are kept clean of debris, which lends itself to fast riding. Don't develop a false sense of security, however. Trees may still block the trail, so stay vigilant.

The scenery around the Nordic Centre is splendid. Although many of the trails are in treed areas and most of the riders at this facility are interested in speed, the local landscape rewards those who take the time to look around. To the south, the community of Canmore is nestled beneath the towering slopes of the Fairholme Range. To the north, the jagged walls of Mount Rundle form an impenetrable barrier.

General location: The Canmore Nordic Centre is located above the town of Canmore, approximately 80 km west of Calgary, Alberta.

Elevation change: The elevation change varies with the trails; however, it is often steep and sudden. The rolling nature of the trails means significant

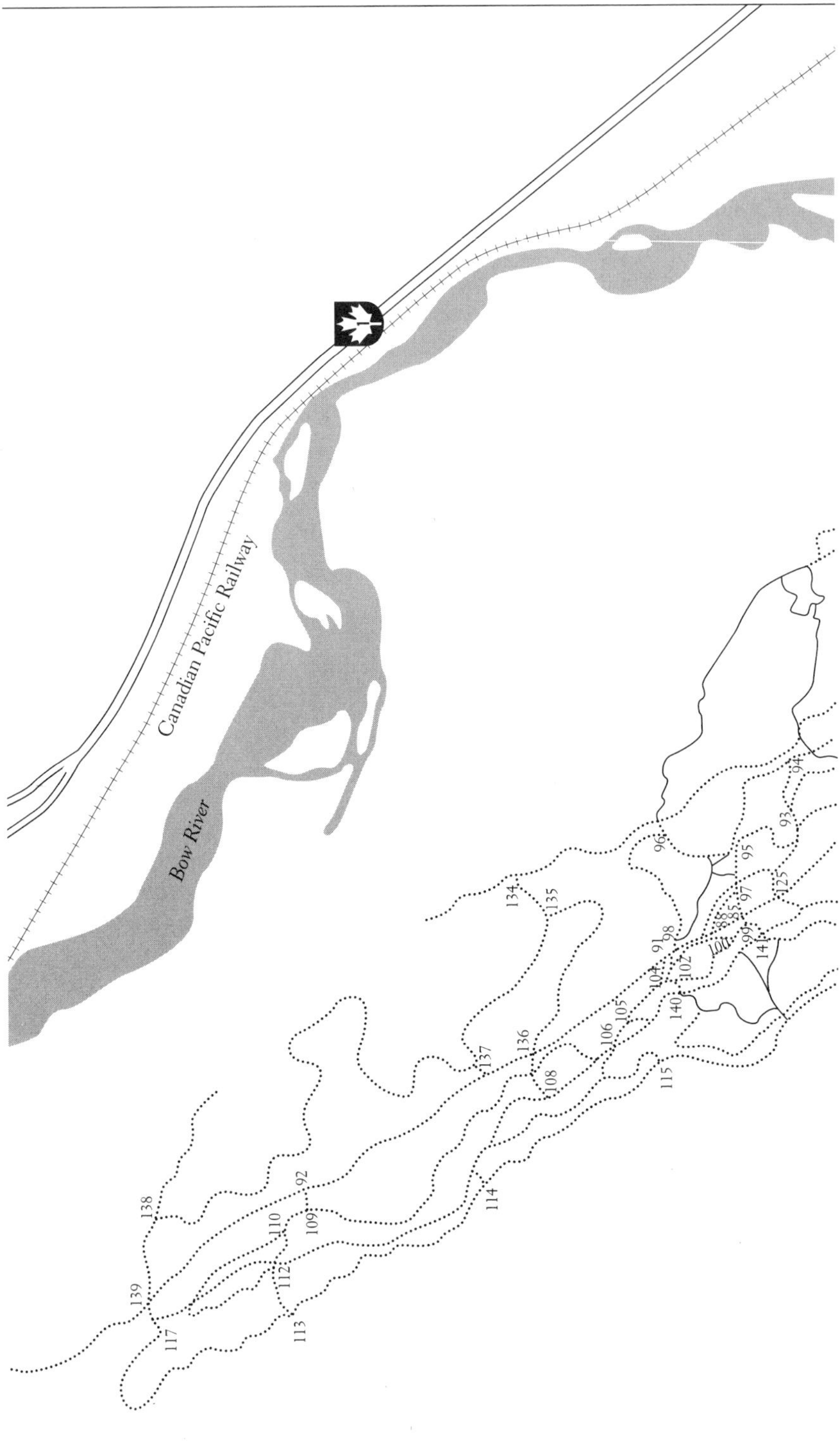

Canadian Pacific Railway

Bow River

134 135

96

95 93 94

97

98 91 99 100 141 125

104 102 90 140 105

137 136 106 115

108

92

138 110 109 114

139 112

117 113

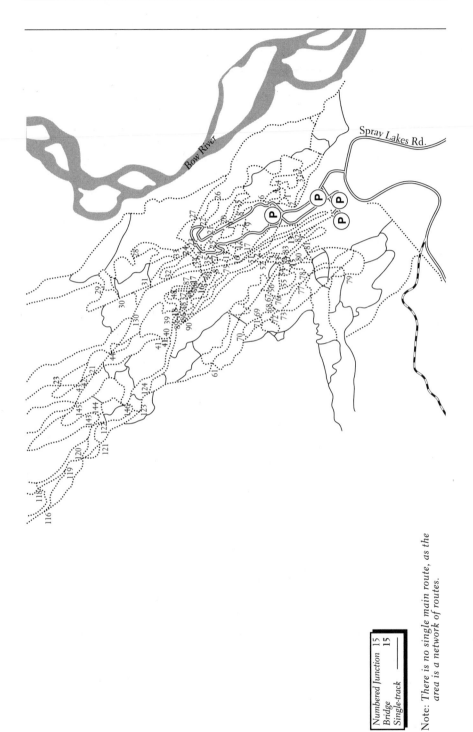

Note: *There is no single main route, as the area is a network of routes.*

Numbered Junction	15
Bridge	15
Single-track	———

amounts of elevation are never achieved, but the lengthy uphill nature of some climbs will test even the strongest lungs.

Season: The trail system is available from early June to mid-October.

Services: All services are provided in the town of Canmore.

Hazards: This trail network is well maintained and kept relatively clear of debris. But don't let this fool you into thinking that you don't have to be wary of freshly fallen trees or loose rock debris. As with any trail, obstacles may need to be negotiated. Also, some riders don't heed the one-way designation of some trails, so be cautious of the occasional rider going the wrong way. Since riders of varying skills ride this network, you must keep your eyes open on blind hills — someone may be stopped at the bottom. Although the network is clearly signed, it can still be confusing. Dozens of junctions must be properly negotiated, each with a number of signs indicating the various loop routes. As you pass each junction, make sure to look for the coloured arrow that indicates your particular route. Finally, roller-skiers also use the paved section of this trail. Please be especially cautious of these rolling obstacles. This network of trails was designed for such users, and if mountain bikers want to continue to benefit from the use of the trail network, they need to be sensitive to the facility's principal purpose.

Rescue index: You can contact emergency assistance at the day lodge. In addition, the trails tend to be very popular, so it is rarely difficult to get assistance. If the day lodge is closed, a pay phone outside the building will provide you with a means to obtain assistance.

Land status: Canmore Nordic Centre Provincial Park is operated as a part of Kananaskis Country Provincial Recreation Area.

Maps: The 1:50,000 scale topographic map for this trail is 82 O/3 Canmore. Map Town's "Kananaskis Country-Spray Lakes and Canmore Region" also covers the area. The Canmore Nordic Centre has produced a good trail map, but the best map is called "Canmore Albera Recreation Map" and has been produced by TerraPro Recmaps, P.O. Box 1016, Whistler, British Columbia, V0N-180. It is available at most local bike shops.

Finding the trail: From Canmore, follow the signs to the Canmore Nordic Centre. From the day lodge, all trails are well signed.

Sources of additional information: Contact the Canmore Nordic Centre directly at (403) 678-2400, or mail inquiries to the Kananaskis Country address listed in the introduction to this section.

Notes on the trail: The trails vary from moderate to blood-tasting expert level. Some of the most challenging mountain bike competitions in the country have been hosted at this facility, so be prepared for challenges. The main trail system is generally clear of obstacles, and every junction is well signed.

RIDE 3 · CNC World Cup Route

AT A GLANCE

Length/configuration: 8.67-km (5.2-mi.) figure-eight loop.

Aerobic difficulty: The ride includes some sharp climbs from the trailhead to the top of The Oven at km 2.12 (1.27 mi.). The remainder of the trail challenges your technique more than your lungs.

AB

Technical difficulty: This is a World Cup route designed to challenge the best riders. Nevertheless, most of the route is rideable by intermediate cyclists. There are several steep, rooted drops, though, so read the ride description carefully.

Scenery: The trail stays mostly in the trees, but you'll get a few brief views of Mount Rundle's towering face.

Special comments: Many recreational riders focus on the upper part of the course because it offers more variety. The lower section, with the exception of a technical start, is of less interest.

This is an awesome, technical ride. While this 8.67-km (5.2-mi.) figure-eight loop was designed to test the world's best riders, it is largely passable by intermediate-level cyclists. The trail climbs sharply from the trailhead, cresting atop a section known as The Oven. You then drop down Nectar Noodle, bounce through The Albertan, Nordic Norm, The Chute, and finally pass back over the starting point of the ride.

The lower section of the ride begins with the sheer descent of the Devonian Drop, after which it becomes an intermediate ride with only moderate technical challenge. The World Cup route is short, but it's a great way to see some of the hidden single-track of the Canmore Nordic Centre. Keep in mind, though, that none of the single-track is signed in any way. This description should help, but you may need to experiment to discover the actual route. The best option is to head out with a local and let that person show you the route.

Keep in mind that this trail goes up several trails in opposition to one-way signs. These signs are intended to ensure that cross-country skiers do not run into each other, but the Nordic Centre does not encourage cyclists to ride against the grain, either. Please be cautious of oncoming riders when you're on these sections of trail.

General location: Adjacent to the town of Canmore.

Elevation change: From the trailhead at approximately 1,430 m (4,690 ft.), the trail climbs steadily to the top of The Oven at 1,570 m (5,150 ft.). It then descends to the starting point and continues to drop 55 m (180 ft.), bottoming out at approximately 1,375 m (4,510 ft.). The last section of the ride regains that loss to return to the trailhead.

Season: Late May to mid-October.

Services: All services are available in the town of Canmore.

RIDE 3 · CNC World Cup Route

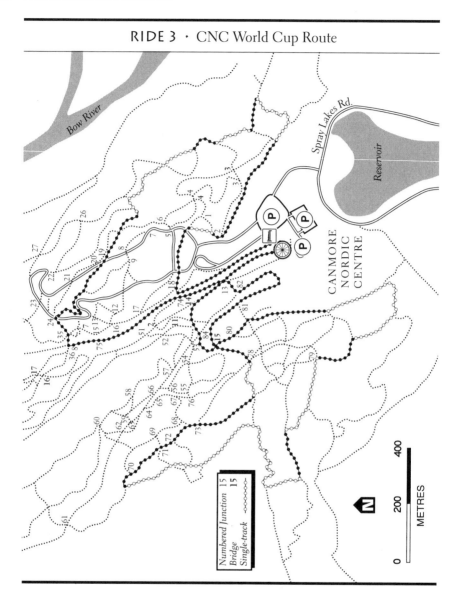

Hazards: The main challenges on this ride occur during the descent. Numerous rooted drops occur, with several exceedingly steep, rutted descents. You will also need to yield to other riders on the few stretches where you travel counter to the signed cross-country routes. On the pavement, roller-skiers, who will also be traveling in the opposite direction to you, are not able to stop suddenly—yield to them.

Rescue index: In an emergency, return to the day lodge, where help can usually be found. If it is closed, a pay phone outside will allow you to call 911. The trails are also popular with local cyclists, who can also offer assistance.

Aydin Odyakmaz grinds his way toward the top of the Oven on the CNC World Cup Route.

Land status: The trail is within Canmore Nordic Centre Provincial Park.

Maps: The NTS 1:50,000 Series topographic map for this trail is 82 O/3 Canmore; however, this route is not marked on it. A better option is the Canmore Alberta Recreation Map produced by TerraPro Recmaps, P.O. Box 1016, Whistler, British Columbia, V0N-1B0.

Finding the trail: In Canmore, follow signs to the Canmore Nordic Centre. The trail begins in the main arena area behind the day lodge.

Sources of additional information: Contact the Canmore Nordic Centre at (403) 678-2400, or address mail to Canmore Nordic Centre, Suite 100, 1988 Olympic Way, Canmore, Alberta, T1W-2T6. You may also want to visit Altitude Sports on Canmore's main drag for a copy of the Canmore Recreation Map.

Notes on the trail: This route, which is unusually difficult to follow, begins in the main arena area behind the day lodge. As you leave the day lodge, stay to the left and pass under Bridge 13 and leave the day lodge behind. As you pass under the bridge, you'll climb a short, sharp hill. At the top of this hill, make an immediate left following an unsigned route. Climb up this trail, passing to the right of Junction (Jcn) 84 (do not approach the junction; instead, stay on the unmarked route) at km 0.22 (0.13 mi.). Continue climbing after the route crosses a major trail. As you meet a T intersection with a culvert to the right at km 0.33 (0.2 mi.), climb up to the left and cross over Bridge 15. As you make the crossing, you'll see some pipes sticking up vertically from the ground. Ride past these pipes and take the right fork at km 0.57 (0.34 mi.) and begin climbing a single-track. If you pass a sign indicating "Access Road," you have missed this unmarked junction. As you climb, stay to the left at the first junction and left again at km 0.85 (0.51 mi.).

As you wind your way along the single-track, you may pass a pile of rolled-up blue plastic fencing and a blue board at km 1.11 (0.67 mi.). The trail makes a hard right at this point as you begin to round the outer portion of the Killer B's Loop. This point marks the start of a rooted, technical climb until you meet a T intersection at km 1.41 (0.85 mi.). Turn left at this junction and continue until you meet Jnc. 79 on the cross-country ski trails. Do not stay on the wide trail; instead, take the rough single-track that forks off just beside the junction sign. This marks the beginning of Ziggy's and the start of a tricky, rooted uphill. At km 1.93 (1.16 mi.), the trail joins a wider single-track. Follow this trail around to the left and enjoy an excellent view of Mount Rundle through the trees. This viewing spot marks the beginning of The Oven, which will continue to take you uphill while the sun bakes you. At another junction at km 2.12 (1.27 mi.), turn right onto the unmarked single-track of the Nectar Noodle and descend this winding, rooted single-track. As you meet a wider junction at km 2.6 (1.56 mi.), go left and bounce your way over the roots and bumps. Take the next right at 2.87 km (1.72 mi.) and finally cross a wide cross-country trail at 2.92 km (1.75 mi.). As you continue to drop, you'll see a log at head height leaning across the trail. Just in case you aren't quick enough, the log has been padded with ensolite and painted orange. At 3.2 km (1.92 mi.), take a right onto the first major trail you find. Continue to follow the wide cross-country trail as you pass Jcns 70, 71, 72, and 73. At the 3.8-km (2.28-mi.) mark, the original World Cup route drops down to the left to descend The Chute. It is closed for reclamation, but if you continue on the cross-country trail, you can take the next sharp drop to the left. Although it's easy to miss, this sharp drop is only 0.1 km beyond The Chute. This drop is a steep, rutted, expert-level descent, so be careful. Turn left at the bottom to return to the base of The Chute. The main route can be picked up again at this point. Turn right just beyond Jcn 78 (the base of The Chute) and drop down a sharp single-track, which brings you back to Bridge 15. This time, go under the bridge and follow the trail as it winds to the right. Stay straight on the high trail and go over the Camel's Hump. This fast stretch allows you to scream your way to Coaches Corner. Pass Jcn 81 at km 4.46 (2.68 mi.). Beyond this point, a hairpin turn will either send you into the bush or wind you to the left and bring you to the score clock above the day lodge. Beyond the score clock, the trail crosses another main route just to the right of Jcn 82, where it takes you on a short single-track descent. You're now back to the point where you began the ride, but this time, you continue over Bridge 13 and begin the lower part of the course.

As you cross the bridge, roll your way for 0.18 km (0.1 mi.) and pass under Bridge 14. Beyond the bridge, take a sharp right and head toward the shooting range. Follow the pavement as you pass the range. As you approach Bridge 12, turn left onto a rough single-track rather than continuing on the paved trail that winds beneath the bridge. As the trail you've taken parallels the training centre, stay to the right at the first junction, cresting a small wood-chip-covered uphill at km 5.75 (3.45 mi.). As the wood-chips route makes a switchback to the left, stay straight on a narrow single-track, then go left over a gravel hump and be prepared for a sudden drop. Part of the route has been fenced off, but you can get around it on the left. This is a serious, expert-level descent known as the Devonian Drop. Halfway down, a tree has fallen, leaning across the trail at head level. At the base of this drop the trail winds around a small pond and then joins the Canmore Trail at a T intersection.

Turn left almost 180 degrees onto this wide gravel trail. As you crest a loose uphill, the trail bounces down a small dip at km 6.4 (3.84 mi.). At the bottom of the dip is a fork in the trail that's almost hidden. Be sure to take the right fork, which will join a cross-country trail at 6.56 km (3.94 mi.). Follow the double-track for a moment, then take the first single-track on the right and begin the Disk Drive. The single-track crosses a wide cross-country trail and continues on the opposite side. Join a wide trail again at km 7.17 (4.3 mi.). Follow this route under Bridge 5, where the trail crosses the paved path, and continue climbing. You'll pass a "Do Not Enter/One Way" sign. As the trail makes a sharp switchback to the left, stay straight on a short section of single-track. Rejoin the paved path at km 7.69 (4.65 mi.). Be cautious since you are riding the wrong way on a path that may have roller-skiers coming toward you—yield to these athletes. As the pavement makes a hard right, leave the pavement near Jcn 24, turning left onto a wide gravel trail. As you roll past Jcn 35, go up and over Bridge 8 (again passing a "Do Not Enter" sign) as it crosses the wide gravel of the Banff Trail. Immediately over the bridge, turn left and take the trail that parallels the wide Banff Trail.

The route enters the homestretch now. Continue to follow the trail that parallels the Banff Trail, crossing a wide trail at km 7.94 (4.76 mi.). Just beyond this crossing, a major trail comes in from the right. You'll see a bridge up and to the right as the trail joins a smooth, wide, sawdust-covered route. Climb up over Bridge 14 and drop back down into the arena area, finishing at km 8.67 (5.2 mi.).

RIDE 4 · CNC Canada Cup Route

AT A GLANCE

Length/configuration: 9.18-km (5.51-mi.) loop, though various configurations are possible.

Aerobic difficulty: Moderate, with limited elevation gain.

Technical difficulty: While most of the ride stays on wide trails, there are several difficult single-track sections, including the expert-level drop of the T2 Trail.

Scenery: The trail is generally tree-bound, with a few views of the surrounding peaks of Mount Rundle to the west and the Fairholme Range to the east.

AB

Special comments: This route tends to change regularly as race orga-
nizers modify the routing and erosion closes damaged sections. Do not go
into areas marked as closed.

Another of the Canmore Nordic Centre Race Courses, the Canada Cup
Route uses a large portion of the network to make a loop of approximately
9.18 km (5.51 mi.). The Canada Cup is a series of seven races held at different
locations nationwide. It attracts a huge number of expert riders, and this route
provides a challenging way to follow their tracks. While the actual routing of the
course changes over time, this description provides a rideable option as of
November 1999. At that time, the steep drop of the Coal Chutes was closed off
due to erosion and downed trees. This closing not only eliminated this technical
drop, but it also removed the long climb of the Georgetown Hill. With the
almost endless range of possibilities on this network, however, you can vary this
route as the mood takes you. Just keep a copy of the trail map handy so that you
can regain your bearings when you return to the main trail network.

Keep in mind that this trail goes up several trails in opposition to one-way signs.
These signs are intended to ensure that cross-country skiers do not run into each
other, but the Nordic Centre does not encourage cyclists to ride against the grain,
either. Please be cautious of oncoming riders when on these sections of trail.

General location: Adjacent to the town of Canmore.

Elevation change: From the trailhead at approximately 1,430 m (4,690 ft.), the
trail climbs slightly before dropping toward the bottom of the Nordic Centre
trails, bottoming out at approximately 1,375 m (4,510 ft.). The last section of the
route regains that loss to return to the trailhead.

Season: Late May to mid-October.

Services: All services are available in the town of Canmore.

Hazards: The main challenges on this ride occur during the descent. There are
many rooted drops with several extremely short, rutted descents. You'll also need
to yield to other riders on the few stretches where you travel counter to the
signed cross-country routes.

Rescue index: In an emergency, return to the day lodge, where help can usually
be found. If it is closed, a pay phone outside will allow you to call 911. The trails
are popular with local cyclists, who can also offer assistance.

Land status: The trail is within Canmore Nordic Centre Provincial Park.

Maps: The NTS 1:50,000 Series topographic map for this trail is 82 O/3 Canmore; however, this route is not marked on it. A better option is the Canmore
Alberta Recreation Map produced by TerraPro Recmaps, P.O. Box 1016,
Whistler, British Columbia, V0N-1B0. The Canmore Nordic Centre has produced its own map, but sections of this trail are not indicated on it.

Finding the trail: In Canmore, follow signs to the Canmore Nordic Centre.
The trail begins in the main arena area behind the day lodge.

Sources of additional information: Contact the Canmore Nordic Centre at
(403) 678-2400, or address mail to Canmore Nordic Centre, Suite 100, 1988

RIDE 4 · CNC Canada Cup Route

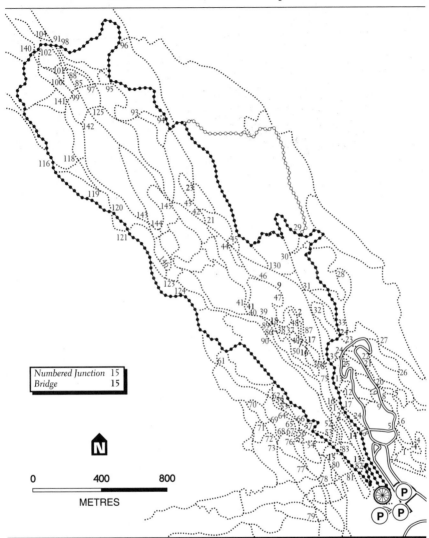

Numbered Junction 15
Bridge 15

N

0   400   800

METRES

Olympic Way, Canmore, Alberta, T1W-2T6. You may also want to visit Altitude Sports on Canmore's main drag for a copy of the Canmore Recreation Map.

Notes on the trail: This route varies from year to year, largely because some of the single-track sections have been damaged by excessive erosion, along with windstorms that brought down hundreds of trees at the Nordic Centre. As of November 1999, this version of the route was open and available.

Beginning in the main stadium, behind the day lodge, roll away from the day lodge and climb the trail beneath the bridge. As you crest this hill, make a sharp left and continue climbing on an unsigned trail. As you make your way, you'll

The author takes a break on the Canada Cup Route at Canmore Nordic Centre.

meet a **T** intersection at km 0.42 (0.25 mi.). Turn left and then right onto a wide trail just to the left of Junction (Jcn) 82. Turn right onto a trail with a "More Difficult" sign as you pass two tall water pipes used in the lodge's snowmaking operations. Almost immediately, join a wide trail just above Jcn 84. Stay to the right on this trail, and go right again at Jcn 53 just after the sign for the 15 km Special Loop. At Jcn 57, at km 0.63 (0.38 mi.), make a sharp right, following the 15 km Special Loop. This trail climbs a short hill and then rolls to the left. Stay right (straight) at Jcn 58, despite all the arrows pointing to the left. At km 1.06 (0.64 mi.), you'll see the fork of Jcn 60. At this fork, you'll leave the wide trails behind. If you look straight ahead, a bit of orange flagging tape marks a single-track leaving the groomed trails—take this trail. The high-quality single-track rolls along the edge of an embankment and bounces over numerous small trees and roots. Turn left as the single-track forks at km 1.41 (0.85 mi.). The single-track meets the wide cross-country trails again at km 1.52 (0.91 mi.), but you want to avoid joining these wide trails. If you look to the right, you'll see the single-track continue; you want to stay on it. You do finally rejoin the wide cross-country network at km 1.72 (1.03 mi.). As you emerge, turn right, and this trail will merge with an even wider trail by 1.79 km (1.07 mi.).

Ride the wide trail for 0.16 km (0.1 mi.), where another single-track will fork to the left just before you reach Jcn 124. This single-track climbs at right angles to the wide cross-country trail, eventually rolling right and dropping back to the winter ski network. Turn left on the wide trail at km 2.33 (1.4 mi.) after a technical, rooted descent. Kick into high gear at this point and enjoy the double-track for a while. Stay straight at Jcn 120, then at Jcn 121 wind uphill to the left at this three-way junction. Essentially, you'll be taking the middle trail past a "Do Not Enter" sign. As you meet Jcn 116, follow the red arrow for the 15 km Special Trail and drop off to take the lower trail, paralleling the route you've been riding. This section provides access to the Terminator and T2 single-tracks. Keep an eye to the right as you ride this section, and at km 3.55 (2.13 mi.) turn right as a trail crosses the wide route. To the right, you'll see a small downed log and a small uphill. Climb this hill. As you crest the top, turn left onto the unmarked single-track of T2. Terminator drops straight down the slope, and T2 takes the high line atop the embankment. Novices can avoid this extreme expert section by merely ignoring this last junction and staying straight on the main trail. The two trails soon meet again.

T2 begins deceptively as it rolls along the top of the steep embankment, but at km 3.71 (2.23 mi.) it heads straight down the fall line for an expert-level descent. Do not do this section unless you feel very comfortable dropping along nearly vertical fall lines. This sharp descent spits you back onto the cross-country network at km 3.93 (2.36 mi.). Turn right and come to another junction at km 4.03 (2.42 mi.). While numerous trails arrive at this junction, you want to stay straight across it to take the narrowest trail on the opposite side. While not a single-track, it is narrower than the others, and it will bring you to Jcn 102. As you approach it, turn left and drop down to Jcn 104 and then go right. Cross the wide Banff Trail at a diagonal at Jcn 91 and almost immediately meet Jcn 98. Go left and pass another "Do Not Enter" sign.

Enjoy the pleasant descent along this next section, which rolls you to an unmarked junction at km 4.71 (2.83 mi.). Here, the Banff Trail is about 50 m ahead, but you want to roll right and begin climbing. At Jcn 96, this route continues climbing to the right. An alternative route would have you turn left here, cross the Banff Trail, and then join the challenging single-track of Skull Mountain. For the ride described here, though, avoid the temptation and continue climbing. Stay left on the main trail at a rough junction at km 4.87 (2.92 mi.) and ignore a single-track coming in from the right soon after. As the trail crests at Jcn 95, stay to the far left as several trails join here. At 5.34 km (3.2 mi.), the trail approaches the Banff Trail. Do not go down to this wide trail; instead, wind to the right to drop down a steep gully as you pass a wooden retaining wall on your right. Climb the opposite side and stay straight at the unmarked junction at the crest of this short ride/push, then go left at the next junction. At Jcn 94, stay to the right, ignoring trail signs pointing to the left, and drop down a small gully. Almost immediately, as you climb a short hill, a single-track crosses the trail. Head left on this single-track and drop down to the Banff Trail.

The traditional Canada Cup Route crosses the Banff Trail on the single-track of the Coal Chutes. These trails were closed in 1999 due to excessive erosion and dozens of fallen trees. Instead, roll to the right and follow the wide track of the Banff Trail, keeping your eye out for single-tracks off to the left. After passing a brown "2 KM" sign, a single-track drops to the left at km 6.58 (3.95 mi.). Take this trail and enjoy a short single-track diversion. Emerge onto a wide trail at km 6.81 (4.09 mi.), then turn left. This trail drops down and winds to the right to join the top of the Georgetown Hill at Jcn 29. Stay straight, crossing this trail, and follow it as it winds to the right. As you make the turn, you'll notice a single-track forking to the left—ignore it. However, you will take a second single-track to the left just as the trail crests a hill after straightening out. Stay on this single-track as it crosses the main trail, and remain on it as it winds to the left and levels out. After a pleasant roll, it drops sharply down to a small bridge before climbing back up the opposite side. Rejoin the cross-country network at km 7.79 (4.67 mi.) just as the trail makes a long loop. Take the upper trail on this corner, and avoid the temptation to continue on the single-track that makes a hard right at this point.

As you approach Jcn 33 at km 8.0 (4.8 mi.), turn left and begin following the route of the Lower 5 km Trail (red arrow). Simply follow the red arrows for the rest of the route. They will direct you over Bridge 24 to a left turn at Jcn 34, a right at Jcn 35, a left at Jcn 15, a right at Jcn 17, and finally a left at Jcn 18. This will drop you back down to the starting area at km 9.18 (5.51 mi.).

RIDE 5 · CNC Georgetown Trail

AT A GLANCE

Length/configuration: 5.76-km (3.46-mi.) loop.

Aerobic difficulty: The climb up the Georgetown Hill is enough to humble the most fit rider. Don't feel bad if you end up pushing the top section.

AB

Technical difficulty: The steep climb requires good technique along with strong lungs, but the vast majority of the trail is easy.

Scenery: There are great views of the Fairholme Range and the Bow River to the east.

Special comments: This trail has a secondary purpose as a self-guided interpretive trail. Take the time to read some of the many interpretive panels along the route.

While this trail is a very popular 5.76-km (3.46-mi.) loop, it also reflects the history of an area that was built on coal mining. This trail has two main access points. The principal access is from the Nordic Centre itself, and this is the trail as described here. Most Canmorites, however, access the trail by climbing the long staircase from the Rundle Power Plant on the Canmore Townsite Trails. This offers quick access to the Nordic Centre without a car.

In the early 1880s the railway made its way into the mountains and brought coal-hungry locomotives with it. Over time, numerous mines opened up within this coal-rich valley to provide this essential fuel to the Canadian Pacific Railway. Mines like Bankhead, Anthracite, Canmore, and Georgetown competed to supply the railway. While Georgetown was abandoned after only four years, it was a bustling community during its heyday, boasting a company store, school, and bunkhouses, all with electricity and running water. When the mine closed, some of the buildings were moved to Canmore, and a few of them are still used today.

RIDE 5 · CNC Georgetown Trail

General location: Adjacent to the town of Canmore.

Elevation change: From the trailhead at approximately 1,420 m (4,658 ft.), the trail drops steadily to a minimum elevation of 1,300 m (4,264 ft.). It then turns uphill and reclaims all the elevation, most of it along the challenging climb of the Georgetown Hill.

Season: Late May to mid-October.

Services: All services are available in the town of Canmore.

Hazards: The trail is wide, with few hazards.

Rescue index: In an emergency, return to the day lodge, where help can usually be found. If it is closed, a pay phone outside will allow you to call 911. The trails are popular with local cyclists, who can also offer assistance.

Land status: The trail is within Canmore Nordic Centre Provincial Park.

Maps: The NTS 1:50,000 Series topographic map for this trail is 82 O/3 Canmore; however, this route is not marked on it. A better option is the Canmore Alberta Recreation Map produced by TerraPro Recmaps, P.O. Box 1016, Whistler, British Columbia, V0N-1B0. The Canmore Nordic Centre has also produced a free map, which shows this route well.

Finding the trail: In Canmore, follow signs to the Canmore Nordic Centre. The trail begins in the main arena area behind the day lodge.

Sources of additional information: Contact the Canmore Nordic Centre at (403) 678-2400, or address mail to Canmore Nordic Centre, Suite 100, 1988 Olympic Way, Canmore, Alberta, T1W-2T6. You may also want to visit Altitude Sports on Canmore's main drag for a copy of the Canmore Recreation Map.

Notes on the trail: Beginning at the day lodge, ride along the paved access roads toward the line of flags. This route will take you past the Bill Warren Training Centre and the parking lot for the Biathlon Team Rooms. Just beyond the parking lot, join the paved trail and wind to the right, paralleling the parking lot. From here, the route will take you under the bridge with the shooting range off to your left. After you go under the bridge, you'll see a trail leaving the pavement and heading to the right. Take this trail, following the sign for the Georgetown Trail. Meet Jcn 1 at km 0.51 (0.31 mi.). The Georgetown Trail stays straight, following a green sign. Another sign will beckon you to the left at km 0.58 (0.35 mi.). As the trail meets a bridge at km 0.71 (0.43 mi.), avoid the temptation to cross it. Instead, turn left, then immediately right on a narrow trail that essentially goes beside the bridge. A sign indicates the Canmore Trail. At this point, the Georgetown Trail and the Canmore Trail are the same trail. At km 1.06 (0.64 mi.), the trail forks, with the Georgetown Trail going left and descending sharply. Stay left at another junction at km 1.15 (0.69 mi.). This brings you onto the main stretch of the Georgetown Trail. Some cyclists access the trail from the town of Canmore and will come in from the right as you meet this junction.

The trail begins to parallel a steep embankment on your right, with views of the river below. After some moderate climbing, the trail forks after passing some chin-up bars on your right. Take the right fork and begin descending on a wide, gravel double-track. Pass numerous interpretive signs on the descent, and cross a rocky runoff channel at km 2.68 (1.61 mi.). The drop bottoms out at km 2.88 (1.73 mi.), rolling along toward a meadow at km 3.67 (2.2 mi.). The meadow has several interpretive signs, and to your left you'll see a steep climb up a loose slope of coal. Thus begins the infamous Georgetown climb.

Drop into your granny gear and prepare to grind. The slope is misleading, with several false summits, before finally peaking as you meet Jcn 29 at km 4.39 (2.63 mi.). To continue on the Georgetown Trail, cross this **T** intersection and continue on a very gradual uphill gradient. At Jcn 30, stay left following the red arrow for the Lower 5 km Trail. At Jcn 31, the trail climbs to join the Banff Trail, which rolls along back to the trailhead. If you want to stay on the trails, another option is to continue following the Lower 5 km Trail. This route will also take you back to the trailhead. Once you've joined the Banff Trail, you'll follow the wide gravel until km 5.41 (3.25 mi.). At this point, the Banff Trail takes a left fork and leaves this wide, gravel access road. As you wind around to Jcn 18, take a left and drop down to join the paved path. Turn right and return to the Biathlon Centre at km 5.76 (3.46 mi.).

RIDE 6 · Canmore Canalside

AT A GLANCE

Length/configuration: 4.69-km (2.81-mi.) point-to-point.

Aerobic difficulty: The trail is level with a few short uphill sections.

Technical difficulty: The trail offers few technical challenges.

Scenery: While rolling along the reservoir, you'll have a view in all directions. To the east, the reservoir reflects the peaks of the Fairholme Range, while Mount Rundle and Ha Ling Peak own the western sky.

Special comments: A dip at Quarry Lake makes for a great finish.

This trail is a favourite of locals because of its endless views and pleasant demeanor. Along this 4.69-km (2.81-mi.) point-to-point, you are treated to some of the best views of the many peaks of the Bow Valley. Along the way, the ride passes Quarry Lake, one of Canmore's most popular summer hangouts. What more could you possibly want from a beginner ride. Bring the kids . . . and don't forget to pack your swimsuit.

Beginning at the entrance to the new Peaks of Grassi subdivision, the trail rolls along behind this quiet residential area before passing within view of Quarry Lake on your right. After passing another small pond, the trail rolls along beneath the power lines to eventually join the canal at km 2.64 (1.58 mi.). Across the spillway, many Trans Alta Utilities homes can be seen. To the west and southwest, the winding canal reflects the humplike summit of Ha Ling Peak (formerly Chinaman's Peak) and the long range of Mount Rundle. Across the valley, the peaks of the Fairholme Range complete the panorama. After winding along the canal, the trail ends at a junction with Spray Lakes Road.

General location: Within the town of Canmore.

Elevation change: Very little.

Season: Late May to mid-October.

Services: All services are available in the town of Canmore.

RIDE 6 · Canmore Canalside

Hazards: The trail is wide, with few hazards.

Rescue index: In an emergency, either return to the Peaks of Grassi subdivision or continue toward the day lodge of the Canmore Nordic Centre, where help can usually be found. If it is closed, a pay phone outside will allow you to call 911. This ride is popular with local cyclists and dog walkers, who can also offer assistance. Quarry Lake, is very popular on sunny summer days, so help is always close by.

Land status: Town of Canmore.

Grotto Mountain towers above the quiet serenity of the Canmore Canalside trail.

Maps: The NTS 1:50,000 Series topographic map for this trail is 82 O/3 Canmore; however, this route is not marked on it. A better option is the Canmore Alberta Recreation Map produced by TerraPro Recmaps, P.O. Box 1016, Whistler, British Columbia, V0N-1B0. The trail is not accurately marked on this map either, however, it is still the most up-to-date map of the area.

Finding the trail: From Canmore's Main Street, turn left onto 8th Avenue and follow this road as it winds over the Bow River Bridge. It continues to wind until it meets at **T** intersection with Three Sisters Drive. Turn left and continue climbing. As the road forks, stay to the left until this road ends near the newly opened Marriott Residence Inn. Turn right onto Peaks Drive and climb toward the Peaks of Grassi subdivision. As you approach the power line, the trail heads to the right, beneath the power lines. Park your car and take this trail.

Sources of additional information: Contact Tourism Canmore/Kananaskis at 801 8th Street, Canmore, AB, T1W-2B3, or call (403) 678-1295.

Notes on the trail: The wide trail begins beneath the power lines and follows them westward. Stay to the left at a fork with Quarry Lake, which is visible to the right at km 0.55 (0.33 mi.). Another fork goes to the left at km 0.77 (0.46 mi.). Stay to the right at this junction and continue following the power lines. Take the fork to the right at km 0.97 (0.58 mi.) since a deep runoff channel blocks the path ahead. Taking this right fork provides a bypass of this deep gouge. As you roll right, you'll see a path going to the left as you approach a wire fence. Cross the channel and follow the trail as it climbs back to the main trail at km 1.17 (0.7

mi.). Stay left at a trail fork at km 1.44 (0.86 mi.) and resume climbing. The trail descends slightly at km 2.06 (1.24 mi.), and soon the runoff channel for the reservoir comes into view on the right. After climbing again, you'll meet a final junction at km 2.49 (1.49 mi.). Turn right at this junction and begin rolling along the edge of the reservoir. Follow the wide path until you meet the junction with Spray Lakes Road at km 4.69 (2.81 mi.). You can either retrace your steps or turn right to return to Canmore.

RIDE 7 · Benchlands Trail Network

AT A GLANCE

Length/configuration: 8.96-km (5.38-mi.) loop, but distances can vary with the routing options you select.

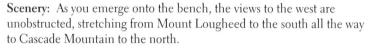

Aerobic difficulty: The trail has a stiff climb at the beginning, followed by moderate gains until the climbing crests at km 2.67 (1.6 mi.).

Technical difficulty: The trail has some highly technical descents along with great amounts of exposure.

Scenery: As you emerge onto the bench, the views to the west are unobstructed, stretching from Mount Lougheed to the south all the way to Cascade Mountain to the north.

Special comments: While this is a classic advanced ride, intermediate riders comfortable with exposure will also want to take it in.

For many years this ride remained one of the secrets of Canmore's hard-core elite, but with the publishing of the Canmore Alberta Recreation Map in 1999, the secret is out. Riders from all areas are learning to appreciate the magic offered by this narrow single-track network. While the distances can be varied, this sample loop stretches for 8.96 km (5.38 mi.), but distances can be easily doubled by staying on the high line of the bench and winding all the way to the community of Harvey Heights.

Along the way, the views are fabulous, highlighted by all the most famous peaks of the Bow Valley. To the south, the snowcapped peak of Mount Lougheed peaks out from behind the triple summit of the Three Sisters, easily the most photographed mountain in the Canmore Corridor. Directly across the valley, the rolling summit of Ha Ling Peak (formerly Chinaman's Peak) pays tribute to a Chinese miner who climbed it in order to win a bet more than a hundred years ago. To the right of Ha Ling Peak is the long ridge of Mount Rundle. To the north, the defiant peak of Cascade Mountain stands above the town of Banff. Below your feet, you can almost feel the town of Canmore growing, slowly, relentlessly. In just ten years, it has tripled its population. It's not difficult to understand how habitats like this one can easily be threatened by development. With this in mind, the Benchlands form a critical wildlife corridor for large car-

RIDE 7 · Benchlands Trail Network

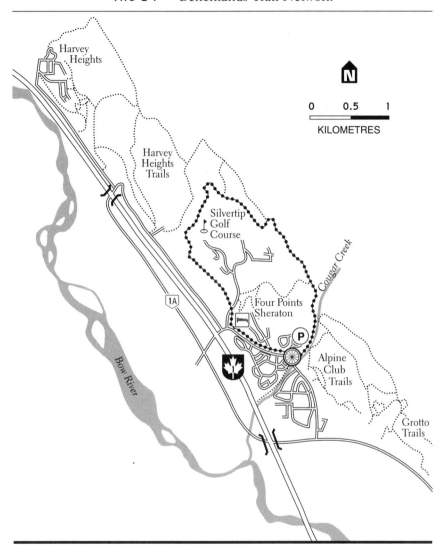

nivores, and as such, it may be closed to hiking and biking at some point. Be sure to check its status before heading out.

General location: Within the town of Canmore.

Elevation change: From the trailhead at 1,370 m (4,497 ft.), the trail climbs steadily to a maximum elevation of 1,600 m (5,248 ft.). From there, it's downhill all the way until you emerge at the Four Points Sheraton Hotel at 1,350 m (4,428 ft.). A final stretch of gradual uphill along Benchlands Trail will bring you back to the trailhead.

Season: Late May to mid-October.

Services: All services are available in the town of Canmore.

Hazards: This ride involves a steep push to access the bench, after which it traverses the slopes of Lady MacDonald. The exposure along these side-cuts may intimidate novices, but the views easily compensate. The descent off the bench is also very steep, so be cautious.

Rescue index: In an emergency, you'll need to decide whether to return toward the trailhead or continue toward one of the other exits from the trail. The trail is popular with hikers and cyclists, so you may be able to find assistance en route. Also, a great cellular signal is available throughout the ride.

Land status: Town of Canmore land. The trail status is uncertain, though, as talk has been heard of closing this area to hiking and biking since it forms a critical wildlife corridor. It may become subject to development as well, so check for current status.

Maps: The NTS 1:50,000 Series topographic map for this trail is 82 O/3 Canmore; however, this route is not marked it. A better option is the Canmore Alberta Recreation Map produced by TerraPro Recmaps, P.O. Box 1016, Whistler, British Columbia, V0N-1B0.

Finding the trail: In Canmore, follow Benchlands Trail to the main Cougar Creek trailhead. It's on the left side of the road as it makes a sharp right turn to become Elk Run Boulevard. Park in the trailhead parking lot and begin by rolling along the pavement.

Sources of additional information: Contact Tourism Canmore/Kananaskis at 801 8th Street, Canmore, AB, T1W-2B3, or call (403) 678-1295.

Notes on the trail: The trail heads upstream on wide pavement that almost immediately fades to gravel. As you continue upstream, the trail quickly deteriorates into a narrow single-track that parallels the rocky riverbed. At km 0.95 (0.57 mi.), you'll see a small rock cairn and a fork in the trail. Take the left fork and leave the river behind. This trail begins a steep switchback up the embankment. Push/ride your way as the trail climbs. Soon after your first open views of Three Sisters and two informal junctions, the actual trail forks to the left at km 1.21 (0.73 mi.). The trail becomes rideable again almost immediately as you start the traverse of the upper bench. Stay right at a rough junction at km 1.44 (0.86 mi.). The left fork drops sharply down the bench toward Silvertip Drive. After this junction, the trail climbs gradually, with some incredible views across the valley to the west. Stay left at another informal junction at km 2.05 (1.23 mi.) and continue climbing until you crest the main uphill at 2.67 km (1.6 mi.). A highly exposed section of side-cut carries you around a river channel at km 2.9 (1.74 mi.), which then brings you to another junction at km 2.96 (1.78 mi.). The right junction continues on to more great views along the bench, and eventually it continues toward Harvey Heights. For this route, turn left and drop down the steep fall line.

The drop bottoms out at 3.13 km (1.88 mi.). Head right and stay on the single-track as it parallels some of the fairways of Silvertip Golf Course. As you leave the golf links behind, the trail becomes a pleasant single-track, rolling along on a carpet of needles. The trail makes a sharp downhill drop at km 3.85

CANMORE/KANANASKIS COUNTRY **37**

(2.31 mi.), and, after leveling out, it brings you to another junction. Turn left here. If you head to the right, the trail climbs back up to the bench. Beyond this junction, the trail retains its marvelous rolling character as it descends. Off to the right, the trail is bordered by a steep streambed. The trail slowly rolls around to the southeast, which brings you to an informal junction at km 5.0 (3.0 mi.). Stay right and quickly drop down a sheer descent toward another junction. Again, stay right and continue the steady descent. At km 5.65 (3.39 mi.), you'll encounter a very tricky drop down to yet another junction. Stay straight and climb up onto the lower bench. This route takes you along the lower bench with views of Canmore to the right and one putting green of Silvertip Golf Course to the left. Enjoy this final stretch of bench because it ends all too soon. The trail emerges atop a steep embankment at km 7.1 (4.26 mi.) with no other way but down. You can either drop straight down the fall line to the right, or you can head left on a slightly easier drop. Either way, you'll emerge onto Silvertip Trail at approximately 7.48 km (4.49 mi.). If you want to return to the trailhead, cross the road and follow a trail that winds past the cemetery and then parallels Benchlands Trail. Arrive back at your vehicle at km 8.96 (5.38 mi.).

RIDE 8 · Baldy Pass

AT A GLANCE

Length/configuration: 17.0-km (10.6-mi.) point-to-point.

Aerobic difficulty: The trail has a sharp climb of 458 m (1,500 ft.) to crest the pass. A strong set of lungs is a prerequisite.

Technical difficulty: The drop down the south side of the pass includes a sharp descent along a very loose scree slope. While expert riders will be able to ride this short section, most riders will push their bike down it.

Scenery: The view from the summit is limited by the high peak of Mount Baldy to your right, but there are nice views toward the rolling foothills behind you and the rugged peaks around Mount Allan to the southwest.

Special comments: This challenging ride crests a rugged mountain pass. The loose rock descent can easily eject novices. Therefore, this ride is for experts only.

This 17.0-km (10.6-mi.) out-and-back takes you over a saddle on the southeast end of Mount Baldy. In the north-south direction it's an expert-level trail with a long, grinding uphill to a dramatic, rocky summit. This stretch is followed by an extremely technical descent that has body-slammed the best of riders.

The trail begins as a nice double-track as it climbs toward the summit of Baldy Pass. From the pass, the summit of Mount Baldy rises sharply to the northwest, and Wasootch Towers can be seen to the southwest. To the east, the rolling foothills slowly give way to the seemingly endless plains. This is a world of steep, stark contrast. Mount Baldy is sharp and rocky with scant vegetation.

From the pass, the trail descends a precariously rideable scree slope until it enters the forest beneath the summit. As it traverses the slopes of Mount Baldy, it becomes very narrow along the edge of a steep embankment. Most riders, including myself, take their lumps here. Endless possibilities for disaster exist here, so be especially cautious. Don't even think of riding this trail without a helmet unless you have a death wish! At the 12.0-km (7.5-mi.) mark, the trail begins to level out, and at km 17.5 (mi. 10.9) it becomes a double-track again.

This mountain was named by German prisoners kept in a camp at its base during World War II. To relieve the boredom of a POW camp, they were allowed to leave its confines and climb this mountain—as long as they promised not to escape while outside camp gates. Not one of them ever attempted to flee while on one of these passes. In addition, since POWs were required to be fed the same quantity of food as that fed to overseas Canadian troops, many locals complained that the prisoners were treated better than home-front Canadians, who were subjected to severe rationing.

General location: The trail is located within the Kananaskis Valley, one of the best-known areas of Alberta's Kananaskis Country.

Elevation change: Beginning at a relatively low 1,373 m (4,500 ft.), this trail moves steadily uphill. But the difficult climbing awaits you at the 5.6-km (3.5-mi.) mark. By the time you reach the summit, you've climbed a total of 458 m (1,500 ft.) to max out at 1,830 m (6,000 ft.). From the summit, it drops off suddenly down a steep scree slope. This slope is rideable for expert bikers, but most riders will want to walk their bikes down the steepest part of the slope.

Season: This high-elevation trail is passable only during the warmest part of summer. It remains snowbound until mid-June. After the first snowfall of autumn, the trail remains snowbound.

Services: You can find the nearest services at the centres of Dead Man's Flats and Canmore. Both are located west of the junction between Highway 40 and Highway 1. Dead Man's Flats is primarily a roadside service centre with little more than several service stations and motel accommodations. Canmore offers all services.

Hazards: This trail has hazards galore. Relatively safe until you reach the summit, it becomes an expert-only trail from that point. Dropping suddenly, it is rideable but incredibly tricky. It traverses a steep embankment strewn with loose rocks and other obstacles that have dumped many a rider. If you survive this descent, the trail eventually smoothes out again at km 12 (mi. 7.5).

Rescue index: This trail is not heavily traveled, so you may not always encounter other traffic. It starts and finishes along major roadways, however, so you can usually flag down vehicles. The nearest access to rescue services is at the Barrier Lake Visitor Information Centre. If it is closed, a pay phone outside provides 24-hour access to emergency services.

Land status: This area is part of Kananaskis Country, a 4,250-square-kilometre provincial recreation area.

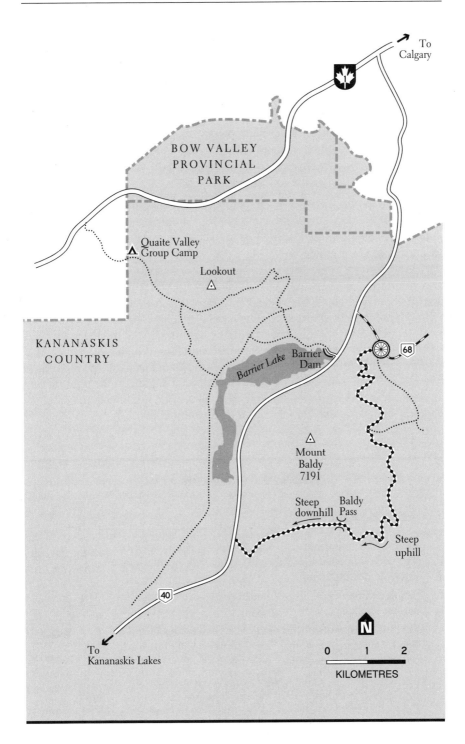

To
Calgary

BOW VALLEY
PROVINCIAL
PARK

Quaite Valley
Group Camp

Lookout

KANANASKIS
COUNTRY

Barrier Lake Barrier
Dam

68

Mount
Baldy
7191

Steep   Baldy
downhill Pass

Steep
uphill

40

To
Kananaskis Lakes

N

0   1   2

KILOMETRES

Maps: The 1:50,000 scale topographic maps for this trail are 82 O/3 Canmore and 82 J/14 Spray Lakes Reservoir. Map Town produces an excellent trail map called "Kananaskis Country—Spray Lakes and Canmore Region."

Finding the trail: Head west from Calgary on Highway 1 until its junction with Highway 40 (the Kananaskis Trail). Head south to the junction with the Sibbald Creek Trail. There, turn left and travel a short distance to the Stoney Creek trailhead.

Sources of additional information: The Kananaskis Country address is listed in the introduction to this section. For up-to-date trail conditions, contact the Barrier Lake Travel Information Centre at (403) 673-3985.

Notes on the trail: The trail begins as a nice wide fire road through a mixture of trembling aspen and lodgepole pine. There are several junctions in the first kilometre (0.6 mi.); bear left at each of these. At km 2.6 (mi. 1.6), you'll pass a junction to Stoney Creek, and a bit farther, at km 4.4 (mi. 2.7), you'll see the junction to Lusk Pass–Link Trail. This first stretch is smooth, but steadily uphill. At km 5.6 (mi. 3.5) a steep stretch passes through some old fire scars. The climbing is unrelenting as you pass an unsigned junction at km 8.1 (mi. 5.0). From this point, the route becomes steep single-track. As you approach the summit at km 10.4 (mi. 6.5), you'll find yourself pushing a bit as you do the final climbing.

From the summit, the drop is treacherous, sudden, and steady for km 1.3 (0.8 mi.). It traverses a lengthy side-cut, which constitutes one of the most technical stretches. Watch for loose rocks as you travel along this narrow ledge. After approximately 3.0 km (1.9 mi.), the trail levels out and parallels the highway to Wasootch Creek. You can also exit the trail down a cut-line to the right, 3.0 km (1.9 mi.) from the summit. This trail will shorten the ride if you are using the highway to make a loop completely around Mount Baldy.

RIDE 9 · Stoney Trail

AT A GLANCE

Length/configuration: 16.5-km (10.25-mi.) point-to-point. The wide shoulder of Highway 40 can serve to create a loop of just over 30 km (18 mi.).

Aerobic difficulty: This is a moderately level trail with little aerobic challenge.

Technical difficulty: Most of the ride follows the wide power line access road. A few small hills are strewn with loose rock, but otherwise the challenges are limited.

Scenery: The open character of this ride offers many views of Barrier Lake and Mount Baldy on its eastern shoreline. To the west, Mount Lorette borders the trail. As you near the southern end of the ride, the Olympic ski hill, Nakiska at Mount Allan, comes into view.

Special comments: This is an excellent early season ride. While trails at higher elevations are still snowbound, Stoney Trail receives generous amounts of sunlight, often clearing it of snow ahead of its neighbouring rides.

This 16.5-km (10.25-mi.) point-to-point or out-and-back begins at the north end of Barrier Lake and follows its shores for 7 km (4.4 mi.). It then leaves the lake behind and parallels the Kananaskis River. For strong riders, this trail will take about 90 minutes one-way to complete. Although the trail is an out-and-back, it turns into an enjoyable loop when combined with a return ride on Highway 40. In addition, it can form a challenging loop with Prairie View and Jewell Pass trails.

Scenically, the trail is superb. Riding along the shores of emerald-green Barrier Lake, you'll look across toward the steep slopes of Mount Baldy and south toward Mount Lorette. Mount Baldy was named by German POWs in remembrance of a similar mountain in Germany. A prison camp was located beneath its towering slopes, and the site still houses a museum highlighting this colourful bit of history. The prisoners were allowed to leave the camp to climb this mountain—as long as they promised not to escape while outside camp fences. Believe it or not, no prisoners tried to run while out on passes. Many enjoyed the scenery of the Rockies so much that they tried—unsuccessfully—to stay on after the war.

As you leave the south end of the lake, the southern vista begins to include the Olympic Ski Hill on Mount Allan and the Wasootch Valley to the east. Nakiska at Mount Allan, as this Olympic development is known, is still a popular winter ski destination. Its slopes also hold the highest hiking trail in the Canadian Rockies, the Mount Allan Centennial Trail. With a maximum elevation in excess of 2,800 m (9,186 ft.) and a gain of 1,400 m (4,593 ft.), it's a trail for only the most determined hikers. It was developed in celebration of Canada's Centennial in 1967.

The Stoney Trail is ideal for riders who don't get an evil glow in their eyes whenever they strap on a helmet. It is a moderate route with a wide track for its entire length. The climbs are virtually all rideable, and the downhills are generally smooth.

General location: The trail is located in the Kananaskis Valley, within Kananaskis Country, approximately an hour west of Calgary, Alberta.

Elevation change: Although this is a rolling trail, the actual elevation gain is virtually zero. Some of the hills are a steep uphill grind, but they are short, and some enjoyable downhills compensate for the steepness.

Season: This trail is relatively open and can be ridden from the early part of May to mid-October.

Services: The nearest services are in Dead Man's Flats and Canmore. However, near the south end of the trail lies the Kananaskis Village with accommodations, basic supplies, and restaurants. In addition, the Kananaskis Valley has hundreds of campsites.

Hazards: Several junctions on this trail are not clearly visible, particularly if you are riding fast. You'll need to keep your eyes open for the dark green trail signs to

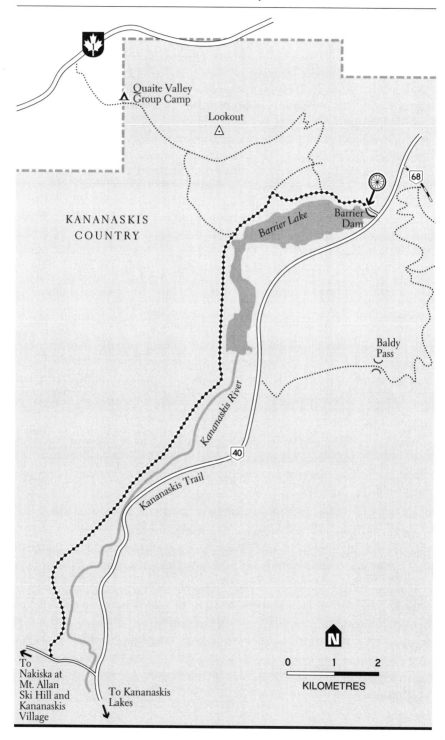

Quaite Valley
Group Camp

Lookout

KANANASKIS
COUNTRY

Barrier Lake

Barrier
Dam

68

Baldy
Pass

Kananaskis River

40

Kananaskis Trail

N

0   1   2
KILOMETRES

To
Nakiska at
Mt. Allan
Ski Hill and
Kananaskis
Village

To Kananaskis
Lakes

ensure that you stay on the route described here. It is difficult to get truly lost, but you can end up losing time if you take a wrong turn. Since you are riding in the mountains, make sure you bring along proper clothing for the sudden storms that sometimes blow in. During autumn, hunters may be using this trail as a staging area, so wearing bright colours is a good idea. Also, since this trail does allow for some speed, keep your eyes open for animals on the trail. This trail is also used by horses. Please be courteous when you encounter them, as horses may spook when riders come up too quickly from behind.

If you're thinking of taking the highway back north, a wide paved shoulder is available, but it is still a busy highway, so be cautious. As is common in areas of scenic splendor, drivers don't always watch the road as closely as they should, so be extra vigilant on this stretch of road.

Rescue index: This popular trail generally has other cyclists who can lend a hand, and both the north and south ends provide quick access to emergency services. Just north of the trailhead at Barrier Dam Day Use Area is the Barrier Lake Visitor Information Centre. From this office you can access park rangers and emergency services. If the centre is closed, a pay phone is outside. From the south end of the trail, you can flag down vehicles along the road. If the road is quiet, turn left when you reach pavement, and, in a short distance, you'll meet Highway 40. Just south of this junction is the headquarters of the valley's emergency services. You can always find assistance there.

Land status: The area is operated as part of Kananaskis Country. This is a provincial recreation area.

Maps: The 1:50,000 scale topographic maps for this trail are 82 O/3 Canmore and 82 J/14 Spray Lakes Reservoir. Map Town produces an excellent trail map entitled "Kananaskis Country—Spray Lakes and Canmore Region."

Finding the trail: Finding this trail is very easy. Heading west from Calgary on the Trans Canada Highway (Highway 1) for 45 minutes, you'll see the junction for the Kananaskis Trail (Highway 40). Head south for 8.4 km (5.2 mi.) to Barrier Dam Day Use Area. From the parking lot, cross the dam, and the trail begins on the opposite side. As you climb the hill to the first junction, turn left onto Stoney Trail.

Sources of additional information: The Kananaskis Country address is listed in the introduction to this section. For up-to-date trail conditions, contact the Barrier Lake Travel Information Centre at (403) 673-3985.

Notes on the trail: From the parking lot, cross the dam and climb a slight hill to the first junction at km 1.1 (mi. 0.7). Turn left onto Stoney Trail and begin to head south. The next junction is at km 2.2 (mi. 1.4). Although this juncture is unmarked and appears to go straight, take the right-hand branch to avoid a steep gully. At km 2.7 (mi. 1.7), turn left at a signed junction. If you're heading north on the trail, missing this turn can mean missing the trailhead, which will cause you to continue well beyond the northern parking lot. The trail makes its way back toward the shoreline, and at km 4.2 (mi. 2.6) you pass the junction with Jewell Pass Trail. Continue on Stoney Trail, and at km 6.7 (mi. 4.2) a short, steep climb takes you above the south end of Barrier Lake. It quickly drops off this ledge for a short distance before climbing back again. Shortly after this second climb, at km 8.3 (mi. 5.2), a dead-end trail descends to the left—keep right at this point. The rest of the ride is along rolling terrain with impressive views to the south and east. At km 15.4 (mi. 9.6), the trail becomes a gravel access road, and at km 16.6 (mi. 10.3) you join the paved road to Nakiska at Mount Allan, the Olympic ski hill. If you're cycling the road loop, turn left at this point for 1.0 km (0.6 mi.) to a **T** intersection with Highway 40. Turn left on the paved highway, and the rolling route back will add another enjoyable 15.0 km (9.3 mi.) to your ride.

RIDE 10 · Prairie View Trail

AT A GLANCE

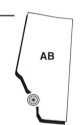

Length/configuration: 16.11-km (10.0-mi.) loop. The technical sections can be avoided by riding the road to the vista point and then returning along the same route for an 11.02-km (6.61-mi.) out-and-back.

Aerobic difficulty: The climb to the vista point ascends 538 m (1,765 ft.) in 5.51 km (3.4 mi.), so a good level of fitness is required.

Technical difficulty: The ride includes a tricky hike-a-bike section along with a rocky descent into the trees. It becomes a challenging trip once you pass the vista point.

Scenery: The view from atop Prairie View is spectacular.

Special comments: However you ride it, the view from the top is worth every inch of the climb. There are few rides that provide a panorama equal to this one.

If you like climbing high above the valley to attain excellent alpine panoramas, this 16.11-km (10.0-mi.) loop is for you. It's a beginner trail to the viewing point, but it becomes an expert-level trail beyond that point.

The trail climbs a good fire road to a ridge above Barrier Lake. From there, the emerald-green waters of the lake are unimaginably brilliant. Across the valley, the imposing face of Mount Baldy juts above the valley.

From the main viewing point, the trail climbs a small rock face before descending steeply to the valley bottom. A winding, technical, roller-coaster stretch takes you through the trees and eventually joins with the Stoney Trail, a good fire road, to bring you back to the trailhead at Barrier Dam.

General location: Prairie View Trail is located on Highway 40 in Kananaskis Country Provincial Recreation Area.

Elevation change: The trail climbs from 1,384 m (4,540 ft.) to the summit at 1,922 m (6,305 ft.) before descending to the valley bottom.

RIDE 10 · Prairie View Trail

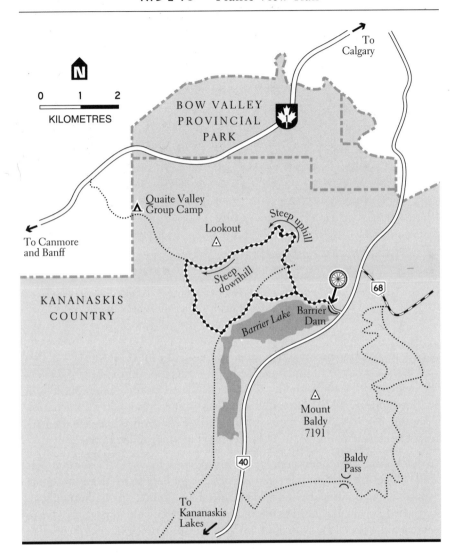

Season: This trail is rideable from early June to mid-October.

Services: All services are available in the community of Canmore, a 30-minute drive from the trailhead. Visitors may use the telephone at the Barrier Lake Information Centre, just north of the trailhead on Highway 40.

Hazards: This trail begins moderately, with few hazards. However, the climb to the summit has the potential for a fall if you aren't confident in carrying your bike up a small rock face. From the summit, the descent on the north side of the vista point is narrow and winding. If you pick up too much speed, you could eas-

The climb is steady as you creep toward Prairie View, but the rewards make the work well worth the effort as Barrier Lake and Mount Baldy spread out beneath you.

ily hit one of the aspens that border the trail. From the junction with Jewell Pass Trail to the Stoney Trail junction, the route is a technical mixture of excellent riding and tricky, rooty washouts. Caution is advised for this stretch. Finally, as you ride Stoney Trail back toward the trailhead, the last junction is easy to miss. If you ride past it, the trail continues along the power line well beyond the trailhead. Pay close attention to the distances listed in the trail description.

Rescue index: This trail is popular for out-and-back hiking to the summit vista point. Along this stretch, it is often possible to get help from hikers and other cyclists. Once you drop down the south side of the summit, the trail is not heavily traveled, so you may need to travel some distance for help. If necessary, when you reach the Jewell Pass junction, turn right instead of left as described in the "Notes on the trail" section. This will take you to the Trans Canada Highway in approximately 5 km (3.1 mi.). You can contact help by dialing (403) 591-7767 — remember, 911 does not apply.

Land status: This trail is operated as part of Kananaskis Country.

Maps: The 1:50,000 scale topographic map for this trail is 83 O/3 Canmore. Map Town produces a superior trail map entitled "Kananaskis Country — Spray Lakes and Canmore Region."

Finding the trail: From the entrance to Kananaskis Country on Highway 40, continue south for 2.9 km (1.8 mi.) to Barrier Dam Day Use Area. From the parking lot, the trail begins on the far side of the dam. You can ride your bike across.

Sources of additional information: The Kananaskis Country address is listed in the introduction to this section. For up-to-date trail conditions, contact the Barrier Lake Travel Information Centre at (403) 673-3985.

Notes on the trail: From the trailhead, ride your bike across Barrier Dam at elevation 1,384 m (4,540 ft.). The trail continues on the far side along a high-quality gravel road at km 0.9 (mi. 0.5). From here, the trail crosses a power line, climbs a short hill, and meets a junction at km 1.43 (mi. 0.9). Prairie View Trail crosses this trail on a diagonal. At another junction at km 2.05 (mi. 1.3), turn right for about 10 m and you'll see Prairie View Trail taking off to the left at a signed junction.

From this point on, the trail is distinct all the way to the main viewpoint at km 5.51 (mi. 3.4) and elevation 1,871 m (6,140 ft.). From the vista point, follow the trail along the ridge for a short distance. At km 5.69 (mi. 3.53), the trail encounters a rocky ridge, where you'll need to portage your bike for a short distance. At km 5.91 (mi. 3.66), you'll reach a concrete platform that bears a large white panel. If you want to scramble to the summit, the site of an old lookout, park your bike there and follow the hiker-defined trail to the right of the panel. To continue on the trail, veer to the left at this point and you'll notice a trail dropping off the summit on the far side. The trail drops down the scree, so you'll have to carry or push your bike for a short distance. At km 6.36 (mi. 3.9), the trail re-enters the woods, and the Prairie View Trail is signed. From this point to km 7.12 (mi. 4.4), the trail is a steep, narrow, downhill slalom through an aspen forest. At km 8.44 (mi. 5.23), turn left at the Quaite Valley–Jewell Pass junction. At km 10.04 (mi. 6.22) and an elevation of 1,560 m (5,120 ft.), a short, steep descent is followed by a narrow bridge. This begins a technical stretch including many narrow bridges, easily bypassed in dry weather. At km 10.94 (mi. 6.8) there is a short, steep uphill push along an embankment. The trail joins the Stoney Trail at km 11.53 (mi. 7.15); turn left. At km 13.06 (mi. 8.1), turn right at an important junction. If you miss the turn and go straight, the trail continues for another 7 km (4.34 mi.), away from your destination.

Stay right at the final junction to Barrier Dam at km 14.63 (mi. 9.1). The trailhead is reached at km 16.11 (mi. 10.0).

RIDE 11 · Jewell Pass

AT A GLANCE

Length/configuration: 16.1-km (10.0-mi.) point-to-point.

Aerobic difficulty: The trail climbs 85 m (285 ft.) from the Trans Canada Highway before descending toward Barrier Dam.

Technical difficulty: The ride passes through some narrow sections, with rocky and rooted stretches.

Scenery: While the trail spends most of its length winding through the trees, it meets the shoreline of Barrier Lake at the

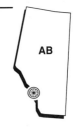

AB

south end of the ride. This point provides excellent views of Mount Baldy across the lake.

Special comments: This popular afternoon ride offers access to the spectacular shoreline of Barrier Lake.

This intermediate point-to-point or out-and-back climbs from the Trans Canada Highway over a low, rideable pass and finishes at Barrier Dam Day Use Area at km 16.1 (mi. 10.0). It offers a combination of fire road and technical riding. As the trail approaches the shores of Barrier Lake, you'll notice the emerald waters of this dammed reservoir sparkling in the afternoon sunlight.

General location: Jewell Pass is south of Lac des Arcs, along the Trans Canada Highway, east of Canmore, Alberta.

Elevation change: The trail begins at 1,320 m (4,330 ft.) and climbs to 1,405 m (4,610 ft.) at Quaite Valley Campground. It then drops slightly before climbing to 1,631 m (5,350 ft.).

Season: This trail is at its best between early June and early October. Jewell Pass holds snow in the early season, so don't try the trail too early.

Services: All services are available in the town of Canmore, a 15-minute drive west of the trailhead.

Hazards: This trail passes some rough, rooty terrain, so beware of sudden changes in conditions and react accordingly. It is also a popular hiking route, so be courteous to other trail users.

Rescue index: This trail begins and ends along major highways. The main trailhead is along the Trans Canada Highway (Highway 1), and the terminus is along the Kananaskis Trail (Highway 40). Other hikers or cyclists can often be found along this route. Not as heavily traveled is the stretch between the Prairie View and Stoney Trail junctions.

Land status: This trail is operated as part of Kananaskis Country.

Maps: The 1:50,000 scale topographic map for this trail is 82 O/3 Canmore, but Map Town's "Kananaskis Country—Spray Lakes and Canmore Region" is superior.

Finding the trail: The trail begins at the Heart Creek parking lot, which is well signed along the Trans Canada Highway. It is adjacent to Lac des Arcs, between Canmore and the main Kananaskis Highway (Highway 40).

Sources of additional information: The Kananaskis Country address is listed in the introduction to this section. For up-to-date trail conditions, contact the Barrier Lake Travel Information Centre at (403) 673-3985.

Notes on the trail: From the trailhead on the Trans Canada Highway, the trail parallels the highway for 3.0 km (1.86 mi.) then heads inland toward Jewell Pass.

As the trail climbs along a wide double-track, it passes Quaite Valley Campground at km 4.7 (mi. 2.9). From there, it continues to climb to an elevation of 1,631 m (5,350 ft.).

RIDE 11 · Jewell Pass

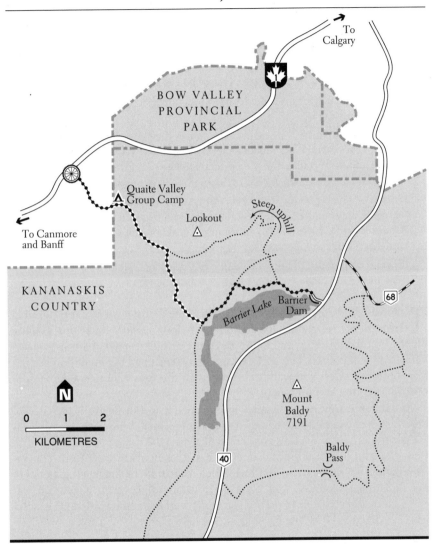

At km 7.7 (mi. 4.77), stay straight at the Jewell Pass–Prairie View junction. At km 10.04 (mi. 6.22) and an elevation of 1,560 m (5,120 ft.), a short, steep descent is followed by a narrow bridge. This begins a technical stretch, including numerous narrow bridges easily bypassed in dry weather. At km 10.94 (mi. 6.8), there is a short, steep uphill push along an embankment. At km 11.53 (mi. 7.15), the trail joins the Stoney Trail; turn left. At km 13.06 (mi. 8.1), the trail passes an important junction. Turn right at this point. If you miss the turn and go straight, the trail continues for another 7 km (4.34 mi.), away from your destination.

Stay right at the final junction to Barrier Dam at km 14.63 (mi. 9.1). The trailhead is reached at km 16.11 (mi. 10.0).

RIDE 12 · Terrace Trail

AT A GLANCE

Length/configuration: A 9.0-km (5.6-mi.) point-to-point or a 24.8-km (15.4-mi.) loop using the Evan-Thomas Bike Path.

Aerobic difficulty: This is moderately level trail that requires little aerobic fitness.

Technical difficulty: The main trail traverses the lower slopes of Mount Kidd and has a moderate level of exposure. While it is not technically difficult, some novices will be uncomfortable with the sharp drop to the Kananaskis River to your left.

Scenery: The exposed nature of this trail is also its greatest asset in terms of scenic opportunities. The view across the valley toward the Kananaskis Country Golf Course and the surrounding peaks of Mount McDougall and The Wedge are spectacular.

Special comments: This is a favourite of many local riders. It offers a nice mix of moderate challenge with breathtaking views.

Traversing the imposing slopes of Mount Kidd, this trail is one of my personal favourites. It is perfect for beginners, as long as they don't mind riding slightly exposed side-cuts, and it provides some excellent views of the Kananaskis Valley and golf course. The trail ends at the Galatea parking lot at km 9.0 (mi. 5.6), but most riders will want to link up with the Evan-Thomas Bike Path to make a 24.8-km (15.4-mi.) loop.

As the trail leaves the Kananaskis Village area, it quickly begins to traverse the lower slopes of Mount Kidd, named after an early settler. A fire lookout, visible on the north shoulder, provides a constant vigil against the danger of forest fires. The views along the length of the trail are spectacular, particularly of the Evan-Thomas Valley and The Wedge to the southwest. Below the trail, the manicured greens of the Kananaskis Country Golf Course are always abuzz with activity. It was designed by Robert Trent Jones Sr., one of the world's foremost golf course architects. He described it as "the finest location I have ever seen for a golf course."

General location: Terrace Trail is adjacent to the Kananaskis Village Resort along Highway 40 in Alberta's Kananaskis Country.

Elevation change: The trail has very moderate change in elevation. It begins at the Kananaskis Village at 1,517 m (4,980 ft.) and finishes at the Galatea parking lot at 1,524 m (5,000 ft.).

Season: The trail is at its best between early June and early October.

Services: The Kananaskis Village offers basic supplies. For bike repairs, you'll need to travel to Canmore, 40 minutes from the trailhead.

Hazards: The main hazard on this trail relates to the side-cuts across the lower slopes of Mount Kidd. They're not particularly challenging, but they are exposed

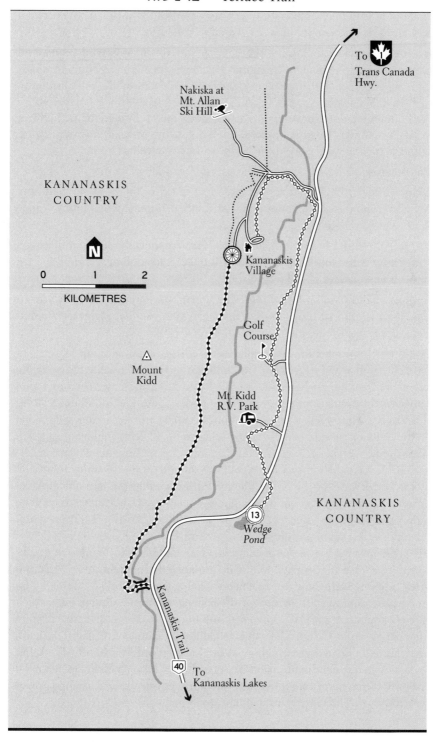

To
Trans Canada
Hwy.

Nakiska at
Mt. Allan
Ski Hill

KANANASKIS
COUNTRY

N

0   1   2

KILOMETRES

Kananaskis
Village

Golf
Course

△
Mount
Kidd

Mt. Kidd
R.V. Park

13
*Wedge
Pond*

KANANASKIS
COUNTRY

Kananaskis Trail

40   To
Kananaskis Lakes

and require confidence. In addition, with the magical views down the valley, bikers tend to lose their concentration, which can lead to a fall. Also, beware of numerous runoff channels that may be difficult to cross.

Rescue index: This trail passes above the picturesque Kananaskis Country Golf Course. In case of emergency, you may be able to attract the attention of golfers. Otherwise, I have rarely met other riders along this trail. At the southern terminus, you can flag down a vehicle on the busy Kananaskis Trail (Highway 40).

If something does go wrong on this trail, don't try to shortcut to the highway, as the Kananaskis River is impassable except at the bridged crossings. Either return to the trailhead or continue to the southern terminus.

Land status: This trail is operated as part of Kananaskis Country.

Maps: The 1:50,000 scale topographic map for this trail is 83 0/3 Canmore. Map Town produces a superior trail map entitled "Kananaskis Country—Spray Lakes and Canmore Region."

Finding the trail: From the Kananaskis Village, follow the signs for the paved Rim Trail. As you follow the pavement, Terrace Trail continues beyond the end of the pavement and is well signed.

Sources of additional information: The Kananaskis Country address is listed in the introduction to this section. For up-to-date trail conditions, contact the Barrier Lake Travel Information Centre at (403) 673-3985.

Notes on the trail: From the Kananaskis Village, at an elevation of 1,517 m (4,980 ft.), follow the paved Rim Trail as it carries you past excellent views of the valley and golf course below. At km 0.42 (mi. 0.26) the trail becomes a wide gravel road heading south above the Kananaskis Country Golf Course. At km 0.59 (mi. 0.37), stay left at a trail junction and follow the edge of the steep slope. At the junctions at km 0.68, 0.71, and 1.06 (mi. 0.42, 0.44, and 0.66), stay left. After the last junction, Terrace Trail becomes a wide single-track. At km 1.14 (mi. 0.71), take the left fork again, but stay straight at the junction at km 2.04 (mi. 1.26). At km 2.12 (mi. 1.31), the trail crosses a bridge over a runoff channel. At km 2.3 (mi. 1.43), it opens up to a picturesque view of a marsh below, with the golf course in the distance. After this point, until km 2.67 (mi. 1.66), the climb is uphill, with a bit of pushing. At km 2.92 (mi. 1.8), you'll pass the best view of the golf course, with some impressive views of Mount Evan-Thomas in the distance. The lower slopes of Mount Kidd dominate to the right. At km 4.26 (mi. 2.64), a short, washed-out but rideable stretch occurs. At km 5.61 (mi. 3.5), the trail passes a fire succession forest, with evidence of burned stumps and straight lodgepole pine. At km 7.07 (mi. 4.38), you'll make a short push across a runoff channel. At km 8.45 (mi. 5.24), turn left at the junction with Galatea Trail and cross a small bridge over a tributary of the Kananaskis River. Shortly thereafter, cross a rugged suspension bridge. You'll reach the Galatea parking lot at km 9.0 (mi. 5.6). From here, a short highway ride north provides access to a loop option with the Evan-Thomas Bike Path at km 14.13 (mi. 8.76).

RIDE 13 · Evan-Thomas Bike Path

AT A GLANCE

Length/configuration: 11.46-km (7.11-mi.) point-to-point, but it has access points along the way that provide many riding options.

Aerobic difficulty: The trail is smooth and rolling. The only significant uphill occurs near its northern end, rising from the Ribbon Creek Trailhead to the Kananaskis Village.

Technical difficulty: The trail is paved for its entire length, making it perfect for families.

Scenery: Winding through a mixed forest of aspen and lodgepole pine, the trail provides regular breaks in the canopy to allow striking views of Mount Kidd, The Wedge, and other local peaks.

Special comments: This trail is very popular for cyclists as well as for inline skaters and hikers. Be sure to share with these other users.

This is the premier family trail within Kananaskis Country. Its smooth pavement and gentle gradient brings out riders of all abilities—you don't even need a real mountain bike. It runs 11.46 km (7.11 mi.) one-way and will require a vehicle at both ends, or a return on the same trail. You can make an excellent loop with the Terrace Trail.

The views toward Mount Kidd dominate the western skyline, and, to the north, Mount Lorette looms. The river passes all the major facilities along this stretch of highway, including the Mount Kidd RV Park, where a small store offers supplies and even ice cream. How many rides offer ice cream midway through?

General location: The trail parallels Highway 40 in Kananaskis Country Provincial Recreation Area.

Elevation change: This trail exhibits only moderate changes in elevation. From the trailhead at 1,533 m (5,030 ft.), it drops gradually until it reaches the Kananaskis Village access road at 1,444 m (4,740 ft.). From this point, it climbs to the hotels at 1,517 m (4,980 ft.).

Season: The bike path usually becomes snow-free by late May and remains clear until early October.

Services: The Kananaskis Village offers basic supplies. For bike repairs, you'll need to travel to Canmore, 40 minutes from the trailhead.

Hazards: Many people feel that because this trail is paved, they don't need to wear a helmet. For that very reason, people have died on this route. With a gravel shoulder, it's easy to lose your concentration, hit the gravel, and go down. Helmets should always be worn. Occasionally, someone will try to ride too fast on the trail and miss one of the sudden corners; never ride so fast that you cannot

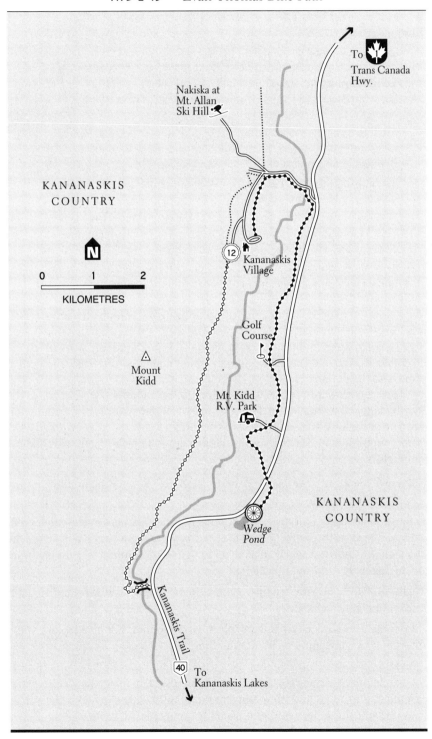

respond to unknown factors. Also, make sure you stay to the right-hand side, as this trail can become busy on a sunny weekend.

Rescue index: This very urban trail is usually packed with other cyclists, so it's never difficult to find help. It also parallels the Kananaskis Trail (Highway 40), where you can flag down vehicles. If this safety net isn't enough, the trail passes a major campground and the Kananaskis Country Golf Course. Also, at the terminus of this trail, at the Kananaskis Village, you can contact emergency services.

Land status: This trail is operated as part of Kananaskis Country.

Maps: The 1:50,000 scale topographic map for this trail is 83 0/3 Canmore. Map Town produces a superior trail map entitled "Kananaskis Country—Spray Lakes and Canmore Region."

Finding the trail: Travel south on Highway 40 to Wedge Pond Day Use Area at the 30.9-km (19.2-mi.) mark. From this pleasant, man-made lake, the winding pavement of the bike path heads north.

You can also access this trail at numerous points along its length, including the Kananaskis Village and the Ribbon Creek trailhead.

Sources of additional information: The Kananaskis Country address is listed in the introduction to this section. For up-to-date trail conditions, contact the Barrier Lake Travel Information Centre at (403) 673-3985.

Notes on the trail: From Wedge Pond, the trail climbs slightly to its junction with Highway 40 at km 0.8 (mi. 0.5). The trail is a winding, paved path running through the trees. At km 1.67 (mi. 1.04), the trail twice crosses the access road for Mount Kidd. At km 2.27 (mi. 1.41), the bridge over Evan-Thomas Creek was damaged during the floods of 1995; a temporary replacement is to the right of the main bridge. At km 2.69 (mi. 1.67), the trail passes the junction for the Kananaskis Country Golf Course. At km 4.32 (mi. 2.7), the trail leaves the golf course and parallels a gravel road to its left for a short distance. At km 6.18, 6.57, 6.72, and 7.62 (mi. 3.83, 4.07, 4.17, and 4.72), you'll find more bridge crossings. The trail turns left at a stop sign at km 7.84 (mi. 4.86). This is the junction with the Kananaskis Village Road. Cross the bridge, and a left fork brings you back onto the bike path on the far side. At km 8.5 (mi. 5.26), the trail becomes gravel for a short distance, and at km 8.84 (mi. 5.48) it takes a left fork again. At km 10.72 (mi. 6.65), the trail passes the helipad junction, crosses a bridge shortly after, and at km 11.46 (mi. 7.11) meets the Kananaskis Village parking lot.

RIDE 14 · Skogan Pass

AT A GLANCE

Length/configuration: 20.33-km (12.6-mi.) point-to-point that requires a long vehicle shuttle.

AB

Aerobic difficulty: With a climb of 677 m (2,221 ft.) in only 9.85 km (6.11 mi.), this trail is reserved for riders with good lungs and big water bottles.

Technical difficulty: While the climb is steady, the trail follows a wide fire road. This makes it perfect for physically fit riders looking for a cardio workout without a correspondingly difficult technical challenge.

Scenery: As you approach the summit, the views to the northwest stretch all the way to Canmore and beyond to Cascade Mountain in Banff. Beyond the summit, the view focuses on Mount Allan (the Olympic ski hill) and the Kananaskis Valley to the southwest.

Special comments: This is an excellent trail for physically fit riders looking to gain some elevation. Few rides offer a wider diversity of views.

This 20.33-km (12.6-mi.) point-to-point or out-and-back takes you from the Trans Canada Highway over Skogan Pass and before descending to the Kananaskis Valley near the 1988 Winter Olympic downhill site. It is almost all wide fire road, so it's passable for beginners—as long as they have a high fitness level. The climb is 677 m (2,221 ft.) in only 9.85 km (6.11 mi.) between the trailhead and the pass.

As you climb, the views to the east stretch to Canmore and beyond—all the way to Cascade Mountain near the town of Banff. Later, as the trail drops down the north side of the pass, the views of Mount Kidd and The Wedge open up, and the Kananaskis Valley unfolds in front of you.

The base of the trail takes you past the Mount Allan Ski Area. This site played host to the alpine events of the 1988 Winter Olympics and is still a popular winter ski hill.

General location: Skogan Pass is located east of Canmore near Dead Man's Flats, Alberta.

Elevation change: From the trailhead, at 1,383 m (4,540 ft.), it climbs to Skogan Pass at 2,060 m (6,760 ft.) before descending to the north trailhead at 1,450 m (4,920 ft.).

Season: This trail is at its best between mid-June and late September.

Services: The Kananaskis Village offers basic supplies. For bike repairs, you'll need to travel to Canmore, 40 minutes from the trailhead.

Hazards: There are few hazards along this trail. One of the stream crossings is a little tricky, but it requires only caution. Once you crest the pass, the descent is

RIDE 14 · Skogan Pass

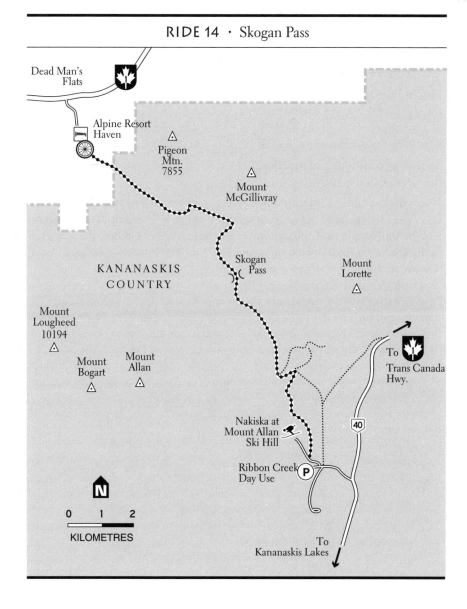

fast and furious. Avoid the temptation to attain warp speed, and keep your eyes open for hikers on the trail.

Rescue index: At the north trailhead, at the Alpine Resort Haven, you can contact emergency services. Along the trail you may find few other riders until you crest the pass. The south side of the pass brings you into a network of trails that offers many opportunities for hiking and mountain biking, so chances for assistance are greater. At the southern base of the pass, the trail passes Nakiska Ski Hill, where you can contact emergency assistance.

Land status: This trail is operated as part of Kananaskis Country.

Maps: The 1:50,000 scale topographic maps for this trail are 82 O/3 Canmore and 82 J/14 Spray Lakes Reservoir. The best map for this area is Map Town's "Kananaskis Country—Spray Lakes and Canmore Region."

Finding the trail: The trailhead is located at the Alpine Resort Haven. Follow the signs for this resort facility just south of Dead Man's Flats. As you climb the hill to the resort, go right at the "Resort" sign and follow the gravel road to the right. The trailhead is at the end of this short access road.

Sources of additional information: The Kananaskis Country address is listed in the introduction to this section.

Notes on the trail: From the trailhead, at 1,384 m (4,540 ft.), the wide-track takes you quickly past a junction at km 0.15 (mi. 0.1). Stay left at this junction, and the trail begins to climb steeply. At km 0.41 (mi. 0.25), follow the main trail to the left rather than stay on the overgrown trail that continues straight. Again, remain on the main trail at the junction at km 1.03 (mi. 0.64).

The trail enters Kananaskis Country at km 1.26 (mi. 0.8) and continues to climb, passing a black metal gate. At km 1.67 (mi. 1.04) the Mount Allan Centennial Trail forks to the right. Stay to the left for Skogan Pass. The trail briefly leaves the power line at km 2.8 (mi. 1.74) and heads into the woods. The climbing is steady all the way to the pass. Take the left fork at km 4.25 (mi. 2.63) and head into the woods. The trail opens to a beautiful meadow area at the 5.45-km (3.4-mi.) mark, with a small stream supporting alpine forget-me-nots, cow parsnip, horsetail, and spirea.

At km 6.44 (mi. 4.0) the trail crests a small summit. The rest doesn't last long, but the views are superb. The climbing is gradual until a rough trail forks from the main trail at km 8.76 (mi. 5.4). Stay straight, crest another mini-summit, and begin a short descent. Finally, at km 9.85 (mi. 6.11), the true pass is reached, and the view toward Mount Allan to the northwest opens up.

From the summit, the trail crosses a tricky but rideable stream crossing at km 10.6 (mi. 6.6). Stay right at the fork ahead and stay left at another junction at km 11.73 (mi. 7.27). The trail drops down a cut-line on the north side of the pass and occasionally leaves it for the woods.

The first winter cross-country trail junction is at km 13.64 (mi. 8.46) as you pass High Level Trail. At km 15.62 (mi. 9.7), the trail passes the junction with Sunburst Trail. You'll pass Marmot Basin Trail at km 17.1 (mi. 10.6), and shortly thereafter you'll pass a gate to the Mount Allan Ski Area. At km 17.4 (mi. 10.8), you'll pass the junction with Ruthie's Trail; turn left and leave the road for the trail at km 18.4 (mi. 11.4). Stay on this trail until km 19.8 (mi. 12.3), where you'll make a right. Cross the road and continue to the Ribbon Creek parking lot at km 20.33 (mi. 12.6).

RIDE 15 · Whiskey Jack–Pocaterra Loop

AT A GLANCE

Length/configuration: 25.6-km (15.9-mi.) loop.

Aerobic difficulty: The first 3.7 km (2.3 mi.) climbs 225 m (738 ft.) to the junction with the Pocaterra Trail. From here the trend is downhill and rolling.

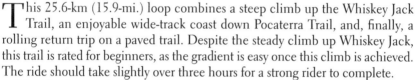

Technical difficulty: The climb up Whiskey Jack Trail has some challenging sections where drainage channels have been carved across the trail. Novice riders may find themselves pushing if they don't keep up their momentum. Other than this minor annoyance, the ride is technically easy.

Scenery: Periodic views open up toward the surrounding peaks of the Opal Range to the east and the Spray Mountains to the west.

Special comments: Check for spring wildlife closures before riding.

This 25.6-km (15.9-mi.) loop combines a steep climb up the Whiskey Jack Trail, an enjoyable wide-track coast down Pocaterra Trail, and, finally, a rolling return trip on a paved trail. Despite the steady climb up Whiskey Jack, this trail is rated for beginners, as the gradient is easy once this climb is achieved. The ride should take slightly over three hours for a strong rider to complete.

The climb up Whiskey Jack Trail begins with a short ride through Boulton Creek Campground before climbing steeply to its junction with Pocaterra Trail. George Pocaterra was an early settler in the area. He once recalled his first meeting with "real" Indians shortly after his arrival in the West in 1903. He was working on his homestead, to the south of this point, when he stopped for a cigarette. Suddenly five heavily armed Indians walked out of the woods and approached him. As he put it: "Somehow I managed not to be startled. One living in those conditions was usually ready to meet sudden crises. I smiled and, handing my tobacco pouch to the nearest Indian, said 'Have a smoke with me.' All five broke into a smile. One said some strange words (later when I had learned to speak the Stoney's language) I found out what the Indian had said meant: This white man is not afraid of anything."

This chance meeting led to a lifelong friendship. In fact, one of these Indians took him as a son, while his other son, Spotted Wolf, became Pocaterra's blood brother. Ironically, although Pocaterra opposed the hydro developments in Kananaskis Country, one of the dams is named after him.

After turning right onto Pocaterra Trail the ride becomes a pleasant downhill coast for almost 9 km (5.6 mi.) to its terminus at Pocaterra Day Use Area. The trail is a wide double-track that allows you to pick up a fair bit of speed. Beware of a few runoff channels that have been cut across the trail; they can catapult you off your bike if you hit them with too much speed. The staging area is surrounded by an old beaver pond that attracts plenty of wildlife. If you happen to

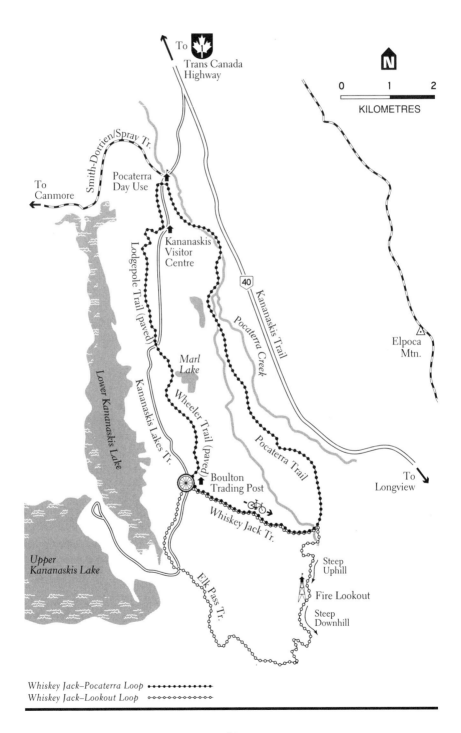

Whiskey Jack–Pocaterra Loop •••••••••••
Whiskey Jack–Lookout Loop ∘∘∘∘∘∘∘∘∘∘∘∘

be riding in the early morning, you can occasionally see moose along this trail. They frequent the marshy habitat so common in this part of Kananaskis Country.

Take some time in the Visitor Centre; its displays and films, along with its well-versed information attendants, will provide you with answers to just about any question about the area.

General location: The trail is located near the Kananaskis Lakes in the heart of Alberta's Kananaskis Country. It is only an hour south and west of Calgary, Alberta.

Elevation change: Climbing up Whiskey Jack you will rise from just under 1,700 m (5,575 ft.) to 1,925 m (6,300 ft.) in 3.7 km (2.3 mi.). The climb is steep but generally rideable. From the junction with Pocaterra Trail, there is little in the way of uphill riding for the duration. On Pocaterra you drop from 1,925 m (6,300 ft.) to 1,616 m (5,300 ft.). The cycle path is nicely rolling with little significant gain or loss.

Season: This ride is at its best from early June to early October. Since these trails are also used in the winter for cross-country skiing, the snowfall is heavily packed, so it lasts well into spring. Once the snow has disappeared, it is an all-weather ride.

Services: Information and maps are available at the Kananaskis Visitor Information Centre. In addition, campgrounds are abundant in this spectacular valley, but they do fill early on weekends. Plan to come out Thursday evening if you want a good selection. The nearest service station is the Kananaskis Junction Petro Canada just a few kilometres north of the junction of Highway 40 and the Kananaskis Trail.

Hazards: This trail is generally smooth, so the hazards are few. Be cautious of runoff channels cut across the trail, as these act as a catapult when hit with the high speeds possible on this trail. In addition, keep your eyes open for hikers and animals on the trail. Bears are not commonly a problem, as the trail travels through some heavily populated areas, but be vigilant when riding at high speed.

The paved bike trail can get busy during the summer months, so stay to the right to avoid collisions. Like all trails, helmets are essential on this ride. A fall on pavement can be, and has been, fatal.

This trail lies within Kananaskis Country, but it is also within Peter Lougheed Provincial Park. Hunting and horses are not allowed, so you need not worry about these potentially conflicting uses.

Rescue index: This route is well used, making it easy to find assistance when necessary. The Kananaskis Visitor Information Centre is a good start. You can contact an ambulance from here. In addition, during the summer months, the cabin at Pocaterra Day Use serves as the Park Interpreter's Office. They can also contact park rangers for assistance. Finally, at the Whiskey Jack trailhead, located at the Boulton Creek Trading Post, assistance can be enlisted.

Land status: This ride lies within Peter Lougheed Provincial Park, which, in turn, lies within Kananaskis Country Provincial Recreation Area.

Maps: The 1:50,000 scale topographic map for this trail is 82 J/14 Kananaskis Lakes. Map Town produces an excellent trail map entitled "Kananaskis Country—Kananaskis Lakes and Region." Kananaskis Country also has a simple trail map for this area.

Finding the trail: Head west from Calgary on the Trans Canada Highway (Highway 1) for 45 minutes, then south on Highway 40 (The Kananaskis Trail). Approximately 52 km (32 mi.) south, turn right on the Kananaskis Lakes Trail. As you drive this winding road, you will pass the Pocaterra Day Use Area and the Kananaskis Visitor Information Centre. The trailhead is located at the Boulton Creek Trading Post. This is well signed approximately 10 km (6.2 mi.) down this road. To the rear of this parking lot, the trail begins by traveling through Boulton campground before climbing toward its junction with Pocaterra Trail.

Sources of additional information: The Kananaskis Country address is listed in the introduction to this section. For up-to-date trail conditions, contact the Barrier Lake Travel Information Centre at (403) 673-3985.

Notes on the trail: The trail climbs through the Boulton Campground before leaving civilization on its upward trend. The climbing begins right away. At km 0.2 (mi. 0.1) you'll reach the top of a short, steep hill. From here, the trail parallels the road for a short distance before leaving the campground. At km 2.4 (mi. 1.5) the steep climbing begins as you leave an old-growth spruce forest covered in lichens that resemble the beard of an old man. The climb is regularly bisected by deep runoff channels. As you ride uphill, they are so deep that you may lose your momentum trying to ride them. If that happens, you may have to push for a while until you can find a spot level enough to remount your bike. The junction with Pocaterra is at km 3.7 (mi. 2.3). Turn left and enjoy a smooth downhill for a little over 8 km (5.0 mi.). After passing through the Pocaterra Group Camp, the trail enters low wetlands until it finally ends at Pocaterra Day Use at km 13.6 (mi. 8.5).

Turn left on the Kananaskis Lakes Trail. Ride the road until it meets with the paved bike path at the Information Centre. From here, a pleasant, rolling paved path takes you the final 11 km (0.7 mi.) back to the trailhead.

RIDE 16 · Whiskey Jack–Lookout Loop

AT A GLANCE

Length/configuration: 19-km (11.8-mi.) loop.

Aerobic difficulty: Like the Whiskey Jack–Pocaterra Loop, the first 3.7 km (2.3 mi.) climbs 225 m (738 ft.) to the junction with the Pocaterra Trail. From here the climbing continues for an additional 189 m (620 ft.) over 1.8 km (1.1 mi.). Finally, you can head downhill and let gravity do the work.

AB

Technical difficulty: The climb is challenging, but the real difficulty begins on the descent, with steep drops, sharp corners, and sudden obstacles.

Scenery: From the summit, the view west toward the Upper and Lower Kananaskis Lakes is superb.

Special comments: This challenging loop starts with a sharp but smooth climb and then drops into a difficult expert-level descent.

If the Whiskey Jack–Pocaterra Loop is too tame for you, this may be just what you need. This 19-km (11.8-mi.) loop provides everything from an incredible alpine panorama to tame paved meandering. It is an intermediate-advanced ride because of its steep gradient and technical downhills.

Beginning at the Boulton Creek Trading Post and climbing Whiskey Jack to its intersection with Pocaterra Trail, this route is identical to Ride 15. But the similarity ends at this junction. Instead of turning left onto Pocaterra, head right onto the Fire Lookout Trail. After making this turn, the trail winds through some old-growth forest before turning right and climbing straight up to a fire lookout perched high above the turquoise waters of the Kananaskis Lakes.

To say the view is dramatic would be an understatement. From the lookout, at an altitude of almost 2,114 m (7,000 ft.), you can see both the Upper and Lower Kananaskis Lakes spread out below you. Beyond the Upper Lake, Mount Lyautey stands defiantly. Between the two lakes, living up to its name, is Mount Indefatigable. The lake levels have been raised through hydro developments, but they still hold the eye of even the most jaded observer. To the east lie the Elk Range with Mount Tyrwhitt, forming the boundary of Peter Lougheed Provincial Park as well as the boundary of Alberta and British Columbia. The solid wall of mountains behind Mount Lyautey complete this boundary.

The trail surface varies widely along this route. To the lookout, it is wide double-track, but that quickly changes as you drop off the summit. Here, the condition varies from wide-track to swamp. The ride also includes a rideable stream crossing, but it will leave your feet wet. After the solid drop down Lookout, Hydroline, and Elk Pass Trails, you'll arrive at the Elk Pass parking lot. A short ride on the paved road will bring you to the paved bike path. Follow this pleasant route back to the trailhead at Boulton Creek Trading Post.

General location: The trail is located within Peter Lougheed Provincial Park, which is located within Kananaskis Country. This large recreation area lies approximately an hour south and west of Calgary, Alberta.

Elevation change: Whiskey Jack Trail climbs from 1,700 m (5,575 ft.) to 1,925 m (6,300 ft.) in 3.7 km (2.3 mi.). The climb is steep but generally rideable. From here, after a 0.5-km (0.3-mi.) stretch of relatively level trail, you begin the assault of the summit at an elevation of 2,114 m (7,000 ft.). This ends the uphill. The trail heads solidly, and technically, downhill from this point.

Season: Because of the high elevation of this trail and the fact that such trails are used by winter cross-country skiers, winter is reluctant to give up its hold on this area. Generally, it's best to wait until June before attempting these higher

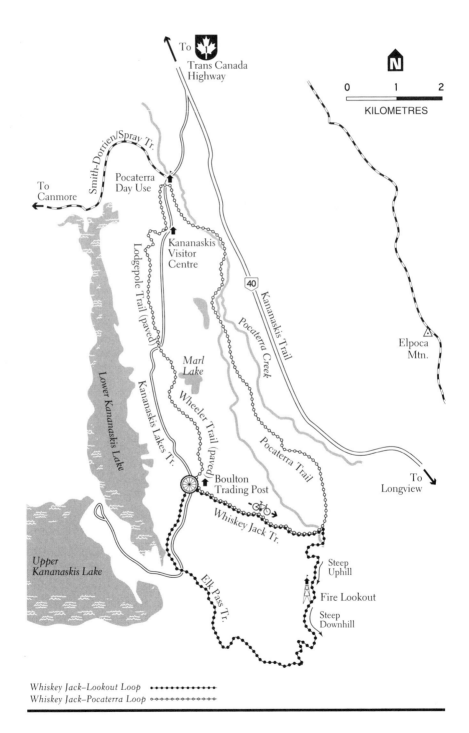

To
Trans Canada
Highway

N

0   1   2
KILOMETRES

Smith-Dorrien/Spray Tr.

To
Canmore

Pocaterra
Day Use

Kananaskis
Visitor
Centre

Lodgepole Trail (paved)

40

Kananaskis Trail

Pocaterra Creek

Marl
Lake

Wheeler Trail (paved)

Kananaskis Lakes Tr.

Lower Kananaskis Lake

Pocaterra Trail

Elpoca
Mtn.

To
Longview

Boulton
Trading Post

Whiskey Jack Tr.

Upper
Kananaskis Lake

Elk Pass Tr.

Steep
Uphill

Fire Lookout

Steep
Downhill

Whiskey Jack–Lookout Loop   ••••••••••••
Whiskey Jack–Pocaterra Loop ∘∘∘∘∘∘∘∘∘∘∘∘

trails. Depending on conditions, it might be best to wait until even later. The season will then stretch into October.

Services: The Boulton Creek Trading Post has a grocery store and restaurant. The nearest service station is the Kananaskis Junction Service Station a few minutes north of the junction of Highway 40 and the Kananaskis Lakes Trail. Many campgrounds can be found within the area. The town of Canmore, about an hour away, can provide all other services.

Hazards: This trail is chock-full of potential hazards. It includes steep, technical downhill stretches that offer ample opportunities to launch yourself into the stratosphere. A helmet is essential. You will find yourself riding through a swamp, possibly deadfall, and even crossing a stream that could necessitate a portage in high water. Some of the downhill stretches may require sudden stops as obstacles and runoff channels interrupt the path with little or no warning. Loose rocks are also a danger. Sitting at the fire lookout, you are atop a very high summit; this exposes you to extremely serious inclement weather. Thunderstorms can blow in without warning, so be prepared to exit the summit if the weather changes. Also, be on the lookout for hikers who may be making their way up to the lookout as well. You needn't watch for horses, as they are forbidden within the provincial park, but other animals may be using the trail. Always be vigilant for bears, and make sure your bike is equipped with a bell to sound warning of your approach on long, steep, blind downhills. This will help you avoid running into a fellow biker or, even worse, Master Bruin.

On the roadway, watch for traffic. Once you enter the bike path, stay to the right, as it can get crowded on a sunny weekend.

Rescue index: You'll often encounter other riders. As you approach the lookout, you can have the person in charge radio for assistance. At the Whiskey Jack trailhead, at the Boulton Creek Trading Post, help is close at hand.

Land status: This trail lies within Peter Lougheed Provincial Park, which is within the 4,000-square-kilometre Kananaskis Country.

Maps: The 1:50,000 scale topographic map for this trail is 82 J/14 Kananaskis Lakes. Map Town produces an excellent trail map called "Kananaskis Country—Kananaskis Lakes and Region." Kananaskis Country has a simple trail map for this area.

Finding the trail: Head west from Calgary on the Trans Canada Highway (Highway 1) for 45 minutes and then go south on Highway 40 (The Kananaskis Trail). Approximately 52 km (32 mi.) south, turn right on the Kananaskis Lakes Trail. As you drive this winding road, continue to Boulton Creek Trading Post. It is well signed, approximately 10 km (6.2 mi.) down this road. To the rear of the parking lot you will see the trail. It begins climbing through the Boulton Campground before continuing toward its junction with Pocaterra.

Sources of additional information: The Kananaskis Country address is listed in the introduction to this section. For up-to-date trail conditions, contact the Barrier Lake Travel Information Centre at (403) 673-3985.

Notes on the trail: Like the Whiskey Jack–Pocaterra Loop, this route climbs through the Boulton Campground before leaving civilization on its upward trend. The climbing begins right away. At km 0.2 (mi. 0.1), you'll reach the top of a short, steep hill. From there, the trail parallels the road for a short distance before leaving the campground. At km 2.4 (mi. 1.5), the steep climbing begins as you leave an old-growth spruce forest covered in lichens. The climb is regularly bisected by deep runoff channels. As you ride uphill, these channels are so deep that you may lose your momentum trying to ride through them. If that happens, you may have to push for a while until you can find a spot level enough to remount your bike. The junction with Pocaterra is at km 3.7 (mi. 2.3).

At this junction, turn right and enjoy a level ride for all of 0.6 km (0.4 mi.), where the trail turns right and begins climbing to the fire lookout. Your lungs will be tested as you climb 220 m (720 ft.) in 1.8 km (1.1 mi.). From the lookout, the trail runs around the building to its left and then drops suddenly. The next 3.5 km (2.2 mi.) are very rough with swampy sections and numerous chances for sudden ejection from the saddle. At km 7.0 (mi. 4.4), you may have to walk a short swamp. After a bumpy ride, you'll join the Hydroline at km 9.6 (mi. 5.6). The ride becomes much smoother as it descends beneath the power line to its intersection with Elk Pass at km 11.5 (mi. 7.2). A final steep drop brings you to the bottom of the valley, where a short uphill followed by a similar descent ends at the Elk Pass parking lot at the 13-km (8.1-mi.) mark.

Turn left on the Kananaskis Lakes Trail for 1 km (0.6 mi.) until you meet the paved Lakeside Trail at Mount Sarrail Campground. A final, pleasant 5 km (3.1 mi.) will bring you back to your vehicle at km 19 (mi. 11.8).

RIDE 17 · Burstall Pass

AT A GLANCE

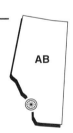

Length/configuration: A 4-km (2.48-mi.) out-and-back one-way, with a 3.5-km (2.1-mi.) one-way hike.

Aerobic difficulty: The riding portion of this trail is relatively level and requires little effort.

Technical difficulty: This is an easy ride along a wide double-track, followed by a steep but fabulous hike.

Scenery: This is one of the most popular hikes in Kananaskis Country. The views from the hiking trail are superb. Mount Birdwood, with its triple summit, dominates with Mount Chester to the east. From the pass, look down toward the Palliser Valley and Leman Lake.

Special comments: While many cyclists avoid combination trails, this one should be at the top of every rider's list.

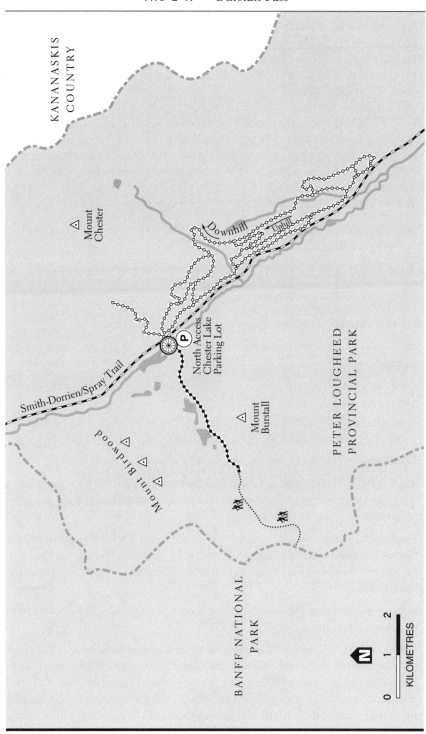

KANANASKIS
COUNTRY

Mount
Chester

Downhill

Uphill

Smith-Dorrien/Spray Trail

North Access
Chester Lake
Parking Lot

Mount
Burstall

Mount Birdwood

PETER LOUGHEED
PROVINCIAL PARK

BANFF NATIONAL
PARK

N

0   1   2
KILOMETRES

This beginner trail works best as a combination of mountain biking and hiking. It begins on a level fire road and passes three tiny alpine lakes along the base of Mount Birdwood. The ride is approximately 4 km (2.48 mi.) before you'll need to park your bike and continue on foot. From here, the hiking trail climbs to a lower bowl at the base of Mount Birdwood before climbing to the true pass at an elevation of 2,380 m (7,808 ft.). The total distance from the trailhead to the pass is 7.5 km (4.65 mi.).

In fall, as you pass this lower area and begin climbing toward the true pass, the bowl is filled with the golden colours of the alpine larch. The only evergreen that isn't green, the larch loses its needles each fall.

The pass is an explorer's dream. The view back to three-summit Mount Birdwood and Mount Chester in the distance are remarkable. To the west, the deep blue waters of Leman Lake and Mount Leman pay tribute to General Gerard Mathieu Leman, who helped defend Belgium during World War I.

General location: Burstall Pass is along the Smith-Dorrien/Spray Trail, south of Canmore in Alberta's Kananaskis Country.

Elevation change: The trail climbs from the trailhead at 1,898 m (6,230 ft.) to 1,981 m (6,500 ft.) where the hiking begins. From there, the hiking trail climbs to the pass at 2,380 m (7,808 ft.).

Season: This trail is at its best from mid-June to late September.

Services: All services are available in Canmore, 45 km (28 mi.) north of the trailhead.

Hazards: There are few hazards on this trail. The cycling portion is along wide gravel roads, and the hiking is well defined.

Rescue index: The trail to Burstall Pass is popular, so it's rarely hard to find assistance. The trailhead is also very busy, and the highway is heavily traveled.

Land status: This trail is operated as part of Kananaskis Country.

Maps: The 1:50,000 scale topographic map for this trail is 82 J/14 Spray Lakes Reservoir; however, Map Town's Kananaskis Lakes Map is a superior guide for this route.

Finding the trail: From Canmore, follow the signs to the Canmore Nordic Centre. Continue past this former Olympic site and climb the steep hill toward the Smith-Dorrien/Spray Trail. Follow this road for 45 km (28 mi.) to the Burstall Pass trailhead.

Sources of additional information: The Kananaskis Country address is listed in the introduction to this section.

Notes on the trail: Follow the high-quality gravel road leading away from the highway. It turns to the left where another old road heads toward French Creek. Stay on the main trail and follow it as it winds toward the right. The road stays wide and smooth as it passes three small lakes, seen just through the trees to the right of the trail. The Burstall lakes are worth a look. You should dismount and wander their shorelines, as Mount Birdwood reflects in their frigid waters.

After leaving your bike behind, the hike up toward the summit of Burstall Pass provides a pleasant conclusion to an excellent bike/hike.

As the road leaves the final lake, it quickly narrows and enters the trees for a short distance before breaking out on wide, gravel flats. The ground is carpeted with yellow mountain avens, one of the most rugged of plants, and the trail continues across these flats toward the trees on the far side. As you cross the flats, look to the left for a view of Robertson Glacier sitting atop a narrow, dark valley. As you reach the woods, you'll see a trail sign heading into the forest. Park your bike and begin hiking toward the pass.

The hiking trail climbs rapidly, following Burstall Creek, until it levels off in a bowl beneath the true pass. After a short, moderately level stretch, the final climb toward the pass begins. As it crests the summit of the pass, the views to the west complement the steady panoramas to the east. You'll reach the pass at km 7.5 (mi. 4.65).

RIDE 18 · Sawmill Trails

AT A GLANCE

Length/configuration: Variable from a few km up to as much as 15 km (9 mi.).

Aerobic difficulty: This is a tight network of trails with some short, sharp uphills. Overall, though, the network does not gain a large amount of elevation, so the aerobic rating is only moderate.

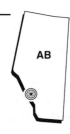

Technical difficulty: Depending on the loop chosen, this network offers beginner-, moderate-, and expert-level challenges.

Scenery: Most of the rides are in the trees, but a few spots offer views across the valley toward Mount Birdwood and the peaks of the Spray Mountains.

Special comments: This is a great network over which to crank out some miles. The variety keeps things fresh, and the gradients are all bearable.

If you're looking for a workout and have some excess energy to burn off, why not try the Sawmill Trails? Following many old logging roads, the trail system provides an intricate network of signed trails with something for everyone. You'll be able to choose either beginner, intermediate, or expert routes. In addition, these trails are less popular with hikers, so it is possible to use a little more speed and a lot more aggression. They vary in quality from good gravel to soupy mud and can be linked together to create loops of various distances.

Although this system of trails is generally in the trees, as you climb to the upper reaches, views to the west toward Mount Murray and the Spray Mountains provide extra incentive. Feeling energetic? Why not take the yellow loop, which totals 12 km (7.44 mi.)? You can link it with numerous other trails to increase the total distance of the ride.

General location: This network lies along the Smith-Dorrien/Spray Trail south of Canmore, Alberta.

Elevation change: The elevation change varies with the trails chosen.

Season: Take these trails from June to September.

Services: All services are available in Canmore, 45 km (28 mi.) north of the trailhead.

Hazards: Since these trails vary in quality, you'll need to be ready for anything. Trees may be down, and the trail may deteriorate suddenly. They are a challenge and enjoyable to ride, but make sure you watch the coloured markers on the trees to maintain your route.

Rescue index: This trail system is not extensively used, with the exception of the Chester Lake Trail, which can be accessed from the northern trailhead. This trailhead is generally very busy, and the highway is heavily traveled, so you can usually find help with relative ease.

Land status: This trail is operated as part of Kananaskis Country.

Maps: The 1:50,000 scale topographic map for this trail is 82 J/14 Spray Lakes Reservoir; however, Map Town's Kananaskis Lakes Map is a better trail map. The ideal map for this trail is Kananaskis Country's map called "X-Country Skiing and Mountain Biking Trails—Smith Dorrien."

Finding the trail: From Canmore, follow the signs to the Canmore Nordic Centre. Continue past this former Olympic site and climb the steep hill toward the Smith-Dorrien/Spray Trail. Follow this road for 45 km (28 mi.) to the Chester Lake trailhead. This is the north access point for the trail system. A second trailhead, a few kilometres south, is signed as "Sawmill Day Use."

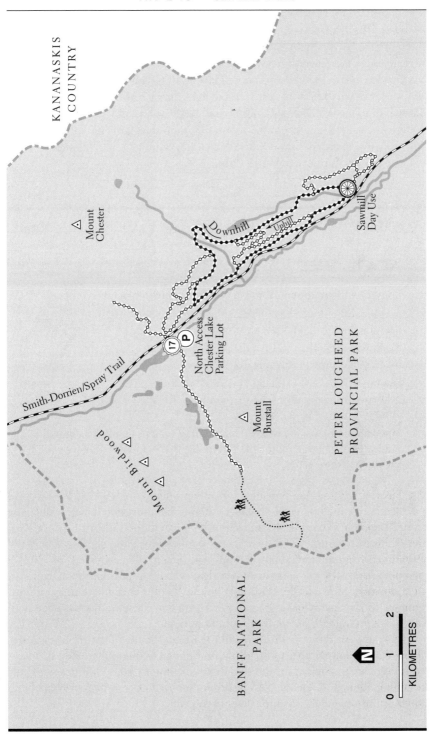

Sources of additional information: The Kananaskis Country address is listed in the introduction to this section.

Notes on the trail: It is difficult to describe this ride, as it is more a series of linked trails than a single route. Traveling the yellow trail in a clockwise direction, it leaves the Sawmill Parking lot and rapidly climbs a moderate uphill for 5.2 km (3.2 mi.) to the lower reaches of Headwall Creek. It crosses the creek and drops back down toward the rest of the system. After a short distance, stay straight at two junctions with the orange trail and make an abrupt left at approximately 7.4 km (4.6 mi.). The trail climbs a short hill, then stays fairly level until km 10.8 (mi. 6.7), where another short hill will have you puffing. A final kilometre brings you back to the trailhead at km 12.2 (mi. 7.56).

RIDE 19 · Mount Shark to Spray Lake Westside Road

AT A GLANCE

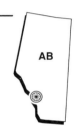

Length/configuration: 31.48-km (18.89-mi.) point-to-point.

Aerobic difficulty: The trail has some moderate climbing near the trailhead, but it is easy overall.

Technical difficulty: Most of the route stays on wide fire roads, making for an easy ride.

Scenery: The views of the Spray Lakes Reservoir and the peaks of the Goat Range keep you company for the ride's duration.

Special comments: This ride has numerous options to link it with other routes. The preferred route links this trail with Goat Creek Trail for an extended point-to-point.

This wide, rolling trail provides a great combination of wide tracks and spectacular views along its 31.48-km (18.89-mi.) point-to-point length. The Spray Lakes Reservoir was artificially created in 1951 when the Canyon and Three Sisters Dams came online. This hydro-generating system, when combined with the Whiteman Dam above Canmore, supplies sufficient power for a city of 100,000 people. Originally, the lakes were merely a collection of small, marshy ponds that provided some excellent fishing along with an unbearable number of mosquitoes. Today, the flying pests are less of a problem, since mosquitoes need shallow, stagnant water to breed. But the trout remain.

Many cyclists discover this trail after learning that two former classic rides, Bryant Creek and Spray Fire Road, are now closed to mountain bikes. However you discover it, you'll want to take plenty of time to enjoy the peaceful surroundings along the Spray Lakes Reservoir. Soon, there may be tour boat operations on this quiet lake, so enjoy it while you can.

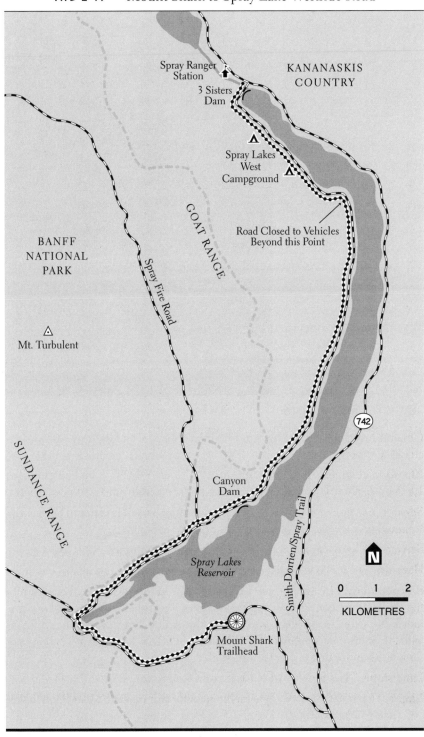

Spray Ranger
Station

KANANASKIS
COUNTRY

3 Sisters
Dam

Spray Lakes
West
Campground

Road Closed to Vehicles
Beyond this Point

BANFF
NATIONAL
PARK

GOAT RANGE

Spray Fire Road

Mt. Turbulent

742

SUNDANCE RANGE

Canyon
Dam

Smith-Dorrien/Spray Trail

N

Spray Lakes
Reservoir

0   1   2
KILOMETRES

Mount Shark
Trailhead

Susan Cameron takes in the view on the Mount Shark to Spray Lake Westside Road.

General location: Along the Smith-Dorrien/Spray Trail Highway within Kananaskis Country.

Elevation change: From the trailhead at 1,774 m (5,820 ft.), the trail climbs to 1,835 m (6,020 ft.) before dropping down to the lakeshore at 1,710 m (5,609 ft.).

Season: Because of the high elevation of this trail, save it for later in the season. It should be passable between late May and late September.

Services: All services are available in the town of Canmore.

Hazards: The trail is wide and easy for its entire length, with few serious obstacles.

Rescue index: This route is not well traveled. You may need to either return to the trailhead or continue to the Spray Lakes Westside Campground for assistance. No cellular service is available in this valley. Just north of the junction with the Smith-Dorrien/Spray Trail Highway, help may be found at a park ranger station. Be aware that it is not always staffed.

Land status: The trail is part of Kananaskis Country.

Maps: The 1:50,000 scale topographic map for this trail is 82 J/14 Spray Lakes

Reservoir. Map Town has produced an excellent trail map entitled "Kananaskis Country—Spray Lakes and Canmore Region."

Finding the trail: In Canmore, follow signs for the Canmore Nordic Centre. Continue past this former Olympic Site. To reach the trailhead, follow the winding course of this road for 36 km (21.6 mi.) to the Mount Shark Road. Turn right on this gravel road and follow it for 5.6 km (3.4 mi.) to the parking lot trailhead. Park here.

Sources of additional information: The Kananaskis Country address is listed in the introduction to this section. For up-to-date trail conditions, contact the Barrier Lake Travel Information Centre at (403) 673-3985.

Notes on the trail: From the parking lot, begin following the gated access road to the west. The trail begins with an uphill climb that quickly offers views toward the Spray Lakes to the north. Cross over a small stream at km 1.69 (1.01 mi.) and continue on the uphill trend until km 2.36 (1.42 mi.). While many winter cross-country ski trails branch off from this route, the main trail is always clearly visible and clearly signed. As you approach Watridge Lake, the Karst Trail forks off the left at km 3.62 (2.17 mi.). Pass the boundary with Banff National Park at km 4.55 (2.73 mi.) and soon begin dropping down toward the junction with Bryant Creek. After descending 67 m (220 ft.), you'll cross over the first of two bridges. A bridge over Bryant Creek after another 0.7 km (0.42 mi.) brings you to a Y intersection. The left fork, now closed to mountain bikes, goes to Bryant Creek and Mount Assiniboine. Take the right fork toward Canyon Dam and the Spray Lakes Westside Road. The trail gets sloppy for a short distance, but it quickly returns to a wide, comfortable gradient. The views toward the southern end of Spray Lakes Reservoir begin right away. At first, it appears to be a small lake, but after going over another bridge at km 10.35 (6.21 mi.), you come out on the shores of this very large lake. Roll your way along the lake, meeting Canyon Dam at km 14.56 (8.74 mi.). Like Bryant Creek Trail, the Spray Fire Road Trail is also closed to mountain bikes for the time being. Stay right on the Spray Lakes Westside Road. Soon you'll pass through a gate and join the Spray Lakes Westside Campground. For the first time you may meet vehicles as they bounce their way to this rustic camping site. Cross over Spray Dam at km 28.82 (17.29 mi.) and meet the Smith-Dorrien/Spray Trail Highway at km 31.48 (18.89 mi.).

You can continue north to Canmore and make a 47.0-km (28.2-mi.) point-to-point. Another option includes linking it with Goat Creek Trail, bringing you to the Banff Springs Hotel in 60.57 km (36.34 mi.). Should you wish to make a loop with the Smith-Dorrien/Spray Trail Highway, head south and return to the trailhead at km 59.0 (35.4 mi.).

RIDE 20 · Loomis Lake

AT A GLANCE

Length/configuration: 22.34-km (13.4-mi.) out-and-back with a 1.5-km (0.9-mi.) hiking option up to Loomis Lake at the far end.

AB

Aerobic difficulty: The climbing is moderate throughout the ride.

Technical difficulty: The trail involves a seemingly endless number of fords, including one major ford of the Highwood River.

Scenery: The views up the valley toward Mount Bishop and the peaks of the Elk Range are dramatic. If you decide to do the hike/bushwhack up to Loomis Lake at the far end, you'll be amazed at the incredible colour of this alpine gem.

Special comments: Save this ride for late in the season, preferably August, when the level of the Highwood River will make it safer to ford.

This is a great ride that takes you into a wilderness valley with plenty of opportunities for exploration. Along this 22.34-km (13.4-mi.) out-and-back, you're treated to exquisite views of Mount Bishop and the peaks of the Elk Range. Adventurous souls may choose to continue beyond trail's end and hike to Loomis Lake itself. The lake has a magical emerald-green colour and also contains cutthroat trout—so bring your rod and your fishing licence. What's the catch? Well, you need to cross a major ford of the Highwood River along with a seemingly endless number of crossings of Loomis Creek. The lake option also requires being comfortable with map and compass as you will be following a rough, hiker-defined trail. Despite these obstacles, it's a great place to explore and a fun, if wet, ride.

General location: Highwood Region of Kananaskis Country Provincial Recreation Area.

Elevation change: From the trailhead at 1,662 m (5,450 ft.), the trail climbs gradually up the valley of Loomis Creek, reaching a maximum elevation of approximately 1,950 m (6,396 ft.).

Season: Because of a major ford of the Highwood River, this trail is best left for August and early September.

Services: At Highwood Junction, a few miles farther south on Highway 40, gas and food are available, but for more substantial supplies you'll need to head north to the town of Canmore.

Hazards: This trail involves a major ford of the Highwood River and many smaller fords. Not a ride for those who don't like to get their feet wet! Even in August the Highwood River can be thigh deep. Don't even think of trying this ride until at least late July. Save it for dry weather; cattle can make a mess of the trail's surface when it's wet. Since the trail is lined with buffaloberries, it is a favourite location for bears. Be cautious.

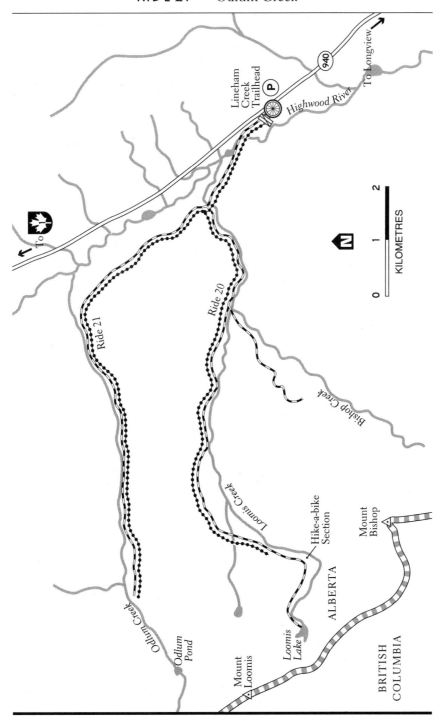

The author descends the double-track of the Loomis Lake trail.

Rescue index: Since you long ago have left any cellular signal behind, you'll need to backtrack toward Highway 40 to find assistance. If you're unable to flag down any vehicles, you can head south to Highwood Junction where a gas station and a small ranger station will be able to organize any needed assistance.

Land status: Within Kananaskis Country Provincial Recreation Area.

Maps: The NTS 1:50,000 Series topographic map for this trail is 82 J/07 Mount Head.

Finding the trail: Drive south on Highway 40 (Kananaskis Trail) for 90 km (54 mi.) and turn left into the Lineham Creek parking lot. From the parking lot, ride across to the other side of the highway, turn right, and follow the highway for 0.28 km (0.17 mi.) until you see a locked gate on your left. This is the trail.

Sources of additional information: The Kananaskis Country address is listed in the introduction to this section. For up-to-date trail conditions, contact the Barrier Lake Travel Information Centre at (403) 673-3985.

Notes on the trail: From the parking lot, the locked gate is at km 0.49 (0.29 mi.). Beyond the gate, the trail begins as a wide former fire road lined with buffaloberry. Stay straight as a rough trail forks to the left at km 1.05 (0.63 mi.). While it looks tempting to take the left fork, the trail ahead does continue after bouncing over a small gravel hump. Beyond the hump, ride over a short, rocky runoff channel as the trail begins to parallel the highway. A short, sandy stretch may bog down your tire just as you approach the Highwood River at km 1.65 (0.99 mi.). Even in August, it is still a thigh-deep ford over slippery rocks. Once you make it across the frigid ford, the trail becomes a wide double-track. After leaving the river behind, the trail climbs gradually. Stay straight as a rough trail forks off to the left at km 2.05 (1.23 mi.).

The trail approaches the double ford of Loomis Creek at km 3.19 (1.91 mi.). The remains of an old bridge will keep your feet dry on the first crossing; the second ford, however, is calf deep, but only a few metres across. As you reach the opposite side, the trail forks with Odlum Creek going to the right and Loomis Creek to the left. Stay left at this junction and begin climbing from the river valley. As you make your way up this valley, some sections have become sloppy as the result of cattle churning up the mud. Stay to the left as a trail joins in from the right at km 3.72 (2.23 mi.). As you continue, the trail descends back toward the creek at the base of a steep embankment on your left. This drops you down to a double ford, one at km 4.35 (2.61 mi.) and the other at 4.41 km (2.65 mi.). The river snakes back and forth across the trail, so your feet will remain wet for the duration of this ride. The trail makes a rough bypass of the river at km 4.6 (2.76 mi.), returning to the wide trail for another ford at 5.12 km (3.07 mi.). Beyond the ford, there is a stretch of trail where the river has eroded much of the road, causing you to creep along the edge of a quickly disappearing surface. Make your final ford at km 5.53 (3.32 mi.), then begin climbing to some great views of the many peaks of the Elk Range.

The road passes a rustic horse camp at km 5.7 (3.42 mi.), and the quality of the road improves with the increases in elevation. A rough trail forks off to the left along this stretch, heading up the drainage of Bishop Creek. Stay on the main road to the right. Another rough junction occurs at km 8.24 (4.94 mi.), when another rough trail forks off to the left. Once again, stay on the main trail. The trail begins a moderate uphill grade soon after this junction, cresting at 8.99 km (5.39 mi.), where it meets a nice open meadow, the site of an old sawmill, at km 10.07 (6.04 mi.). Beyond this point, the trail deteriorates as it heads through some very mucky sections where the water flows directly down the trail. By km 11.17 (6.7 mi.), it becomes a hike-a-bike. To continue to Loomis Lake, park your bike and follow this rough trail for an additional 1.5 km (0.9 mi.) before finally arriving at the serene beauty of Loomis Lake. Retrace your path, returning to the trailhead at km 22.34 (13.4 mi.).

RIDE 21 · Odlum Creek

AT A GLANCE

Length/configuration: 23.9-km (14.34-mi.) out-and-back with a 3.0-km (1.8-mi.) out-and-back hiking option to Odlum Pond at the far end of the ride.

Aerobic difficulty: This trail is exceptionally smooth and rolling.

Technical difficulty: Three fords must be negotiated at the start of the ride, including a major ford of the Highwood River.

Scenery: The views of the surrounding avalanche slopes are pleasant, and the distant Elk Range forms a defiant barrier on the western horizon.

Special comments: Save this ride for late in the season, preferably August, when the level of the Highwood River will make it safer to ford.

Odlum Creek is a pleasant ride along a smooth road without the elevation gains so prominent on many other mountain trails. It takes you into a wilderness valley, past several abandoned sawmill sites. Along its 23.9-km (14.34-mi.) route you pass some incredibly lush avalanche slopes, which highlight the dual character of this winter phenomenon. To your right, the rich summer growth of these slopes makes for excellent summer habitat for animals such as grizzlies. To your left, you cross an avalanche slope where the power of avalanches is highlighted. Large trees have been snapped off as if they were matchsticks. It's amazing how humans can look at an avalanche slope and see devastation, while nature, in effect, sees opportunity. At the far end of the valley, you have the option of parking your bike and hiking a rough trail for approximately 2.5 km (1.5 mi.) up to Odlum Pond, a tiny alpine lake at the base of the Elk Range.

General location: Highwood Region of Kananaskis Country Provincial Recreation Area.

Elevation change: From the trailhead at 1,662 m (5,450 ft.), the trail climbs gradually up the valley of Odlum Creek, reaching a maximum elevation of approximately 1,925 m (6,314 ft.).

Season: Because of a major ford of the Highwood River, this trail is best left for August and early September.

Services: At Highwood Junction, a few miles farther south on Highway 40, gas and food are available, but for more substantial supplies you'll need to head north to Canmore.

Hazards: This trail involves a major ford of the Highwood River. Even in August it can be thigh deep. Don't even think of trying this ride until at least late July or, even better, August. Save it for dry weather since cattle can make a mess of the trail's surface when it's wet. Since the trail is lined with buffaloberries, it is a favourite location for bears. Be cautious.

Get ready for cold feet in the Highwood River.

Rescue index: Since you long ago have left any cellular signal behind, you will need to backtrack toward Highway 40 of find assistance. If you're unable to flag down any vehicles, you can head south to Highwood Junction, where a gas station and small ranger station will be able to organize needed assistance.

Land status: Within Kananaskis Country Provincial Recreation Area.

Maps: The NTS 1:50,000 Series topographic map for this trail is 82 J/07 Mount Head. See also trail map on page 77.

Finding the trail: Drive south on Highway 40 (Kananaskis Trail) for 90 km (54 mi.) and turn left into the Lineham Creek parking lot. To begin the ride, cross the highway, turn right, and follow the highway for 0.28 km (0.17 mi.) until you see a locked gate on your left. This is the trail.

Sources of additional information: The Kananaskis Country address is listed in the introduction to this section. For up-to-date trail conditions, contact the Barrier Lake Travel Information Centre at (403) 673-3985.

Notes on the trail: From the parking lot, the locked gate is at km 0.49 (0.29 mi.). Beyond the gate, the trail begins as a wide fire road lined with buffaloberry. Stay straight as a rough trail forks to the left at km 1.05 (0.63 mi.). While it seems tempting to take the left fork, the trail ahead does continue after it bounces over a small gravel hump. Beyond the hump, youi ride over a short, rocky runoff channel as the trail parallels the highway. A short, sandy stretch may bog down your tire just as you approach the Highwood River at km 1.65 (0.99 mi.). Even in August, it's still a thigh-deep ford over slippery rocks. Once you make it across the frigid ford, the trail becomes a wide double-track. After leaving the river behind, the trail climbs gradually. Stay straight as a rough trail forks off to the left at km 2.05 (1.23 mi.).

The trail approaches the double ford of Loomis Creek at km 3.19 (1.91 mi.). The remains of an old bridge will keep your feet dry on the first crossing. The second ford, however, is calf deep, but only a few metres across. As you reach the opposite side, the trail forks with Odlum Creek going to the right and Loomis Creek to the left. Stay right at this junction and climb away from Loomis Creek. The trail levels out at km 3.32 (1.99 mi.) and begins rolling on a smooth, if over-grown, logging road. While the trail climbs for most of its length, the grade is pleasant and hardly noticeable. Be cautious of a deep washout on the right at km 4.71 (2.83 mi.). You can ride around it to the left, but it is somewhat hidden by overgrown vegetation. Stay to the right as a trail forks off to the left at km 5.91 (3.55 mi.), and slow down for a drainage channel crossing the trail at 6.07 km (3.64 mi.). The trail you're on begins to descend slightly and wind to the west to head up the valley of Odlum Creek. Ignore another trail coming in from the left at km 6.58 (mi. 3.95). You are now enclosed within the Odlum Creek drainage as the trail cuts across a high avalanche slope coming down from your left; on the opposite side, the valley is covered with other lush avalanche slopes.

As the trail rolls uphill, you'll come on a deep hole in its center at km 8.11 (4.87 mi.). It could easily swallow your front tire and is partially hidden by new growth. Be very cautious along this stretch, as two more washouts occur over the next 0.5 km (0.3 mi.). A fork at km 8.92 (5.35 mi.) indicates your arrival at an old sawmill site. It makes no difference which fork you take, as they both seem to dead-end in a large meadow. As you get to the meadow, simply make your way directly across to the opposite side, and you'll see the trail continue up the valley. It also takes on a much more overgrown character as it begins to choke with grass and other foliage. There are two washed-out culverts and a stream-crossing over the next 0.75 km (0.45 mi.). As you cross the stream, several logs have been placed sideways making a functional but tricky bridge. You ride through a mucky stretch at km 11.16 (6.7 mi.); not long after the path dries out, you'll cross a bad washout. It is rideable but quickly eroding. The trail ends in some marshy meadow at km 11.95 (7.17 mi.). A bridge to the right beckons, but that route doesn't take you to Odlum Pond-where you want to go. Staying on the same side of the creek, you'll find a rough route that continues to the pond, but you'll also find yourself hiking the final kilometre or so. The lake is at approximately km 14.45 (8.67 mi.). Retrace your route and return to your car at km 23.9 (14.34 mi.)

RIDE 22 · Rye Ridge

AT A GLANCE

Length/configuration: 32.77-km (19.66-mi.) loop.

Aerobic difficulty: The trail climbs 630 m (2,066 ft.), most of it within 3 km (1.8 mi.), as you approach the summit or Rye Ridge.

AB

Technical difficulty: The drop off the summit is steep, but most of the ride is wide and smooth.

Scenery: From Rye Ridge, the views toward the Continental Divide and the High Rock Range are superb.

Special comments: Be cautious of washouts along upper Cataract Creek and along Etherington Creek Road.

This pleasant, intermediate-level loop provides a combination of impressive mountain faces and streamside cycling. The total loop is 32.77 km (19.66 mi.) and seems just the right length.

The trail begins with a short road roll along lazy Cataract Creek, after which the route follows a wide gravel logging road. The quality of the road varies with the weather. When I rode it, a cat tractor had previously been there, leaving behind petrified tracks. I'm sure I lost a few fillings as I rattled along the rough route.

As the trail passes an old logging site, it climbs more steadily. The steep climb toward Rye Ridge is signaled by Perkinson's Cabin, an old range rider's lodging. Just before the crest, the ride becomes a push as you puff your way to the pass at km 18.6 (mi. 11.2). From there, the views west toward the High Rock Range and north to Mount Armstrong open up. Take some time on the grassy meadow to drink in this wide vista, as it ends all too soon when the trail quickly drops off the summit and heads down steeply.

From the base of the ridge, it follows Etherington Creek back toward the trail-head.

General location: Rye Ridge is located at the southern extent of Highway 40 along the Forestry Trunk Road, within Kananaskis Country Provincial Recreation Area.

Elevation change: The trail begins at 1,719 m (5,325 ft.) and climbs to the summit of Rye Ridge at 2,349 m (7,160 ft.).

Season: This is a good summer trail. It is best not ridden until well into the season, from mid-July to mid-September. The late start will allow the level of some of the river crossings to drop.

Services: The nearest services are at the Highwood Junction, 4.5 km (2.8 mi.) north of the trailhead at Etherington Creek Campground. They provide basic supplies, maps, and gas. You'll need to be self-sufficient regarding your bicycle maintenance.

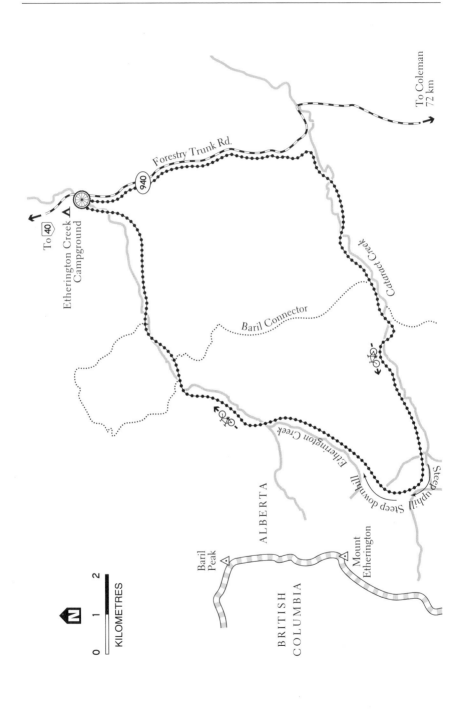

Hazards: This trail has many hazards. At some points, route finding is a challenge. In particular, on the Etherington Creek side, at km 29.23 (mi. 17.5), the entire trail vanishes in a washout from the floods of 1995.

The descent to Etherington Creek can be intimidating for novice riders. It's steep and long. The tendons in your wrists will scream from the long period of hard braking.

Rescue index: This route takes you along several former fire roads, and the possibility of meeting other riders is moderate. A few intrepid hikers also use it, so stay on their good side; you may need their help. Along Cataract Creek, you'll pass several buildings operated during logging in the adjacent Lost Creek area. You may be able to get help here in an emergency. Beyond this point, you'll likely meet few people.

Land status: This trail is operated as part of Kananaskis Country.

Maps: The 1:50,000 scale topographic map for this loop is 82 J/7 Mount Head.

Finding the trail: Travel south on Highway 40 or west on Highway 541 from Longview to Highwood Junction. Head south to Etherington Creek Campground and follow the campground road to the far end. Park at a locked gate.

Sources of additional information: The Kananaskis Country address is listed in the introduction to this section. For up-to-date trail conditions, contact the Barrier Lake Travel Information Centre at (403) 673-3985.

Notes on the trail: As you leave the trailhead, follow the campground road to its access with Highway 940 at the 1.4-km (0.9-mi.) mark. Turn right and continue south on the Forestry Trunk Road, climbing 121 m (400 ft.) over the next 4.6 km (2.9 mi.). As you crest this hill, the road drops sharply until you reach a gated road branching off to the right at km 7.5 (mi. 4.6). No sign is at the trailhead, but as you pass the metal gate you'll follow a good-quality logging road that drops to a bridge at km 8.8 (mi. 5.5.). You'll cross a second bridge, a metal grate structure, at km 9.6 (mi. 6.0). You'll notice a road switchbacking up the side of Raspberry Ridge toward the fire lookout located on its summit. Fear not; the correct route stays on this lower road. After km 10.7 (mi. 6.6) the quality of the road slightly deteriorates. When I rode, a tractor had been on the trail, perhaps to do repairs after the floods of 1995. The dried tracks made for some rough riding, but perhaps time will heal the ruts before you encounter them.

At km 11.9 (mi. 7.4), you'll pass a junction with the Baril Connector, a trail heading north to make a shorter loop with Etherington Creek trailhead. Things get slightly confusing at the 12.5-km (7.8-mi.) mark. For a short distance, the trail becomes lost as a result of some logging in the area. Follow the route that takes you slightly to the left of several old buildings, and the main trail picks up again by km 13.0 (mi. 8.1).

At km 13.25 (mi. 8.2) a signed junction indicates Lost Creek Trail to the left; go right at this sign. Shortly after this turn, the trail climbs to 1,804 m (5,920 ft.). Shortly after crossing another bridge, you'll reach another junction at km 14.9 (mi. 9.25), which marks Faller's Trail to the left; go right. Now the trail becomes cattle slop and badly washed out from the floods of 1995. I ended up pushing through much of it until I passed the sharp bend in the stream where the river had overflowed its banks at km 15.3 (mi. 9.5). At km 15.4 (mi. 9.6), a crossing appears to require fording; however, a bridge is located a short distance to the right of the main trail. A junction at km 15.5 (mi. 9.7) beckons you to turn right; avoid the temptation and stay left. At km 15.79 (mi. 9.8), take a right onto a wood-chipped trail. A steep hill from km 16.0–16.1 (mi. 9.9–10.0) brings you up to 1,859 m (6,100 ft.). Stay straight at another junction at km 16.75 (mi. 10.1) and left at the signed junction at km 16.84 (mi. 10.11). Go left at km 17.2 (mi. 10.32) and right at km 17.35 (mi. 10.4).

Perkinson's Cabin, at km 18.15 (mi. 10.9), marks the end of pleasant riding and the beginning of a steep uphill push. This steep climb begins at km 18.6 (mi. 11.2) and continues to the crest at km 21.6 (mi. 13.0). While you're climbing, you'll encounter two junctions; go right at the first and stay straight at the second. The summit is at 2,349 m (7,160 ft.). The exposed slopes of Rye Ridge provide a pleasant, if short, ridge ride with exquisite views to the north and west.

From the ridge, the drop is steep and hard. It begins after a junction at km 22.7 (mi. 13.6). Go right and drop steeply until km 24.8 (mi. 14.9), where the route levels off into a cattle-chewed meadow. The trail fords Etherington Creek half a dozen times, beginning at km 26.9 (mi. 16.15). Go straight at a junction after this first ford. At km 29.23 (mi. 17.5), not only the bridge was damaged during the floods of 1995, but the entire trail disappears at this point. Rather than cross the stream, follow a dry runoff channel to the right of the river until the channel peters out. Some rough tracks left by game animals will continue on until you finally find the track again at approximately km 29.6 (mi. 17.75). From there, conditions improve, and the road becomes easily rideable. At km 30.3 (mi. 18.2), the junction to the Baril Connector branches off to the right. Stay straight and, at km 32.77 (mi. 19.66), you'll return to the trailhead at Etherington Creek Campground.

RIDE 23 · Plateau Mountain

AT A GLANCE

Length/configuration: 7-km (4.2-mi.) point-to-point or 14-km (8.4-mi.) out-and-back.

Aerobic difficulty: The climb is steady but easily rideable.

Technical difficulty: The trail is a wide road with no technical challenge.

Scenery: As you crest the summit, you'll find views to the east toward the rolling foothills and the solid wall of the High Rock Range to the west.

Special comments: Since this summit was not glaciated, it shows evidence of having been in permafrost while the glaciers flowed just below its frigid summit.

RIDE 23 · Plateau Mountain

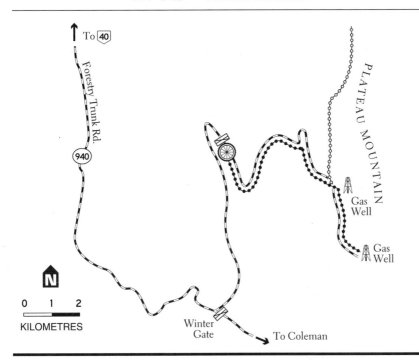

Plateau Mountain is a short, easy out-and-back suitable for all riders. Its entire length lies along good gravel fire road and takes you rapidly above the tree-line. The trail runs for 7.0 km (4.2 mi.), but the options for exploration at the summit are endless.

The peak forms a unique combination of geology and biology. As a nunatak (a high point that rose above the glaciers during the Ice Age), Plateau Mountain forms an unusual landmark. Most of the areas below 2,285 m (7,500 ft.) were scoured by the action of glaciers. This summit stood as an island above the ice. The result is that today the summit shows evidence of land forms found only in a permafrost environment. These colder climatic conditions were found here when the summit was surrounded by ice. Many of the plants are not found on nearby summits, and some are normally found only in areas some distance to the north.

From the summit, the views open up in all directions. To the west, the sheer faces of the High Rock Range form the Continental Divide, the boundary between Alberta and British Columbia. To the east, the lonely Hailstone Butte Fire Lookout stands atop a neighbouring peak.

The summit is also the site of numerous Husky Oil gas wells. You'll follow the oil well access road to the summit. Geologically, this mountain has trapped natural gas below thick layers of rock. That gas is one of Alberta's most important exports and travels through pipelines all the way south to California and east across Canada.

General location: This trail is located at the southern extent of Highway 40 along the Forestry Trunk Road, within Kananaskis Country Provincial Recreation Area.

Elevation change: The trail climbs from the trailhead at 2,262 m (7,420 ft.) to the summit at 2,566 m (8,420 ft.).

Season: The trail is rideable from early June to late September.

Services: The nearest services are at the Highwood Junction, 23.7 km (14.7 mi.) north of the trailhead. They provide basic supplies, maps, and gas. You'll need to be self-sufficient regarding your bicycle maintenance.

Hazards: The sour gas wells on this mountain are very safe and are operated under strict guidelines. However, the best-laid plans can go wrong; hence, the warning sign at the trailhead. It is always good to be cautious.

The summit is constantly whipped by strong west winds. When I was on the summit, there were times when the wind almost blew my bike over. Make sure you have some wind protection; bring some gloves for your hands and something to keep your ears warm.

Rescue index: This trail takes you to the top of a windswept summit, but it isn't as remote as it seems. With many natural gas wells at the summit, service vehicles often use this route. It is not a busy recreational trail, but you may meet other riders on busy weekends.

Land status: This trail is operated as part of Kananaskis Country.

Maps: The 1:50,000 scale topographic map for this trail is 82 J/2 Fording River.

Finding the trail: Travel south on Highway 40 for 110 km (68 mi.) to Highwood Junction. Turn right onto the good gravel of the Forestry Trunk Road for an additional 23.7 km (14.7 mi.) to the south winter gate. As you pass the winter gate, you'll see a road branching off to the left. Follow this road past a dire warning about hydrogen sulphide and climb for 3.8 km (2.36 mi.) to a second gate. Park here and follow the road on your bike.

Sources of additional information: Information for contacting Kananaskis Country is listed in the introduction to this section.

Notes on the trail: From the gate, follow the good gravel road as it rapidly climbs the remaining elevation toward the summit. At km 1.26 (mi. 0.78), the road switchbacks to the left and continues climbing. At km 1.76 (mi. 1.1), the road levels out slightly and heads toward a final switchback to the summit.

At km 5.09 (mi. 3.16), the trail passes a gas well on the summit of Plateau Mountain. The summit is level and windswept, with the potential for extensive exploration. At km 5.81 (mi. 3.6), the road passes a sour gas pipeline operated by Husky Oil as part of its Savannah Creek Gas project. Just beyond it, you'll find a large windmill and weather station.

Once you are on the crest of Plateau Mountain, you can ride in many directions and explore the extent of this large, flat mountain. When you're ready, follow the road back to the trailhead.

RIDE 24 · Cataract Creek to Upper Falls

AT A GLANCE

Length/configuration: 3.5-km (2.2-mi.) point-to-point or 7-km (4.4-mi.) out-and-back.

Aerobic difficulty: Easy.

Technical difficulty: There is a little route finding required, but little technical challenge.

Scenery: The falls are picturesque.

Special comments: Quick but pleasant.

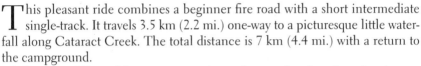

This pleasant ride combines a beginner fire road with a short intermediate single-track. It travels 3.5 km (2.2 mi.) one-way to a picturesque little waterfall along Cataract Creek. The total distance is 7 km (4.4 mi.) with a return to the campground.

The waterfall tumbles over two resistant layers of rock as it makes its way toward the Highwood River to the north. As you head out on the trail, Mount Burke to the west dominates the skyline. It was named after Denis Charles Burke, a Northwest Mounted Policeman from 1896 until 1901. He later ranched in this area and also spent time as a forest ranger.

General location: This trail is located at the southern extent of Highway 40 along the Forestry Trunk Road, within Kananaskis Country Provincial Recreation Area.

Elevation change: The trail exhibits little change in elevation.

Season: The trail is at its best from late June to early October. It does require a ford of Cataract Creek, so avoid the trail in very wet weather and in early June.

Services: The nearest services are at the Highwood Junction, 11.8 km (7.3 mi.) north of the trailhead at Cataract Creek Campground. They provide basic supplies, maps, and gas. You'll need to take car of your own bicycle maintenance.

Hazards: As the fire road disappears, it takes a few minutes to discover the single-track that continues on to the falls. Patience will be rewarded.

The falls lie in a narrow canyon along Cataract Creek. Be careful when trying to find the best vantage point.

Rescue index: This trail is short and sweet. It's not overly difficult and doesn't take you far from the road. However, you won't find many riders on it. Since it begins in Cataract Creek Campground, it shouldn't be difficult to find assistance.

Land status: This trail is operated as part of Kananaskis Country.

Maps: The 1:50,000 scale topographic map for this trail is 82 J/7 Mount Head.

Finding the trail: Travel south on Highway 40 or west on Highway 541 from Longview to Highwood Junction. Travel south to Cataract Creek Campground. Follow the campground road to site 27. A gated road beside the campsite is the beginning of the trail.

RIDE 24 · Cataract Creek to Upper Falls

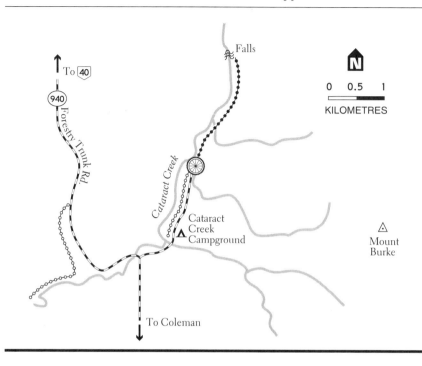

Sources of additional information: The Kananaskis Country address is listed in the introduction to this section. For up-to-date trail conditions, contact the Barrier Lake Travel Information Centre at (403) 673-3985.

Notes on the trail: Follow the good gravel road for approximately 2.5 km (1.55 mi.). After a ford of the creek, the road seems to end abruptly. After a few minutes of exploring, you'll find a narrow single-track continuing on to the falls, 1 km (0.6 mi.) distant.

RIDE 25 · Powderface Creek Trail

AT A GLANCE

Length/configuration: 8.6-km (5.3-mi.) point-to-point but you can make a 22-km (13.7-mi.) loop by linking it with Powderface Trail Road and Prairie Creek Trail.

Aerobic difficulty: The trail has a gradual climb of 396 m (1,300 ft.) and requires a strong set of lungs.

Technical difficulty: The trail has some sudden washouts along with some rapid drops in elevation on the return trip.

Scenery: From the summit of Powderface Creek, it is worth parking your bike and climbing to the summit of Powderface Ridge where the view west toward the peaks of the Front Ranges of the Rockies (in particular Mounts Cornwall and Glasgow along with Banded Peak) contrast with the rolling foothills to the east.

Special comments: This is best done in combination with Prairie Creek and Powderface Trail Road to make a great loop.

This 8.6-km (5.3-mi.) point-to-point or out-and-back traverses the foothills of the Elbow Valley and climbs toward the lower slopes of Powderface Ridge. It descends quickly to its terminus at the Powderface Trail Road. Most of the trail is good single-track, with some sections that tend to get muddy. Due to the solid climb toward the summit of Powderface Creek, this trail requires a high fitness level. However, if you are fit and don't mind some lengthy uphill climbing, it's an enjoyable test for your legs at the beginning of the season. Since the trail lies in the foothills, it's often free of snow long before some of the more remote, high-elevation trails.

Although the earlier sections of the trail are heavily treed, you'll quickly get some glimpses of the very imposing Powderface Ridge in front of you. Pace yourself, because you'll need to climb much of that elevation before dropping toward Powderface Trail Road. As you slowly gain the summit of Powderface Creek, you'll be rewarded with some spectacular views to the west and north. Slightly southwest, you'll notice a knife-blade ridge. This is Nihahi Ridge; it forms the official start of the Front Ranges of the Rocky Mountains. Its name is derived from the Stoney Indian word that means "rocky." As you look toward this sharp ridge, you'll notice that you're riding the last remnant of the foothills, as only the jagged Rockies lie to the west.

This trail has several loop options. You can link it with Powderface Trail Road and Prairie Creek Trail to make a 22-km (13.7-mi.) loop. Since most riders prefer to create loops that bring them back to their vehicles, this is a most enjoyable option.

Another option includes riding Powderface Creek Trail to its junction with Powderface Ridge Trail. From here, you'll ride/push your bike up another 91 m (300 ft.) in approximately 1.5 km (0.9 mi.). From the summit, you'll discover a full panorama. To the east, you can barely spot Calgary more than 60 km (37 mi.) distant. To the west, you'll see Nihahi Ridge. To the south and north, you can watch the transition of foothill to mountain. From this point, the ride heads relentlessly downhill for 5 km (3.1 mi.), during which you'll drop 615 m (2,000 ft.). This option is for expert riders of questionable sanity. Keep your eyes open for hikers as you scream downhill.

General location: The trail begins approximately 20 km (12.4 mi.) southwest of Bragg Creek on Highway 66.

Elevation change: The elevation gain rises from 1,524 m (5,000 ft.) to a maximum elevation of 1,920 m (6,300 ft.). If you decide to climb to the summit of

RIDE 25 · Powderface Creek Trail

Powderface Ridge, you'll gain an additional 91 m (300 ft.) to a maximum elevation of approximately 2,011 m (6,600 ft.).

Season: Like most rides in the mountains, this trail requires waiting until the snow leaves the more sheltered areas. I rode the trail in early May and still had to push my way through many areas. Near the summit it was still very snowy. This route clears before many of the higher mountain trails and should be rideable by late May. It stays clear of snow until mid-September.

Services: Bragg Creek has several restaurants, a grocery store, gas station, and a variety of craft stores. The nearest bike shop is in Calgary. The Elbow Valley includes more than 600 campsites for primitive-style camping. Only a very limited number of sites have electricity, and these are in McLean Creek Campground.

Hazards: This trail's main hazards are its steep gradients and sometimes sudden washouts during equally steep downhills. Riding a trail like this one requires constant vigilance and care. Also, consider the hunting season. Although it is illegal to shoot from or across a trail, bright clothing may be a good idea.

Rescue index: This trail is sporadically busy. On weekends, it sees lots of traffic, but during the week it is remarkably quiet. At the west end, you can often get assistance in the Little Elbow Campground, or, if you're lucky, you might flag down one of the rare vehicles along the Powderface Trail (Road). The east trailhead is along a fairly busy road (Elbow Falls Trail/Highway 66); you'll have a better chance of stopping cars on this road.

Land status: This trail is within Kananaskis Country Provincial Recreation Area.

Maps: The 1:50,000 scale topographic map for this trail is 82 J/15 Bragg Creek. Map Town produces an excellent trail map entitled "Kananaskis Country—Bragg Creek and Elbow Falls."

Finding the trail: From Bragg Creek, travel through the town site for 3.2 km (2 mi.) to a **T** intersection with Highway 66 (Elbow Falls Trail). Head west for 16.3 km (10.1 mi.) to the Powderface Day Use Area. Keep in mind that the Elbow Falls Trail closes from December 1 until May 15 every year at Elbow Falls, 0.2 km (0.1 mi.) east of the trailhead.

Sources of additional information: The Kananaskis Country address is listed in the introduction to this section. For up-to-date trail conditions, contact the Elbow Valley Information Centre at (403) 949-4261 or the Elbow Ranger Station at (403) 949-3754.

Notes on the trail: As you leave the trailhead on a good, wide single-track, the climbing begins almost immediately. At km 1.6 (mi. 1), Powderface Creek seems to meld with the trail for a short distance during wet weather, and you may need to walk for a short bit. The trail passes the junction with Prairie Link Trail at km 2.3 (mi. 1.4). Stay left at this junction; you will quickly find yourself traveling through some horse-churned stretches. Hang on; they don't last long. At km 4.0 (mi. 2.5), the steep climbing begins. The next 2 km (1.2 mi.) will be a mixture of riding and pushing as you climb a steep rock face. As you crest the first long hill, the view to the rear opens up, and you are treated to a vista of gently rolling foothills. At km 5.7 (mi. 3.5), you'll reach the summit of Powderface Creek. From there, you'll continue down through a tight slalom of trees and roots. At km 7.0 (mi. 4.5), you may need to make a quick stop as the creek takes over the trail for a short distance. At km 7.3 (mi. 4.54), the trail turns right and follows the north-south valley for a short distance before finally dropping to the valley floor. At km 8.6 (mi. 5.4), you'll meet Powderface Trail Road. To link up with Prairie Creek, head north on Powderface Trail Road for slightly more than 2.5 km (1.5 mi.) to its intersection with Prairie Creek.

RIDE 26 · Prairie Creek Trail

AT A GLANCE

Length/configuration: 9.9-km (6.2-mi.) point-to-point, but you can make a 22-km (13.7-mi.) loop by linking it with Powderface Trail Road and Powderface Creek Trail.

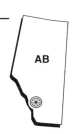

Aerobic difficulty: The trail climbs a moderate 180 m (590 ft.) before descending back toward Highway 66 (Elbow Valley Trail).

Technical difficulty: A few sudden drops and muddy sections will challenge your skills.

Scenery: From the summit of the trail, you'll have some good views of the rolling foothills to the east and west.

Special comments: For riders interested in seeing the handiwork of busy beavers, the trail passes many beaver dams.

This 9.9-km (6.2-mi.) point-to-point or out-and-back follows the course of Prairie Creek to its junction with the Elbow River. I have described it here in a west-to-east direction, as it is often used in conjunction with Powderface Creek Trail to make a 21.3-km (13.2-mi.) loop. It can, however, be ridden in either direction.

From the trailhead, it travels beside and above an old beaver marsh. If you, like many people, are fascinated by these industrious rodents, this may be the trail for you. Although no signs of recent activity are evident, it is still a pleasant place to observe the significant changes a family of beavers can produce. Far more than merely benefiting the beavers, a beaver marsh creates an entire ecosystem.

Prairie Creek gains its name from its proximity to the seemingly endless plains of western Canada. From the junction of the prairies with the foothills, they stretch across most of the province of Alberta in addition to the provinces of Saskatchewan and Manitoba. Driving across the prairies takes more than 15 hours.

Riding east on this trail gives you excellent views of the foothills. So often, trails focus on mountains to such a degree that riders rarely give the rolling foothills a second thought. Today, the mountains are at your back.

The vegetation along this ride is a mixture of trembling aspen and lodgepole pine. Keep your eyes open for some mule deer or elk, as this is ideal habitat for these common ungulates.

The first steep climb is at km 6.1 (mi. 3.8). Keep your ears open in the spring for the low, rumbling sound of a ruffed grouse drumming. Male grouse have developed a technique of using old logs as an amplifying drum. By beating his wings rapidly against his side, the sound seems to echo through the whole valley. Once you find a spot within earshot of a favourite log, it is fairly predictable that each year you'll hear the drumming from the same spot.

RIDE 26 · Prairie Creek Trail

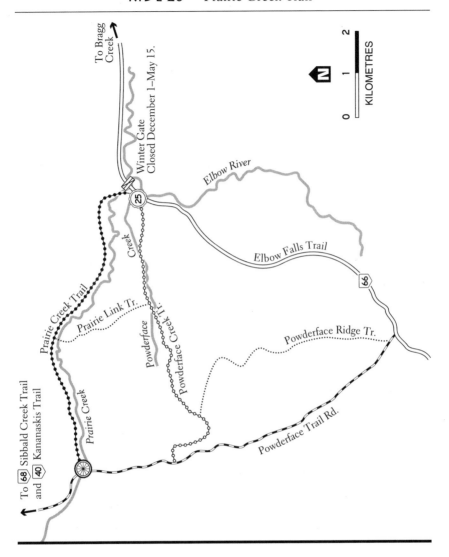

At km 7.9 (mi. 4.9), the trail climbs under a rocky outlier of Prairie Mountain. As you puff your way up this steep push, the whole nature of the trail changes from marsh and meadow to rocky and sheer. At the summit, the trees appear stunted as they crouch low to avoid the strong winds that regularly sweep across.

From the top of the hill, a quick, steep, technical downhill brings you to the junction of Elbow Falls Trail just slightly east of Powderface Day Use.

General location: The trail is within the Elbow Valley, approximately 20 km (12.4 mi.) southwest of Bragg Creek on Highway 66 (Elbow Falls Trail).

Elevation change: This trail climbs a total of 180 m (590 ft.) from its trailhead to the rocky height of land at km 7.0 (mi. 4.4). From here it drops until it joins Highway 66 at km 9.9 (mi. 6.2).

Season: This trail is snow-free from early May until the first snowfalls of October or November. Unlike Powderface Creek Trail, it doesn't tend to hold snow for long periods in sheltered areas.

Services: Bragg Creek has several restaurants, a grocery store, a gas station, and a variety of craft stores. The nearest bike shop is in Calgary. The Elbow Valley includes more than 600 campsites for primitive-style camping. Only a handful of sites have electricity, and these are found in McLean Creek Campground.

Hazards: This trail's main hazards are its steep gradients and sudden washouts during steep downhills. Riding such a trail requires constant vigilance and care. Also, consider the fall hunting season. Although it is illegal to shoot from or across a trail, bright clothing may be a good idea.

Rescue index: This trail is moderately busy with some potential to attract the assistance of others. In case of an accident, the eastern end of the trail is along Highway 66, which generally sees a fair amount of traffic—especially on weekends. If there is little action on the highway, just head a few hundred metres to the east of the highway junction and you'll encounter a popular picnic site at Elbow Falls. The western end of the trail is located along a winding gravel road, which sees little traffic. It may take some patience to flag down a vehicle.

Land status: This trail is within Kananaskis Country Provincial Recreation Area.

Maps: The 1:50,000 scale topographic map for this trail is 82 J/15 Bragg Creek. An excellent recreational map produced by Map Town is entitled "Kananaskis Country—Bragg Creek and Elbow Falls."

Finding the trail: To find the east trailhead, travel to the community of Bragg Creek. Turn left onto the continuation of Highway 22 until the road comes to a T intersection with Highway 66 (Elbow Falls Trail). From there, turn right and continue west for 16.2 km (10.1 mi.) to Powderface Day Use. Park there and follow the road east for approximately 100 m (109 yards) to its junction with Prairie Creek. You'll see the trail head into the woods.

To find the west trailhead, follow Highway 66 until you reach Little Elbow Campground. From there, follow Powderface Trail north until you meet Prairie Creek. The signage here is poor, but you'll notice a bridge off to the right near the creek. Head straight to it and you'll be on the correct trail. From this point the trail is well marked.

Sources of additional information: The Kananaskis Country address is listed in the introduction to this section. For up-to-date trail conditions, contact the Elbow Valley Information Centre at (403) 949-4261 or the Elbow Ranger Station at (403) 949-3754.

Notes on the trail: From the trailhead, follow the single-track as it quickly climbs above the valley to skirt a large beaver marsh. For the next 0.6 km (0.4

mi.), the trail periodically returns to the marsh as you follow this artificially flooded valley. A stream at km 1.1 (mi. 0.7) will get your feet wet, but the route is generally rideable. Watch for changing water levels, particularly in the spring when depths may be greater.

The enjoyable roller coaster you've been riding to this point will now deteriorate quickly. Horses have churned the trail beyond this ford into a muddy mess. The scenery and the convenience of the trail's loop with Powderface Creek make it worth enduring the slop.

At km 3.77 (mi. 2.3), you'll pass the junction with Prairie Link Trail. At km 6.1 (mi. 3.66), the first long climb begins. Just beyond the summit, at km 7.0 (mi. 4.4), you'll pass a horse gate. A sign asks you to keep it closed, but it has been permanently wired open. Following a steep downhill, your tires will point back uphill at the 7.6-km (4.7-mi.) mark. The rocky summit of this hill is followed by the final descent to the highway at km 9.9 (mi. 6.2).

RIDE 27 · Cox Hill Ridge

AT A GLANCE

Length/configuration: 19.5-km (11.7-mi.) loop.

Aerobic difficulty: The ride grinds uphill for 700 m (2,275 ft.).

Technical difficulty: Although you'll face a few very steep sections, the trail is generally wide and smooth.

Scenery: This trail crests a wonderful foothill summit with a full panorama. To the west, the high peaks of the Fisher Range mark the beginning of the Front Ranges of the Rocky Mountains.

Special comments: Link this trail with Jumpingpound Ridge for an even longer ridge-top ride.

How are your climbing legs? They better be in prime condition before you attempt this 19.5-km (11.7-mi.) grunt. The trail is a loop that climbs over the ridge and brings you back on the good gravel of Powderface Trail Road. If you endure the 700-m (2,275-ft.) ride/push to the summit, you'll be rewarded with a panoramic view and options for some extended ridge-top riding.

I highly recommend this trail for expert riders looking for a challenge. Almost from the start, you'll find yourself pushing your bike a lot more than riding it, and this continues for the first 6.6 km (4.1 mi.). The climbing is steep, unrelenting, and exhausting. The views provide ever-widening vistas, culminating in the 360-degree view from the true summit of Cox Hill Ridge. At 2,250 m (7,382 ft.) it provides unobstructed views all the way to the prairies to the northeast and east. To the south, the main peaks of the Elbow Valley, Banded, Cornwall, and Glasgow dominate. To the west, Mount Yamnuska forms the official start of the Front Ranges of the Rocky Mountains.

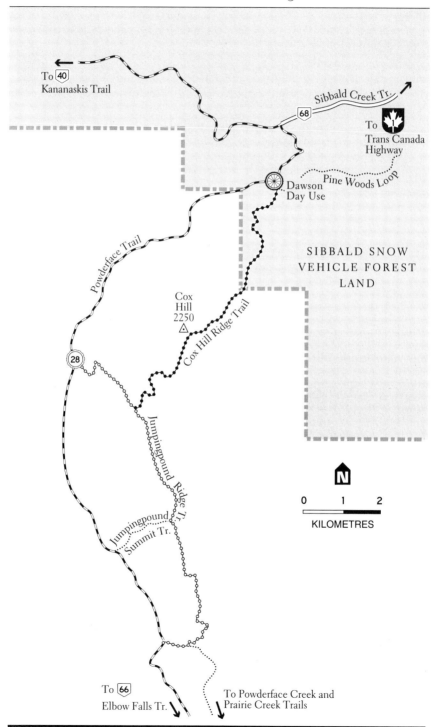

To 40
Kananaskis Trail

Sibbald Creek Tr.

68

To
Trans Canada
Highway

Pine Woods Loop

Dawson
Day Use

SIBBALD SNOW
VEHICLE FOREST
LAND

Powderface Trail

Cox
Hill
2250
△

Cox Hill Ridge Trail

28

Jumpingpound Ridge Tr.

Jumpingpound
Summit Tr.

N

0   1   2
KILOMETRES

To 66
Elbow Falls Tr.

To Powderface Creek and
Prairie Creek Trails

The trail exhibits some sections that have been churned by horses' hooves. This damage is largely during the long uphill push to the summit. Once you reach the summit, the trail is generally rideable.

General location: The trailhead is within the Sibbald Creek area of Kananaskis Country. It is accessed most easily from either the Trans Canada Highway or via Highway 40 (the Kananaskis Trail).

Elevation change: The climb to the summit at 2,198 m (7,210 ft.) is a steep 700 m (2,275 ft.).

Season: This is a summer-only trail. Wait until the snow has had enough time to disappear from some of the sheltered areas before riding. Generally, it is at its best from early June to mid-September.

Services: Few services are available in the area. The nearest services are located in Dead Man's Flats and Canmore. In Canmore, you'll find full services. Dead Man's Flats is merely a highway service centre with some motels, restaurants, and gas stations.

Hazards: The hazards here include loose rocks and steep corners on the long descent off the pass. Helmets are a must for some of the steep, technical downhill stretches.

This trail has a variety of users, including both horses and hikers. Please be cautious and courteous. In addition, during the autumn, hunters may use this trail. Although they are not allowed to fire their guns within 100 m (109 yd.) of the trail or across the trail bright colours at this time of year are well advised.

If you're riding Powderface Trail Road back to the trailhead, watch for vehicles along some of the winding stretches. This is an unmaintained road, and drivers often don't expect to see cyclists.

Rescue index: This trail is located in remote country, so be extra cautious. Although the trail begins and ends along a road, the Powderface Trail, it is a winding gravel route with little traffic. You may be able to flag down a vehicle, but it will take patience. In an emergency, follow the Powderface Trail to the north to its junction with Sibbald Creek Trail (Highway 68), and your chances of flagging down assistance will be greatly improved. On weekdays, the road is almost deserted. The trail is equally quiet. It sees more riders each year as mountain biking becomes more and more popular, but it is not a busy trail.

Land status: This is part of Kananaskis Country.

Maps: The 1:50,000 scale topographic maps for this trail are 82 J/15 Bragg Creek and 82 O/2 Jumpingpound. Map Town produces a recreation map entitled "Kananaskis Country—Bragg Creek and Elbow Valley."

Finding the trail: Heading west from Calgary, take the Sibbald Creek Trail exit, approximately 30 minutes west of Calgary. Follow this road past the Sibbald Lake Campground until you notice a gravel road heading south. This is the Powderface Trail Road. It is signed as unsuitable for travel, but in dry weather it's fine, and you need to travel only a few kilometres until you see a sign for the Dawson Day Use Area. Park there. Powderface Trail Road can also be accessed by traveling south on Highway 40 and turning left onto the Sibbald Creek Trail.

Sources of additional information: The Kananaskis Country address is listed in the introduction to this section. For up-to-date trail conditions, contact the Barrier Lake Travel Information Centre at (403) 673-3985.

Notes on the trail: From the trailhead at Dawson Day Use, you'll pass a junction with the Tom Snow Trail at km 0.25 (mi. 0.15). Stay to the right and begin climbing almost immediately. You'll be jumping on and off your bike for the next 6.4 km (4.0 mi.) as a combination of gradient and horse churn overcomes your ability to ride. The push culminates at the true summit of Cox Hill Ridge. Just before the summit, a push so steep that it's difficult to negotiate with a bike is rewarded with a dramatic panorama.

When you leave the summit, make sure to don your helmet, because the trail drops steeply on a narrow, rocky, technical stretch. From km 8.75 (mi. 5.4) you climb again to the junction with the Jumpingpound Ridge Trail. Turn right if you want to exit the ride at this point. The Powderface Trail Road junction is another 3 km (1.9 mi.) along a winding, switchbacking trail. From there, turn right onto Powderface Trail Road for 7.7 km (4.8 mi.) to the Dawson trailhead. Before you take this exit, take your pulse. If your heart and lungs still have some strength left, continue and ride Jumpingpound Ridge Trail (see Ride 28).

RIDE 28 · Jumpingpound Ridge Trail

AT A GLANCE

Length/configuration: 12.5-km (7.8-mi.) point-to-point.

Aerobic difficulty: A steep climb for 3 km (1.9 mi.), after which it moderates.

Technical difficulty: The trail is generally wide and smooth.

Scenery: The trail straddles the boundary of foothills and mountain. To the west, the jagged ridge of Nihahi Ridge and the Fisher Range mark the eastern boundary of the Front Ranges. To the east, the rolling foothills gradually fade out toward Calgary.

Special comments: Link this trail with Cox Hill Ridge for an even longer ridge-top ride.

This trail can be ridden on its own or as part of an extended ridge ride by incorporating Cox Hill Ridge. It's a point-to-point, but Powderface Trail Road provides a handy loop back to your vehicle. The trail condition is good single-track for the entire route and will be an enjoyable ride for intermediate to expert riders. The gradient is steep and the trail challenging, but the views are worth it.

This trail provides ridge-riding at its best. When linked with Cox Hill Ridge, the summit ride seems to go on forever. The Jumpingpound Ridge section runs for 7.15 km (4.4 mi.) along the ridge top with intermittent stretches through the trees. The ridge is heavily windswept with some stunted vegetation. In spring and early summer, wildflowers find shelter in the rocks and explode into a variety of

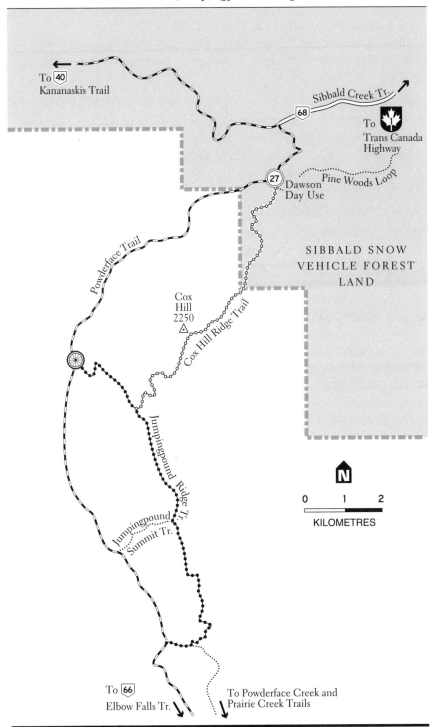

To 40
Kananaskis Trail

Sibbald Creek Tr.

68

To
Trans Canada
Highway

27

Dawson
Day Use

Pine Woods Loop

SIBBALD SNOW
VEHICLE FOREST
LAND

Powderface Trail

Cox
Hill
2250

Cox Hill Ridge Trail

N

0   1   2
KILOMETRES

Jumpingpound Ridge Tr.

Jumpingpound
Summit Tr.

To 66
Elbow Falls Tr.

To Powderface Creek and
Prairie Creek Trails

colours. To the southwest, the Little Elbow River winds its way from the west. Also to the west, six clear-cuts are visible. This limited resource extraction is part of the multiple-use mandate of Kananaskis Country.

Heading into the trees for the last few kilometres, the trail drops steeply to its junction with Prairie Creek Trail. Turning right brings you to Powderface Trail Road at km 12.5 (mi. 7.8).

General location: The trail is along Powderface Creek Trail, bordering the boundary between foothills and mountain.

Elevation change: The trail climbs approximately 535 m (1,738 ft.).

Season: This is a summer-only trail. You must wait until all the snow has melted to ride. In addition, the Powderface Trail Road does not open to vehicles until May 15. It is usually snow-free from June to September.

Services: No services are available in this area.

Hazards: This trail involves a steep climb uphill, much of which you will likely push, followed by a rocky ridge ride, and it finishes with a steep drop to the Powderface Trail Road. Strong lungs are required, along with the ability to negotiate tight turns with some loose rock debris. If you're planning on riding the Powderface Trail Road back to the north trailhead, be cautious of vehicles whose drivers may not be expecting to encounter cyclists along this narrow, winding road. During the autumn hunting season, you should wear bright clothing since hunters may be using this trail. They are not allowed to shoot within 100 m (109 yd.) of the trail, or across it, but caution is important at this time of year.

Rescue index: This trail, like Cox Hill, is located in remote country, so caution is vital. Although the trail begins and ends along a road, the Powderface Trail, it is a winding, gravel route with little traffic. You may be able to flag down a vehicle, but it will take patience. In an emergency, follow the Powderface Trail to the north to its junction with Sibbald Creek Trail (Highway 68), and your chances of flagging down assistance are greatly improved. On weekdays, the road is almost deserted. The Jumpingpound Ridge Trail is moderately busy, so you may find assistance on it.

Land status: This trail is operated as part of Kananaskis Country.

Maps: The 1:50,000 scale topographic map for this trail is 82 J/15 Bragg Creek. Map Town produces a recreation map called "Kananaskis Country—Bragg Creek and Elbow Falls."

Finding the trail: Access to this trail is via the Powderface Trail. From Calgary, travel to Bragg Creek and continue west on Highway 66 (Elbow Falls Trail) for approximately 32 km (19.9 mi.) to its junction with Powderface Trail Road. Head north up this road 24 km (14.9 mi.) to the trailhead on the east side of this road.

You can also access it via the Trans Canada Highway and Sibbald Creek Trail. From the junction with Powderface Trail Road, head south for 11 km (6.8 mi.).

Sources of additional information: The Kananaskis Country address is listed in the introduction to this section. For up-to-date trail conditions, contact the Barrier Lake Travel Information Centre at (403) 673-3985.

Notes on the trail: Beginning with a long uphill push/ride along a single-track, switchbacking trail, the first 3 km (1.9 mi.) are hard work. From the junction with Cox Hill Ridge, turn right and climb to the ridge top at km 4.1 (mi. 2.5). The ridge runs for 7.15 km (4.4 mi.) before descending sharply to its junction with Canyon Creek and Creek Trail at km 11.25 (mi. 7.0). Turn right and ride for 0.7 km (0.4 mi.) to Powderface Trail Road.

If you need to exit early, a junction with Summit Trail at km 6.6 (mi. 4.1) provides a steep drop for 2.5 km (1.6 mi.) to its junction with Powderface Trail Road at km 9.1 (mi. 5.64).

RIDE 29 · Tom Snow Trail

AT A GLANCE

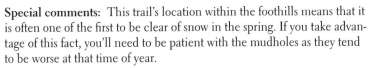

Length/configuration: 16.3-km (9.78-mi.) point-to-point.

Aerobic difficulty: The trail is generally level, with only a few short uphill sections.

Technical difficulty: Many mudholes, a rutted downhill, and one difficult river crossing will test your patience.

Scenery: While much of the trail remains in the trees, it does have some excellent views of Moose Mountain to the south.

Special comments: This trail's location within the foothills means that it is often one of the first to be clear of snow in the spring. If you take advantage of this fact, you'll need to be patient with the mudholes as they tend to be worse at that time of year.

Tom Snow Trail is one of those rides that are rarely used, but it provides a great link between the Sibbald and Elbow Districts of Kananaskis Country. Along its 16.3-km (9.78-mi.) point-to-point route, you get some views of Moose Mountain to the south. Atop its rolling summit sits the highest fire lookout in Alberta. Although much of the ride remains in the trees, it is a pleasant woodland roll. The north section tends to be much muddier than the south. While this description takes you from the north to the south, it can be done in either direction.

General location: West of the community of Bragg Creek, Alberta.

Elevation change: From the trailhead at approximately 1,400 m (4,592 ft.), the trail climbs gradually to 1,550 m (5,084 ft.), before descending toward the south trailhead at 1,425 m (4,674 ft.).

Season: This trail is rideable from mid-June to early October.

Services: With the exception of a bike shop, all services are available in the community of Bragg Creek, a 30-minute drive from the trailhead. The nearest bike shop is in Calgary, a 1-hour motor from the trailhead.

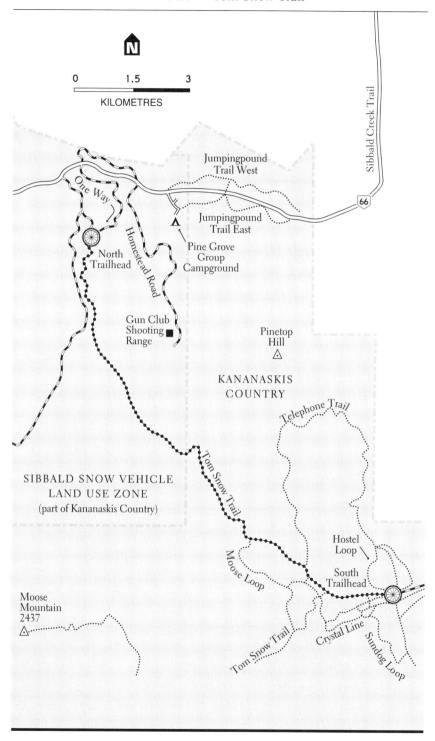

Susan Cameron
pushes through
some mud on the
Tom Snow Trail.

Hazards: The greatest challenges on this ride are the numerous mudholes that must be dealt with. Beyond these, you make one challenging river crossing near the south trailhead where a bridge has been washed out. Also, beware of horses throughout the season and hunters in the autumn.

Rescue index: On this ride, in case of an emergency, you need to decide which trailhead is closer. The south trailhead tends to see more use than the north one. You may also be able to get a weak cellular signal along high points on the trail.

Land status: This trail is operated as part of Kananaskis Country.

Maps: The 1:50,000 scale topographic map for this trail is 82 J/15 Bragg Creek. Gem Trek has produced an excellent trail map called "Kananaskis Country—Bragg Creek and Elbow Falls."

Finding the trail: To find the north trailhead, from the Trans Canada Highway, head south on Highway 40 (the Kananaskis Trail) for 7.7 km (4.62 mi.), and turn left onto the gravel of Sibbald Creek Trail (Highway 66). Follow this road for 19.2 km (11.52 mi.) and turn right onto the Jumpingpound Demonstration Forest Road. This road winds around in a large loop. Follow it until you arrive at the Spruce Woods Trailhead. Park here. To find the south trailhead, as Highway 22 approaches the town of Bragg Creek, take the right fork in the road and pass the shopping mall. Cross the bridge over Bragg Creek and make a left. Wind along this high-quality road, continuing as the pavement ends at km 6.8 (4.08 mi.). You'll pass a Texas gate (cattle guard) at the entrance to Kananaskis Country at km 8.5 (5.1 mi.). Finally, at km 9.6 (5.76 mi.), turn right into the West Bragg Creek parking lot. The trail begins by following the road beyond its terminus at the trailhead parking lot.

Sources of additional information: The Kananaskis Country address is listed in the introduction to this section. For up-to-date trail conditions, contact the Elbow Valley Information Centre at (403) 949-4261 or the Elbow Ranger Station at (403) 949-3754.

Notes on the trail: From the trailhead, drop down a long series of steps and cross a bridge over Moose Creek. After the bridge, take the right fork along a nicely carpeted trail. After passing interpretive marker 1, the trail winds to the left and a rough single-track forks off to the right. Stay left on the main trail, and after crossing a log bridge you'll meet another trail junction. While it may be tempting to turn right, the correct trail stays straight at this junction and begins climbing. The trail parallels the road off to the right, winding its way to the correct route—the Tom Snow Trail junction—at km 1.2 (mi. 0.72). After this junction, the trail continues to parallel the road until it passes a gas well. Beyond the well, it begins climbing and leaves the road behind. By km 2.0 (mi. 1.2), the trail levels out into a secondary forest of lodgepole pine that rolls through a muddy stretch. At km 2.2 (mi. 1.32), the trail drops down a sharp, rutted hill toward a short bridge. Stay right at the junction beyond the bridge, heading toward an orange diamond with a horse on it. These markers will periodically let you know you are on the right track. The trail soon widens until you reach a short, generally rideable ford at km 3.9 (mi. 2.34). Beyond the ford, a boot sucking mudhole presents a challenge, and the trail remains muddy until you enter a clear-cut at km 5.7 (mi. 3.42). Stay to the left at a fork in the trail at km 6.1 (mi. 3.66), using a red arrow sign as a marker. Soon after this junction, ride across another shallow ford and meet another fork in the trail. While an obvious trail seems to go right, it has been blocked by some downed logs. The correct trail goes to the left, marked by another orange diamond.

The trail climbs briefly and begins to roll comfortably through an alder thicket. Unfortunately, it heads back down into the muck at km 7.6 (mi. 4.44). This drop brings you to a closed barbed-wire gate at km 8.1 (4.86 mi.). Be sure to close the gate again once you are through. The trend becomes a gradual downhill roll until you meet a major washout at km 9.2 (mi. 5.52). When I did the ride, a large orange roadblock gate marked it. Beyond the washout, the trail climbs to parallel a large marsh off to the right. Several mudholes will slow you down before you emerge into a pleasant meadow at km 10.75 (mi. 6.45). Simply roll your way across the meadow, following a rough, grassy trail and meet the junction with the Moose Loop Trail at km 11.4 (mi. 6.84). Turn left at this junction and follow the wide trail. Soon after passing a picnic bench to the right of the trail, you'll see a trail going into the bush on the right at km 12.5 (mi. 7.5). Ignore it and stay to the left on the wide trail. As this trail forks again at km 12.8 (mi. 7.68), take the right fork. This will carry you back to a signed junction with the base of the Telephone Trail at km 13.5 (mi. 8.1). Stay straight and follow a now wide double-track.

Enjoy the wide trail until km 14.5 (mi. 8.7) where a bridge has washed out over Bragg Creek. This crossing can seem very puzzling, but if you search around, you'll find several places to cross—none of them welcoming, however. Once you make it across, the trail joins a major road coming in from the right, goes through two metal gates, and meets the West Bragg Creek trailhead at km 16.3 (mi. 9.78).

RIDE 30 · Telephone Trail

AT A GLANCE

Length/configuration: 16.05-km (9.63-mi.) loop.

Aerobic difficulty: The climbing is gradual, making for a pleasant ride.

Technical difficulty: Many mudholes require a certain amount of finesse, along with a very challenging crossing near the trail's end.

Scenery: There are some great views toward the eastern foothills as the trail rolls around the outer edge of this rounded knoll.

Special comments: Keep in mind that these trails are not maintained for summer use, so the conditions may vary dramatically.

This 16.05-km (9.63-mi.) loop makes for a pleasant foothill roll, despite some bad mudholes along its length. Beginning at the West Bragg Creek trailhead, it climbs gradually, passing through a muddy stretch, and climbs onto a high knoll on the edge of the foothills. As you reach the northern extent of the ride, you begin to roll along the edge of this knoll and get some great views toward the rolling country to the north and east of the ride. To the north, the aspen-coated slopes of the Jumpingpound River Valley lie just beyond Pinetop Hill. To the east, you look out toward some of the surrounding ranchlands of West Bragg Creek.

General location: West of the community of Bragg Creek, Alberta.

Elevation change: The gains are moderate on this ride, rising from the trailhead at 1,425 m (4,674 ft.) to a maximum of 1,575 m (5,166 ft.). This climb is spread over almost 11 km (6.6 mi.), making for a nice, slow climb.

Season: This trail is rideable from mid-June to early October.

Services: With the exception of a bike shop, all services are available in the community of Bragg Creek, a 10-minute drive from the trailhead. The nearest bike shop is in Calgary, a 1-hour drive from the trailhead.

RIDE 30 · Telephone Trail

Hazards: This trail is not maintained for summer use, so some of the mudholes may get larger over time. Be aware that two barbed-wire fences block the trail.

Rescue index: In case of emergency, you may need to return to the trailhead for assistance. If nobody is in the parking lot to offer help, head toward Bragg Creek where shops and telephones make for a quick rescue.

Land status: This trail is operated as part of Kananaskis Country.

Maps: The 1:50,000 scale topographic map for this trail is 82 J/15 Bragg Creek. Gem Trek has produced a superior trail map called "Kananaskis Country— Bragg Creek and Elbow Falls."

Rolling through the aspen woods on the Telephone Trail.

Finding the trail: As Highway 22 approaches the town of Bragg Creek, take the right fork in the road and pass the shopping mall. Cross the bridge over Bragg Creek and make a left. Wind along this high-quality road, continuing as the pavement ends at km 6.8 (mi. 4.08). You'll pass a Texas gate (cattle guard) at the entrance to Kananaskis Country at km 8.5 (mi. 5.1). Finally, at km 9.6 (mi. 5.76), turn right into the West Bragg Creek parking lot. Look for a trail sign on the far side of the lot. This is the trailhead.

Sources of additional information: The Kananaskis Country address is listed in the introduction to this section. For up-to-date trail conditions, contact the Elbow Valley Information Centre at (403) 949-4261 or the Elbow Ranger Station at (403) 949-3754.

Notes on the trail: The trail begins as a wide single-track that climbs to the right as it leaves the parking lot. Stay straight at a junction with the Hostel Loop Trail at km 0.65 (0.39 mi.). The next section of trail has many mudholes that can vary from passable to quicksand. You'll simply need to take them as they come. Stay straight at the upper junction with the Hostel Loop at km 1.45 (mi. 0.87). The mudholes continue until you meet a short, sharp drop down a gully, with a steep climb up the opposite side. At km 4.15 (mi. 2.49), the trail's character changes as it dries out and begins rolling along the edge of this upland with some views down to the right. The next section is rolling, with a downhill trend. At km 4.55 (mi. 2.73), you'll want to slow down as a sign indicates a barbed-wire fence. Just beyond this sign, you'll meet the fence, which completely blocks the trail. An angular gate allows you to get through, but you definitely want to be prepared for this sudden barrier.

Beyond the barbed wire, the trail continues its pleasant, rolling character. At km 5.05 (mi. 3.03), a winter sign indicates "Ice Flows" just at the top of a downhill. As you scream your way down the hill, a washed-out culvert appears at the bottom. Be cautious. The trail climbs briefly after the washout, eventually meeting a corduroy bridge at km 5.45 (mi. 3.27). The centre log has sunk into the mud, so watch that it doesn't grab your front tire as you cross. The trail begins to descend and wind to the left, bringing you to a rough junction at km 6.45 (mi. 3.87). Stay on the main trail and soon meet an old logging site with a sign indicating "B7-L6 Homestead Road Area." Cross this open area and begin a short, sharp climb. Once you crest this hill, the trail becomes a pleasant roll again, crossing a high-quality bridge at km 9.35 (mi. 5.61).

The fast pace is slowed once more as you approach a horrible section of muck at km 9.85 (mi. 5.91). It's very tough to keep your feet dry on this short section, but it is possible. The bog takes only a short time to cross, though, and you are quickly rolling along again when you meet another barbed-wire fence at km 10.95 (mi. 6.57). You can bypass this one by crawling under a few logs and continuing on your way. After an uninterrupted downhill roll, you meet another bad mudhole. This one extends until you cross a high-quality bridge at km 12.35 (mi. 7.41). Beyond the bridge, a "Danger" sign warns of a tricky stream crossing. This hazard is quickly followed by another bad washout, after which conditions improve again.

You'll pass a "Dangerous Hill" sign at km 12.85 (mi. 7.71), but the danger refers to cross-country skiing. It is not difficult on a mountain bike, just a bit steep and loose. This section brings you down to the junction with Mountain Road Trail to the left and access to the Tom Snow Trail and Moose Loop to the right. Turn left on the wide gravel and roll back toward the trailhead. While this is a nice wide double-track, one final obstacle must be faced before you reach the trailhead. At km 14.05 (mi. 8.43), the bridge over Bragg Creek is out. It can be very challenging to find a way across, but a little searching will get you past this hazard. Once you are across, the trail joins a major road coming in from the right. Join with this route, cross a good bridge over the creek, and meet a locked gate at km 15.65 (mi. 9.39). Pass through this gate and another soon after, and meet the parking lot at km 15.85 (mi. 9.51). Reach the trailhead at 16.05 km (mi. 9.63).

RIDE 31 · McLean Creek Off-Highway Vehicle Zone

AT A GLANCE

Length/configuration: Variable—up to 20 km (12 mi.) or more.

Aerobic difficulty: The gradients can be anything from flat to extremely steep.

Technical difficulty: The trails vary from wide roads to narrow, rough single-track.

Scenery: Some great views are available from some of the high ridges within the off-highway vehicle zone.

Special comments: Keep your eyes open for wild horses that call this area home.

The McLean Creek area provides an opportunity for riders to travel just about anywhere they like. This 200-square-kilometre (77.22-square-mile) area was set aside for motorcycles and four-wheel-drives. It provides a unique network of trails and lots of mountain bike action as well. It is best to ride the trails on weekdays if possible; they are much busier with motorized users on weekends.

Some of the trails provide access to some wonderful high country, and most of the major trails are in generally good condition, with wide tracks and solid gravel. Mud, though, is a way of life in this area, so avoid it if you're shy about getting a little dirty.

General location: This area is west of Bragg Creek in the Elbow Valley of Kananaskis Country.

Elevation change: The elevation change varies with the trails chosen.

Season: The season opens earlier here, in late May, and continues into early October.

Services: All services are available in Bragg Creek, with the exception of a bike shop. You'll need to travel to Calgary, a distance of 61 km (37.8 mi.) from the trailhead, for bike repairs.

Hazards: The trail system is used by both motorized and nonmotorized travelers. Be courteous and give the dirt bikes plenty of room to move. Some of the trails have deep mud holes from the vehicle traffic. They may be far deeper than they appear at first glance. Be cautious before you head full speed into a long mud hole—you might just disappear. Some of the trails have eroded badly, so you'll need to be wary of roots and other trail damage.

Rescue index: Many vehicles share the area during summer weekends. Most of them can either offer assistance in the way of evacuation or provide a way to signal for emergency help. These areas see little traffic, and the farther you head from the main staging areas, the less traffic you'll encounter.

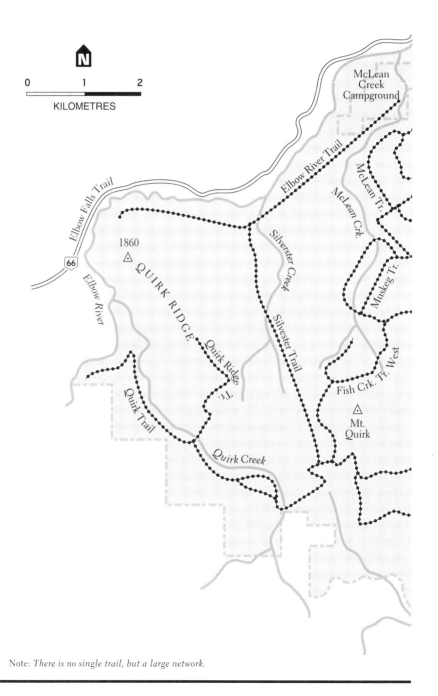

Note: *There is no single trail, but a large network.*

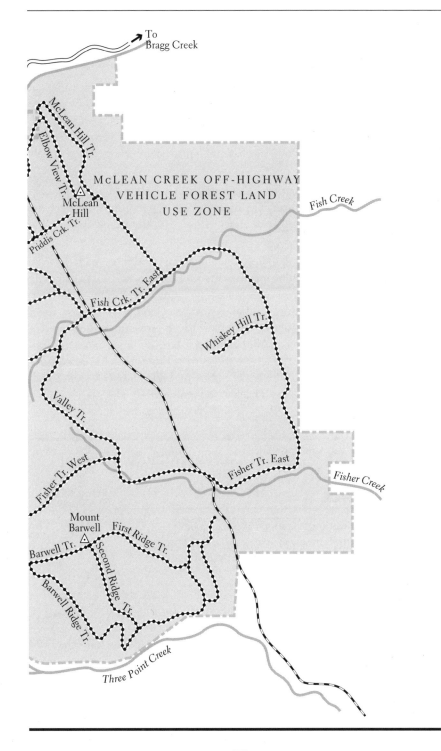

To
Bragg Creek

McLean Hill Tr.

Elbow View Tr.

McLEAN CREEK OFF-HIGHWAY
VEHICLE FOREST LAND
USE ZONE

Fish Creek

McLean
Hill

Priddis Crk. Tr.

Fish Crk. Tr. East

Whiskey Hill Tr.

Valley Tr.

Fisher Tr. West

Fisher Tr. East

Fisher Creek

Mount
Barwell

First Ridge Tr.

Barwell Tr.

Second Ridge Tr.

Barwell Ridge Tr.

Three Point Creek

Land status: This trail is operated as part of Kananaskis Country.

Maps: The 1:50,000 scale topographic map for this trail is 82 J/15 Bragg Creek. Map Town produces a trail map for this area called "Kananaskis Country — Bragg Creek and Elbow Falls." In addition, Kananaskis Country produces its own trail map of the McLean Creek Trail System.

Finding the trail: From Bragg Creek, follow the signs to the Elbow Valley on Highway 66. From the entrance to Kananaskis Country, indicated by a large sign, continue west for 3.6 km (2.23 mi.) to the McLean Creek Campground. Day — use access is also along this road. Make sure you get a McLean Creek trail map, either at the Elbow Valley Information Centre or the campground checking station.

Sources of additional information: The Kananaskis Country address is listed in the introduction to this section. For up-to-date trail conditions, contact the Elbow Valley Information Centre at (403) 949-4261 or the Elbow Ranger Station at (403) 949-3754.

Notes on the trail: It's difficult to describe individual trails here, so I'll describe the system of trails. From the day-use area, the McLean Creek Trail (a driveable road) heads south and provides access to trails radiating from this main corridor. You can also mount your saddle right away and head west on the Elbow River Trail. This westbound route follows the Elbow River, providing some excellent views toward the western peaks. After riding 4.5 km (2.7 mi.), Silvester Trail branches off to the south. It has loop options with Fish Creek Trail or Fisher Trail West, both of which make their way east to the McLean Creek Trail. Heading north on this road will take you back to the trailhead.

RIDE 32 · Quirk Creek–Wildhorse Loop

AT A GLANCE

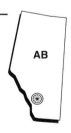

Length/configuration: 25.5 km (15.9 mi.) loop.

Aerobic difficulty: The trail climbs steadily to its junction with Wildhorse Trail, but it is wide and smooth for its duration.

Technical difficulty: A challenging ford of the Elbow River marks the beginning and end of this ride. Wildhorse Trail is a winding, single-track slalom. Watch for obstacles and trees.

Scenery: Most of the ride, which is within the trees, focuses on fun rather than scenic views.

Special comments: This great loop offers a smooth ascent followed by a rapid, single-track return route.

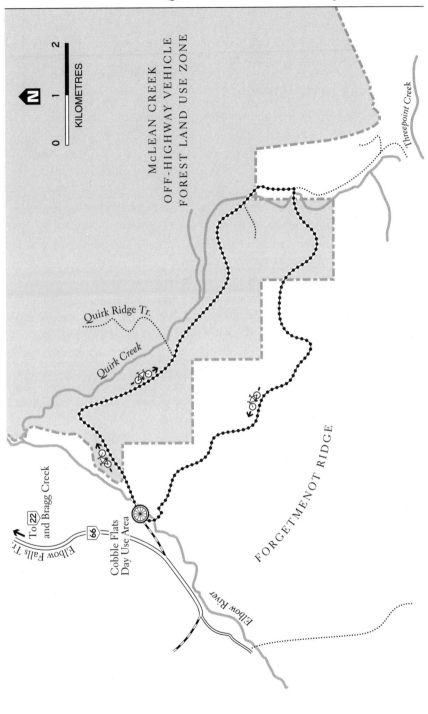

An intermediate rider's dream, this 25.5-km (15.9-mi.) loop climbs gradually up an old gas exploration road and then winds its way back on a narrow, wilderness roller coaster.

The trail provides some excellent views of the surrounding foothills and returns along the base of Forgetmenot Mountain. A frigid ford of the Elbow River is required at both ends of the ride, but nothing will wake you up like a wade through a mountain stream.

General location: The trail lies west of Bragg Creek in the Elbow Valley.

Elevation change: From the trailhead at 1,591 m (5,220 ft.), the trail climbs steadily as it rises to the top of the Quirk Trail. At the junction with Wildhorse Trail, it has gained 214 m (702 ft.). From this point, the ride is downhill.

Season: This trail is rideable from mid-June to early October; however, the ford over the Elbow River suggests leaving it until late July, when the water levels have dropped. During spring floods, it can be extremely dangerous to attempt this ford.

Services: All services are available in Bragg Creek, with the exception of a bike shop, which is 30 minutes east of the trailhead.

Hazards: The ford over the Elbow River can be treacherous with high water. Wait until later in the season for lower water levels. Once you begin descending the Wildhorse Trail, some of it is quite narrow, and rooty stretches are common. It also makes some quick slalom turns, so you'll need to be able to respond quickly.

Rescue index: This trail is not heavily traveled. The first half, climbing along the Quirk Road, offers the possibility of encountering other riders, as well as off-highway vehicle users. Once you turn onto the Wildhorse Trail, you'll likely need to continue to the end before you can find assistance. The trailhead is at a busy picnic area.

Land status: This trail is operated as part of Kananaskis Country.

Maps: The 1:50,000 scale topographic map for this trail is 82 J/15 Mount Rae; however, Map Town's map entitled "Kananaskis Country—Bragg Creek and Elbow Falls" is superior.

Finding the trail: From Bragg Creek, follow Highway 22 to its junction with Highway 66. Turn right, and within a few minutes a sign will indicate the entrance to Kananaskis Country. Travel west for 22.6 km (14 mi.) to Cobble Flats Day Use Area. The trail begins at the picnic site at the far end of the access road.

Sources of additional information: The Kananaskis Country address is listed in the introduction to this section. For up-to-date trail conditions, contact the Elbow Valley Information Centre at (403) 949-4261 or the Elbow Ranger Station at (403) 949-3754.

Notes on the trail: From the day-use area, a short trail across a bridge brings you onto a wide gravel wash. Strike out across the wash and you'll see the Quirk Road heading off on the opposite side of the river. Ford the cold Elbow River, and the road will bring you smoothly but steadily uphill for 10.24 km (6.35 mi.), where you'll see an overgrown access road heading to the right. Follow this road and quickly pass beyond the boundary of the Off-Highway Vehicle Zone. As you follow the good trail, it meets the Wildhorse Trail at km 14.24 (mi. 8.83). Take the right-hand turn to begin Wildhorse Trail and immediately notice the difference. From the open nature of the Quirk Trail, the Wildhorse becomes a narrow, winding single-track that will run you downhill at a fast and furious pace. Watch for obstacles and roots, as the riding is fast. The trail crosses several streams coming from the back side of Forgetmenot Mountain and then makes the final descent into the valley. At a junction at km 24.7 (mi. 15.3), turn right. The trail reaches the Elbow River almost immediately. A quick ford brings you back to the trailhead at km 25.5 (mi. 15.9).

RIDE 33 · Moose Mountain Fire Road

AT A GLANCE

Length/configuration: 5.6-km (3.5-mi.) point-to-point followed by a 1-km (0.6-mi.) hike to the lookout. Total out-and-back distance is 13.2 km (7.9 mi.).

Aerobic difficulty: The trail climbs moderately until the final summit push. This is a good place to park your bike and hike the remainder of the trail.

Technical difficulty: There are few technical challenges.

Scenery: The panorama from the fire lookout stretches east to Calgary and west all the way to Mounts Glasgow and Cornwall at the west end of the Elbow Valley.

Special comments: Do this ride! The views are fabulous.

Moose Mountain Fire Road provides riders of beginner to expert ability an opportunity to ride the ridges while climbing toward Moose Mountain Fire Lookout. This out-and-back is composed of a 5.6-km (3.5-mi.) ride, followed by a 1-km (0.6-mi.) hike. The last stretch to the lookout is best done on foot. The total riding distance is 11.2 km (7 mi.). The combination of riding and hiking provides excellent access to the highest fire lookout in Alberta.

From the summit, the views to the east stretch all the way to Calgary approximately 50 km (30 mi.) distant. To the west, the transition from foothills to mountain is clearly displayed. This is one of the premier viewing points in the valley, and it is one of only two mountain summits in the valley accessible by bike (the other is Powderface Ridge).

Please respect the privacy of the lookout. It is not a public building and is the lookout's home. A sign at the trailhead asks visitors to stay away from the actual building.

General location: This trail lies west of Bragg Creek, Alberta.

Elevation change: The trail begins at 1,975 m (6,480 ft.) and climbs 914 m (3,000 ft.).

RIDE 33 · Moose Mountain Fire Road

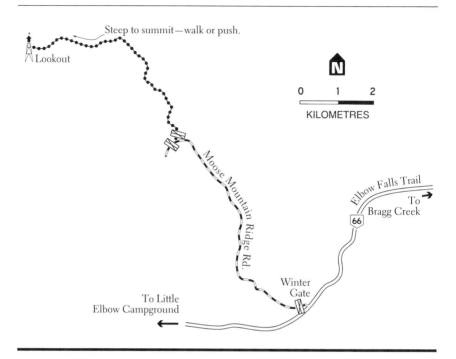

Season: This trail is rideable from mid-June to early October.

Services: With the exception of a bike shop, all services are available in Bragg Creek, a 30-minute drive from the trailhead. The nearest bike shop is in Calgary, a 1-hour drive from the trailhead.

Hazards: Some sections of trail are rocky, with loose material that can throw an unwary rider.

Rescue index: Moose Mountain Fire Road is a very popular ride and hike. It is rarely difficult to get assistance. In addition, the fire lookout at the summit has a two-way radio and can contact park rangers if necessary. The trailhead lies along a winding access road for the gas wells on Moose Mountain and sees a lot of sightseeing traffic, along with the official gas company vehicles. Any of these can initiate a rescue.

Land status: This trail is operated as part of Kananaskis Country.

Maps: The 1:50,000 scale topographic map for this trail is 82 J/15 Bragg Creek. Map Town produces an excellent trail map called "Kananaskis Country—Bragg Creek and Elbow Falls."

Finding the trail: From Bragg Creek, follow the signs to the Elbow Valley on Highway 66. From the entrance to Kananaskis Country, indicated by a large sign, continue west for 9.5 km (5.7 mi.) to the Moose Mountain Ridge Road. Turn right onto this gravel road and climb for 7.5 km (4.5 mi.) to the trailhead. No sign indicates the trail; however, a gated fire road branches off the main road at this point and is clearly visible.

Sources of additional information: The Kananaskis Country address is listed in the introduction to this section. For up-to-date trail conditions, contact the Elbow Valley Information Centre at (403) 949-4261 or the Elbow Ranger Station at (403) 949-3754.

Notes on the trail: From the trailhead, at an elevation of 1,975 m (6,480 ft.), the road is an excellent gravel fire road. The trail quickly provides views of your destination, the twin-humped summit of Moose Mountain. At km 0.61 (mi. 0.4), there is a short, moderately steep uphill to an elevation of 2,011 m (6,600 ft.). The trail then drops 61 m (200 ft.) on a technical rocky section before climbing again. The climbing is a first-gear grind with some excellent views of the surrounding Elbow River Valley. At km 3.74 (mi. 2.3) the trail passes the junction to Moose Packer's Trail; stay straight.

Shortly after the junction, the trail provides a welcome downhill break until km 4.4 (mi. 2.7). It drops from 2,213 m (7,260 ft.) to 2,079 m (6,820 ft.) and is followed by a steep uphill. Shortly after the trail begins climbing, distant switchbacks show their intimidating face. At km 5.62 (mi. 3.5) and an elevation of 2,194 m (7,200 ft.), I parked my bike and hiked the last kilometre (0.6 mi.) to the lookout at the summit. Return on the same trail.

RIDE 34 · Forgetmenot Rounder

AT A GLANCE

Length/configuration: 48.9-km (29.4-mi.) loop.

Aerobic difficulty: There are some steep climbs, and the distance will challenge novices.

Technical difficulty: Some of the trail sections have been badly chewed up by cattle, making for a rough ride.

Scenery: The trail moves from in and out of the trees, with periodic views. The view of Threepoint Creek Gorge is spectacular.

Special comments: This trail is long and remote, but it makes for a great follow-up to the Big Elbow-Little Elbow Loop.

This 48.9-km (29.4-mi.) loop route takes the rider into remote country and through some difficult terrain. It is for advanced and intermediate riders only. By the end of the ride, you'll have completely circumnavigated Forgetmenot Ridge.

From the trailhead at 1,591 m (5,220 ft.), the trail climbs to a high point of 1,957 m (6,420 ft.). This high elevation provides some wide-open views of the surrounding peaks, including the Elbow's most famous peaks, Banded, Cornwall, and Glasgow. Cornwall and Glasgow commemorate ships engaged in the Battle of Jutland during World War I. Although World War I was not a naval war, Jutland was the only major sea engagement and formed a turning point in the conflict. The Allies suffered greater casualties, but the Germans never again tried to break the Allied blockade.

As you move away from the western peaks, the trail enters the foothills and exhibits the rolling character so often associated with this area. You also encounter something else often connected to the foothills—cows. This region of Kananaskis has a seemingly endless number of grazing cattle, and parts of this trail will suffer as a result. The views easily make up for the challenges, and the steep gorge of Threepoint Creek alone is worth the ride. Bring lots of water and pack a lunch, as this is a long, adventurous ride.

General location: This trail lies west of Bragg Creek in the Elbow Valley of Kananaskis Country.

Elevation change: The trail begins at 1,591 m (5,220 ft.) and climbs to a high point of 1,957 m (6,420 ft.). From this height of land, the general trend is downhill, with a few short, steep climbs.

Season: This trail is rideable from mid-June to early October.

Services: All services are available in Bragg Creek, with the exception of a bike shop, which is 30 minutes east of the trailhead.

Hazards: As you wind along this route, the junctions are sometimes confusing, with signs indicating campgrounds that don't appear and junctions with only one trail. Follow the directions listed here in "Notes on the trail."

When riding past the cattle, try not to harass them. They have the potential to get aggressive, but they rarely do. Since this is not heavily traveled country, keep your eyes open for other wildlife as well.

Much of the trail is technical and cattle-chewed. It is easy to lose control, especially on some of the badly damaged sections of trail. The final ford over the Elbow River can be treacherous early in the season. Don't ride this trail until mid-July to allow the water level to drop. Even then, it is a thigh-deep crossing.

Rescue index: This trail is not heavily traveled. I didn't encounter any other riders while I was out. You have to assume you'll be on your own while riding it. Your chances of meeting other riders are better near both ends of the trail. It begins along a popular route and ends at a busy picnic area. From the junction with Threepoint Mountain Trail to the junction with the McLean Creek Off-Highway Vehicle Zone, you'll encounter little assistance.

Land status: This trail is operated as part of Kananaskis Country.

Maps: The 1:50,000 scale topographic map for this trail is 82 J/15 Bragg Creek. Map Town produces an excellent trail map called "Kananaskis Country—Bragg Creek and Elbow Falls."

Finding the trail: From the entrance to Kananaskis Country along Highway 66, continue 23.7 km (14.7 mi.) to the Little Elbow Campground. A few hundred metres beyond the checking station you'll see a large suspension bridge crossing the river. Near this bridge is a small parking lot.

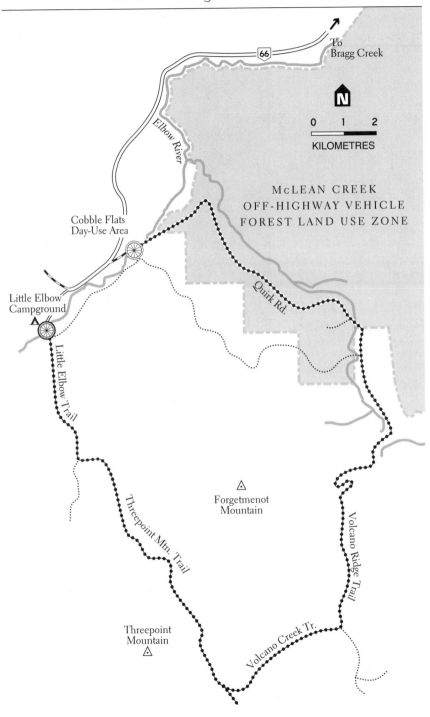

To
Bragg Creek

66

N

0   1   2
KILOMETRES

Elbow River

McLEAN CREEK
OFF-HIGHWAY VEHICLE
FOREST LAND USE ZONE

Cobble Flats
Day-Use Area

Quirk Rd.

Little Elbow
Campground

Little Elbow Trail

Forgetmenot
Mountain

Threepoint Mtn. Trail

Volcano Ridge Trail

Threepoint
Mountain

Volcano Creek Tr.

Forgetmenot Rounder provides everything from steep pushing to wide track to rooty ruts. Here, Sue Baker rolls across a wide meadow.

Sources of additional information: The Kananaskis Country address is listed in the introduction to this section. For up-to-date trail conditions, contact the Elbow Valley Information Centre at (403) 949-4261 or the Elbow Ranger Station at (403) 949-3754.

Notes on the trail: Cross the suspension bridge over the Little Elbow River and go straight at the first junction at km 0.51 (mi. 0.3). This junction provides one of the return options. Over the next several kilometres the trail opens up to provide views of the slopes of Forgetmenot Mountain. A small ford, the result of a washout at km 3.5 (mi. 2.1), is rideable. Keep your eyes open as the junction to Forgetmenot Mountain Trail is easy to miss—I missed it. At km 4.3 (mi. 2.58), a small trail branches off to the left of the main trail. A green post with an orange diamond has Threepoint Mountain written on it. This is the correct junction. Over the next kilometre, turn right, then left, at two junctions. Several shallow fords are followed by some rooty single-track. Before long, you'll start climbing steeply. The climb begins at approximately km 5.72 (mi. 3.43) and continues until km 8.49 (mi. 5.1). As you near the crest, the views open up to the west. Dropping off the shoulder, a small ford is followed by some badly cattle-chewed trail. The trail remains in poor riding condition until the junction with Volcano

Ridge Trail at km 19.7 (mi. 11.8). Before reaching the junction, several confusing signs test your confidence. A sign at km 13.6 (mi. 8.2) indicates Threepoint Campground, but no evidence of a campground is apparent. Don't fear, you're heading in the right direction. Another confusing sign at km 14.8 (mi. 8.9) indicates that you should go left, but there is no sign of another trail.

Drop down to the creek again at km 19.7 (mi. 11.8) and the junction with Volcano Ridge Trail.

Beginning with a steep climb out of the river valley, Volcano Creek signals an improvement in the trail condition. The sloppy nature of this cattle range hardens up, and the trail becomes a smoother ride. Parts of Volcano Ridge Trail follow old seismic lines, so they are almost perfectly straight. At km 25.9 (mi. 15.55), the floods of 1995 have eaten away at the road. The traverse of the river's cut-bank makes for a tricky 100 m. An old campsite at km 29.4 (mi. 17.6) seems to beckon the rider straight on. Avoid the temptation and take a right turn at this point. Before long, your faith is rewarded with views to the deep valley of Threepoint Gorge. A closed gate at km 28.93 (mi. 17.4) is followed by a signed junction at km 29.3 (mi. 17.6). Go right at this marker and straight at the junction for Wildhorse Campground.

The left junction takes you down Wildhorse Trail. This alternate exit provides a slalom trail that eventually returns you to the trailhead at Little Elbow Campground. I chose to continue straight and exit through the McLean Creek Off-Highway Vehicle Zone. The boundary of the Off-Highway Zone is reached at km 32.96 (mi. 19.8), followed by a road at km 33.3 (mi. 20.0). Go left on the road as it winds farther to the left, toward the junction with Quirk Ridge Trail at km 37.26 (mi. 22.4). A side road at km 41.0 (mi. 24.6) climbs to a gas well on Quirk Mountain; go straight. A left junction at km 43.0 (mi. 25.8) takes you to a frigid ford over the thigh-deep Elbow River. After the ford, cross straight over the gravel wash, and you'll enter Cobble Flats Day Use Area on the opposite side. Go left on the day-use area road until it meets the Elbow Falls Trail (Highway 66) at km 45.75 (mi. 27.5). Go left on the highway and left again into the Little Elbow Campground at km 46.9 (mi. 28.1). You'll reach the trailhead at the 48.9-km (29.35-mi.) mark.

RIDE 35 · Big Elbow–Little Elbow Loop

AT A GLANCE

Length/configuration: 43.6-km (27.1-mi.) loop.

Aerobic difficulty: This is a long ride with lots of elevation gain. Save it for later in the season when you're pumped.

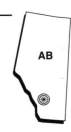

AB

Technical difficulty: There are some tricky, technical sections on this ride, especially between the Big Elbow Campground and the Elbow Pass Junction.

Scenery: The ride straddles the boundary of foothill and mountain with vistas in all directions, including excellent views of the valley's dominant western peaks, Banded, Cornwall, and Glasgow.

Special comments: This is one of the Rockies' greatest rides. You'll likely find yourself doing it over and over.

If you want a trail with a bit of everything, this is the perfect ride for you. This 43.6-km (27.1-mi.) loop includes smooth fire road, technical stretches, a blood-tasting uphill, all of it topped off with an incredible alpine setting. The level of difficulty is rated as intermediate due to the long distance and wilderness nature of the trail. However, physically fit beginners can easily complete the loop if they are cautious and don't mind walking their bikes on some of the technical stretches. This is one of my favourite rides, although I question my preference each time I attempt the climb to Elbow Pass. This temporary loss of confidence is quickly corrected when the panorama of the pass swings into view.

Beginning at the western end of the Elbow Valley, this trail circumnavigates three of the most prominent mountains visible from Calgary. Banded Peak, Glasgow, and Cornwall are three of the first mountains of the Front Range of the Rockies. To the east lie the foothills, which slowly give way to the plains. To the west, the peaks are craggy examples of true Front Range mountains. Standing just under 3,050 m (10,000 ft.), these three peaks form an impressive backdrop for this circular route.

The first 8.9 km (5.5 mi.) follow the dividing line between foothill and mountain as the trail hugs the shoreline of the Elbow River. The gradient is smooth and quick on this former four-wheel-drive route. Shortly after the Big Elbow Campground, the trail follows the river west and passes between Banded Peak and Cougar Mountain. The panorama opens up as you look toward jagged faces of limestone and shale.

From the junction with Tombstone Campground at km 19.4 (mi. 12.1), prepare yourself for hardship as your wheels head steeply uphill for the next 4.5 km (2.8 mi.) to the summit of Elbow Pass. For a side trip, park your bike and hike the short distance to Tombstone Lakes. These beautiful lakes, lying in a textbook example of a glacial bowl (or cirque), are definitely worth the diversion. Acquiring their name from some rocky pillars resembling grave markers, these lakes must be seen to be believed. The summit of Elbow Pass at 2,225 m (7,300 ft.) provides dramatic views of Tombstone Mountain to the west. Along the pass, alpine larch, the only coniferous tree in the mountains to lose its needles every year, provide a pleasant foreground. In the meadow, flowers like the alpine forget-me-not poke their blue heads above the grasses.

From the pass, drop your head and get ready to rock. From here it's a downhill run almost all the way to the end of the ride. The drop in elevation is quick but smooth on this old access road. Passing Mount Romulus Campground at km 31.5 (mi. 19.6) gives you excellent views of its namesake mountain and its counterpart, Mount Remus. As the trail continues toward its Little Elbow Campground terminus, you'll pass several lush avalanche slopes and cross several good bridges over the Little Elbow River.

General location: The trail begins in Little Elbow Campground, approximately 32 km (19.9 mi.) west of Bragg Creek along Highway 66 (Elbow Falls Trail).

Elevation change: The trail climbs over Elbow Pass, which provides a total elevation gain of 625 m (approximately 2,000 ft.).

Season: A summer trail only, it heads into high country, so you must wait until the last snow leaves the Rockies in June. The trail becomes snowbound by mid-September because of its high elevation.

Services: Bragg Creek boasts a grocery store, a gas station, and several restaurants. Within the Elbow Valley, more than 600 campsites are available for those who wish to spend a few days exploring the area. The nearest bike shop is in Calgary.

Hazards: This is a remote ride, so be prepared for any contingency with a good repair kit and a first-aid kit. As you ride this trail, the main hazards are along the rocky, technical stretch between the Big Elbow Campground at km 8.9 (mi. 5.5) and the junction with Elbow Pass Trail at km 20.7 (mi. 12.9).

Rescue index: Beginning and ending at the Little Elbow Campground, the trail offers assistance at the campground registration building. A pay phone, located near the registration building, can be used during the off-season. Along the trail, which is moderately busy, you can occasionally flag down other mountain bikers or horseback riders. Several campgrounds are located along the route.

Land status: This land is operated as part of Kananaskis Country.

Maps: The 1:50,000 scale topographic maps for this trail are split between 82 J/10 Mount Rae and 82 J/15 Bragg Creek. Map Town produces an excellent recreational map entitled "Kananaskis Country—Bragg Creek and Elbow Falls."

Finding the trail: Head west from Bragg Creek approximately 32 km on Highway 66 (Elbow Falls Trail) to the Little Elbow Campground. As you drive through the campground, you'll notice a rust-coloured bridge over the Little Elbow River. A parking lot is adjacent to this bridge.

Sources of additional information: The Kananaskis Country address is listed in the introduction to this section. For up-to-date trail conditions, contact the Elbow Valley Information Centre at (403) 949-4261 or the Elbow Ranger Station at (403) 949-3754.

Notes on the trail: From the trailhead, at the bridge over the Little Elbow River, follow the wide fire road as it heads south between Forgetmenot Ridge to the east and Mount Glasgow to the west. The trail is well marked and provides few navigational difficulties. All junctions are marked with trail maps and signs.

Along this first stretch, the trail is primarily a former fire road, but it does cross several rocky gravel washes. You'll pass Big Elbow Campground at km 8.9 (mi. 5.5), and shortly afterward, at km 10.5 (mi. 6.5) the trail heads westward as the Elbow River begins to cut across the mountains. After a steep climb, the trail drops to river level and begins to exhibit a more rolling, technical, and rocky nature. Along the next 7.0 km (4.4 mi.), several difficult technical stretches may cause novices to dismount.

Note: *All double-track (former fire road) except where indicated.*

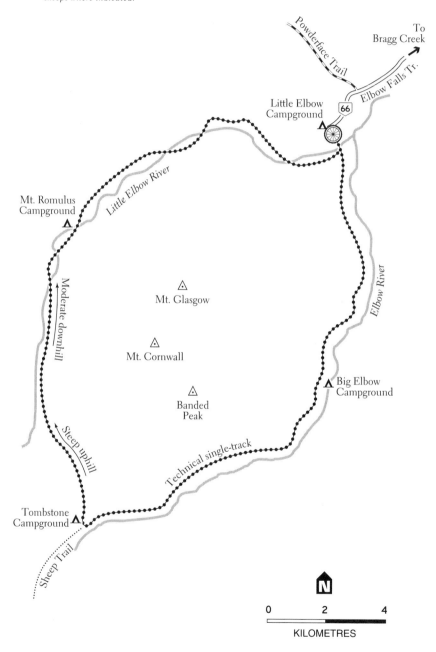

The Big Elbow–Little Elbow Loop follows the water all the way around. Here the Elbow River flows beneath Forgetmenot Mountain.

Km 19.4 (mi. 12.1) brings you to the next important junction. Head right at the trail sign toward Tombstone Creek. At km 21.9 and 24.8 (mi. 13.6 and 15.4), two different trailheads provide you with access to Tombstone Lakes. This 1.0-km (0.6-mi.) side trip must be done on foot, but it is well worth the effort.

The climb to the pass is extremely difficult and the hardiest riders wheezing as the final push culminates at the summit at the 23-km (14.3-mi.) mark. The trail drops here and heads quickly downhill, following the Little Elbow River. Crossing several avalanche slopes, the route passes Mount Romulus Campground at km 31.5 (mi. 19.6). From there, the trail is wide, smooth, and rolling for the final 12.1 km (7.5 mi.) to the Little Elbow Campground.

RIDE 36 · Elbow-Sheep Trail

AT A GLANCE

Length/configuration: 42.8-km (26.54-mi.) point-to-point.

Aerobic difficulty: The trail climbs gradually, although the total elevation gain is 625 m (2,050 ft.).

AB

Technical difficulty: The section between Big Elbow Campground and the Elbow Pass Junction is narrow and technical. In addition, the section between Sheep Pass and Bluerock Campground includes many creek crossings, so save this trail for late in the season when the water level has dropped.

Scenery: This ride follows the official start of the Front Ranges of the Rockies. The views are regular and dramatic.

Special comments: This is a point-to-point, with a long vehicle shuttle.

This 42.8-km (26.54-mi.) point-to-point or out-and-back takes you from the valley of the Elbow River south to the valley of the Sheep. It traverses some challenging terrain along its northern section, so it's rated as intermediate. Beginner riders can complete this trail if they don't mind walking some of the rough stretches. Outside the technical stretches, it follows an old four-wheel-drive road the entire way.

From the north trailhead, it passes beneath the three main peaks of the Elbow Valley: Banded, Cornwall, and Glasgow. Banded Peak has a steep band of rock near the summit. Since it is too steep to hold snow in winter, the mountain generally has a dark band near the peak. Mounts Cornwall and Glasgow commemorate battleships from the Battle of Jutland in World War I, the only major naval battle during that war and one that was a turning point. The Allies sacrificed more men but managed to keep the main German fleet from breaking their blockade. The German fleet stayed in harbour for the rest of the war.

At the Tombstone Campground the Elbow River is traded in for the Sheep. At the same time, the trail begins traversing the Misty Range to the west and Cougar Mountain to the east. A strong cougar population is present in the Rockies. Studies in this area in the early 1980s used dogs to track cougars. During the study's four-year duration, 28 different cats were radio-collared. This provided an abundance of information about this reclusive resident.

The trail passes the old Burns Mine site, where several old buildings still stand. Harry Denning, a friend of Pat Burns, used these cabins when grazing his cattle back in the 1930s and 1940s. In 1947, he built a new log cabin and put up a sign that read "You are welcome to use this cabin. Leave things as you found them with a little food and dry firewood," and was signed H. E. Denning. The land is still owned by the Burns family.

From the mine site, the trail passes below the towering face of Gibraltar Mountain and arrives at Bluerock Campground at km 42.8 (mi. 26.54).

General location: This trail joins the Elbow and Sheep River valleys from their western extents.

Elevation change: From the trailhead at 1,600 m (5,249 ft.) the trail climbs to a maximum elevation of 2,225 m (7,300 ft.) at Sheep Pass. It finishes at Bluerock Campground at 1,603 m (5,260 ft.).

Season: This is a summer trail only. Since it heads into relatively high country, you must wait until the last snow leaves the Rockies in June. The trail will also become snowbound by mid-September because of its high elevation.

Services: In Bragg Creek, you'll find a grocery store, a gas station, and several restaurants. Within the Elbow Valley, more than 600 campsites are availablefor those wishing to spend a few days exploring the area. The nearest bike shop is in Calgary.

Hazards: Since this is a remote wilderness ride, make sure you have a good repair kit; you'll be a long way from civilization. As you ride this trail, be cautious along the rocky, technical stretch beyond the Big Elbow Campground at km 8.9 (mi. 5.5). For approximately 7 km (4.4 mi.) the trail has rough stretches that may require a bit of pushing to negotiate. The trail crosses the Sheep River a seemingly endless number of times. Save this trail for later in the season when the river becomes shallow and sluggish. It can be a frustrating ride early in the season.

Rescue index: This trail provides a mixture of popular trail and quiet riding. As a point-to-point, there may be long stretches where you encounter few riders. Both ends of the trail provide access to busy roads and campgrounds for assistance. The trail passes many campgrounds along the way, which may offer options for attracting help.

Land status: This land is operated as part of Kananaskis Country.

Maps: The 1:50,000 scale topographic maps for this trail are split between 82 J/10 Mount Rae and 82 J/15 Bragg Creek. Map Town produces an excellent recreational map entitled "Kananaskis Country—Bragg Creek and Elbow Falls"; however, it only shows the northern part of the route.

Finding the trail: For the north trailhead, head west from Bragg Creek approximately 32 km on Highway 66 (Elbow Falls Trail) to the Little Elbow Campground. As you drive through the campground, you'll notice a rust-coloured bridge over the Little Elbow River. A small parking lot is adjacent to this bridge.

To access the south trailhead, travel west from the town of Turner Valley, following signs to Kananaskis Country. Drive all the way to the western end of the Sheep Valley and the Bluerock Campground. Park at the trailhead at the end of the main road.

Sources of additional information: The Kananaskis Country address is listed in the introduction to this section. For up-to-date trail conditions, contact the Elbow Valley Information Centre at (403) 949-4261 or the Elbow Ranger Station at (403) 949-3754.

Notes on the trail: Along its first stretch the trail is primarily old access road, but it does cross several rocky gravel washes. Cross the bridge over the Little Elbow

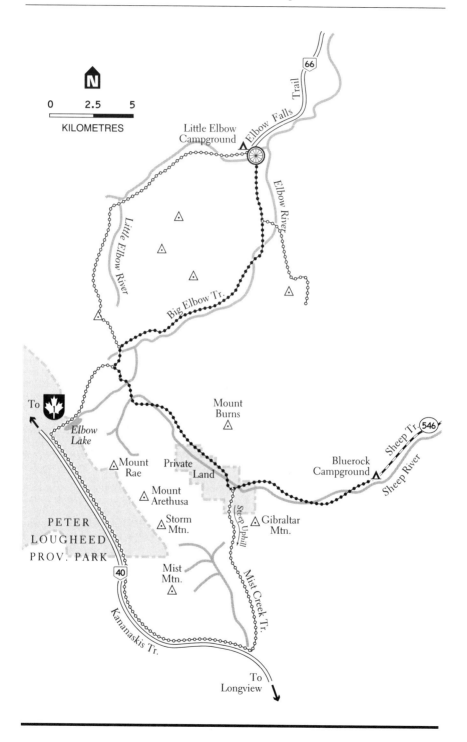

River and follow this former fire road as it travels south. You'll pass Big Elbow Campground at km 8.9 (mi. 5.5), and shortly afterward, at km 10.5 (mi. 6.5), the trail heads westward as the Elbow River begins to cut across the mountains. After a steep climb, the trail drops back down to river level and begins to exhibit a more rolling, technical, and rocky character. Along the next 7 km (4.4 mi.), several difficult technical stretches may cause novices to dismount.

Km 19.4 (mi. 12.1) brings you to the next important junction. Turn left to descend toward Tombstone Campground at km 20.1 (mi. 12.46) and continue south on the Sheep Trail. The trail passes the junction to Elbow Pass at km 20.8 (mi. 12.9). The Sheep Trail follows its namesake river, crossing it numerous times. During spring, this can be a wet ride. At km 30.5 (mi. 18.9), the trail passes the old cabins of the Burns Mine. Continue past the buildings toward the sheer face of Gibraltar Mountain. The trail reaches Bluerock Campground on Highway 546 at km 42.8 (mi. 26.54).

RIDE 37 · Junction Mountain Fire Lookout

AT A GLANCE

Length/configuration: 24.3-km (17.6-mi.) out-and-back; 14.15 km (8.8 mi.) one-way.

Aerobic difficulty: This steep trail climbs 670 m (2,200 ft.), making for a difficult challenge.

Technical difficulty: Moderate, on a wide fire road.

Scenery: Fabulous views of Pyriform and Junction Mountains to the west and Mount Ware to the north.

Special comments: Don't forget to pack an extra water bottle for this sharp climb.

This intermediate-level trail climbs 670 m (2,200 ft.) to a lonely fire lookout atop an outlier of Junction Mountain. The trail is 14.15 km (8.8 mi.) one-way, making for a total distance of 24.3 km (17.6 mi.) out-and-back.

The trail parallels the Sheep River for a short distance before fording Dyson Creek. Just below the ford, a pleasant falls represents one of the first refrigerators in the mountains. Back in the 1940s the foreman of one of the logging camps along Dyson Creek used a small cave underneath and behind the falls to store game meat. The cave's moist, cool environs kept the meat fresh while keeping it safe from scavengers.

Just above the crossing, a lonely chair sits on a long pole. This is used by biologists studying Columbian ground squirrels. By sitting in these chairs, they get a panoramic view of the colony and can collect more accurate data.

From the river, the trail makes one additional right-hand turn and then begins climbing in earnest. The climb is steady and unrelenting. As you pass the 8.8-km

(5.5-mi.) point, the views finally open up, and the sights to the west are pristine. The steep faces of Pyriform and Junction mountains dominate the western horizon, while Missinglink Mountain and Mount Ware hold the northern skyline. Mount Ware was named in honour of Alberta's most famous black cowboy, John Ware. Born into slavery, he eventually made his way to Canada in 1882 and quickly began working for the large Quorn Ranch to the south of this mountain. In 1885 he filed his own homestead, and his "9999" brand became famous in this area. He died in 1905 — the same year that Alberta became a province.

As the trail climbs past the first viewpoint, the slope is covered with hedysarum, locoweed, buttercups, and chickweed. The pleasant nature of this meadow distracts you from the steep climbing ahead. As the trail finally crests the summit, and the fire lookout is reached, it's tempting to announce your presence and visit the lookout. However, this is not a public building, and the Alberta Forest Service asks that riders not approach the building. Drink in the views and prepare for a rock-and-roll screamer of a downhill back to the trailhead.

General location: The trail lies south of the Sheep Trail and west of Turner Valley, Alberta.

Elevation change: The trail begins at 1,560 m (5,120 ft.) and climbs to the fire lookout at 2,230 m (7,316 ft.).

Season: This trail is at its best between mid-June and mid-September.

Services: All services are available in Turner Valley, 30 minutes to the east of the trailhead.

Hazards: This trail follows a good grade for most of its length. When crossing Dyson Creek, be cautious. The stream is not deep, but the current is strong.

As you drop back down from the lookout, there are many areas where the old roadbed has been eroded by heavy spring runoff. If you pick up speed on the way down, you'll need to watch for these sudden washouts.

Rescue index: This trail takes you to a lonely lookout atop Junction Mountain. Along the way, I didn't meet any other riders, so you can't assume you'll find assistance. The trailhead is along a moderately busy highway, making it possible to flag down help on the road. Also, the lookout at the end of the trail has a two-way radio, affording help in an emergency.

Land status: This trail is operated as part of Kananaskis Country.

Maps: The 1:50,000 scale topographic map for this trail is 82 J/10 Mount Rae.

Finding the trail: From Turner Valley, follow the signs to Kananaskis Country. As you enter the Sheep River Valley, you will pass the Information Centre. Continue west for 16.9 km (10.5 mi.) to the Indian Oils trailhead. Park there and drop down to a bridge over the Sheep River.

Sources of additional information: Information for contacting Kananaskis Country is listed in the introduction to this section.

Notes on the trail: Dropping down from the trailhead, the trail crosses the Sheep River over a high-quality bridge at km 0.3 (mi. 0.19). As you cross the bridge,

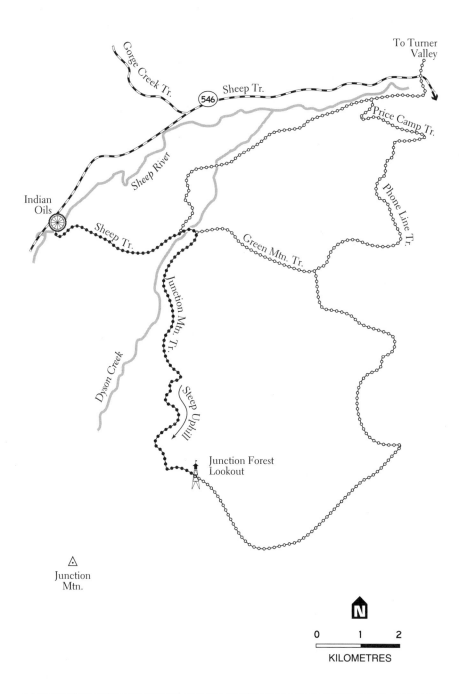

To Turner
Valley

Gorge Creek Tr.

546

Sheep Tr.

Price Camp Tr.

Sheep River

Phone Line Tr.

Indian
Oils

Sheep Tr.

Green Mtn. Tr.

Junction Mtn. Tr.

Dyson Creek

Steep Uphill

Junction Forest
Lookout

Junction
Mtn.

N

0   1   2

KILOMETRES

follow the road up to the left. It climbs briefly to rise above the river valley and levels off at km 1.0 (mi. 0.6), where it begins to follow the river downstream.

The trail becomes a wide single-track at km 2.0 (mi. 1.2). It passes some badly cattle-chewed areas for the next several kilometres and proceeds through some fields that are alive with Columbian ground squirrels. Parts of this stretch tend to get very sloppy in wet weather. At km 3.44 (mi. 2.13) a trail forks to the left; stay on the fire road. At a muddy junction at km 4.06 (mi. 2.5), stay right on the Green Mountain Trail. The trail fords Dyson Creek at km 4.3 (mi. 2.7). The ford is 10 m (30 ft.) wide and knee deep.

Across the stream, the trail climbs slightly to 4.67 km (2.9 mi.), where the Junction Mountain Fire Lookout Trail takes off to the right. Follow this trail through some cattle slop until it climbs slightly out of the valley and dries out at km 5.11 (mi. 3.2). The climbing is steady from this point. It passes a small, marshy pool and starts climbing more steeply. As it climbs, it improves in quality to become a good fire road.

At km 8.8 (mi. 5.5), views begin to open up to the west as the trail slowly climbs out of the trees. At km 9.2 (mi. 5.7), the trail pulls out onto an exposed meadow with excellent views to the west. You also get your first views of the lookout in the distance.

As the trail climbs, it winds to the left of a small knoll before making a hard right to approach the lookout from the west side at km 9.92 (mi. 6.15). At km 10.06 (mi. 6.24), a very steep climb begins and continues until km 10.25 (mi. 6.35). The trail then traverses a ridge, with a valley down to the left. After a short distance, the climbing resumes. At km 10.6 (mi. 6.6), a small stream crosses the trail and tumbles down the ridge. At km 11.32 (mi. 7.02), the trail makes a sharp right and climbs moderately. At km 11.85 (mi. 7.35), it passes an old rock cairn. The steep climbing (some will likely require pushing) continues to the lookout at km 14.15 (mi. 8.8) and an elevation of 2,230 m (7,316 ft.).

BANFF NATIONAL PARK
AND AREA

As Canada's oldest national park, Banff is known as a place of splendid scenery and endless opportunities for outdoor recreation. At 6,641 square kilometres (2,564 square miles), this park covers a vast area. Long before Canadian Pacific Railway (CPR) surveyors arrived, the area around Banff had been visited by local natives, missionaries, and fur traders.

The Stoney Indians were very familiar with this area. They had traveled its valleys for generations before George Simpson made his way here. Simpson, known as the "Little Emperor," was in charge of the Hudson Bay Company and was also one of Canada's greatest travelers. He passed through this area during a trip around the world and covered countless miles of Canada's wilderness during his career.

Missionary Robert T. Rundle arrived on the scene in 1847. This Methodist minister, after whom Mount Rundle is named, did extensive work with the local Indians and may have traveled as far as present-day Lake Louise. Ironically, neither Simpson nor Rundle made any mention of hot springs in the area, yet it would be these warm waters that would eventually spawn development here.

It wasn't until the railway chugged its way west that development of the springs became inevitable. With this development came more and more people. On a cold morning in November 1883, three workers, Frank McCabe and William and Thomas McCardell, noticed steam rising from the side of Terrace (now Sulphur) Mountain. As they checked out the source of the steam, they became the modern discoverers of the Cave and Basin hot springs.

Being good capitalists, they quickly built a small bathhouse and filed a homestead claim. Unfortunately for them, homesteads weren't recognized in the Rockies. They then tried a mineral rights claim. Unfortunately again, mineral springs were not considered a mineral resource. All of this brought the area to the attention of William Pearce, the mine superintendent in Calgary. Upon investigation, he was so impressed that he, along with William Van Horne, general manager of the CPR, began to agitate for the creation of a park.

Finally, on November 2, 1885, the Banff Hot Springs Preserve was set aside. It was only 26 square kilometres (10 square miles), but two years later it was enlarged to include Lake Louise and renamed Rocky Mountains Park — Canada's first national park. It was the third such park in the world, behind only Yellowstone in the United States and Royal National Park in Australia.

For more than a hundred years the hot springs in Banff have attracted untold numbers of visitors to their healing waters. There's something soothing about soaking in a pool of water heated by the earth's primordial heat. Today, Banff looks very different than it did a hundred years ago. With several million visitors a year making their way through the gates, the connection that these pools provide to the early days becomes more and more vital. We need to ensure that these landmarks continue to soothe the aches and pains of travelers for many years to come.

For the mountain biker, Banff, like parks elsewhere, has seen backcountry cycling as a threat and has closed many of its most attractive trails to cyclists. Some enjoyable rides remain within the park, but most are either fire roads or areas used extensively by the four-legged nemesis of mountain bikes—horses. Mountain bikes are even banned from some areas in which horses are allowed—despite the fact that horses produce measurably more impact, introduce non-native species through their droppings, and remove local flora through their constant feeding. With this adversarial atmosphere in our national parks, it becomes crucial that cyclists stay away from closed trails, respect other users on the trail systems, and follow safe and ethical riding practices.

All services are available in the town of Banff. Most of the cycle shops provide maps and local guidebooks as well as advice on some trails to get you started. In the case of emergencies, call (403) 762-2000 for an ambulance or (403) 762-4506 for the Banff National Park Warden's Office.

For further information, contact:

Banff National Park
Box 900
Banff, Alberta
T0L-0C0
(403) 762-1550

Map Town Publishing
(403) 266-2356

Banff/Lake Louise Tourism Bureau
Box 1298
Banff, Alberta
T0L-0C0
(403) 762-0270

Gem Trek Publishing
640 6 Avenue, SW
Calgary, Alberta
T2P-0S4
(403) 266-2523

Mountain Magic Equipment
Box 1901
Banff, Alberta
T0L-0C0
(403) 762-2591

Altitude Sports
Canmore, Alberta
T0L-0M0
(403) 678-6272

RIDE 38 · Spray Loop

AT A GLANCE

Length/configuration: 12-km (7.2-mi.) loop.

Aerobic difficulty: While it is a rolling trail, it is generally easy.

Technical difficulty: Few serious challenges make this a ride for all abilities.

Scenery: The trail is largely in the trees, but views abound. The towering slopes of Mount Rundle rise to the northeast, and Sulphur Mountain stands to the southwest.

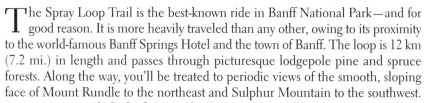

AB

Special comments: This is often one of the first rides for visitors to Banff. It is a classic because of its rolling character and its proximity to the town.

The Spray Loop Trail is the best-known ride in Banff National Park—and for good reason. It is more heavily traveled than any other, owing to its proximity to the world-famous Banff Springs Hotel and the town of Banff. The loop is 12 km (7.2 mi.) in length and passes through picturesque lodgepole pine and spruce forests. Along the way, you'll be treated to periodic views of the smooth, sloping face of Mount Rundle to the northeast and Sulphur Mountain to the southwest.

As you approach the bridge over the Spray River, you'll notice an old outhouse on the edge of a forest clearing. This lonely shack is all that remains of the Spray River Hostel, which for many years was the town of Banff's only hostel. When Banff completed its present hotel, this rustic cabin became unneeded. It was demolished, and all evidence of the structure was removed. While the hostel is long gone, the valley remains a critical corridor for wildlife moving between the Bow and Spray Valleys.

General location: Adjacent to the town of Banff.

Elevation change: The trail, which has little net change in elevation, is rolling and has no significant climbs.

Season: This trail opens in mid-June and is rideable until early October.

Services: All services are provided in the town of Banff.

Hazards: Most of this ride is very smooth and clean. Its second half, once you cross the bridge over the Spray River, is rougher. There are a few runoff channels and sections with loose rocks.

Rescue index: With civilization at either end of the trail, it's usually easy to obtain emergency services. In addition, the many people on this trail provide added security.

Land status: Banff National Park.

Maps: The 1:50,000 scale topographic map for this trail is 82 O/4 Banff. Gem Trek has produced the best map for this trail, called "Banff Up-Close." It can be ordered from the source listed in this section's introduction.

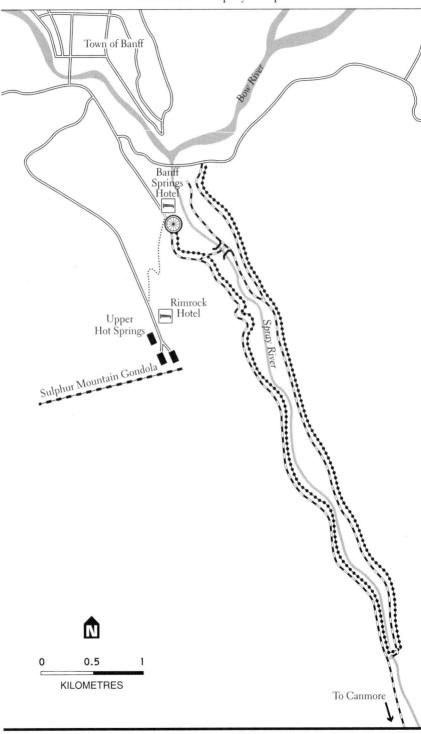

Town of Banff

Bow River

Banff
Springs
Hotel

Rimrock
Hotel

Upper
Hot Springs

Spray River

Sulphur Mountain Gondola

N

| 0 | 0.5 | 1 |

KILOMETRES

To Canmore

Susan Cameron
on the Spray Loop,
one of Banff's most
popular rides.

Finding the trail: In the town of Banff, follow Banff Avenue toward the Parks Administration Building. As you cross the bridge over the Bow River, turn left. Stay left as Spray Avenue brings you to the Banff Springs Hotel. When you arrive at the hotel, drive past the traffic circle, heading under the hotel arch farthest to the right. Beyond this point, pass the parkade on your right. Beyond this building, a road branches off to the right and connects with the trailhead parking lot. Park here.

Sources of additional information: Information for contacting Banff National Park is listed in the introduction to this section.

Notes on the trail: From the Banff Springs Hotel, follow the Spray Loop Trail as it radiates from the day-use parking lot. This wide fire road has little worth mentioning until you roll your way to the 6-km (3.6-mi.) point. Keep your eye open for this junction, as the trail continues an additional 12 km (7.2 mi.) toward the Goat Creek Trailhead, should you miss this important junction.

Cross the bridge over the Spray River and roll your way back toward the Banff Springs Golf Course. Just after passing below the base of an avalanche slope on your right, you meet SPR-06 Mount Rundle Campground at km 6.5 (mi. 3.9). After a short uphill at km 7.1 (mi. 4.26), you'll come upon a short gravel wash where a runoff channel brings rocks across the trail. It is easily rideable, though.

Beyond the campground the trend continues uphill as the river drops well below the trail and the sound of water becomes fainter. Stay to the right as a narrow trail forks to the left at km 10.3 (mi. 6.2), then continue on to meet the Banff Springs Golf Course at km 11.5 (mi. 6.9). Roll your way toward the golf links road (watching for flying objects), and follow this road to the left over the Bow River Bridge. To return to the parking lot, turn left after the bridge and wind your way along the pavement as the road climbs back toward the trailhead. Meet your car at approximately 12 km (7.2 mi.).

RIDE 39 · Goat Creek Trail

AT A GLANCE

Length/configuration: 19.8-km (12.3-mi.) point-to-point.

Aerobic difficulty: Easy, with a net elevation loss of 292 m (958 ft.).

Technical difficulty: The trail follows the wide path of a former fire road.

Scenery: Periodic views toward the long range of Mount Rundle.

Special comments: This trail is one of the most popular rides in the Rockies.

One of the most well-traveled trails in the Banff-Canmore area, this point-to-point is 19.8 km (12.3 mi.) long and is a quick downhill ride to Banff along the back of Mount Rundle. It varies between wide single-track and deluxe fire road riding. Riders of all abilities will enjoy this trail; it provides a pleasant introduction for novices, while giving expert riders some exhilarating options for a quick downhill ride. Preferably, have a vehicle drop you off at the trailhead; otherwise, you'll need to climb a steep, dusty, 7.7-km (4.8-mi.) gravel road rising 366 m (1,200 ft.) to access the trailhead.

Beginning on the Spray Lakes Road, high above the community of Canmore, the ride is almost entirely downhill, dropping from an elevation of 1,675 m (5,495 ft.) to Banff, at an elevation of 1,384 m (4,538 ft.). It's possible to make a loop with the Banff Trail and return to Canmore.

The scenery is pleasant, although not spectacular, along this ride. Paralleling the length of Mount Rundle, you are treated to numerous views of its steeply bedded slopes. This mountain, one of the most photographed in the Rockies, is a classic example of a Front Range peak. Although more of a range than a single peak, Mount Rundle exhibits rock layers thrust up at steep angles. It gains its name from one of the first white men to set foot in this area way back in 1847, the Rev. Robert T. Rundle, a Methodist missionary who worked extensively with the local Stoney Indians. On numerous occasions, the trail crosses well-bridged stream crossings as it follows Goat Creek and later the Spray River. Thus, the sound of rushing water is a common and pleasant feature of this ride.

RIDE 39 · Goat Creek Trail

BANFF
NATIONAL PARK

Banff Springs
Hotel

Bow River

Mount
Rundle
9673

Canmore

Chinaman
Peak
8790

To
Calgary

SUNDANCE RANGE

Sp 15

Sp 33

KANANASKIS
COUNTRY

Smith-Dorrien/Spray Trail

N

0 2 4
KILOMETRES

General location: The trail joins the towns of Canmore and Banff, Alberta, by following the back side of Mount Rundle.

Elevation change: If you decide to begin riding in the town of Canmore, the trail begins at 1,309 m (4,297 ft.). As you climb up the Spray Lakes hill, you reach the trailhead at 1,675 m (5,495 ft.). From here, it is almost all downhill to Banff at 1,383 m (4,538 ft.).

Season: This trail opens in mid-June and is rideable until early October.

Services: All services are provided in the towns of Canmore and Banff.

Hazards: Parts of this trail are single-track with some loose rock. Also, some of the stream crossings are at the bottom of long downhill gradients. Don't go so fast that you can't make a quick turn for a bridge at the bottom of a long hill.

This trail is popular with hikers, particularly as you approach Banff. Since it ends at the Banff Springs Hotel, you can bet that people will be walking the trail. It is also very popular with cyclists, so be watchful. Occasionally, you'll see horses.

In spring, certain stretches of the trail can exhibit washouts or ice flows. Always watch for rapid deterioration of the trail.

Rescue index: With civilization at either end of the trail, it generally isn't difficult to contact emergency services. In addition, the many people on this trail provide added security.

Land status: The Goat Creek Trailhead is within Kananaskis Country Provincial Recreation Area, but the trail quickly enters Banff National Park.

Maps: The 1:50,000 scale topographic maps for this trail are 82 O/3 Canmore and 82 O/4 Banff. Map Town produces a trail map entitled "Banff-Canmore." Finally, Parks Canada produces a large-scale trail map called "Banff/Yoho/Kootenay."

Finding the trail: From Canmore, follow the signs to the Canmore Nordic Centre. Pass this former Olympic site and climb all the way up Spray Lakes Hill toward its gap at Whiteman Pass. From the summit, continue another 1.6 km (1 mi.) to the trailhead. The trail is clearly signed.

Sources of additional information: Information for Banff National Park is listed in the introduction to this section.

Notes on the trail: The trail begins with wide single-track and quickly begins its descent. The first crossing is km 5.9 (mi. 3.7) from the trailhead. Crossings also occur at km 6.8 (4.2 mi.), km 7.4 (4.6 mi.), and km 9.4 (5.8 mi.). All crossings are well bridged.

As you travel along the trail, you'll drop down a steep, loose rock hill just before the third bridge. Be cautious, since a sudden turn is required to safely negotiate the bridge. Beyond the final crossing, a short, steep hill brings you to the junction with Spray River Fire Road at km 9.75 (mi. 6.1).

After turning right onto Spray River Fire Road, the trail becomes smooth double-track for the remainder of its run into Banff. At km 13.8 (mi. 8.6), a bridge to the right of the trail provides a single-track optional trail that takes you to the Banff Springs Golf Course. Staying on the fire road will bring you to the Banff Springs Hotel at km 19.8 (mi. 12.3).

RIDE 40 · Spray Fire Road

AT A GLANCE

Length/configuration: 51.5-km (32.0-mi.) point-to-point.

Aerobic difficulty: While the trail is wide, the length of this ride adds to the challenge, making for a moderate rating.

Technical difficulty: The trail is wide and smooth.

Scenery: Periodic views of the Goat Range to the east and the Sundance Range to the west.

Special comments: This trail is presently closed to mountain bikes, but it may reopen at some future time.

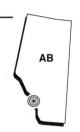

If you enjoy riding fire roads, don't miss this one. Traveling the Goat Creek Trail gives you a taste of the smooth grade of this former fire access route. Most fire roads in the Rockies have become unneeded since the advent of the helicopter, which has relegated them to nonmotorized traffic only. This wide, gravel road provides you with 51.5 km (32.0 mi.) of excellent point-to-point or out-and-back riding. Before you decide to ride this trail, keep in mind that it may be closed to riding by the time you arrive in the area. It has been closed since 1994 as part of an extensive ecosystem study and may or may not be reopened.

The trail begins at the Banff Springs Hotel, and the first 10.1 km (6.3 mi.) follow the Goat Creek Trail. Beyond this point, the quality is maintained for the trail's entire length as it climbs approximately 380 m (1,250 ft.) along its route.

Leaving the Goat Creek Trail, you follow the Spray River as it cuts across the formerly continuous Goat Range. This notch now separates Sulphur Mountain from its parent range. Sulphur Mountain is named for seven sulphur hot springs along its slopes. These springs led to Banff National Park being set aside in 1885 as the first national park in Canada. Unfortunately, the Spray River is anything but a hot spring. Its frigid waters flow to their junction with the Bow River just beyond this trail's origin at the Banff Springs Hotel.

Once through this pass, the trail turns south again to stay with the Spray River. To your left is the now familiar Goat Range, and to your right stands the Sundance Range. Indian sun dances were an important part of native culture prior to the arrival of the white man and the subsequent outlawing of this tradition.

Heading south, you view Turbulent Mountain, named after a destroyer engaged in the Battle of Jutland during World War I. This battle, which took place off the coast of Jutland, Denmark, on May 31 and June 1, 1916, ended as a draw, but it was recognized as a turning point in the war. To commemorate it, a seemingly endless number of peaks in this area have been named for the various ships and commanders that took part.

General location: This trail travels from the town of Banff and follows the Spray River to its source in the Spray Lakes. It finishes at the Mount Shark Trailhead in Kananaskis Country Provincial Recreation Area.

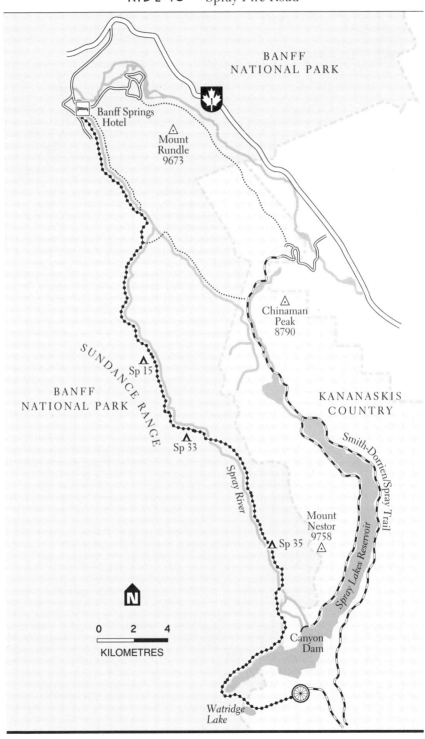

BANFF
NATIONAL PARK

Banff Springs
Hotel

Mount
Rundle
9673

Chinaman
Peak
8790

SUNDANCE RANGE

Sp 15

BANFF
NATIONAL PARK

Sp 33

KANANASKIS
COUNTRY

Smith-Dorrien/Spray Trail

Spray River

Mount
Nestor
9758

Sp 35

Spray Lakes Reservoir

N

0   2   4
KILOMETRES

Canyon
Dam

Watridge
Lake

Elevation change: The north end of the trail begins at 1,383 m (4,538 ft.) and climbs to 1,763 m (5,785 ft.) at the south trailhead, Mount Shark Trailhead.

Season: The trail is rideable from mid-June to early October.

Services: All services are available in the communities of Banff or Canmore, Alberta.

Hazards: This trail has few physical hazards. It does, however, travel through very remote country and, as such, must be respected. All the sun dances in the world won't keep you dry if a sudden storm blows in as you travel beneath the Sundance Range, so be prepared for changeable weather.

Since this route is shared by horses and some intrepid backpackers, be watchful and courteous. Within Banff National Park, more and more trails are being closed to mountain bikes, so we can use all the goodwill we can get.

Rescue index: This trail is remote. You'll encounter few people along the way, but you will pass several campgrounds. Some vistors may be using these sites as you pass them. In Banff, full paramedic response service is available by dialing 762-2000. Remember, 911 does not apply here. From the south trailhead, the nearest emergency assistance is at the Mount Engadine Lodge near the junction of the Smith-Dorrien/Spray Trail. The lodge has a radio telephone, and someone can call for help if needed.

Land status: This trail traverses portions of Banff National Park and Kananaskis Country Provincial Recreation Area.

Maps: The 1:50,000 scale topographic maps for this trail are 82 O/4 Banff, 82 J/14 Spray Lakes Reservoir, and 82 O/3 Canmore. Another trail map is Parks Canada's "Banff/Yoho/Kootenay Map."

Finding the trail: Within Banff, drive to the Banff Springs Hotel. Just beyond this historic structure is a backcountry parking lot.

Sources of additional information: The information for Banff National Park is listed in the introduction to this section.

Notes on the trail: From the trailhead, follow the wide, gravel road for 10.1 km (6.3 mi.) until it passes the junction with Goat Creek Trail. Stay to the right on the gravel road. The next junction is the intersection of Spray Valley and Sundance Creek. Follow the road to the left and remain true to it until it meets the headwaters of the Spray River at Spray Lakes at km 39.1 (mi. 24.3).

At this point, avoid the temptation to follow the Spray Lakes West Road and turn right. Instead, you should head toward the south end of Spray Lakes, where you'll pass two junctions. Turn left at each. Less than a kilometre (0.6 mi.) beyond this last junction, you'll come to a bridge over the Spray River. Turning left and crossing the bridge will take you up a steep hill and onto the Watridge Lake Trail. The ride finishes at the Mount Shark Trailhead at km 51.5 (mi. 32).

RIDE 41 · Rundle Riverside Trail

AT A GLANCE

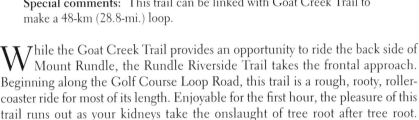

Length/configuration: 14.1-km (8.75-mi.) point-to-point.

Aerobic difficulty: The trail has little change in elevation, making for a rating of easy.

Technical difficulty: The trail bounces over an endless number of roots and rocks. The challenge is moderate.

Scenery: Some pleasant views along the Bow River look toward the Fairholme Range to the north.

Special comments: This trail can be linked with Goat Creek Trail to make a 48-km (28.8-mi.) loop.

While the Goat Creek Trail provides an opportunity to ride the back side of Mount Rundle, the Rundle Riverside Trail takes the frontal approach. Beginning along the Golf Course Loop Road, this trail is a rough, rooty, roller-coaster ride for most of its length. Enjoyable for the first hour, the pleasure of this trail runs out as your kidneys take the onslaught of tree root after tree root. Despite its roughness, however, it does provide a highway-free loop option to the Goat Creek.

Scenically, the trail follows the Bow River along the front side of Mount Rundle toward Canmore. The slopes of Rundle on this side are steep and sharp, quite a contrast to the smooth, angled slopes along its Goat Creek side. Across the valley, the Fairholme Range juts 2,995 m (9,826 ft.) above sea level. This range was named for Grace Fairholme by her brother, John Palliser, who did some of the first surveys of this area in 1858.

As you pass km 8.6 (mi. 5.3), the trail becomes smoother as it joins the Canmore Nordic Centre and becomes a gravel access road. From the Nordic Centre's day lodge, at km 14.1 (mi. 8.75), it is a quick, downhill 4 km (2.5 mi.) to the town site. The Canmore Nordic Centre was the site of all cross-country and biathlon events during the 1988 Winter Olympics. Riding through this area, you will see numerous junctions for the well-developed system of trails used by skiers in the winter and mountain bikers in the summer. The Nordic Centre has hosted a large number of mountain bike races, including the western Canada championships.

General location: This trail begins in Banff National Park, along the Banff Springs Golf Course and finishes at the Canmore Nordic Centre in the town of Canmore, Alberta.

Elevation change: The trail exhibits little change in elevation as it hugs the valley bottom. It does require a short climb to access the Canmore Nordic Centre at the eastern end of the trail.

Season: This trail is rideable from early June to mid-October.

Services: All services are available in the communities of Canmore and Banff.

RIDE 41 · Rundle Riverside Trail

Hazards: This trail is extremely rough and rooty, so caution is advised. A helmet is absolutely essential. Watch for loose rocks as you cross several rocky washouts.

Rescue index: Rescue services are available at either end of the trail. Since the trail has a sheer mountain face to one side and a major river to the other, you'll need to complete one direction to get help. It is not a heavily traveled route because of its rugged character.

Land status: The trail begins within Banff National Park, travels briefly within Kananaskis Country Provincial Recreation Area, ending in the town of Canmore.

Maps: The 1:50,000 scale topographic map for this trail is 82 O/3 Canmore; however, Map Town produces "Banff-Canmore Recreational Map," which is more up to date. You may also use Parks Canada's "Banff/Yoho/Kootenay Trail Map."

Finding the trail: In Banff, follow the signs to the Banff Springs Golf Course. From the bridge that crosses the Bow River, follow the paved loop road for 3.0 km (1.9 mi.) until it branches. From here, take the right fork for an additional 1.4 km (0.9 mi.) to the Rundle Riverside Trailhead.

Sources of additional information: The information for Banff National Park is listed in the introduction to this section.

Notes on the trail: The trail follows the lower slopes of Mount Rundle over numerous washouts and through a roller coaster of tree roots and rolling terrain for 8.6 km (5.3 mi.) to its boundary with the Canmore Nordic Centre. After a short uphill, the trail becomes a smooth access road, and in 5.5 km (3.4 mi.) you arrive at the Main Lodge of the Canmore Nordic Centre.

RIDE 42 · Banff Springs to Gondola Trail

AT A GLANCE

Length/configuration: 1.4-km (0.84-mi.) point-to-point.

Aerobic difficulty: From the Banff Springs Hotel, the trail steadily climbs 155 m (508 ft.).

Technical difficulty: The trail is a winding single-track, with a few loose sections and tight turns.

Scenery: This wooded trail has few open panoramas.

Special comments: The trail is generally used as an access between the Banff Springs Hotel and the Upper Hot Springs or Sulphur Mountain Gondola.

While this 1.4-km (0.84-mi.) point-to-point is rarely a destination in itself, it forms an important link between the Banff Springs Hotel and two of the main sightseeing destinations in the Banff town site area—the Upper Hot Springs Pool and the Sulphur Mountain Gondola. Rare is the ride with a naturally heated hot spring at its terminus. After riding the Spray Loop or the Goat Creek Trail, riders may wish to finish with a relaxing soak. After taking in the pool, it's a quick downhill roll back to the Banff Springs Hotel.

General location: Within the town of Banff.

Elevation change: From the Banff Springs Hotel trailhead at 1,400 m (4,592 ft.), the trail climbs 155 m (508 ft.) to its junction with Sulphur Mountain Road.

Season: Mid-May to mid-October.

Services: All services are available in the town of Banff.

Hazards: A rutted section along with some sharp corners will be encountered

RIDE 42 · Banff Springs to Gondola Trail

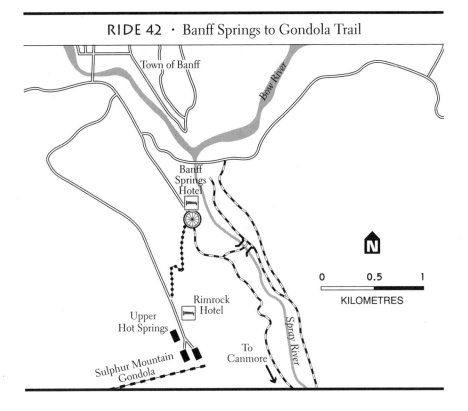

along this trail. This is also a popular walking and horseback trail, so be cautious of other users.

Rescue index: This is a very popular access trail, which begins and ends at urban areas. You are rarely far from civilization.

Land status: Banff National Park.

Maps: The 1:50,000 scale topographic map for this trail is 82 O/4 Banff. Gem Trek has produced the best map for this trail, called "Banff Up-Close." It can be ordered from the source listed in this section's introduction.

Finding the trail: In the town of Banff, follow Banff Avenue toward the Parks Administration Building. As you cross the bridge over the Bow River, turn left. Stay left as Spray Avenue brings you to the Banff Springs Hotel. When you arrive at the hotel, drive past the traffic circle, heading under the right-most hotel arch. Beyond this point, pass the parkade on your right. Beyond this building, a road branches off to the right to access the trailhead parking lot. Park here.

Sources of additional information: Information for contacting Banff National Park is listed in the introduction to this section.

Notes on the trail: From the trailhead at the Spray Loop Trailhead, the trail begins climbing gradually as it makes its way toward the Upper Hot Springs and the Sulphur Mountain Gondola. Cross over a small corduroy bridge at km 0.2 (0.12 mi.), then make a hard switchback to the right. A left switchback counters at km 0.35 (0.21 mi.). Avoid the temptation to take shortcuts en route, as these spur channels are doing increasing damage the trail. Stay to the right as a horse trail forks to the left at km 0.8 (0.48 mi.), and be cautious of some rutting through the next section. An access road joins in at km 0.9 (0.54 mi.) as you pass under the power lines. You'll find a jumble of junctions at this point. As the wide cut-line trail rolls to the left, the first single-track to the right is the correct trail. This road will wind toward Sulphur Mountain Road at km 1.4 (0.84 mi.).

RIDE 43 · Stoney Squaw

AT A GLANCE

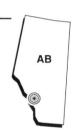

Length/configuration: 3.6-km (2.16-mi.) out-and-back.

Aerobic difficulty: The climb is steady and steep, rising 184 m (604 ft.) over 1.8 km (1.08 mi.).

Technical difficulty: The climb is steep and narrow and the descent very challenging. For expert riders only.

Scenery: The views from the summit stretch from the Fairholme Range in the east to the Vermillion Lakes to the southwest.

Special comments: This trail is best left to expert riders.

Stoney Squaw is a locally well-known trail. In a park where most of the single-track has long since been closed, it stands alone as a great technical route. Total distance for this out-and-back is 3.6 km (2.16 mi.), and it is basically uphill to 1.8 km (1.08 mi.), followed by a descent over the same route. The first views focus to the southwest toward the sparkling waters of the Vermillion Lakes. Some of the most famous photographs of Banff have been taken on the shores of these lakes, with the towering face of Mount Rundle (the major peak to the southeast) reflected in their waters. As you reach the high point on the trail, the views roll toward the Cascade Valley and Cascade Mountain to the north and the Fairholme Range in the east.

The name "Stoney Squaw" came from a native legend about a Stoney Indian couple who lived at the base of the mountain. When her husband became ill, the squaw took care of him by hunting along the slopes of this mountain.

General location: Above the town of Banff, Alberta.

Elevation change: From the trailhead at 1,700 m (5,576 ft.), it is a steady climb to the summit at 1,884 m (6,180 ft.).

Season: Late May to late September.

Services: All services are available in the town of Banff.

RIDE 43 · Stoney Squaw

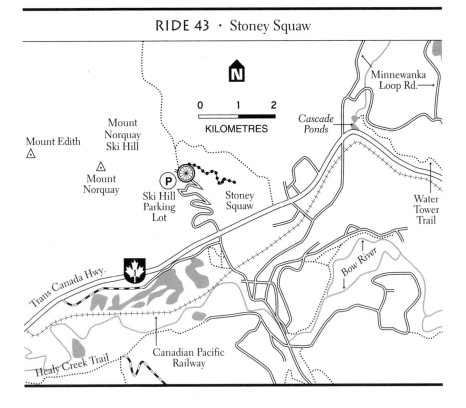

Hazards: Since this trail drops through a single-track lodgepole pine slalom, the potential exists for you to smack into an immovable object—be careful. Some of the openings between the trees are extremely narrow, and the gradient at times is quite steep.

Rescue index: While this trail is popular, you may not encounter other riders while you're out. A good cellular signal is available, so don't leave your phone in the car.

Land status: Banff National Park.

Maps: The 1:50,000 scale topographic map for this trail is 82 O/4 Banff. Gem Trek has produced the best map for this trail, called "Banff Up-Close." It can be ordered from the source listed in this section's introduction.

Finding the trail: From the west exit to the town of Banff, the Mount Norquay Road climbs 5.5 km (3.3 mi.) along a switchbacking road. Follow this pavement until you reach the main ski hill parking lot. Immediately as you enter the parking lot, the Stoney Squaw Trail is to your right.

Sources of additional information: Information for contacting Banff National Park is listed in the introduction to this section.

Notes on the trail: This winding single-track begins climbing immediately through a dense lodgepole pine forest. Grind your way up the steep single-track, taking a rest on a small false summit at km 0.6 (mi. 0.36). Beyond this point, the trail drops down a narrow trail and over many exposed roots. By km 0.8 (0.48 mi.) the trend has returned to the uphill direction. Take a break on a sunny outcrop at km 1.2 (mi. 0.72) before starting the final climb. The first real views are at km 1.5 (mi. 0.90) as you come out on a small cliff band. The main trail ends at km 1.8 (mi. 1.08) as the views open up to the east. Turn around and enjoy the downhill slalom back to your car at km 3.6 (mi. 2.16).

RIDE 44 · Fenland Trail

AT A GLANCE

Length/configuration: 1.9-km (1.14-mi.) loop.

Aerobic difficulty: Very easy.

Technical difficulty: The trail is flat and wide—great for all levels.

Scenery: Some nice views are available along the shoreline of Echo Creek, as are brief views of Mount Norquay and the Vermillion Lakes.

Special comments: This is a marsh; if you plan on relaxing on the many benches en route, don't forget your insect repellent.

The Fenland Trail is short but sweet. Along its 1.9-km (1.14-mi.) length, the trail winds through some pleasant wetlands as it follows the winding course of Echo Creek. As you roll your way through the old-growth forest, keep your eyes open for wildlife. It's common to spot elk and deer along the trail, as well as waterfowl, belted kingfishers, and even an occasional eagle.

To really appreciate this trail, stop at the Park Information Centre and pick up a self-guiding trail brochure. While you'll find a dispenser at the trailhead, it rarely contains brochures. Keep in mind that this route traverses a favourite calving area for the local elk population, and since people regularly get injured during the spring, the most sensitive time, the wardens close the trail for several weeks. Check with the information centre to make sure the trail is open.

General location: Within the town of Banff, Alberta.

Elevation change: Virtually nil.

Season: Mid-June to mid-October. It is closed every spring during the elk calving season.

Services: All services are available within the town of Banff.

Hazards: The trail is wide and smooth with few challenges.

RIDE 44 · Fenland Trail

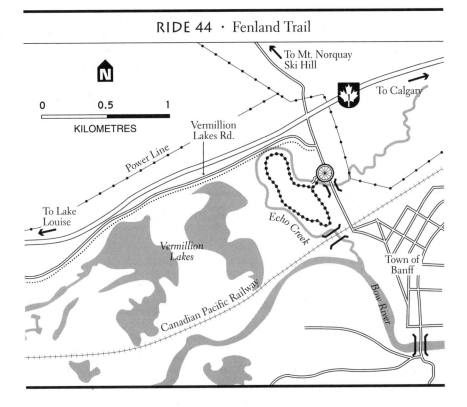

Rescue index: Simply return to the trailhead, where you can flag down a vehicle. A great cellular signal is available, so bring along your phone.

Land status: Banff National Park.

Maps: The 1:50,000 scale topographic map for this trail is 82 O/4 Banff. Gem Trek has produced the best map for this trail, called "Banff Up-Close." It can be ordered from the source listed in this section's introduction.

Finding the trail: In the town of Banff, follow Lynx Street as it winds left to become Gopher Street and then Mount Norquay Road. Just before reaching the Trans Canada Highway (Highway 1), a signed parking lot is on the left. This is the trailhead for Fenland Trail.

Sources of additional information: Information for contacting Banff National Park is listed in the introduction to this section.

Notes on the trail: From the trailhead, follow the wide single-track to cross a bridge almost immediately. On the opposite side of the bridge, stay straight at the three-way junction. You will later return on the trail to your left. The trail is well marked, making it difficult to lose your way. At another trail junction at km 0.4 (mi. 0.24.), stay to the right. The left fork takes you out to the road. Cross over two small bridges in succession at km 0.65 (mi. 0.39) and follow the trail as it winds to the right. The trail follows the winding course of Echo Creek, and beyond the creek the first views of the Vermillion Lakes open up at km 0.89 (mi. 0.53). Another trail junction comes at km 1.33 (mi. 0.8). At this point, a bridge crosses Echo Creek on your left. While the main trail continues straight, this bridge provides convenient access to the Vermillion Lakes Road for riders wishing to extend their excursion. To remain on the Fenland Trail, stay straight at this junction, which will quickly bring you back to your first junction at km 1.81 (mi. 1.09). Turn left over the bridge and return to the parking lot at km 1.9 (mi. 1.14).

RIDE 45 · Vermillion Lakes Road

AT A GLANCE

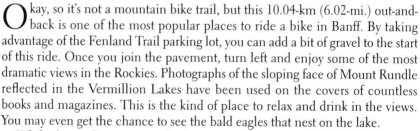

Length/configuration: 10.04-km (6.02-mi.) out-and-back.

Aerobic difficulty: Flat and easy.

Technical difficulty: Perfect for riders of all levels.

Scenery: This ride takes you past one of the most famous views in the Canadian Rockies—Mount Rundle reflected in the waters of Vermillion Lakes.

Special comments: While not a trail, this ride is one of the most popular places that cyclists travel in Banff National Park.

Okay, so it's not a mountain bike trail, but this 10.04-km (6.02-mi.) out-and-back is one of the most popular places to ride a bike in Banff. By taking advantage of the Fenland Trail parking lot, you can add a bit of gravel to the start of this ride. Once you join the pavement, turn left and enjoy some of the most dramatic views in the Rockies. Photographs of the sloping face of Mount Rundle reflected in the Vermillion Lakes have been used on the covers of countless books and magazines. This is the kind of place to relax and drink in the views. You may even get the chance to see the bald eagles that nest on the lake.

While the road is open to vehicles, it is not a thoroughfare, and most of the cars will be doing the same thing that you are—moving slowly and stopping regularly for photographs. Keep your eyes open for elk along the far shoreline. As the pavement ends at km 4.46 (mi. 2.68), a gravel track continues for another 0.56 km (mi. 0.34) before ending at a gate on the busy Trans Canada Highway. Watching vehicles scurry about provides a great feeling of peace as you turn your bike around and return along the same peaceful route.

General location: Adjacent to the town of Banff.

Elevation change: Virtually nil.

Season: While cyclists ride this stretch during winter and summer, the snow-free season runs from late April or early May until late November. In spring, the

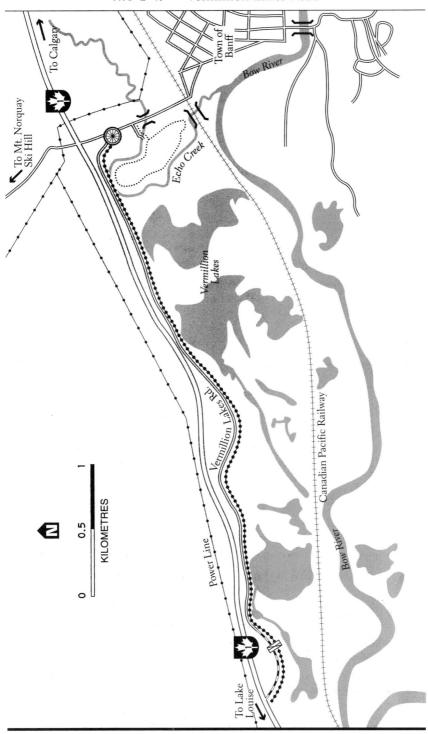

To Calgary

To Mt. Norquay
Ski Hill

Town of
Banff

Bow River

Echo Creek

Vermillion
Lakes

Vermillion Lakes Rd.

Power Line

Canadian Pacific Railway

Bow River

To Lake
Louise

N

0   0.5   1
KILOMETRES

Fenland Trail will be closed because of the elk calving season. At this time you'll need to drive to the actual road and begin your ride there.

Services: All services are available within the town of Banff.

Hazards: Simply watch for other vehicles—and enjoy the ride.

Rescue index: You should see other drivers, walkers, or cyclists en route who can offer assistance. Good cellular coverage can be found along this route.

Land status: Banff National Park.

Maps: The 1:50,000 scale topographic map for this trail is 82 O/4 Banff. Gem Trek has produced the best map for this trail, called "Banff Up-Close." It can be ordered from the source listed in this section's introduction.

Finding the trail: In the town of Banff, follow Lynx Street as it winds left to become Gopher Street and then Mount Norquay Road. Just before reaching the Trans Canada Highway (Highway 1), a signed parking lot is on the left. This is the trailhead for Fenland Trail. If the Fenland Trail is closed because of the elk calving season, simply drive past the trailhead parking lot, and the proper start for the Vermillion Lakes Road will be the next left turn (just before the highway exit).

Sources of additional information: Information for contacting Banff National Park is listed in the introduction to this section.

Notes on the trail: From the Fenland Parking lot, you can either follow the trail clockwise for quick access to the road or ride the loop and extend on to the Vermillion Lakes Road. For the quick-access road, follow the wide single-track as it crosses the first bridge. On the opposite side, turn right and follow the trail until you meet another bridge at km 0.56 (mi. 0.34). Turn right over the bridge and join the Vermillion Lakes Road. Take a left as you reach the pavement and soon begin to enjoy the views along the lakes. The classic view of Vermillion Lakes found on many postcards and brochures of Banff is at km 2.36 (mi. 1.42). You'll see a path going down toward the water and several large logs coming out of a small pond. The pavement ends at km 4.46 (mi. 2.68). If you're not ready to turn around, you can continue on a wide double-track and follow this route to its terminus at a gate on the Trans Canada Highway at km 5.02 (mi. 3.01).

RIDE 46 · Sundance Canyon

AT A GLANCE

Length/configuration: 7.2-km (4.32-mi.) out-and-back with an optional 2.1-km (1.26-mi.) interpretive walk (loop) at the terminus.

Aerobic difficulty: With little change in elevation, this ride is rated easy.

Technical difficulty: The entire length is paved, making it great for the whole family.

Scenery: The views along this trail stretch from Cascade Mountain all the way to the eastern edge of the Sawback Range. This open panorama keeps you company for much of the ride's length.

Special comments: This is the perfect ride for a lazy, sunny day when you can ride a bit and then take in the view from park benches placed along the river.

On a sunny day Sundance Canyon Trail is a popular destination. Along this 7.2-km (4.32-mi.) out-and-back, you'll pass hikers, inline skaters, horseback riders—oh, and yes, cyclists. The paved trail may be the initial attraction, but the open panorama alongside the lazy channel of the Bow River brings riders back time and again. Rolling your way along this trail, there are endless views of Cascade Mountain and Mounts Norquay, Edith, and Louis. Benches placed strategically along the river make for a pleasant place to get off your bike and simply drink in the magic around you. The ride is best done as a hike-and-bike. Ride for 3.6 km (2.16 mi.) to the end of the pavement; then walk the 2.1-km (1.26-mi.) interpretive trail around the actual canyon.

Sundance Canyon was formed thousands of years ago when a much larger river flowed down this valley. The moving water eroded a soft layer of rock that is angled sharply. This undercutting is clearly visible as you hike this short interpretive trail and clamber past delicate waterfalls and rapids. In more recent times, glaciers left debris behind, damming the traditional flow down this valley and diverting it to the upper Spray River.

General location: Adjacent to the town of Banff, Alberta.

Elevation change: This trail climbs all of 35 m (115 ft.), making it a very easy ride.

Season: Because of the heavy dose of sunshine received by this route, you can generally ride it from early to mid-May all the way until mid- to late October.

Services: All services are available in the town of Banff.

Hazards: The main challenge on this trail is negotiating a diverse group of other trail users. Be sure to yield to hikers, horseback riders, and skaters.

Rescue index: You can generally rely on the assistance of other trail users. Cellular coverage is good, and a pay phone can be found at the trailhead.

Land status: Banff National Park.

Maps: The 1:50,000 scale topographic map for this trail is 82 O/4 Banff. Gem Trek has produced the best map for this trail, called "Banff Up-Close." It can be ordered from the source listed in this book's introduction.

Finding the trail: In the town of Banff, follow Banff Avenue toward the Parks Administration Building. As you cross the Bow River Bridge, turn right onto Cave Avenue. Follow this road to its terminus at the Cave and Basin Centennial Centre. The trail begins to the right of the centre.

Sources of additional information: Information for contacting Banff National Park is listed in the introduction to this section.

Notes on the trail: Beginning at the Cave and Basin Centennial Centre, the Sundance Canyon Trail begins on the wide pavement to the right of this distinctive

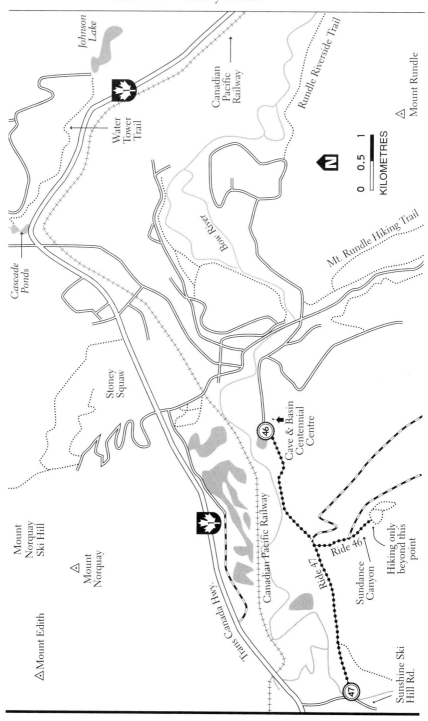

Johnson
Lake

Canadian Pacific
Railway

Rundle Riverside Trail

Mount Rundle

Water
Tower
Trail

KILOMETRES
0   0.5   1

N

Bow River

Mt. Rundle Hiking Trail

Cascade
Ponds

Stoney
Squaw

Cave & Basin
Centennial
Centre

46

Mount
Norquay Ski Hill

Mount
Norquay

Canadian Pacific Railway

Ride 46

Ride 47

Hiking only
beyond this
point

Mount Edith

Sundance
Canyon

Trans Canada Hwy.

Sunshine Ski
Hill Rd.

47

Sundance Canyon
carves its way
through soft layers
of vertical rock.

building. The pavement continues and becomes the Sundance Canyon Trail. Pass
a trail kiosk at km 0.3 (mi. 0.18). Simply stay on the pavement at all junctions and
you can't get lost on this ride. After passing two sets of benches down by the river,
the trail begins climbing gradually to its junction with Healy Creek Trail at km 2.5
(mi. 1.5). Stay left on the pavement, passing several buildings that can be seen
through the trees. They are part of a local horseback riding operation. Just before
the trail ends, you'll come upon a picnic shelter and public washrooms. Keep riding. At km 3.6 (mi. 2.16), the trail is closed to cyclists.

Park your bike in the rack (you did remember your lock . . . right?). After riding
all this way, be sure to take the time to walk this pleasant 2.1-km (1.26-mi.) loop.

When you've completed the hike, retrace the pavement back to the trailhead
at km 7.2 (mi. 4.32).

RIDE 47 · Healy Creek

AT A GLANCE

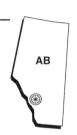

Length/configuration: 7.4-km (4.44-mi.) point-to-point or 14.8-km (8.88-mi.) out-and-back.

Aerobic difficulty: The trail rolls moderately along its way, with little change in elevation.

Technical difficulty: The wide track has few technical challenges, making it a good place to test out your first mountain bike.

Scenery: The paved Sundance Canyon access trail has endless views across the valley to Cascade Mountain and Mount Norquay. Once you leave the pavement behind, the views become sparser, offering only brief views.

Special comments: This trail makes for a great late-afternoon or evening ride when you simply want to put in some miles and burn off steam.

Beginning along the urban pavement of Sundance Canyon Trail, Healy Creek eventually forgoes the pavement for a wide double-track. The total length for this ride is 7.4 km (4.44 mi.) point-to-point or 14.8 km (8.88 mi.) out-and-back. Popular with horseback riders heading on the long trek toward Allenby Pass and Mount Assiniboine, the trail was named in 1884 by George Dawson, one of the area's early surveyors. Captain John Gerome Healy traveled extensively during the late 1800s and visited much of the continent. He worked as a hunter, trapper, prospector, whiskey trader, guide, scout, and even sheriff. Healy had filed several copper claims in this area, which is why many local features were named in his honour.

Along the route you get some good views toward the snowcapped face of Mount Bourgeau to the west, named after Eugene Bourgeau, botanist with the famous Palliser expedition. Bourgeau Mountain is better known today because Sunshine Ski Hill, one of Banff's premier alpine sites, sits at its base.

General location: Adjacent to the town of Banff, Alberta.

Elevation change: The net elevation gain along this route is negligible. As you ride, it rolls up and down 30 m (98 ft.) or so at a time, but the trend is gradual and pleasant.

Season: This trail is generally passable by mid- to late May and remains clear until early October.

Services: All services are available in the town of Banff.

Hazards: Keep your eyes open for horseback riders along this route. Other than the odd stretch of loose rock or mud, few other hazards need to be noted.

Rescue index: Either flag down another trail user or return to either trailhead, where you can usually find assistance.

Land status: Banff National Park.

Maps: The 1:50,000 scale topographic map for this trail is 82 O/4 Banff. Gem Trek has produced the best map for this trail, called "Banff Up-Close." It can be ordered from the source listed in the introduction to this section.

Finding the trail: In the town of Banff, follow Banff Avenue toward the Parks Administration Building. As you cross the Bow River Bridge, turn right onto Cave Avenue. Follow this road to its terminus at the Cave and Basin Centennial Centre. The trail begins to the right of the centre.

Sources of additional information: Information for contacting Banff National Park is listed in the introduction to this section.

Notes on the trail: Beginning at the Cave and Basin Centennial Centre, the Sundance Canyon Trail follows the wide pavement to the right of this distinctive building. The pavement continues and becomes the Sundance Canyon Trail. Pass a kiosk at km 0.3 (mi. 0.18), and simply stay on the pavement at all junctions and you won't get lost. After passing two sets of benches down by the river, the trail climbs gradually to its junction with Healy Creek Trail at km 2.5 (mi. 1.5).

Turn right at this junction and leave the pavement behind. Healy Creek rolls along a wide double-track and begins with a moderate climb. The trail is rolling, with an uphill bias. At km 3.4 (mi. 2.04), you'll notice a small marsh to your left with good views up to Sulphur Mountain in the distance. Several spur trails mark this route, but the main trail is always clearly visible. Beyond the marsh, begin a rolling downhill to km 5.2 (mi. 3.12) where you'll start climbing again. Pass the first junction for Allenby Pass Trail at km 5.5 (mi. 3.3), after which the trail drops down to join Healy Creek. As you approach the river, the trail becomes rougher, but views of Mount Edith across the valley to the north compensate. Pass the second Allenby Pass Trail junction at km 6.8 (mi. 4.08), then soon after rejoin the winding course of Healy Creek. The trail ends as you cross a bridge over Healy Creek at km 7.4 (mi. 4.44) and join the Sunshine Road.

RIDE 48 · Allenby Pass

AT A GLANCE

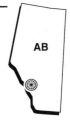

Length/configuration: 73-km (43.8-mi.) out-and-back.

Aerobic difficulty: The extreme length and large gain in elevation make for a difficult ride.

Technical difficulty: Sloppy mud and some steep climbing make this trail an extreme challenge.

Scenery: Fabulous views of the Sundance Range to the east as you follow Brewster Creek. From the pass, you'll be treated to views in all directions, including Og and Cave Mountains on the Continental Divide and Mount Allenby to the south.

Special comments: This is an extremely long wilderness ride. Make sure you're well prepared and very fit before attempting it.

Within the boundaries of Banff National Park, most of the extended wilderness rides have been long closed to mountain bikes. Brewster Creek provides access to the subalpine landscape of Allenby Pass, making for a 73-km (43.8-mi.) out-and-back. While much of the ride remains below the tree line, periodic views show the sharp face of the Sundance Range to the east. As the trail begins to climb toward the pass, it leaves the trees behind and enters an open subalpine world with views stretching in all directions. To the north, the peaks of the Sundance Range dominate, while to the west, Og and Cave Mountains mark the Continental Divide. Mounts Allenby and Mercer rise to the south. Historically, you could drop down the south side of the pass and continue toward Mount Assiniboine Provincial Park. This route, like so many before it, has now been closed to fat-tire travel.

Before undertaking this advanced ride, be sure to pack a complete repair kit, lots of water, and some extra food. Many riders choose to turn around at Sundance Lodge, making a more moderate 18.8-km (11.28-mi.) out-and-back.

General location: Adjacent to the town of Banff, Alberta.

Elevation change: From the trailhead at 1,400 m (4,592 ft.), the trail climbs gradually to Halfway Lodge at approximately 1,980 m (6,494 ft.). Beyond the lodge, the climbing steepens, rising 452 m (1,483 ft.) in just 4.1 km (2.46 mi.). The pass is at 2,432 m (7,977 ft.).

Season: June to early September.

Services: All services are available in the town of Banff.

Hazards: This is a very remote ride. Along the way, sections become severely muddy. When I rode the trail, both wheels continually seized up as muck clogged the bike frame. Be sure to wait for very dry weather. There may also be some route-finding challenges as you near the pass, but the trail is generally well marked. This trail is also used by horses, so be sure to share it.

Rescue index: Be prepared for self-rescue. In this remote wilderness, you may be able to get assistance from horsepack groups or from users of Halfway and Sundance Lodges. There may also be someone at the Sundance warden's cabin. No cellular signal will be available along most of this route.

Land status: Within Banff National Park.

Maps: The NTS 1:50,000 Series topographic maps for this trail are 82 J/13 Mount Assiniboine and 82 O/4 Banff, but the best map has been produced by Gem Trek Publishing and is called "Banff and Mount Assiniboine." Information for contacting Gem Trek is in this section's introduction.

Finding the trail: There are two potential trailheads. Most riders will choose to begin the ride from the town of Banff. Follow Banff Avenue toward the Parks Administration Building. As you cross the Bow River Bridge, turn right onto Cave Avenue. Follow this road to its terminus at the Cave & Basin Centennial Centre. The trail begins to the right of the centre.

An alternative trailhead is located along the Sunshine Ski Hill Road. After approximately 0.4 km (0.24 mi.), Healy Creek Trailhead will branch off to the

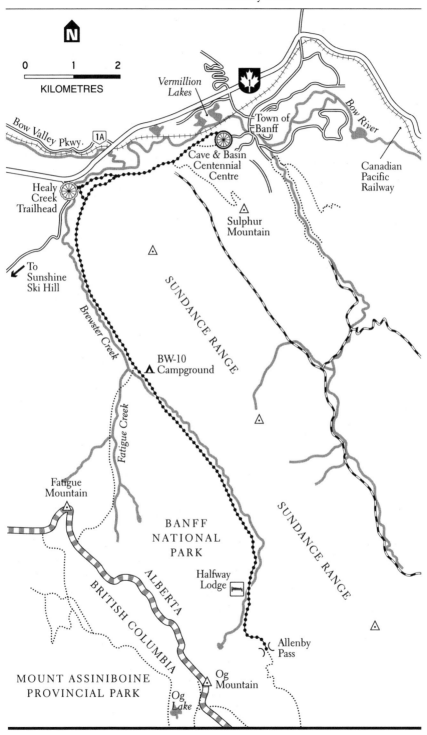

N

0 1 2
KILOMETRES

Vermillion
Lakes

Town of
Banff

Bow River

Bow Valley Pkwy.

1A

Cave & Basin
Centennial
Centre

Canadian
Pacific
Railway

Healy
Creek
Trailhead

Sulphur
Mountain

To
Sunshine
Ski Hill

Brewster Creek

SUNDANCE RANGE

BW-10
Campground

Fatigue Creek

Fatigue
Mountain

BANFF
NATIONAL
PARK

SUNDANCE RANGE

ALBERTA

Halfway
Lodge

BRITISH COLUMBIA

Allenby
Pass

MOUNT ASSINIBOINE
PROVINCIAL PARK

Og
Mountain

Og
Lake

Don't wait too long to ride the high country. The author was caught by several feet of snow while riding Allenby Pass in early September.

left. You can park here. From this trailhead, follow Healy Creek trail until you meet the second junction for Allenby Pass at km 1.9 (mi. 1.14 mi.). This route reduces the trail length by 3.6 km (2.16 mi.).

Sources of additional information: Information for contacting Banff National Park is listed in the introduction to this section.

Notes on the trail: From the Cave and Basin Centennial Centre, follow the wide pavement of the Sundance Canyon Trail for 2.5 km (1.5 mi.), and turn right onto the Healy Creek Trail. Follow the wide gravel, staying straight at an unmarked junction at 3.8 km (1.98 mi.). Turn left at the junction with Allenby Pass Trail at km 5.5 (3.3 mi.). Follow this wide trail, staying straight at a signed junction at km 9.1 (5.46 mi.). At this point the trail heads south toward Allenby Pass. Winding along Brewster Creek, you'll pass Sundance Lodge at km 14.4 (8.64 mi.). At the Fatigue Pass Trail junction at km 15.9 (9.54 mi.), stay left, continuing to follow the winding course of Brewster Creek. After passing the remains of a log cabin, the trail crosses a bridge over Brewster Creek at km 18.8 (11.28 mi.). The character of the ride changes drastically beyond this crossing, becoming a sloppy, muddy horse trail. You may have to persevere as your wheels seize up with the gooey muck. After passing the Sundance warden's cabin at km 26.5 (15.9 mi.), you'll meet Halfway Lodge at km 31.5 (18.9 mi.). Beyond the cabin, the trail takes on a steep, switchbacking course, making its way to the open summit of Allenby Pass at km 36.5 (21.9 mi.). Retrace your route, arriving at the trailhead at km 73 (43.8 mi.).

RIDE 49 · Tunnel Mountain (Hoodoos) Trail

AT A GLANCE

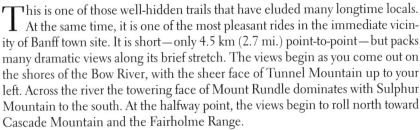

Length/configuration: 4.5-km (2.7-mi.) point-to-point or make a 9.35-km (5.61-mi.) loop, using Tunnel Mountain Drive.

Aerobic difficulty: The rolling character of the trail makes for plenty of breaks in the climbing.

Technical difficulty: Moderate, with few technical challenges.

Scenery: The views change by the minute, gradually stretching from Sulphur Mountain to the Fairholme Range.

Special comments: Within the town of Banff, this trail is a must-do.

This is one of those well-hidden trails that have eluded many longtime locals. At the same time, it is one of the most pleasant rides in the immediate vicinity of Banff town site. It is short—only 4.5 km (2.7 mi.) point-to-point—but packs many dramatic views along its brief stretch. The views begin as you come out on the shores of the Bow River, with the sheer face of Tunnel Mountain up to your left. Across the river the towering face of Mount Rundle dominates with Sulphur Mountain to the south. At the halfway point, the views begin to roll north toward Cascade Mountain and the Fairholme Range.

Tunnel Mountain is an unusual mountain with an unfortunate name—you see, Tunnel Mountain has no tunnel. Early railroad surveyors proposed one, but in the end they were able to go around rather than through the mountain. Unfortunately, the name stuck, and we have almost lost the traditional native name, "Sleeping Buffalo." As you approach the hoodoos viewing point, look back to the southwest and you'll see this amazing likeness. The head is to the right, with the hump behind, then the haunches. The hoodoos are tall columns of glacial material that act as guardians of the Bow Valley. Composed of glacial material cemented by dissolved minerals, the hoodoos erode slower than the rest of the hillside, leaving them behind as erosional remnants. To early natives, they were stone giants that would throw rocks on unsuspecting travelers. To ensure a safe journey, natives would pass them only in daylight, and they would leave gifts of tobacco to appease the spirits.

General location: Within the town of Banff, Alberta.

Elevation change: Over the course of the ride, the trail drops from the trailhead at 1,395 m (4,576 ft.) down to the river level at approximately 1,345 m (4,412 ft.). You then climb back to join Tunnel Mountain at 1,425 m (4,674 ft.).

Season: Mid-May to mid-October.

Services: All services are available in the town of Banff.

Hazards: There are few challenges on this trail. From the trailhead, the drop to river level is moderate. You also have to clamber over a small rock outcrop. The only other challenges are a few roots and loose rocks en route.

RIDE 49 · Tunnel Mountain (Hoodoos) Trail

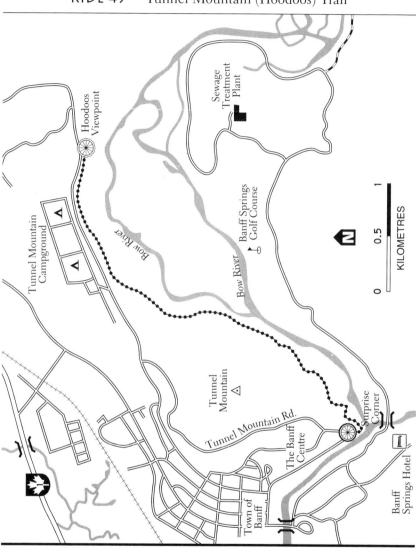

Rescue index: If you don't encounter other trail users, simply choose which end of the trail is closest and head in that direction. Good cellular coverage is available throughout.

Land status: Banff National Park.

Maps: The 1:50,000 scale topographic map for this trail is 82 O/4 Banff. Gem Trek has produced the best map for this trail, called "Banff Up-Close." It can be ordered from the source listed in this section's introduction.

Finding the trail: In the town of Banff, turn left (east) from Banff Avenue onto Buffalo Street. Follow this road until it makes a winding left turn just after you see the classic view of the Banff Springs Hotel. On this corner is a parking lot— use it. Once you have parked, face the back of the lot, and a trail descends from the right corner. This is the trailhead.

Sources of additional information: Information for contacting Banff National Park is listed in the introduction to this section.

Notes on the trail: From the trailhead, descend a set of steps. At the bottom of the steps, you'll find a fork in the trail. Be sure to take the left fork at this point, even though the trail heading straight appears to be the more heavily traveled. It drops down the embankment to a tiny beach on the edge of the Bow River. After taking the correct left trail, you'll pass a sign indicating km 4.0 (2.4 mi.) to the hoodoos. The trail begins with a descent, taking you past a railing at km 0.3 (0.18 mi.). Beyond this point, at km 0.5 (0.3 mi.), is an informal fork. Take the right fork to head closer toward the river. Both trails eventually rejoin. After paralleling a runoff channel, the trail emerges beside the Bow River as you pass beneath the jagged cliffs at the base of Tunnel Mountain. Huge limestone boulders have fallen from the summit to create a powerful setting. Lift your bike up a long series of steps at km 1.2 (0.72 mi.) to climb over a limestone outcrop on Tunnel Mountain. You then drop back down to the valley bottom on a short, technical downhill. As you pass through an open clearing at km 1.9 (1.14 mi.), the views open up and the trail begins to suffer from braiding. Be sure to stay on the main trail to reduce this unwanted erosion. The trail begins to climb toward Tunnel Mountain Drive at km 2.1 (1.26 mi.), and it soon crosses a small bridge over a runoff channel. This climb is a warm-up and levels out a short distance after the bridge. At a fork in the trail at km 2.5 (1.5 mi.), take the right fork to head out onto the escarpment. The views are spectacular along this next stretch. The main climbing begins at km 2.9 (1.74 mi.) and crests at km 3.2 (1.92 mi.). The rustic single-track ends at km 3.8 (2.28 mi.) as the trail joins with the busy pavement of Tunnel Mountain Drive. It parallels the road for a short distance before heading back into the trees for one more premier view at km 4.2 (2.52 mi.). Take a moment to enjoy the peace and quiet; once you arrive at the hoodoos, it is tourism central. Roll your way along the final stretch to arrive at the hoodoos' viewing point at km 4.5 (2.7 mi.). You have a choice of retracing your route or heading east on Tunnel Mountain Drive, followed by a left turn at the Douglas-fir Resort at approximately km 6.7 4.02 mi.). This is still considered Tunnel Mountain Drive, and its winding course will bring you back to the trailhead at 9.35 km (5.61 mi.).

RIDE 50 · Water Tower Trail

AT A GLANCE

Length/configuration: 4.46-km (2.68-mi.) point-to-point or 11.41-km (6.85-mi.) loop, using paved roadways.

Aerobic difficulty: Other than a steep climb at the beginning of the ride, the trail is level and smooth.

Technical difficulty: An easy ride along excellent single-track.

Scenery: The views are spectacular in all directions, stretching from Cascade Mountain to the east, Mount Rundle to the south, and extending all the way to Skogan Pass to the southeast.

Special comments: Ride this trail. The views are grand, and the trail is a magic single-track.

The trail from Cascade Pond to Johnson Lake is a relatively quiet but spectacular 4.46-km (2.68-mi.) single-track. The views include the Fairholme Range and Mount Allan to the east and southeast, Mount Rundle to the south, and Cascade Mountain and Mount Bourgeau to the east. A ride you will want to do again and again, it's relatively quiet, but the views are unsurpassed, focusing on the classic peaks of the Bow Valley.

From Cascade Pond, a popular picnic site and swimming hole, the trail winds around the lake before climbing sharply toward the top of the escarpment. Once you finish the short, steep climb, the trail winds through a forest of Douglas fir with a sparse understory of juniper. I rode the trail in early November through a carpet of fresh snow. In the snow, a steady path of wolf tracks offered pleasant company.

Roll your way along the needled single-track and reach the water tower at km 3.85 (2.31 mi.). The turbines visible to your left, part of the Cascade Dam and Power Plant, generate 35,900 kilowatts, enough power for a community of 24,000 people. Its earthen dam is 579 m (1,900 ft.) long and 35 m (115 ft.) high. Beyond the water tower, the trail widens to a gravel access road winding toward Johnson Lake.

Between 1886 and 1904, miners in the town of Anthracite extracted coal in this area. A small interpretive panel marks a possible burial site for residents of this almost forgotten community. Ride, roll, enjoy.

General location: Adjacent to the town of Banff.

Elevation change: Minimal. One sharp climb from the shores of Cascade Pond at approximately 1,402 m (4,600 ft.) takes you to the top of the escarpment at 1,435 m (4,707 ft.). The remainder of the ride is smooth and pleasant.

Season: Since this route receives plenty of sunlight, it makes for a great early and late season ride. Expect it to be passable from late April or early May until late October or even early November.

RIDE 50 · Water Tower Trail

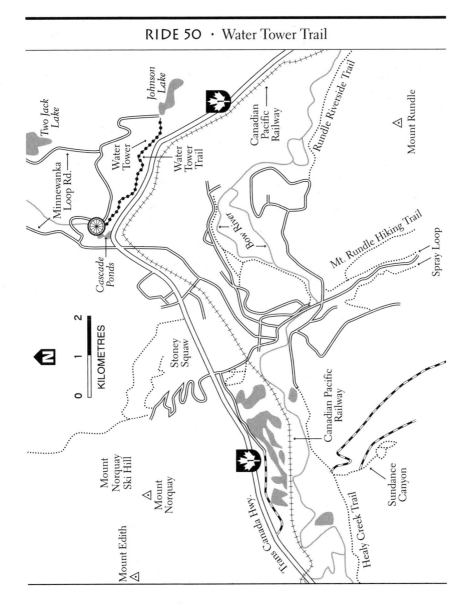

Services: All services are available in the towns of Banff and Canmore.

Hazards: If you ride this trail as described, it is largely hazard-free, with the exception of one steep climb near the beginning.

Rescue index: You may need to choose which trailhead is closest if you need assistance. Since the trail begins and ends at popular summer water holes, plenty of help is usually available. The trail stays largely within cellular range.

Land status: Banff National Park.

Maps: The 1:50,000 scale topographic maps for this trail are 82 O/4 Banff and 82 O/3 Canmore. Gem Trek has produced the best map for this trail, called "Banff Up-Close." It can be ordered from the source listed in this section's introduction.

Finding the trail: Follow Banff Avenue north toward Lake Minnewanka. Pass under the Trans Canada Highway and turn right into the Cascade Ponds picnic area. Park near the lake.

Sources of additional information: Information for contacting Banff National Park is listed in the introduction to this section.

Notes on the trail: From Cascade Pond, follow the trail as it circumnavigates the left-hand shore of the lake. The trail begins as wide pavement winding its way past the picnic shelters. At the final shelter, the trail winds to the right, becoming gravel as it heads toward the opposite shoreline. As you follow the shoreline, cross over the Cascade River bridge where the river enters the pond. Across this bridge, the trail winds left and follows the river upstream for a short distance. At km 0.57 (0.34 mi.), follow the single-track as it turns sharply to the right for the steep climb up the embankment. The climb, while not long, is steep and difficult to ride. Numerous logs have been placed across the trail to act as steps, making it a virtual push to the summit at km 0.78 (0.47 mi.). As you crest the top of the climb, you'll see the pavement of the Minnewanka Loop Road off to the left. Avoid the temptation to climb to the road; instead stay straight on the single-track.

The views open up almost immediately as the trail emerges along the top of the escarpment. To the west, Cascade Mountain rises with its namesake waterfall. Mount Bourgeau and the Bow Valley trend to the southwest, and Sulphur Mountain dominates the southern skyline. Roll your way through the open Douglas fir forest on sweet single-track with a pleasant carpet of needles. As you continue to ride, the views open toward the southeast, including the Fairholme Range and Mount Rundle, stretching all the way east to Mount Allan. At km 2.0 (mi. 1.2), the trail leaves the highway behind for a short distance, returning at km 2.28 (1.37 mi.). The views are grand once again until you leave the highway behind for a final time at km 2.9 (1.74 mi.). The trail widens for a few moments before winding right toward the water tower, which rolls into view just before you approach a short push through a channel filled with limestone blocks. The channel is only a metre wide, and the water tower is now within striking distance. Follow the single-track, reaching the tower at km 3.45 (2.07 mi.).

From the water tower, the trail widens to become a gravel access road. Roll along the gravel toward Johnson Lake. Soon after beginning the access road, at km 3.85 (2.31 mi.), a marker indicates a possible burial site for the town of Anthracite (1886–1904). Meet Johnson Lake at km 4.46 (2.68 mi.). You now have the option of returning along the same route or following the paved roads (staying left at each junction) back to the parking lot at km 11.41 (6.85 mi.).

RIDE 51 · Cascade Fire Road

AT A GLANCE

Length/configuration: 29.2-km (17.52-mi.) out-and-back.

Aerobic difficulty: This trail climbs steadily from the trailhead, making it a challenging test for novices.

Technical difficulty: The trail is strewn with loose gravel and small boulders. These can grab your front wheel if you're not careful. Novices may get frustrated.

Scenery: As you get farther up the valley, the views open to include the long ridge of Cascade Mountain on your left and the summits of the Palliser Range to your right.

Special comments: Make a day out of it and bring along a picnic. The two bridge crossings make for a pleasant spot to sit back and soak in the views.

This well-known Banff trail stays busy year-round. In winter, cross-country skiers head up this valley, and in the summer months it's a favourite of horsepackers and mountain bikers. The trail is a 29.2-km (17.52-mi.) out-and-back, so be sure to bring along some repair gear. It's also a bouncy, bumpy ride that is likely to loosen a bolt (or a filling) or two. While the route is uphill for most of the outride, the views offer plenty of rewards for your hard work. As you pass a marsh at km 3.5 (2.1 mi.), the Palliser Range comes into view to the right. After crossing the Cascade River bridge, the valley opens up with the ridge of Cascade Mountain to your left and the Palliser Range to your right.

Cascade Mountain gains its name from the ribbonlike waterfall that cascades down its face. In winter, ice climbers head straight up the frozen waterfall. To natives, it has had many names. To the Stoney Indians, it was "Minihapa," which means "waterfall place," while to the Cree it was "Nipika-Pakitik," also referring to its waterfall. While the road continues beyond the turnaround at km 14.8 (8.88 mi.), it is closed to cyclists beyond this point because it is critical wildlife habitat. Please respect this designation.

General location: Adjacent to the town of Banff, Alberta.

Elevation change: From the trailhead at 1,455 m (4,772 ft.), the trail climbs steadily to a maximum elevation of 1,655 m (5,428 ft.). It is only a moderate gradient, but it offers little respite along its length.

Season: Late May to late September or early October.

Services: All services are available in the town of Banff.

Hazards: Lots of loose rocks and small boulders that can grab your front tire.

Rescue index: The trail usually hosts many users, so you may be able to get help en route. Should the trail be quiet, your best bet is to return to the trailhead where you will usually be able to attract attention.

RIDE 51 · Cascade Fire Road

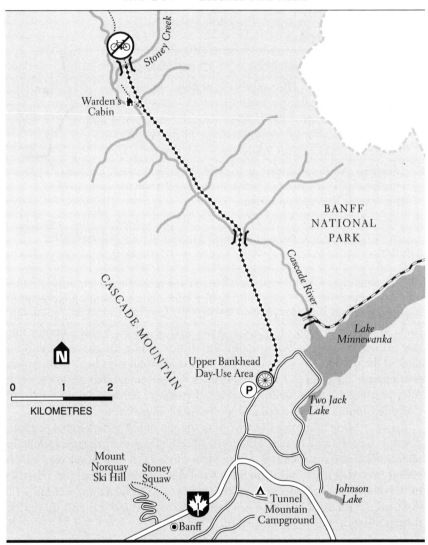

Land status: Banff National Park.

Maps: The 1:50,000 scale topographic maps for this trail are 82 O/4 Banff and 82 O/5 Castle Mountain. Gem Trek has produced the best map for this trail, called "Banff and Mount Assiniboine." It can be ordered from the source listed in this section's introduction.

Finding the trail: From the town of Banff, follow Banff Avenue west through town and leave the hotels and shops behind. Stay on this route as it passes under the Trans Canada Highway, then continue for an additional 3.5 km (2.1 mi.) to the Upper Bankhead parking lot. Watch for the Lower Bankhead parking lot,

Cascade Fire Road
is a popular summer
ride near the town
of Banff.

which comes just before meeting the Upper Bankhead trailhead. As you enter
the lot, park toward the right edge, where the trail heads off from this area.

Sources of additional information: Information for contacting Banff National
Park is listed in the introduction to this section.

Notes on the trail: From the trailhead, a signed single-track heads away from the
parking lot. Be sure that you are not on the C-Level Cirque Hiking trail. That trail
leaves from the opposite end of the parking lot. As you roll along the single-track,
you pass the horse corrals at km 0.8 (0.48 mi.); these mark the start of a short,
sharp climb. As you reach the summit of this hill, you then get to drop down just
as sharply to the junction with the actual Cascade Fire Road. Turn left onto the
wide gravel and begin to bounce your way up this former access road. Horses have
chewed up the gravel badly over the years, and the trail is a challenge of loose
rocks and small boulders. The trail has a steady uphill gradient until km 2.9 (1.74
mi.), after which it takes on a more rolling character. Pass through some picturesque marshes beginning at km 3.5 (2.1 mi.) as the Palliser Range comes into
view, high and to the right. At km 6.2 (3.72 mi.), the trail drops sharply to cross the
bridge over the Cascade River. Beyond the bridge, the trail continues its rolling
uphill trend until km 11.0 (6.6 mi.). You then get a break from the climbing and

drop sharply for 0.4 km (0.24 mi.), only to head back uphill again. As you pass the north end of Cascade Mountain, the trail descends to a trail junction at km 13.4 (8.04 mi.). To the left, the Stoney Creek warden's cabin sits among a picturesque locale, while the fire road beckons you forward (to the right). The mountain bike trail ends at the Stoney Creek Bridge at km 14.8 (8.88 mi.). Retrace your route to return to the trailhead at the 29.2-km (17.52-mi.) mark.

RIDE 52 · Lake Minnewanka

AT A GLANCE

Length/configuration: Variable, with a maximum 35-km (21.7-mi.) point-to-point or 70-km (43.4-mi.) out-and-back.

AB

Aerobic difficulty: Moderate, with a rolling character.

Technical difficulty: The trail winds along some exposed side-cuts and across some rocky washouts.

Scenery: The views are endless, with the peaks of the Fairholme Range paralleling the distant shoreline and Mount Aylmer and the Palliser Range above you to the left.

Special comments: A favourite with locals, this is one of the classic single-tracks in Banff National Park.

This trail is one of my favourite rides in Banff National Park. An out-and-back that can take you as far as 35 km (21.7 mi.) before you need to turn back, it provides both expert and intermediate riders with challenges and views galore. Most riders turn around at the Ghost Lakes at km 24.6 (mi. 15.25).

The ride takes you along the length of Lake Minnewanka toward Devil's Gap. To the early Indians, this body of water was known as Devil's Lake. They believed that a spirit who inhabited the lake took great offense to singing, so please don't sing while you're riding along the shoreline. As the trail progresses, it often traverses steep scree slopes and can be very tricky and technical, but these stretches can be walked.

Originally, the lake was made up of a series of lakes joined by a narrows. Long before highways were built, it was a traditional access route to the mountains. Today, hydro generation has raised the water level approximately 20 m (65 ft.), creating one large lake.

Whoppers lurk in the depths of Lake Minnewanka. Lake trout as large as 20 kilograms (45 pounds) have been caught in recent years. The fishermen go deep with down-riggers, since the lake is almost 183 m (600 ft.) deep.

As you get beyond the 10-km (6-mi.) mark, the face of Devil's Gap becomes dominant ahead of you. It beckons you to continue, the views seeming to improve with every mile. As you arrive at the Ghost Lakes, avoid the urge to go too much farther; remember, you must return whence you came.

RIDE 52 · Lake Minnewanka

GHOST RIVER
WILDERNESS
AREA

Aylmer
Pass △ Mount
Aylmer
3162

BANFF
NATIONAL PARK

Mount
Costigan
2979
△

Stewart Canyon

Lake Minnewanka

Warden's
Cabin

Devil's
Gap

△
Mount
Inglismalde
8964

Mount
△ Girourd
2995

Mount
△ Peechee
2934

△
Saddle
Peak
2819

To Lake
Louise

Johnson
Lake

Town
of Banff

Bow River

Trans Canada Hwy.

To
Calgary

N

0   4   8

KILOMETRES

General location: Lake Minnewanka in Banff National Park.

Elevation change: This trail follows the lake shore, so the change in elevation is minimal. A slight climb at the beginning gains access to the lakeshore, but after that the climbs are very short and rolling.

Season: This trail is rideable from early June to early October.

Services: All services are available in the town of Banff. At the day-use area for Lake Minnewanka, a snack bar offers some junk food and beverages for a celebration after the ride.

Hazards: This trail has numerous hazards. Its character is that of a side-cut trail, which means that it spends much of its time cutting across the side of a long scree slope at the base of several mountains. It's easy to slip and fall down the scree beneath you. Beginners may want to walk some of these stretches.

This trail also gives the illusion of being close to civilization; however, the potential to end up 35 km (21.7 mi.) away from your vehicle is real. Although you can decide the point at which you turn around, treat this trail as a wilderness ride and bring along repair equipment. I ended up pushing 20 km (12 mi.) after breaking an axle.

The outwash channels can be tricky, and you'll need to walk some of these. Between the rough stretches, this trail is a wonderful roller coaster with the potential to pick up some good speed. Watch for hikers along the trail as well as the occasional bighorn sheep. A helmet is an absolute necessity.

Rescue index: Since the trail is popular, you can usually find other people to lend assistance in emergencies. You may even be able to attract the attention of one of the many fishing boats on the lake, which can be a great boon in a true emergency.

Land status: Banff National Park, Parks Canada.

Maps: The 1:50,000 scale topographic maps for this trail are 82 0/6 Lake Minnewanka and 82 0/3 Canmore. You can also use Map Town's Banff-Canmore map. Finally, Parks Canada's Banff/Yoho/Kootenay map is useful as a large-scale, more general guide.

Finding the trail: From the town of Banff, follow the signs to Lake Minnewanka. Then, from the main parking lot, follow the road that goes to the day-use area. At the far end, you'll see the main trailhead.

Sources of additional information: The information for Banff National Park is listed in the introduction to this section.

Notes on the trail: From the day-use area, follow the roadway to the trailhead at km 0.55 (mi. 0.34). Follow the wide track to a bridge over Stewart Canyon at km 1.45 (mi. 0.9). The trail climbs on the opposite side as it makes its way toward the shoreline trail. At a junction at km 1.68 (mi. 1.04), stay to the right. The trail requires a combination of riding and pushing until you crest the shoulder at km 3.0 (mi. 1.86). The next kilometre combines a series of technical, rocky side-cuts across imposing scree slopes above the lake, with roller-coaster rides through the woods. At km 5.19 (mi. 3.22) the trail heads toward the controlled burn along the shores of Lake Minnewanka. The burned trees are visible for some distance, with plenty of new growth evident. At km 6.3 (mi. 3.9) the trail descends to lake level. The first bridge is at km 7.35 (mi. 4.56). At the junction at km 7.84 (mi. 4.86), stay straight. The route to the left is a hiking trail to the summit of Aylmer Lookout.

At km 9.95 (mi. 6.17) the trail passes the first campground along the lakeshore; stay right at the junction. At km 10.42 (mi. 6.46), the trail crosses a narrow, rocky outwash plain. Several of these occur along the trail, so keep an eye out for them. Shortly after this outwash, you climb above the lake and traverse a short distance. At km 11.72 (mi. 7.27), you cross another small runoff channel. At km 11.82 (mi. 7.33), the trail passes the second campground along the lake, LM11. A warden's cabin is located to the left of the trail at km 16.11 (mi. 10.0). The trail gets rougher at km 19.8 (mi. 12.3) as it moves on to another rocky side-cut along the base of the mountain. In a few cases, the trail has been obliterated by rock slides, so be cautious.

A ford at km 20.2 (mi. 12.5) requires a rock-to-rock jump-step to cross, but you can keep your feet dry. You'll pass campground LM20 at km 20.23 (mi. 12.5). Stay left at the fork at this point, although both trails converge again in a short distance. You'll come to another campground, LM22, at km 22.12 (mi. 13.7). After this point, the trail deteriorates into a rougher single-track requiring some pushing across outwash channels. It becomes very bumpy; I broke my rear axle and had to push almost all the way back.

At km 24.6 (mi. 15.25), the trail approaches the end of Lake Minnewanka, with excellent views of the Ghost Lakes. This point forms an ideal turnaround.

Although options include continuing on another 9 km (5.6 mi.) to Ghost River Road, the vehicle shuttle takes several hours. Most riders treat this trail as an out-and-back.

RIDE 53 · Redearth Creek

AT A GLANCE

Length/configuration: 20.6-km (12.4-mi.) out-and-back.

Aerobic difficulty: This is a smooth, gradual climb, suitable for all fitness levels.

Technical difficulty: The trail is a wide fire road with a good surface for its entire length.

Scenery: Along the ride, you are treated to excellent views toward Copper Mountain on your right and Pilot Mountain to the left. Behind you, the sheer cliffs of the Sawback Range dominate.

Special comments: A great ride to simply burn off steam, it is wide and quick, and the scenery is pleasant.

Redearth Creek separates the sheer faces of Pilot and Copper Mountains. While it is not a technically challenging ride, it does offer a pleasant way to roll your way through the mountains of Banff National Park. The riding distance is 10.3 km (6.2 mi.) one-way; however, you'll need to retrace your path to complete the ride for a total distance of 20.6 km (12.4 mi.). This ride also offers possibilities for a great hike-and-bike. From the terminus, hiking trails radiate in many directions. To the west, Shadow Lake is the closest body of water, but longer hikes include Egypt Lake, Ball Pass, and Gibbon Pass. Be sure to have a good map and an early start if you plan to attempt any of these options.

The trail is a former fire road, offering a smooth surface without the crowds found on other local trails. Pilot Mountain, the dominant face to your left as you ascend the trail, formed an important landmark for early travelers. Its distinctive

RIDE 53 · Redearth Creek

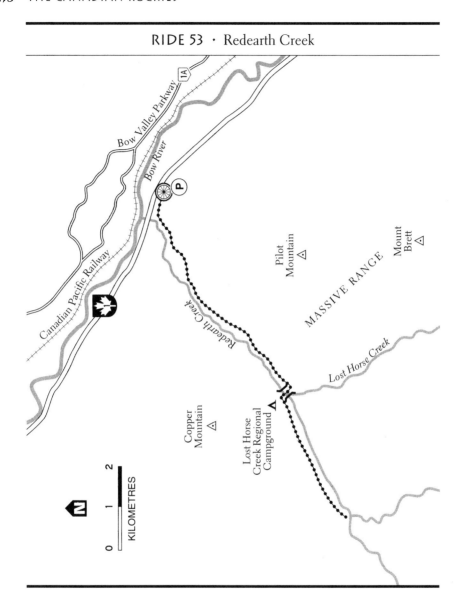

summit was easily recognized from great distances, leading pioneer surveyor George Dawson to christen it Pilot Mountain in 1884. Copper Mountain was named for the deposits of this valuable mineral found near its summit by prospectors Joe Healy and J. S. Dennis.

General location: Banff National Park.

Elevation change: From the trailhead, at 1,410 m (4,510 ft.), the trail climbs gradually to its terminus at approximately 1,745 m (5,724 ft.).

Season: Mid-May to early October.

Services: All services are available in the town of Banff.

Hazards: Few hazards will be encountered on this easy trail.

Rescue index: In an emergency, turn around and head toward the trailhead for assistance. You may also meet other cyclists or equestrian users en route who can offer help.

Land status: Within Banff National Park.

Maps: The NTS 1:50,000 Series topographic map for this trail is 82 0/4 Banff. A better map has been produced by Gem Trek Publishing and is called Banff and Mount Assiniboine. Information for contacting Gem Trek is in this section's introduction.

Finding the trail: From the town of Banff, take the Trans Canada Highway (Highway 1) west toward Lake Louise for approximately 20 km (12 mi.). Redearth Creek will be a signed trailhead immediately west of the second wildlife overpass.

Sources of additional information: Information for contacting Banff National Park is listed in the introduction to this section.

Notes on the trail: After passing through the large metal gate at the trailhead, Redearth Creek Trail follows the fence line and climbs gradually. At km 0.3 (0.18 mi.) the trail winds to the left and leaves the highway behind. Many other roads join with this route near the beginning. They start after you cross a small bridge at km 0.5 (0.3 mi.). At each of these junctions, you'll stay to the left. The junctions end with the crossing of another small bridge at km 1.2 (0.72 mi.).

Beyond this point the road is wide and easily followed. After crossing two bridges across Redearth Creek at km 6.9 (4.14 mi.), you pass RE-6 Lost Horse Creek Campground. With the creek on your left for the remainder of the ride, you'll have excellent views of the sheer slopes of Copper Mountain high to your right. The cycle trail ends at km 10.3 (6.2 mi.) at a signed trail junction. Retrace your route to return to the trailhead.

RIDE 54 · 1A Highway—Lake Louise to Continental Divide

AT A GLANCE

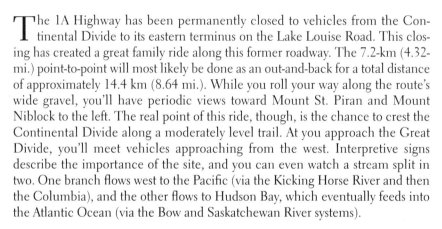

AB

Length/configuration: 7.2-km (4.32-mi.) point-to-point or 14.4-km (8.64-mi.) out-and-back.

Aerobic difficulty: The ride is almost level.

Technical difficulty: None.

Scenery: Periodic views toward Mounts St. Piran and Niblock.

Special comments: This ride gives you the unique opportunity to watch a stream split into two channels, each destined for a different ocean.

The 1A Highway has been permanently closed to vehicles from the Continental Divide to its eastern terminus on the Lake Louise Road. This closing has created a great family ride along this former roadway. The 7.2-km (4.32-mi.) point-to-point will most likely be done as an out-and-back for a total distance of approximately 14.4 km (8.64 mi.). While you roll your way along the route's wide gravel, you'll have periodic views toward Mount St. Piran and Mount Niblock to the left. The real point of this ride, though, is the chance to crest the Continental Divide along a moderately level trail. At you approach the Great Divide, you'll meet vehicles approaching from the west. Interpretive signs describe the importance of the site, and you can even watch a stream split in two. One branch flows west to the Pacific (via the Kicking Horse River and then the Columbia), and the other flows to Hudson Bay, which eventually feeds into the Atlantic Ocean (via the Bow and Saskatchewan River systems).

General location: Near the village of Lake Louise.

Elevation change: From the trailhead at approximately 1,700 m (5,576 ft.) the trail rolls between 1,660 m (5,445 ft.) and 1,710 m (5,609 ft.). The gradual changes are very moderate.

Season: Due to this trail's elevation, you'll need to wait until late May to ride, and it will generally be snowbound by early to mid-October.

Services: All services are available within the town of Banff, while food and supplies can be purchased in the village of Lake Louise.

Hazards: None.

Rescue index: Head back toward the trailhead, where help is always available as vehicles climb toward the famous shore of Lake Louise.

Land status: Within Banff National Park.

Maps: The NTS 1:50,000 Series topographic map for this trail is 82 0/4 Banff, but the best map for this trail has been produced by Gem Trek and is called

RIDE 54 · 1A Highway—Lake Louise to Continental Divide
RIDE 55 · Lake Louise Tramline Trail

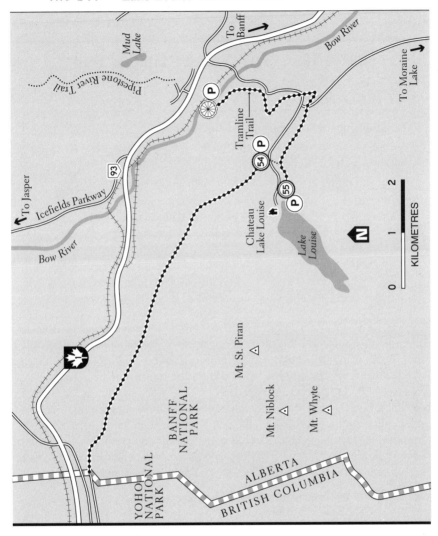

"Guide to Lake Louise Day Hikes." Information for contacting Gem Trek is in this section's introduction.

Finding the trail: From the village of Lake Louise, follow signs for Lake Louise (the actual lake). As you climb the hill toward Lake Louise, the old 1A Highway will be on your right, approximately 1 km (0.6 mi.) past the Moraine Lake Road. Park near the junction and begin your ride at the gate that closes this road to vehicles.

Sources of additional information: Information for contacting Banff National Park is listed in the introduction to this section.

Notes on the trail: This road is easy to follow; simply stay on the wide gravel.

RIDE 55 · Lake Louise Tramline Trail

AT A GLANCE

Length/configuration: 5.0-km (3.0-mi.) point-to-point.

Aerobic difficulty: In the downhill direction it is very easy, but the gain is 209 m (686 ft.) over just 5.0 km (3.0 mi.).

AB

Technical difficulty: The ride is wide and smooth for its entire length.

Scenery: While it begins at Lake Louise, one of the most famous lakes in the Rockies, much of the trail remains in the woods, with a great view at one point across the valley toward Mount Whitehorn.

Special comments: This trail follows the old route from the railway station to the chateau.

Before roads were built and automobiles honked their way through the Rockies, this route was the sole domain of horsepackers and locomotives. Between 1913 and 1930 an open-roofed tram carried visitors from the train station to Chateau Lake Louise along this historic route. While the tracks may be gone, the trail remains, and today it forms a great 5.0-km (3.0-mi.) point-to-point access between the village and the lake. Since the change in elevation between the lower and upper trailheads is 209 m (686 ft.), the ride is preferable in the downhill direction. One advantage to riding the trail uphill is the feeling you have that you're a part of history, following the route of countless early visitors to the chateau. And like those early visitors, you feel awe as you first set eyes on this magical lake.

General location: Adjacent to the village of Lake Louise.

Elevation change: The trail climbs 209 m (686 ft.) from the village to the lakeshore.

Season: Early June to late September.

Services: Between the village of Lake Louise and the town of Banff, all services are available.

Hazards: The only challenge is the gradient if you decide to ride in the uphill direction.

Rescue index: This trail is quite busy, so help can often be found en route. It also parallels the busy road between Lake Louise and the Trans Canada Highway, so there are always vehicles nearby.

Land status: Within Banff National Park.

Maps: The NTS 1:50,000 Series topographic map for this trail is 82 0/4 Banff, but the best map for this trail has been produced by Gem Trek and is called "Guide to Lake Louise Day Hikes." Information for contacting Gem Trek is in this section's introduction. Also, see the trail map on page 182.

Finding the trail: To find the upper trailhead, from the village of Lake Louise, follow signs for Lake Louise (the actual lake). As you approach Chateau Lake Louise, follow the signs for public parking. Entering the parking lot, turn left immediately and park in the far left corner. The trail leaves from here on a route signed with a green "3" and a smaller blue trail sign. If you prefer to ride the trail in the uphill direction, follow signs to the Lake Louise train station. As you approach the station, park in the lot to your left and you'll see a bridge crossing the Bow River. This is the trailhead. To find the lower trailhead, from within the village of Lake Louise, follow the Lake Louise Road as it passes under the railway tracks. At the four-way stop, turn right toward the Lake Louise train station. As you approach the station, turn left into the parking lot. At the far end of the lot, a bridge across the Bow River marks the trailhead.

Sources of additional information: Information for contacting Banff National Park is listed in the introduction to this section.

Notes on the trail: From the trailhead, you'll notice a trail that crosses the parking lot exit road. A small blue sign as well as a more prominent winter cross-country ski sign with a green "3" on it point the way. Almost immediately the trail passes by Deer Lodge and begins its descent toward the village. Take the right fork at the first junction, at km 0.4 (0.24 mi.), and continue to roll your way downhill to the junction with the Moraine Lake Road at km 1.7 (1.02 mi.). You must cross this busy road since the trail continues on the other side. An informal fork branches off to the left, but you want to stay to the right on the main trail. You finally cross Lake Louise Road at km 2.5 (1.5 mi.), and stay straight at the junction that soon appears. Just after crossing a bridge over Louise Creek, take the right fork again at a signed junction. This trail will take you onto an open bench above the access road at km 3.9 (2.34 mi.). This brief view brings you to the final section of trail, finally spitting you out at a bridge behind the Lake Louise train station at km 5.0 (3.0 mi.). You can follow the road to the right to return to the village at approximately 6.1 km (3.66 mi.).

RIDE 56 · Moraine Lake Trail

AT A GLANCE

Length/configuration: 9.76-km (6.05-mi.) point-to-point.

Aerobic difficulty: Moderate elevation gain as you round the lower slopes of Mount Temple.

Technical difficulty: Some exposed and muddy sections mark this moderately challenging ride.

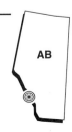

RIDE 56 · Moraine Lake Trail

Scenery: The views toward Moraine Lake and the Valley of the Ten Peaks are some of the best in the Canadian Rockies.

Special comments: In 1999 this trail was closed to mountain bikes. Its future status is unsure, so check with the Lake Louise Information Centre for updates.

This intermediate-level, point-to-point or out-and-back provides 9.76 km (6.05 mi.) of technical riding with unsurpassed views, followed by 8.8 km (5.46 mi.) of fast, downhill pavement pedaling. It allows the rider to parallel the Moraine Lake Road, climb high onto the shoulder of Mount Temple, and descend to Moraine Lake.

The views along the second half of the trail are some of the best in the Rockies. To the southwest, the Valley of the Ten Peaks lies before you. Count them, if you like. At the base of this solid mountain barrier is Moraine Lake, one of the most picturesque gems in the mountains. Until a few years ago it was the scene pictured on the back of the Canadian $20 bill.

The lake is actually misnamed. Not a true moraine, which is a deposit of glacial debris left behind at the toe of a glacier, it is more likely the remains of a landslide off the side of the Tower of Babel. The circular tower is obvious to the left of the lake as you approach from the north.

The Moraine Lake Trail ends at its namesake lake, offering civilized rewards after riding across rugged avalanche slopes.

General location: The trail lies between the village of Lake Louise and Moraine Lake in Banff National Park.

Elevation change: The trail climbs from the trailhead at 1,731 m (5,680 ft.) up to the highest point along the slopes of Mount Temple at an elevation of 2,026 m (6,650 ft.), before dropping down to Moraine Lake at 1,751 m (5,745 ft.).

Season: This trail is rideable from mid-June to late September.

Services: The village of Lake Louise provides all services.

Hazards: This trail contains several technical stretches and has narrow sections interspersed with roots and rocks. As the trail traverses the lower slopes of Mount Temple, it can be tricky at points. You'll need to negotiate some large rocks.

Rescue index: This trail sees a fair number of hikers and bikers, so you may be able to get assistance from a passerby. The terminus at Moraine Lake is always busy, and the trailhead along the Moraine Lake Road provides steady options for hitching a ride in an emergency.

Land status: Banff National Park, Parks Canada.

Maps: The 1:50,000 scale topographic map for this trail is 82 N/8 Lake Louise. However, Map Town's "Lake Louise and Yoho" is superior.

Finding the trail: From the village of Lake Louise, follow the signs toward Lake Louise proper. Take a left turn at the Moraine Lake Road. Drive this road for 2.2 km (1.36 mi.), and the trail will fork off to the right.

Sources of additional information: Information for Banff National Park is listed in the introduction to this section.

Notes on the trail: Follow this trail for 1.6 km (1 mi.) and turn left onto Moraine Lake Trail. At km 1.68 (mi. 1.04), the trail crosses a bridge over Paradise Creek. For the next few kilometres, the trend is uphill through a rough, rooty, narrow trail. Numerous stretches can be very muddy in wet weather, but most of the trail is rideable.

As you reach the shoulder of Mount Temple, the trail makes a gradual right-hand turn to the valley of Moraine Creek. This spot marks the high point in elevation. It also means the trail will open up with some splendid views down the valley toward Moraine Lake. As you continue toward the lake, the trail traverses several winter avalanche slopes; although the slopes provide excellent views, you'll need your concentration to negotiate the rocks along this stretch. The trail finally drops down to the lake at km 9.76 (mi. 6.05). From the lake, follow Moraine Lake Road back to the trailhead at km 18.56 (mi. 11.5).

RIDE 57 · Pipestone River Trail

AT A GLANCE

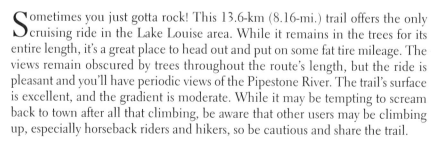

Length/configuration: 13.6-km (8.16-mi.) out-and-back.

Aerobic difficulty: The trail climbs steadily, but moderately.

Technical difficulty: Few real challenges will be met along this wide trail.

Scenery: The trail remains within the trees with the exception of a few picturesque views of the Pipestone River.

Special comments: This is a great cruising ride with a gradual climb and a quick run back to the trailhead.

Sometimes you just gotta rock! This 13.6-km (8.16-mi.) trail offers the only cruising ride in the Lake Louise area. While it remains in the trees for its entire length, it's a great place to head out and put on some fat tire mileage. The views remain obscured by trees throughout the route's length, but the ride is pleasant and you'll have periodic views of the Pipestone River. The trail's surface is excellent, and the gradient is moderate. While it may be tempting to scream back to town after all that climbing, be aware that other users may be climbing up, especially horseback riders and hikers, so be cautious and share the trail.

General location: Adjacent to the Village of Lake Louise.

Elevation change: The trail climbs 130 m (426 ft.) over 6.8 km (4.08 mi.).

Season: Late May to mid- or late September.

Services: In Lake Louise and Banff, all services are available.

Hazards: The ride is wide and smooth for its entire length. Remember that horses, hikers, and other cyclists may be using the trails, so be cautious on the fast downhill.

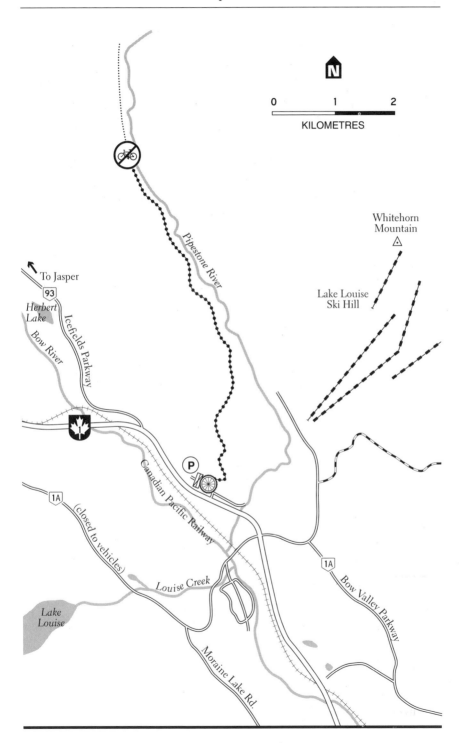

Rescue index: Head back toward the trailhead, which brings you near the busy Trans Canada Highway. Flag down a vehicle. Also, while your cellular signal may fade as you head out on this ride, it returns as you retrace your route.

Land status: Within Banff National Park.

Maps: The NTS 1:50,000 Series topographic map for this trail is 82 0/4 Banff, but the best map has been produced by Gem Trek and is called "Lake Louise and Yoho." Information for contacting Gem Trek is in this section's introduction.

Finding the trail: From the village of Lake Louise, take the Trans Canada Highway (Highway 1) west toward British Columbia. A signed turnoff at km 1.1 (0.66 mi.) indicates Pipestone. Take this right turn, and turn right again into the actual parking lot. At the far end of the lot, a large metal gate indicates the trailhead.

Sources of additional information: Information for contacting Banff National Park is listed in the introduction to this section.

Notes on the trail: Climb under the large gate at the trailhead and follow the wide gravel as it quickly winds left and begins climbing along a winter cross-country trail marked with a green sign indicating the number "1." Almost right away, the trail forks, with trail 2 going left. You want to stay right at this junction, then left at a junction at km 0.3 (0.18 mi.). This one is easy to miss, since it's a single-track to the left while you may be motoring along on the wide access road. After taking this left, the trail begins looping back in the direction of the trailhead. At km 0.8 (0.48 mi.), stay left at the signed junction for Mud Lake. The trail begins climbing moderately until another junction at km 2.2 (1.32 mi.). Stay to the right at this fork, ignoring the green "1" sign beckoning you left. As you begin climbing, you'll see that this trail is also signed as trail "1." Continue climbing, and over the next stretch you'll cross many small bridges. At km 5.7 (3.42 mi.), the trail approaches the river for a short distance. Finally, after a short rough stretch, the bike trail ends at km 6.8 (4.08 mi.). Retrace your route, arriving at the trailhead at km 13.6 (8.16 mi.).

RIDE 58 · Lake Louise Ski Hill—Temple Chalet

AT A GLANCE

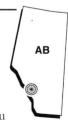

Length/configuration: 8.0-km (4.8-mi.) out-and-back.

Aerobic difficulty: The trail climbs steadily and sharply for its entire length, giving it a difficult rating.

Technical difficulty: The road is wide and smooth for its entire length.

Scenery: The views are fabulous. As you continue to climb, you get views toward Redoubt Mountain in front of you, Lipalian Mountain to your right, and Slate Mountain to your left. The return

AB

RIDE 58 · Lake Louise Ski Hill—Temple Chalet
RIDE 59 · Lake Louise Ski Hill—Whitehorn Lodge

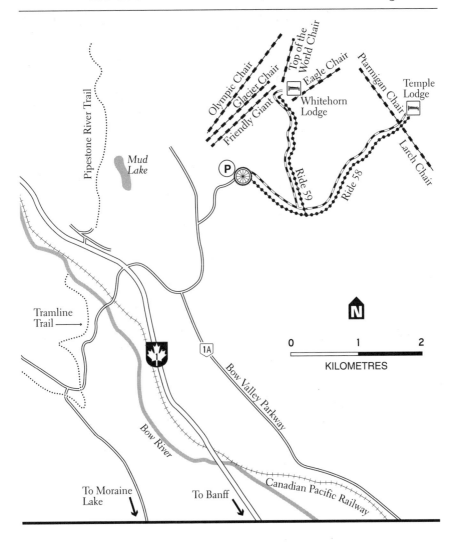

trip is even more spectacular, with views across the valley toward Mounts Temple and Victoria.

Special comments: This trail makes for a great afternoon workout with new views at every turn.

L ake Louise Ski Hill is one of Canada's premier ski destinations. Magazines like *Snow Country* repeatedly rate it the most scenic ski hill on the continent. This trail provides access to the higher reaches of the mountain and fabulous views of

The wide-track of the Tramline Trail follows the original route of the old tram road between the train station and the Chateau Lake Louise.

the surrounding countryside. While the climbing is stiff for the first 4 km (2.4 mi.), the return trip offers both spectacular views and high speed.

As you climb, the waters of Corral Creek will provide some solace to help you build up steam on a heavy uphill grind. Once you begin to gain elevation, the views ahead focus on Redoubt Mountain as well as Slate Mountain on your left and Lipalian Mountain to the right. Take a break on the climb, drinking in the even more superior vista behind you. Mount Temple, at 6,898 m (11,626 ft.), is the highest mountain in this view, with Saddle Mountain and Mount Fairview to its right.

General location: Above the village of Lake Louise.

Elevation change: From the trailhead, at 1,720 m (5,642 ft.), the trail climbs steadily to Temple Lodge at 2,100 m (6,888 ft.).

Season: Early June to mid-September.

Services: Between the village of Lake Louise and the town of Banff, all services are available.

Hazards: This road is open to vehicles with special permits; so keep your eyes open for trucks winding around blind corners.

Rescue index: Your best bet is to head back toward the trailhead. You may meet other users en route who can offer assistance. Otherwise, you can flag down vehicles along the busy ski hill access road. Good cellular coverage can be found throughout.

Land status: Within Banff National Park.

Maps: The NTS 1:50,000 Series topographic map for this trail is 82 0/4 Banff, but the best map has been produced by Gem Trek and is called "Guide to Lake Louise Day Hikes." Information contacting for Gem Trek is in the introduction to this book.

Finding the trail: From Banff, head west on the Trans Canada Highway (Highway 1) to the Lake Louise exit. As you come off of the highway, turn right, following signs for the Lake Louise Ski Hill. Pass the Bow Valley Parkway (Highway 1A) after 0.7 km (0.42 mi.), and continue for an additional 0.9 km (0.54 mi.) to the Fish Creek Road. Wind up this gravel access road for 1.1 km (0.66 mi.) to the Fish Creek Trailhead. Park in this large lot and then continue up the access road on your bike.

Sources of additional information: Information for contacting Banff National Park is listed in the introduction to this section.

Notes on the trail: From the parking lot, continue climbing right away on the wide gravel. At the fork at km 1.2 (0.72 mi.), stay right to continue toward Temple Lodge. At km 1.9 (1.14 mi.), you begin to parallel Corral Creek on your right, and the sound of water will keep you company. Cross the creek on a good-quality bridge at km 2.49 (1.49 mi.) and continue on the steep uphill gradient. The trail winds to the right, then to the left after the bridge, passing a red cabin used for storage and a fenced off area on the right where a gasoline tank is stored. Pass a junction at km 3.4 (2.04 mi.) where the winter ski out (run 29) heads off to the right. Stay left on the wide gravel and you'll soon pass the Larch chairlift and meet Temple Lodge at km 4.0 (2.4 mi.). After a break, turn your wheels downhill and enjoy the effects of gravity on the return trip. Arrive at the trailhead at km 8.0 (4.8 mi.).

RIDE 59 · Lake Louise Ski Hill—Whitehorn Lodge

AT A GLANCE

Length/configuration: 6.6-km (3.96-mi.) out-and-back.

Aerobic difficulty: The trail climbs steadily and sharply for its entire length, giving it a difficult rating.

Technical difficulty: The road is wide and smooth.

Scenery: What can you say? The trail looks out onto Lake Louise, one of the most famous lakes in North America.

Special comments: Another steep climb with an unparalleled view.

The view from Whitehorn Lodge is one of the classics in the Rockies. Across the valley the emerald waters of Lake Louise stand beneath the glacier-covered peak of Mount Victoria. To the right of Lake Louise, Mount St. Piran dominates the skyline. To the south, Mount Temple rises 6,898 m (11,626 ft.) and is capped by the Macdonald Glacier. Named after John A. Macdonald, Canada's first prime minister, it was his national dream to have an all-Canadian railway.

While you will no doubt be dripping sweat, and the salt will be burning your eyes by the time you reach Whitehorn Lodge (closed in the summer), you may be cursing the climb, but your heart will sing praises of the view.

General location: Above the village of Lake Louise.

Elevation change: From the trailhead, at 1,720 m (5,642 ft.), the trail climbs steadily to Whitehorn Lodge at 2,000 m (6,560 ft.).

Season: Early June to mid-September.

Services: Between the Village of Lake Louise and the town of Banff, all services are available.

Hazards: This road is open to vehicles with special permits, so keep your eyes open for trucks winding around blind corners.

Rescue index: Your best bet is to head back toward the trailhead. You may meet other users en route who can offer assistance. Otherwise, you can flag down vehicles along the busy ski hill access road. Good cellular coverage can be found throughout.

Land status: Within Banff National Park.

Maps: The NTS 1:50,000 Series topographic map for this trail is 82 0/4 Banff, but the best map has been produced by Gem Trek and is called "Guide to Lake Louise Day Hikes." Information for contacting Gem Trek is in this section's introduction. See also the trail map on page 189.

Finding the trail: From Banff, head west on the Trans Canada Highway (Highway 1) to the Lake Louise exit. As you come off of the highway, turn right, following signs for the Lake Louise Ski Hill. Pass the Bow Valley Parkway (Highway 1A) after 0.7 km (0.42 mi.), and continue for an additional 0.9 km (0.54 mi.) to the Fish Creek Road. Wind up this gravel access road for 1.1 km (0.66 mi.) to the Fish Creek Trailhead. Park in this large lot, then continue up the access road on your bike.

Sources of additional information: Information for contacting Banff National Park is listed in the introduction to this section.

Notes on the trail: From the parking lot, continue climbing right away on the wide gravel. At the fork at km 1.2 (0.72 mi.), stay left to climb toward Whitehorn Lodge. The trail is wide and smooth for the remainder of the climb, reaching the lodge at 3.3 km (1.98 mi.). Retrace your route, arriving at the trailhead at km 6.6 (3.96 mi.).

RIDE 60 · Saskatchewan Trail

AT A GLANCE

Length/configuration: 7.9-km (4.74-mi.) loop, using the wide pavement of Highway 11.

Aerobic difficulty: Very easy.

Technical difficulty: Very easy.

Scenery: Open views of Mount Murchison to the south, Mount Wilson to the west, and Mount Cline and Resolute Mountain to the north.

Special comments: This is a short but pleasant roll.

This short, 7.9-km (4.74-mi.) beginner loop takes you along the banks of the swift North Saskatchewan River. Since it follows the routes of the early explorers, this is a Canadian Heritage River. From the nearly invisible trailhead, the trail quickly takes you to the water's edge, where views open up along the river.

To the south loom the towering slopes of Mount Murchison. To the northwest, Mount Wilson provides a friendly face, and to the north, Mount Cline and Resolute Mountain dominate. The trail is a quick roller coaster that varies between open panoramas and enclosed, woodsy riding. Shortly after passing a warden's cabin signaling the eastern boundary of Banff National Park, the trail links with the highway. A quick pavement pedal will return you to your car.

General location: This trail lies along Highway 11, west of Saskatchewan River Crossing in Banff National Park.

Elevation change: The change in elevation is nominal. It climbs slightly from the trailhead, but quickly drops back to river level.

Season: This trail is rideable from late May to early October.

Services: Supplies can be purchased at Saskatchewan River Crossing, slightly west of the trailhead. No bike supplies are available nearby.

Hazards: The trail traverses the banks of the North Saskatchewan River, so there is the danger of falling down these sharp slopes. Otherwise, the trail is very easy.

Rescue index: You can contact rescue services at the crossing to the west of the trail. You may also contact the staff at the park gates, which are located halfway between the trailhead and the trail's junction with Highway 11. Since the trail parallels the highway, you can always make a quick exit to flag down a vehicle.

Land status: Banff National Park.

Maps: The 1:50,000 scale topographic map for this trail is 82 N/15 Mistaya Lake, but Gem Trek produces a superior map entitled "Bow Lake and Saskatchewan Crossing." The Parks Canada map, "Banff/Yoho/Kootenay," is also an option, although it is less detailed.

RIDE 60 · Saskatchewan Trail

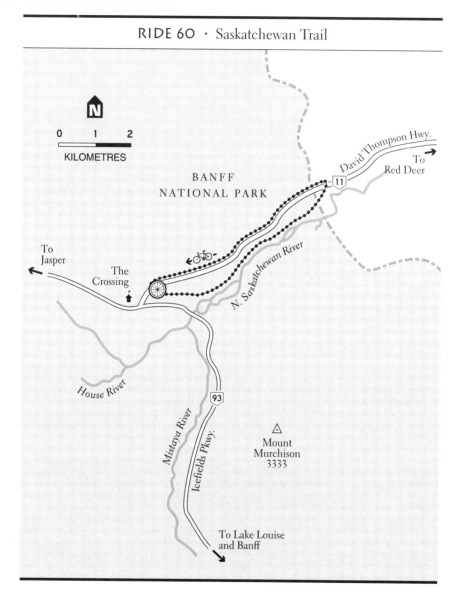

Finding the trail: From the junction with Highways 93 and 11, head east on Highway 11 for approximately 1 km (0.62 mi.). Keep your eyes open and you'll notice a gated, overgrown road branching off to the right. This is the trail.

Sources of additional information: Information for contacting Banff National Park is listed in the introduction to this section.

Notes on the trail: Once you find the obscure trailhead, the trail heads down a slight incline where a cable closes it to vehicles. The first view presents itself at km 0.58 (mi. 0.35), with Mount Murchison dominating. The trail then traverses the riverbank until km 2.62 (mi. 1.6), where it enters the forest and descends. At km

2.93 (mi. 1.75) you'll pass a warden's cabin, and the trail crosses Owen Creek on a rickety bridge. The bridge has partially collapsed, so it may not even exist in the future. Just beyond the crossing are two trails: the left one takes you back to the road, while the trail to the right takes you to the riverbank, where it ends abruptly at km 3.57 (mi. 2.1). If you turn around, you'll pass your original route at km 3.98 (mi. 2.4). At km 4.17 (mi. 2.5), a cable closes this end of the trail to vehicles. If you turn right beyond this barrier, at km 4.34 (mi. 2.7) you can turn left and join the highway, or you can continue on and join the highway at km 4.54 (mi. 2.72). At the highway, turn left back toward your vehicle at km 7.9 (mi. 4.74).

RIDE 61 · Saskatchewan River Excursion

AT A GLANCE

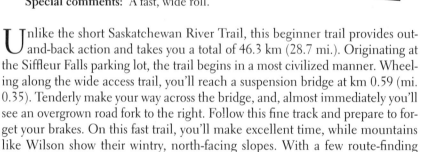

Length/configuration: 46.3-km (28.7-mi.) out-and-back.

Aerobic difficulty: Easy.

Technical difficulty: Easy, with numerous shallow fords.

Scenery: Panoramic views of Mount Wilson to the north and Mount Murchison to the south.

Special comments: A fast, wide roll.

Unlike the short Saskatchewan River Trail, this beginner trail provides out-and-back action and takes you a total of 46.3 km (28.7 mi.). Originating at the Siffleur Falls parking lot, the trail begins in a most civilized manner. Wheeling along the wide access trail, you'll reach a suspension bridge at km 0.59 (mi. 0.35). Tenderly make your way across the bridge, and, almost immediately you'll see an overgrown road fork to the right. Follow this fine track and prepare to forget your brakes. On this fast trail, you'll make excellent time, while mountains like Wilson show their wintry, north-facing slopes. With a few route-finding tricks, this trail provides excellent beginner-level riding and is a must for those who prefer fire roads to single-track.

General location: This trail lies along Highway 11, the David Thompson Highway, at the Siffleur Falls day-use area.

Elevation change: The elevation change is minimal, with the trailhead at 1,340 m (4,396 ft.) and the high point at 1,405 m (4,609 ft.).

Season: This trail is passable from late May to early October.

Services: You can obtain food and supplies at Saskatchewan River Crossing at the junction with Highway 93 and Highway 11. No bike shops are nearby, so you'll need to be self-sufficient with regard to repairs.

Hazards: Few hazards turn up on this pleasant ride. During high water the fords have the potential to be challenging. To avoid this, wait until later in the season when the fords will be more manageable.

RIDE 61 · Saskatchewan River Excursion

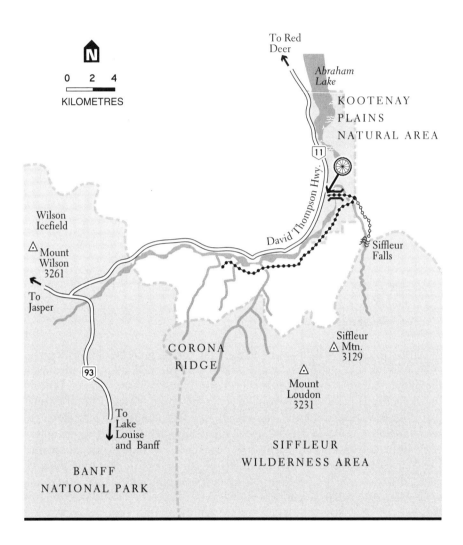

Rescue index: This trail is popular, so assistance is often available. The trailhead is along the busy David Thompson Highway, which always makes it easy to flag down vehicles. A pay phone is located slightly east of the trailhead, along Highway 11. Also to the east, at the Banff Park gates, you can initiate a rescue.

Land status: Alberta Forest Service.

Maps: The 1:50,000 scale topographic maps for this trail are 82 N/15 Mistaya Lake, 82 N/16 Siffleur River, 83 C/1 Whiterabbit Creek, and 83 C/2 Cline River. Gem Trek Publishing's map entitled "Bow Lake and Saskatchewan Crossing"

The author ponders the end of the trail as the Saskatchewan River Excursion suddenly deteriorates in a former clear-cut.

shows part of the route. Finally, Parks Canada's map of Banff/Yoho/Kootenay shows the entire route, but at a large scale.

Finding the trail: From Banff, head west on Highway 1 to the junction with Highway 93 North, the Banff/Jasper Highway. Traveling north on this scenic route, you'll meet the Saskatchewan River Crossing at km 76.7 (mi. 47.7). Head east along the David Thompson Highway beyond the park gates 24 km (14.4 mi.) from the Siffleur Falls trailhead.

Sources of additional information:
Alberta Forest Service
Box 1720
Rocky Mountain House, Alberta
T0M-1T0
(403) 845-8250

Notes on the trail: Beginning at the Siffleur Falls trailhead, drop from the parking lot along the high-quality wide-track. A suspension bridge at km 0.59 (mi. 0.35) takes you across the raging North Saskatchewan River. The wide trail continues on the far side. Keep your eyes out for a faint, overgrown road branching off to the right just beyond the suspension bridge. As the trail begins to follow the river upstream, the view opens up. At km 1.73 (mi. 1.1), the trail forks. Take the left fork and stay straight as the view improves. The first ford is at km 5.72 (mi. 3.43). A bridge was here until the floods of 1995 washed it away. The ford is not difficult — just cold.

At km 7.5 (mi. 4.5), a sign indicates the boundary of the Kootenay Plains Natural Area. Because of the nature of the boundary, you'll pass the boundary again at km 12.2 (mi. 7.3). Prior to passing the boundary, the last 3.27 km (2 mi.) have been within the trees. With the passing of the second boundary sign, you'll come to another ford. It is knee deep in August and about 6 m (20 ft.) wide.

At km 14.9 (mi. 8.9) the trail narrows and makes a small ford. Shortly, you'll come to a clearing, the site of an abandoned sawmill. The trail vanishes in the field; however, if you head to the left of a large cut-bank on the opposite side, you'll find the trail again. It's relatively wide at the start, drops for a while, then narrows to a single-track at km 15.81 (mi. 9.5). At km 17.0 (mi. 10.2), a rideable stream crossing signals the beginning of a formerly logged area. From km 17.5 (mi. 10.5) the view opens to the south, with an excellent panorama of the Wilson Icefield and the mountain of the same name. At km 18.56 (mi. 11.1), the trail enters an old-growth spruce forest for a short distance. Go right at a junction at km 18.93 (mi. 11.36). The trail opens up again at km 19.56 (mi. 11.7). More slash is visible in this logged area.

At km 20.9 (mi. 12.5), the view is dramatic in all directions. The trail now heads toward the lower face of Corona Ridge, disappearing in a cut-block at km 23.15 (mi. 13.9). Turn around at this point and return on the same route.

RIDE 62 · Siffleur Falls

AT A GLANCE

Length/configuration: 6.2-km (3.84-mi.) out-and-back.

Aerobic difficulty: Moderate challenge with a climb of 60 m (197 ft.).

Technical difficulty: The trail is narrow, with one sharp climb. The remainder of the ride is of moderate challenge.

Scenery: The falls are spectacular as they carve their way through a narrow limestone canyon.

Special comments: This short ride makes for a pleasant evening.

This 6.2-km (3.84-mi.) out-and-back makes an excellent evening excursion for intermediate riders. The trailhead is within the Kootenay Plains Natural Area. During the fur trade of centuries past, the Kootenay Indians traded pelts with traders based along the North Saskatchewan River. The Indians traveled inland from the mountains to meet the traders from the Hudson Bay Company post at Rocky Mountain House.

After crossing a high-quality suspension bridge over the North Saskatchewan River, the trail follows a wide track to a second crossing. Turn right at the next junction, and the trail becomes a narrow single-track as it climbs toward the falls.

The low rumble of water tumbling over the falls indicates your proximity to them. The falls have carved a narrow canyon through the limestone. As the

RIDE 62 · Siffleur Falls

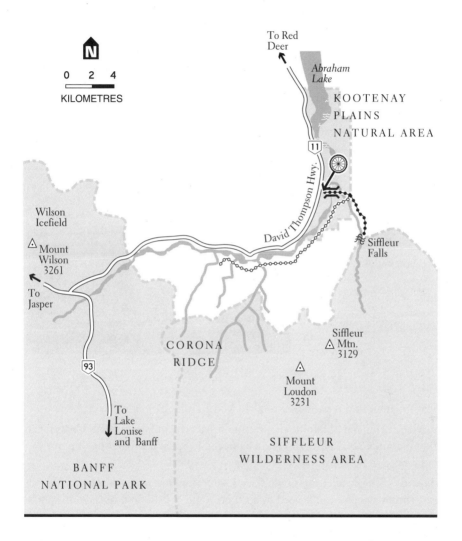

water tumbles over a resistant layer of rock, it cuts away the rock beneath the hard layer and eventually undercuts itself. As the layer collapses, the falls moves a little farther upstream, while at the same time it creates a lengthening canyon beneath it.

General location: The trail is found along Highway 11, the David Thompson Highway, at the Siffleur Falls day-use area.

Elevation change: The trail climbs from 1,340 m (4,396 ft.) at its trailhead to the falls at 1,400 m (4,593 ft.).

Short but sweet. The ride to Siffleur Falls is only 6.2 kilometres, but the intricately carved waterfall and canyon make it well worth the short foray.

Season: This trail is passable from late May to early October.

Services: You can obtain food and supplies at Saskatchewan River Crossing at the junction with Highway 93 and Highway 11. Since no bike shops are nearby, you'll need to be self-sufficient with regard to repairs.

Hazards: Shortly after the single-track begins, the trail makes a narrow side-cut as it climbs steeply. You'll need to push on some of this loose hillside, so watch your footing.

The power of the falls seems to bring out the explorer in most visitors. Scramble around on the rocks to get a better view. Keep in mind that with the mist of the falls constantly bathing the rocks, an extensive growth of moss and algae accumulates on the cliffs. This forms a slippery, potentially hazardous place to wander; be cautious.

Rescue index: This trail is popular since it makes for a perfect family hike. You can usually find help when you need it. The trailhead lies along the David Thompson Highway, which makes it easy to flag down vehicles.

Land status: Alberta Forest Service.

Maps: The 1:50,000 scale topographic map for this trail is 83 C/1 Whiterabbit Creek.

Finding the trail: From Banff, head west on Highway 1 to the junction with Highway 93 North, the Banff/Jasper Highway. Traveling north on this scenic route, you will meet the Saskatchewan River Crossing at km 76.7 (mi. 47.7). Head east along the David Thompson Highway beyond the park gates 24 km (14.4 mi.) to the Siffleur Falls trailhead.

Sources of additional information:

Alberta Forest Service
Box 1720
Rocky Mountain House, Alberta
T0M-1T0
(403) 845-8250

Notes on the trail: From the parking lot, drop down the slope on the wide-track toward a large suspension bridge at km 0.59 (mi. 0.35). After crossing the bridge, stay straight on the wide track. Cross a second bridge at km 1.24 (mi. 0.75) and turn right at the signed junction at km 1.35 (mi. 0.81). At the 1.84-km (1.1-mi.) mark, the trail narrows to a single-track and begins to climb a narrow, steep traverse. The hill is smooth but steep, so you'll do some riding and pushing to the summit at km 2.03 (mi. 1.2). Beyond this point, the trail continues climbing steadily. Most of it is rideable until you reach the falls at km 3.1 (mi. 1.86). Return on the same trail.

JASPER NATIONAL PARK

First established in 1907 on the promise of a railroad heading west from Edmonton, Jasper National Park lies directly north of Banff. Like Banff, it's very large—10,878 square kilometres (4,200 square miles). Farther north and farther than Banff from a major centre, it receives only a fraction of the visitors that its southern neighbour gets. With the park's quiet character comes a wilder reputation. Venturing into the backcountry of Jasper takes you into an area with few other travelers. I once hiked 175 km (109 mi.) along the park's South Boundary Trail and encountered only four people during the entire 12-day journey. Part of this spectacular trail is still open to mountain bikes; however, like Banff, much of the remainder of the park has been closed to two-wheeled exploration.

Although the park was more recently preserved, its history predates Banff. As early as 1811, explorer David Thompson instructed William Henry to build the first trading post in the Canadian Rockies. Henry's House, as it became known, was actually more of a stopping-off place for travelers heading west. It was superseded in popularity by another post, Jasper House, named after its builder, Jasper Hawse. Located at the confluence of the Miette and Athabasca Rivers, it was near the present town site.

In the 1820s, when Yellowhead Pass came into use as a trading route, the junction of the Miette and Athabasca Rivers became the dividing point for parties traveling to Columbia and New Caledonia (central British Columbia). Despite this momentary focus, the area remained relatively undisturbed until rumours of a railroad suddenly brought more attention to this vast wilderness.

Railroad competition was so fierce that two competing companies built lines toward Jasper. In 1911 the Grand Trunk Pacific chugged into town, and four years later the Canadian Northern arrived. With World War I, the redundancy of maintaining two competing lines became apparent, and the railroads were amalgamated into the Canadian National Railway. The iron from the many rails torn up during this merger was used to help drive the dominion's war machine during World War I. The abandoned railbed later proved perfect for the building of the Yellowhead Highway.

Today, the tiny community of Jasper houses 3,000 permanent residents and is much quieter than Banff. Its landscape continues to provide ample excuse for making the journey north, and the enjoyable riding makes the trip highly rewarding.

For more information, contact:

Jasper National Park
Box 10
Jasper, Alberta
T0E-1E0
(403) 852-6176

Freewheel Cycle
611 Patricia Street
Box 2541
Jasper, Alberta
T0E-1E0
(403) 852-5380

RIDE 63 · Athabasca River Trail

AT A GLANCE

Length/configuration: 23.7-km (14.2-mi.) loop.

Aerobic difficulty: Easy.

Technical difficulty: Wide, smooth trail with numerous junctions.

Scenery: Good views along the winding course of the Athabasca River.

Special comments: This is a great fast ride—perfect for an after-work workout.

This pleasant 23.7-km (14.2-mi.) loop is perfect for beginner riders or experts looking for a trail to spin their legs on. It travels through forested country, so the scenery is not as dramatic as trails that climb above the valley bottom, but it is a pleasant ride with some pleasurable riverside cycling.

From the trailhead the trail begins climbing at km 1.6 (mi. 0.96) and continues for another kilometre (0.6 mi.). This takes you past some views of the rolling greens of the Jasper Park Lodge Golf Course. After some forested riding, the trail joins the Maligne Lake Road, follows it for a short distance, then returns to the trailhead along the Athabasca River, past Lac Beauvert and the Jasper Park Lodge.

General location: East of Jasper, Alberta.

Elevation change: Slight.

Season: At a low elevation, the trail is rideable from late May to early October.

Services: All services are available in Jasper.

Hazards: A good ride for beginners, with minimal hazards. Several junctions require that you pay close attention to the trail description; it's possible to take a wrong turn. The most important junction occurs as you approach Jasper Park Lodge. Make sure you stay to the right of Lac Beauvert. Other hazards include hikers on the trail, especially near the day-use areas.

Rescue index: This trail stays close to civilization, passing numerous roads and facilities along its length. Assistance is never far away.

Land status: Jasper National Park, Parks Canada.

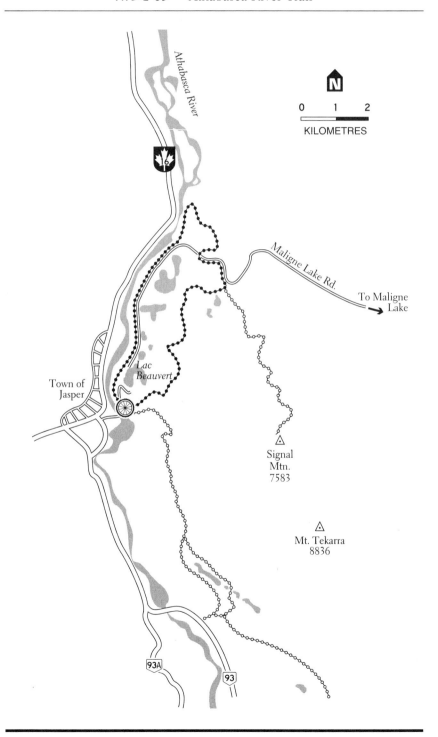

Maps: The 1:50,000 scale topographic map for this trail is 83 D/16 Jasper. How-ever, Gem Trek has produced a superior trail map entitled "Jasper Up-Close." As a third option, Parks Canada has produced a large-scale topographic map of Jasper. Some simple trail maps are put out by the park, but these are poor for visualizing actual features.

Finding the trail: This trail begins at Old Fort Point. On Jasper's main street, Connaught Drive, turn south on Hazel Street (Highway 93A) and follow the signs to Old Fort Point.

Sources of additional information: Information for Jasper National Park is listed in the introduction to this section.

Notes on the trail: Follow the main trail to a junction at km 0.08 (mi. 0.05). Go left at the junction and follow markers for Trail 7. Stay right at another junction at km 0.22 (mi. 0.13) and right again at km 0.47 (mi. 0.28). At km 1.6 (mi. 0.96) a steep hill may require some pushing. Wood chips used to reduce erosion can make it hard to climb. The top of the hill is at km 2.36 (mi. 1.4). From there, you'll have a view above the Jasper Park Lodge Golf Course. A large fence sur-rounds the course as you circumnavigate parts of it. The trail descends 60 m (200 ft.) to join the course at km 4.0 (mi. 2.4). Go straight and then right at the next two junctions. The next stretch is a smooth cruise on excellent wide-track. At km 6.26 (mi. 3.75) go straight. The left junction goes to Lake Annette. If time is lim-ited, this can make for a shorter loop. At km 7.63 (mi. 4.6) you'll meet pavement. The road veers left, but the trail makes a sharp right. After the trail goes around a marshy lake, go straight at km 8.0 (mi. 4.8). The trail climbs a steep hill. At the top the road is visible in the distance. Go left at a final junction at km 9.0 (mi. 5.4) and you'll meet the Signal Mountain trailhead at km 10.13 (mi. 6.0).

Follow the road back to the Fifth Bridge parking lot. From the staging area, cross the bridge. Just before the junction of Fifth Bridge Road, a rider-defined trail cuts off some pavement by making a direct cut toward the staging area. After crossing the bridge, turn right and continue for 0.15 km (0.1 mi.), then turn left at the signed junction. At km 13.84 (mi. 8.3) several small bridges take you through a wet section of trail. After this point, the trail climbs along a ledge over the river and becomes a fast, wide double-track.

At km 14.9 (mi. 8.9) a warden's cabin is visible across the river, and at the 15.5-km (9.3-mi.) mark, you'll cross the river at Sixth Bridge. At km 15.75 (mi. 9.46) ignore the gated route to the left and stay straight on the trail. You'll pass Annette Lake Trail at km 18.25 (mi. 10.9). Go straight at this point and cross Maligne Lake Road at km 19.3 (mi. 11.6). The trail then follows the river to Jasper Park Lodge at km 21.75 (mi. 13.0). Stay to the right of the lodge and Lac Beauvert to arrive back at Old Fort Point trailhead at km 23.7 (mi. 14.2).

RIDE 64 · Valley of Five Lakes and Wabasso Lake

AT A GLANCE

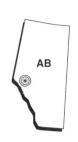

Length/configuration: 22.46-km (13.5-mi.) loop. It can be lengthened 16 km (9.6 mi.) by continuing on to Wabasso Lake farther south.

Aerobic difficulty: After a sharp climb at the start, the trail takes on a moderate downhill trend.

Technical difficulty: Except for one badly eroded downhill, the trail is generally wide and easy.

Scenery: Rolling past many tiny ponds, this is a quiet, scenic ride.

Special comments: Be sure to share the trail with hikers.

This trail is an ideal ride for beginner to intermediate cyclists who are looking for a gentle gradient with some challenges. The 22.46-km (13.5-mi.) loop can be lengthened by 16 km (9.6 mi.) if you continue on to Wabasso Lake farther south.

The trail begins by climbing part of the way to Old Fort Point, one of the most commanding views of the Jasper town site area. It gains its name from the Northwest Company's Old Fort, built nearby in 1812 by William Henry. It was the first fur trading station built in the area. You may want to park your bike and make a short detour to enjoy the view.

From this point, the trail continues past some excellent views of Mount Tekarra to the left. This rocky summit was named in 1858 to honour an Iroquois hunter who accompanied Dr. James Hector on his surveying trips through this area.

Before you know it, the first of the lakes rolls into view to the right. Stay to the left at a junction prior to the first lake. This high route provides views from above all of the lakes in succession. At the last lake, you have the option of continuing on to Wabasso Lake or exiting to the highway. A final paved run brings you back to the trailhead.

General location: The trail is located east of Jasper, Alberta.

Elevation change: From the trailhead at Old Fort Point at 981 m (3,220 ft.) the trail climbs to 1,139 m (3,740 ft.) as it approaches the vista at Old Fort Point. From there it descends toward the lakes at 1,085 m (3,560 ft.).

Season: This low-elevation trail is rideable from late May to early October.

Services: All services are available in Jasper.

Hazards: At km 4.54 (mi. 2.72) is a steep, badly eroded downhill. Novices will want to dismount here to avoid wiping out. Otherwise, the trail is suitable for riders of all abilities.

Rescue index: Like most town-site-area trails, the route to the Valley of Five Lakes is very popular. Hikers and mountain bikers aplenty follow this well-defined route. At the end of the lakes, you can exit to Highway 93 (Jasper/Banff Highway), where it is always easy to flag down vehicles.

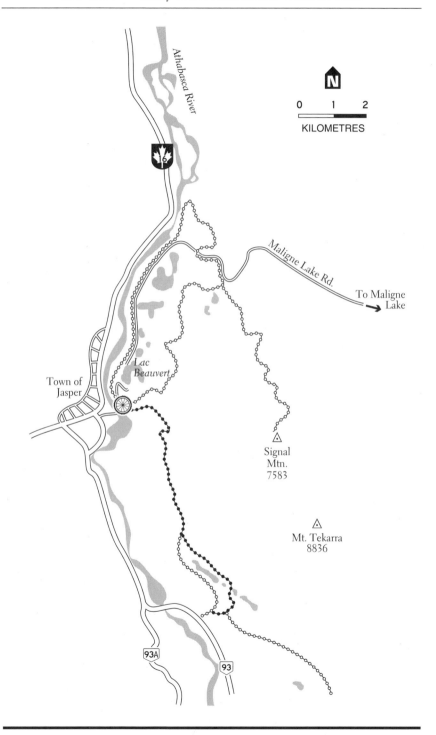

Land status: Jasper National Park, Parks Canada.

Maps: The 1:50,000 scale topographic map for this trail is 83 D/16 Jasper. However, Gem Trek has produced a superior trail map called "Jasper Up-Close." The Wabasso Lake option, though, extends beyond the scope of this map. Gem Trek's larger-scale Jasper and Maligne Lake map shows the entire route. In addition, Parks Canada has produced a large-scale topographic map of Jasper, along with some simple trail maps.

Finding the trail: This trail begins at Old Fort Point. On Jasper's main street, Connaught Drive, turn south on Hazel Street (Highway 93A) and follow the signs to Old Fort Point.

Sources of additional information: The information for Jasper National Park is listed in the introduction to this section.

Notes on the trail: From the trailhead at Old Fort Point, at an elevation of 981 m (3,220 ft.), follow the main trail to a junction at km 0.04 (mi. 0.02) and go right on the trail marked "1A." At a second fork at km 0.97 (mi. 0.6) go right again. Continue trending right when you meet the horse trail at km 1.64 (mi. 0.98). This will keep you on the hiking trail. It also means you'll need to push your bike up a very steep hill to the summit at km 2.18 (mi. 1.3), elevation 1,057 m (3,470 ft.). Turn left and follow the trail marker indicating trail "9" from now on. By km 3.27 (mi. 1.95) the trail becomes a wide-track rolling through a mixed forest of aspen and lodgepole pine.

Another short push, just before km 3.63 (mi. 2.2), forms the start of a pleasant roller-coaster section ending at km 4.54 (mi. 2.72). At this point, the trail begins to drop suddenly. It is badly abraded, and, at km 4.78 (mi. 2.9), novices will want to dismount before reaching a difficult downhill section. At the base of the slope, a crossing over Tekarra Creek is followed by a short, sharp uphill. Km 5.75 (mi. 3.45) takes you past a small, marshy lake at the base of Mount Tekarra. A steep, rooty uphill at km 6.45 (mi. 3.87) has a bypass on the left. It leads to an important junction at km 6.91 (mi. 4.14). At this point, stay left to take the upper trail past the lakes or go right to bypass the lakes on the lower trail. (I am describing the upper trail.)

The first lake becomes visible at km 7.7 (mi. 4.6), where a short spur trail branches off the main trail to provide access to the shoreline. Stay on the main trail; it drops to the shoreline at km 8.27 (mi. 5.0). At km 8.98 (mi. 5.4) turn left at the junction and continue on to the next lake at km 9.14 (mi. 5.84). You'll pass other lakes at km 9.39 and 9.93 (mi. 5.63 and 6.0). This lake is followed by another junction where you'll turn right.

As you drop down from the lakes, you'll cross a bridged creek at km 10.12 (mi. 6.1). After the bridge, a short, steep hill will require a dismount. At km 10.88 (mi. 6.5) you can make a loop by following the bottom of the lakes to join back up with the main trail, or you can return via the highway. I chose to continue down to the highway and follow the roadway back. The final junction at km 11.12 (mi. 6.67) allows you to add significantly to this loop by turning left and continuing on to Wabasso Lake. This route adds an extra 10.5 km (6.3 mi.) of trail riding, followed by an extra 5.5 km (3.3 mi.) of highway riding.

By staying straight at the Wabasso Lake junction, you'll reach the highway at km 12.07 (mi. 7.24). Head north until you meet Highway 93A at km 19.85 (mi. 11.9), then turn right. The final road junction is at km 21.5 (mi. 12.9) at the sign to Old Fort Point Road. The trailhead is at km 22.46 (mi. 13.5).

RIDE 65 · Overlander Trail

AT A GLANCE

Length/configuration: 37.22-km (22.3-mi.) loop, using Highway 16.

Aerobic difficulty: Easy, with little change in elevation.

Technical difficulty: Difficult, with some challenging technical sections and sharp side-cuts.

Scenery: Open views of the Athabasca River and the Colin Range to the east and the peaks of the Victoria Cross Range to the west.

Special comments: This local favourite has great views and a challenging character.

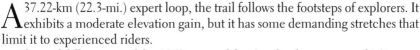

A 37.22-km (22.3-mi.) expert loop, the trail follows the footsteps of explorers. It exhibits a moderate elevation gain, but it has some demanding stretches that limit it to experienced riders.

The trail follows part of the 1862 route of the Overlanders, a party of 150 men, 1 pregnant woman, and 3 children who set out from Fort Garry (Winnipeg, Manitoba) to prospect the gold fields of the Caribou in the interior of British Columbia. The gold rush was short-lived, but rich. One claim alone produced 46 kilograms (102 pounds) of gold in one day and a $10,000 dividend every Sunday for several weeks. The ordeal of the Overlanders, traveling through country devoid of pathways, led them to dismal failure. Traveling across endless plains with no firewood, they burned buffalo dung as fuel. In the end, as one member put it: "Our mining tools were the only articles . . . that we found to be unnecessary." Before the Overlanders' use of this trail, it had been a traditional route for native Indians migrating into the mountains. It was later used by fur traders and explorers.

The route follows the Athabasca River beneath the towering slopes of the Colin Range. It passes the cabins of John Moberly, who settled in the area at the turn of the 20th century and lived here until 1909. Once each year he and his family made the trip to Edmonton to sell their furs. The trip took three months, as no roads existed. From the Moberly cabins the trail passes through the site of a controlled burn, set in 1989 by park wardens to improve wildlife habitat. You can see the rapid regrowth beneath the blackened stumps. Before you know it, the trail is squeezed along narrow side-cuts above the river. It gets technical and challenging, but the views are exquisite.

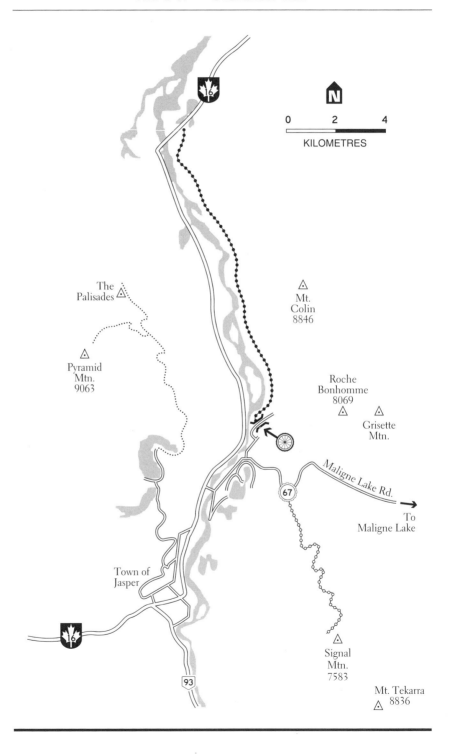

N

0   2   4
KILOMETRES

The
Palisades

Mt.
Colin
8846

Pyramid
Mtn.
9063

Roche
Bonhomme
8069

Grisette
Mtn.

Maligne Lake Rd.

67

To
Maligne Lake

Town of
Jasper

Signal
Mtn.
7583

Mt. Tekarra
8836

93

The Overlander Trail is a wonderful challenge. It travels through a variety of terrain, but often traverses sharp side-cuts.

Eventually, the route joins with Highway 16, then a final 21 km (13 mi.) on pavement returns you to the trailhead.

General location: The trail is located north of Jasper, Alberta.

Elevation change: The trail begins at 1,033 m (3,390 ft.) and climbs to a maximum of 1,060 m (3,480 ft.).

Season: This low-elevation trail is rideable from late May to early October.

Services: All services are available in Jasper.

Hazards: This trail requires the negotiation of numerous technical side-cuts above the Athabasca River. In some cases, you'll find yourself pushing your bike up some steep draws above a high embankment. In other stretches, the trail is badly chewed and will require perseverance. Some of the downhills are steep and challenging. Finally, as the trail joins the highway, you'll need to negotiate a steep ladder to get your bike down to road level.

Rescue index: This trail, which begins at the Sixth Bridge picnic area, a popular day-use site, is a challenging ride and tends to attract serious riders. Once you head out, you'll need to either turn back or continue to the end for help. In most cases, at least until you enter the most difficult stretches, it's an easier return ride. After you reach the highway at km 15.6 (mi. 9.3), it's easy to flag down a vehicle.

Land status: Jasper National Park, Parks Canada.

Maps: The 1:50,000 scale topographic maps for this trail are 83 D/16 Jasper and 83 E/01 Snaring River. However, Gem Trek has produced a superior trail map

entitled "Jasper and Maligne Lake." As a third option, Parks Canada has produced a large-scale topographic map of Jasper. Some simple trail maps are put
out by the park, but they are poor for visualizing actual features.

Finding the trail: From Jasper, head west on Highway 16 to the junction with
the Maligne Lake Road. After crossing the Athabasca River, watch for the sign
for Sixth Bridge. Park at the picnic area. From there, cross the bridge, and the
trail veers off to the left.

Sources of additional information: Information for Jasper National Park is
listed in the introduction to this section.

Notes on the trail: From the Sixth Bridge parking lot, cross the bridge from the
trailhead, then immediately turn left. Between km 0.25–0.34 (mi. 0.15–0.2), the
river has washed away parts of the trail. You'll cross bridges at km 0.48, 0.6, and
1.37 (mi. 0.29, 0.36, and 0.82). During this stretch the trail is rough and rooty. At
a junction at km 1.44 (mi. 0.86), turn left. The trail enters a mixed forest of
spruce and pine for the next little while. A wet-weather washout at km 2.1 (mi.
1.25) requires negotiating as the stream takes over the trail for a short distance.
After a bridge crossing at km 2.45 (mi. 1.5), turn left at the junction. The trail
improves after this junction and enters a dark, old-growth spruce forest. A bridge
over a dry creek at km 3.2 (mi. 1.9) precedes several rideable washouts. At km 3.6
(mi. 2.1) the trail opens into a mix of Douglas fir, aspen, and spruce. There are
good views of Pyramid Mountain and Colin Range. At km 4.5 (mi. 2.7) the trail
descends into a dark spruce forest. After a short downhill push at km 4.8 (mi.
2.9), the trail improves. It becomes a forested roller coaster until km 6.4 (mi.
3.84), where it opens into a clearing. You'll pass the former cabins of John
Moberly at km 7.21 (mi. 4.32). Evidence of a controlled burn is visible on the
slopes of Colin Range.

At km 7.5 (mi. 4.5) the trail enters the forest again until km 8.3 (mi. 5.0).
You'll find yourself pushing a short uphill into the controlled burn site at km
9.12 (mi. 5.47). By km 9.3 (mi. 5.6) the trail has climbed above the river and
offers good views of Roche De Smet in the distance.

The pleasant nature of the trail changes at km 9.7 (mi. 5.82), where the trail
begins a long stretch of technical side-cuts as it traverses the lower slopes of Hawk
Mountain and Morro Peak. The views of the river are pleasant along the final 5
km (3 mi.), but you'll need to concentrate to stay on your bike. At km 10.53 (mi.
6.3) a very difficult side-cut will require you to push/carry your bike to the top of
a steep hill. Once you're at the top of this hill, the trail enters the woods and
drops treacherously from the summit through the fire site. At km 11.2 (mi. 6.7)
stay right at a junction with a lower trail. Another side-cut at km 11.4 (mi. 6.8)
provides good views as the trail climbs above a quiet bay on the Athabasca River.
Another steep, tricky side-cut at km 14.3 (mi. 8.6) will require cautious pushing.
At a junction at km 15.57 (mi. 9.3), head left and you'll find yourself atop a short
ladder above the highway. Scramble down the ladder and take the highway back
to the trailhead.

You'll meet Maligne Lake Road at km 33.47 (mi. 20.0). Turn left again at
Sixth Bridge Road, and the trailhead is at km 37.22 (mi. 22.3).

RIDE 66 · Saturday Night Loop

AT A GLANCE

Length/configuration: 28.9-km (17.3-mi.) loop.

Aerobic difficulty: Moderate difficulty.

Technical difficulty: This challenging ride has a very muddy, technical section near its western extent.

Scenery: Passing many small lakes, the ride has some pleasant views of the surrounding peaks. The dominant peaks are Muhigan Mountain and The Whistlers to the south.

Special comments: This trail is popular with locals, but it lacks some of the great panoramas found on other rides in the area.

If you grind your teeth at night dreaming of a ride designed to break you, this may be the one. A 28.9-km (17.3-mi.) loop that passes many picturesque lakes, it is an expert-level ride with endless mud bogs and extensive root erosion. This trail is so bumpy it rattled my front forks loose.

The trail climbs toward Pyramid Bench before heading west along the base of the Victoria Cross Range. Each peak of this range is named after a winner of the empire's highest award for valor. Most of the lakes are scenic, their waters reflecting the surrounding peaks.

The ride begins innocently enough. The stretch to Cabin Lake is enjoyable, and, for as far as the Saturday Night Lake junction, the trail is rideable. Beyond this junction, however, its true character shows. The trail becomes a mixture of sloppy, muddy stretches mixed with bad root erosion. I rode little of the stretch at the western end of this loop. Once the trail passes the junction to Minnow Lake, it becomes easily rideable again.

General location: The trail is located west of Jasper in Jasper National Park.

Elevation change: From the trailhead at 1,054 m (3,458 ft.), in Jasper, it climbs to 1,585 m (5,200 ft.) as it rounds the western extent of the loop.

Season: Ride this trail in dry weather only, from early June to late September.

Services: All services are available in Jasper.

Hazards: This trail is laced with obstacles. Some stretches traverse narrow sidecuts, while at other times the trail drops into mud bogs. The roots are often eroded, making for bumpy, technical riding.

I met numerous cyclists who had turned around when they found out how unpleasant the far end of this loop can be. It is a ride best left to expert riders who have done the more spectacular trails in the area.

Rescue index: This trail sees plenty of action toward either end. As you head farther out, many bikers turn back, meaning that you see less traffic toward the outer end of the loop. With the trail beginning and ending in Jasper, you'll find help easily at the trailhead.

RIDE 66 · Saturday Night Loop

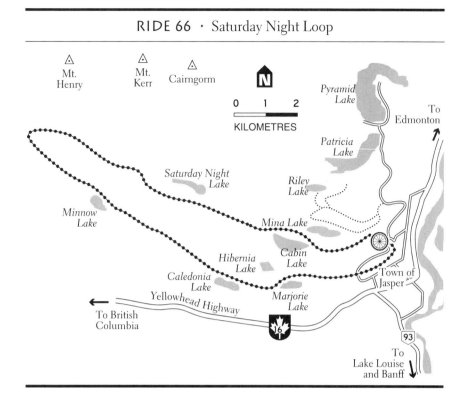

Land status: Jasper National Park, Parks Canada.

Maps: The 1:50,000 scale topographic map for this trail is 83 D/16 Jasper. However, Gem Trek has produced a superior trail map entitled "Jasper Up-Close." As a third option, Parks Canada has produced a large-scale topographic map of Jasper. Some simple trail maps put out by the park are of poor quality for visualizing actual features.

Finding the trail: The trailhead is in the town of Jasper. It is on Pyramid Lake Road in the parking lot across from the Aquatic Centre. Immediately from the trailhead, take the left fork and follow the route as it traverses the slope and climbs above Jasper.

Sources of additional information: Information for Jasper National Park is listed in the introduction to this section.

Notes on the trail: From the start, this trail is confusing. At the trailhead, you'll find two signs; go left. At km 0.37 (mi. 0.22), take the right fork and begin climbing above the town site. As the trail traverses the slope, it gets tricky at points. You'll reach the top of the side-cut at km 0.85 (mi. 0.51). At a junction at km 0.98 (mi. 0.6) go right. A lower trail joins at km 1.19 (mi. 0.7), and quickly the quality of the trail improves and the trail widens. Go right at the junction at km 1.25 (mi. 0.75). When you intersect a fire road at km 1.4 (mi. 0.84), go left.

At km 1.85 (mi. 1.1) stay to the right of a marshy lake. You'll arrive at Cabin Lake at km 3.24 (mi. 1.95). Avoid the temptation to follow the road to the other side of the lake. The trail stays on the right-hand side, picking up at the far end of the parking lot. From this point, follow the signs indicating trail "3." Shortly after the parking lot, the trail traverses some side-cuts that may require pushing. As you leave the end of the lake, the trail becomes good single-track. Trail quality varies over the next stretch, shifting between good single-track and wet, rocky, and rooty. Stay right at a junction sign at km 5.84 (mi. 3.5).

You'll pass a small, marshy pond at km 6.05 (mi. 3.6), and the trail deteriorates into a rocky, rooty, uphill push. At km 7.93 (mi. 4.75), you'll pass a loose rock slope at elevation 1,328 m (4,360 ft.). Stay straight at the Saturday Night Lake junction at km 8.2 (mi. 4.92) and prepare for the condition of the trail to deteriorate severely. Over the next several kilometres, you'll cross numerous bridges. At km 13.55 (mi. 8.1) the bridge crosses beneath a waterfall, turns right sharply, and drops on a steep, rocky hill. Turn right and cross the bridge at a junction at km 14.2 (mi. 8.5). The trail now begins to drop in elevation, varying in quality between rideable and sloppy. The drop is steady until you reach Caledonia Lake at km 21.93 (mi. 13.2). After the ordeal of this trail, it's hard to appreciate the image of The Whistlers reflected in Caledonia Lake, but do take the time. At the signed junction at km 23.3 (mi. 14.0), go left toward Marjorie Lake. Stay right at the Hibernia Lake junction at km 24.7 (mi. 14.8), and go straight at the campground junction at km 25.0 (mi. 15.0). Go straight at another junction at km 26.0 (mi. 15.6), and turn right at a major junction at km 27.2 (mi. 16.3). The trail comes out behind several townhouses along Cabin Creek Drive. Turn left on the road and follow it to the trailhead at km 28.9 (mi. 17.3).

RIDE 67 · Signal Mountain Fire Lookout

AT A GLANCE

Length/configuration: 19.82-km (11.9-mi.) out-and-back.

Aerobic difficulty: Difficult, with a vertical rise of 963 m (3,159 ft.).

AB

Technical difficulty: The gradient is the principal challenge, along with some deep gouges in the trail that may eject riders who descend too rapidly.

Scenery: Dominant views are of The Whistlers to the southwest and Pyramid Mountain (part of the Victoria Cross Range) to the west.

Special comments: This steep climb offers the very best fat-tire panorama of the Jasper town site area.

Signal Mountain Fire Road is perfect for riders of all abilities—as long as their lungs are made of steel. The climb is unrelenting, but the rewards make it all worthwhile. The trail climbs 963 m (3,159 ft.) to the site of an old fire lookout on the lower slopes of Signal Mountain.

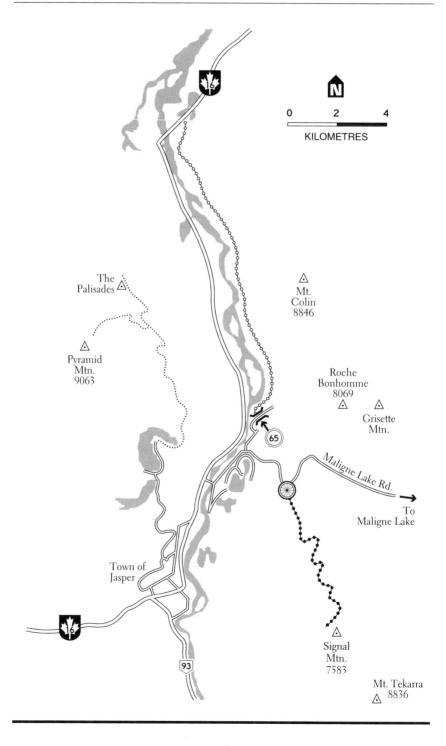

N

0   2   4
KILOMETRES

The
Palisades

Mt.
Colin
8846

Pyramid
Mtn.
9063

Roche
Bonhomme
8069

Grisette
Mtn.

65

Maligne Lake Rd.

To
Maligne Lake

Town of
Jasper

Signal
Mtn.
7583

Mt. Tekarra
8836

93

The quality of the trail is excellent for the entire out-and-back distance of 19.82 km (11.9 mi.). It follows a wide fire road all the way to the top. Just before the summit, the whistling calls of the hoary marmot will tempt you to look for these large rodents. When I rode to the summit, a family of marmots sat patiently beside the trail while I photographed them from only a few feet away.

From the lookout, the views open in all directions. Beneath you sits the town of Jasper and a seemingly endless number of small, sparkling, emerald-green lakes. Beyond Jasper, the peaks of the Victoria Cross Range are visible; each mountain is named for a recipient of the empire's highest award for valor. To the southwest, Whistlers Mountain dominates, with its tramline constantly moving up and down the mountain face. To the south, Mount Edith Cavell's snow-covered summit holds the skyline.

General location: The trail is east of Jasper, Alberta, within Jasper National Park.

Elevation change: The trail climbs relentlessly from the trailhead at 1,182 m (3,880 ft.) to the summit at 2,145 m (7,040 ft.). The total climb is 963 m (3,159 ft.).

Season: You must wait for the snow to melt off the summit before riding. The trail is at its best from early July to mid-September.

Services: All services are available in Jasper.

Hazards: Riding this trail includes few hazards apart from the dangers associated with picking up too much speed on the descent. Watch the trail carefully; a few drainage channels cut across it and offer the opportunity to launch yourself off your bike. This is also a popular hiking route, so be courteous of backpackers trundling up and down the fire road.

Rescue index: Signal Mountain fire road follows the beginning of one of Jasper's busiest hiking trails—the Skyline Trail. Its busy nature means it's always easy to find help. The trailhead is along a busy sightseeing route and is only a few hundred metres from Maligne Canyon. A busy store is located here.

Land status: Jasper National Park, Parks Canada.

Maps: The 1:50,000 scale topographic maps for this trail are 83 C/13 Medicine Lake and 83 D/16 Jasper. However, Gem Trek has produced a superior trail map entitled "Jasper Up-Close." As a third option, Parks Canada has produced a large-scale topographic map of Jasper. Some simple trail maps put out by the park are poor for visualizing actual features.

Finding the trail: From Jasper, head west on Highway 16 to the junction with the Maligne Lake Road. After crossing the Athabasca River, continue 5.8 km (3.6 mi.) and watch for a sign indicating a hiking trailhead on the right-hand side of the road. Park here and follow the good fire road that leads up from the staging area.

Sources of additional information: Information for contacting Jasper National Park is listed in the introduction to this section.

Notes on the trail: From the trailhead along Maligne Lake Road, follow the wide fire road as it slowly climbs the lower slopes of Signal Mountain. As it is no longer used by vehicles, the trail varies between wide road and single-track. By km 3.0 (mi. 1.8) the trail has climbed 241 m (709 ft.) to an elevation of 1,426 m

(4,680 ft.). The climbing continues: at km 4.0 (mi. 2.4), the elevation is 1,530 m (5,020 ft.), and at km 5.0 (mi. 3.0) it's 1,615 m (5,300 ft.). The views begin to open up behind you, with a pleasing view of Pyramid Mountain. A 100-m flat stretch at km 6.13 (mi. 3.7) is all you get, so savour it. By km 8.52 (mi. 5.1) you'll begin to pull out of the trees, and the trail becomes rougher, with loose rocks. The campground is at km 8.84 (mi. 5.3), but stay on the road. Shortly after the campground, at km 8.94 (mi. 5.4), the Skyline Trail branches off to the left. Stay straight at this junction, and the road continues to climb to the summit at 2,145 m (7,040 ft.). The last stretch is loose rock, but take your time and admire the extensive views. The ride down is a scream, but be wary of a culvert that has been partially washed out, leaving a deep gouge in the trail at km 14.04 (mi. 8.42). The trailhead is at km 19.82 (mi. 11.9).

RIDE 68 · Palisades Lookout

AT A GLANCE

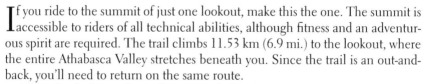

Length/configuration: 23.06-km (13.84-mi.) out-and-back.

Aerobic difficulty: Steep climb of 854 m (2,801 ft.) over 11.53 km (6.9 mi.).

Technical difficulty: Formerly a fire road, the trail is wide with some loose rocks and overgrown foliage.

Scenery: From the former lookout, the entire valley of the Athabasca River spreads out at your feet.

Special comments: The climb is steep, but the view from the summit makes it all worthwhile.

If you ride to the summit of just one lookout, make this the one. The summit is accessible to riders of all technical abilities, although fitness and an adventurous spirit are required. The trail climbs 11.53 km (6.9 mi.) to the lookout, where the entire Athabasca Valley stretches beneath you. Since the trail is an out-and-back, you'll need to return on the same route.

From the lookout, the Colin Range holds the eastern skyline, with Roche Bonhomme, locally known as the "Old Man of the Mountain," resembling a face that looks toward the sky. With its cable car providing access for maintenance of the telecommunications tower at its summit, Pyramid Mountain blocks the western horizon. The town of Jasper and Whistlers Mountain stand out clearly to the south, and Jasper Lake is visible to the north. Few views in Jasper can compete with the awesome spectacle visible from this point.

General location: The trail is north of Jasper at the end of Pyramid Lake Road.

Elevation change: This trail climbs steadily from the trailhead at 1,182 m (3,880 ft.) to the old lookout site at 2,036 m (6,680 ft.).

RIDE 68 · Palisades Lookout

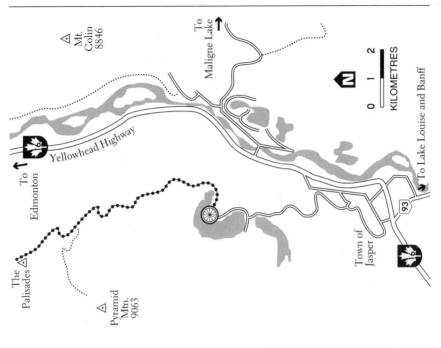

Season: This road ride opens up fairly early in the season, around mid-May, and remains rideable until early October.

Services: All services are available in Jasper.

Hazards: This trail follows a reclaimed fire road; as a result, the condition of the trail varies dramatically. At one point it is wide and clear, while a few minutes later the alders close in to limit visibility.

Some loose rocks are scattered along the road. These can be especially challenging on the descent, where the urge to go fast is almost undeniable on a steep trail like this one. Also, keep in mind that the lower part of the trail, before you head off the main fire road toward the lookout, is still used by staff driving the road to maintain the telecommunications tower on Pyramid Mountain. They don't expect to see a rider screaming downhill in the middle of the road.

Rescue index: Since this trail begins at a busy day-use area, you can generally find help at this point. It is also used by service vehicles, so you may encounter an occasional truck on the trail. Once you fork off the main trail and climb toward the summit, you're on your own. The trail is not heavily traveled, and you may not encounter any hikers. The lookout is no longer present, so no one staffs the summit.

On top of the world. The author takes in the scenery on the top of Palisades Lookout.

Land status: Jasper National Park, Parks Canada.

Maps: The 1:50,000 scale topographic map for this trail is 83 D/16 Jasper. How-ever, Gem Trek has produced a superior trail map (although at larger scale) enti-tled "Jasper and Maligne Lake." As a third option, Parks Canada has produced a large-scale topographic map of Jasper. Some simple trail maps put out by the park are poor for visualizing actual features.

Finding the trail: From Jasper, follow Pyramid Lake Road to its terminus at the far end of its namesake. From there, a gated road continues beyond the parking lot. This is the trail.

Sources of additional information: Information for contacting Jasper National Park is listed in the introduction to this section.

Notes on the trail: From the gate at the end of Pyramid Lake Road, follow the road around the east end of the lake until km 1.9 (mi. 1.14), where the climbing begins. At km 2.9 (mi. 1.74) you'll get a short break as the trail levels out for a short distance at an elevation of 1,316 m (4,320 ft.). At km 3.4 (mi. 2.04), you'll pass a small, marshy pond on your left, followed by a fast downhill to km 4.2 (mi. 2.5). The real climbing begins at km 5.0 (mi. 3.0) and remains unrelenting. Cross a bridge at km 5.9 (mi. 3.6) and, shortly thereafter, enjoy your first views as the valley toward Roche Bonhomme opens up. At this point, the elevation is 1,438 m (4,720 ft.).

At km 8.0 (mi. 4.8), turn right at the gated junction. You'll have achieved an elevation of 1,615 m (5,300 ft.), and the wide road becomes a rough wide-track. Before long, the trail begins to close in as the forest slowly reclaims the track, and you'll ride through some alder thickets. It's rideable all the way, but visibility is limited. It opens up again soon. You'll finally reach the summit at km 11.53 (mi. 6.9) and an elevation of 2,036 m (6,680 ft.).

The ride down is fast and smooth, reaching the trailhead at km 23.0 (mi. 13.8).

RIDE 69 · Celestine Lake Road

AT A GLANCE

Length/configuration: 29.2-km (17.52-mi.) out-and-back, but riders can vary this distance simply by choosing different turnaround points.

Aerobic difficulty: Moderate difficulty, with gradual gains in elevation.

Technical difficulty: Easy, along a wide, gravel road.

Scenery: Panoramas of Jasper Lake and the peaks of the Jacques and Miette Ranges.

Special comments: A perfect early season ride.

The mountains have a funny effect on people—by March we're itching to get our mountain bikes out, and by September we're waxing our skis. We always want to push the season ahead. Well, for mountain bikers, this is the place to do it. This good gravel road crosses a south-facing slope, so it gets most of the day's sunlight, melting the snow by mid- to late April. You can adjust the length of the ride, but the main stretch of road is 14.6 km (8.76 mi.) one-way. It's great for all riders and provides the option of continuing on to Snake Indian Falls at the terminus.

From this road, which traverses the lower slopes of Mount Greenock, the ride follows a narrow road that cuts into the side of this mountain. Appropriately named, this mountain's moniker originates from the Gaelic term *greennoch*, meaning "the sunny knoll." From the roadside, views are impressive. Below, the pristine waters of Jasper Lake tempt you as you drink warm water from your bottle. Across the valley, the slopes of the Jacques and Colin Ranges dominate the skyline.

General location: This trail lies north of Jasper, along Highway 16.

Elevation change: The road climbs from 1,038 m (3,405 ft.) at the trailhead to a high point of 1,247 m (4,091 ft.).

Season: This is one of the earliest rides available in Jasper. Most years, it clears of snow by mid-April and stays snow-free until early October.

Services: All services are available in Jasper.

Hazards: While riding this narrow road, be cautious of traffic winding around blind corners—especially since you may be riding in the opposite direction from that designated by the access control schedule. Also, the quality of the road is good, but the gravel is loose, so watch yourself if you're riding close to the edge; it's easy to slip.

RIDE 69 · Celestine Lake Road

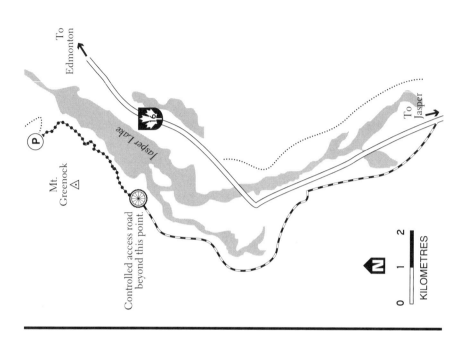

Rescue index: This trail follows a road open to vehicle traffic, and vehicles usually travel along its dusty gravel. In addition, a warden's station lies just south of the point at which access to the road is controlled.

Land status: Jasper National Park, Parks Canada.

Maps: The 1:50,000 scale topographic map for this trail is 83 W/1 Snaring River. Gem Trek's "Jasper and Maligne Lake" also covers this trail. As a third option, Parks Canada has produced a large-scale topographic map of Jasper. Some simple trail maps put out by the park are poor for visualizing actual features.

Finding the trail: From Jasper, head east along Highway 16 to the signed junction for Snaring River Campground. As you travel this gravel road, you'll pass the campground. After 14.8 km (9.2 mi.), you'll reach a point at which access to the road is controlled. Begin riding at this point.

Sources of additional information: Information for contacting Jasper National Park is listed in the introduction to this section.

Notes on the trail: From the access control point, mount your bike and follow this wide gravel road. Cross a bridge over Vine Creek at km 1.5 (mi. 0.9). Shortly after this bridge, the road begins to traverse the lower slopes of Mount Greenock. Throughout the next 4.0 km (2.46 mi.), the trail curls along a narrow road carved

Celestine Lake Road is a summer access road that takes the rider high above the surrounding valleys and provides some exquisite views of Jasper Lake.

into the side of the mountain. After this traverse, the trail drops sharply to km 8.5 (mi. 5.1). You'll pass a gated fire road at km 10.5 (mi. 6.3), and the main road ends at km 14.6 (mi. 8.76). To continue beyond this point, see the description for Ride 70, Snake Indian Falls.

RIDE 70 · Snake Indian Falls

AT A GLANCE

Length/configuration: 50-km (30-mi.) out-and-back.

Aerobic difficulty: Moderate.

Technical difficulty: Easy, along a wide fire road.

Scenery: Snake Indian Falls tumbles over a 120-m (394-ft.) limestone lip.

Special comments: The falls is very easy to miss, so pay close attention to the trail description.

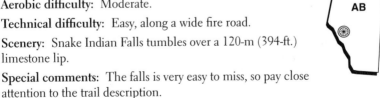

This 50-km (30-mi.) out-and-back is an excellent trek for both beginners and experts. It follows the beginning of the North Boundary Hiking Trail, a 151.5-km (94-mi.) hiking trail that follows the northern boundary of Jasper National Park. Snake Indian Falls is one of the scenic highlights of this route.

The road is wide for its entire length. It trends uphill for the first half, cresting at an elevation of 1,524 m (5,000 ft.) before dropping to Shalebanks Campground. Beyond the campground, an easy ford is necessary before the trail continues on to the falls.

Snake Indian Falls is easy to miss. An insignificant sign hides the impressive nature of it. I rode right by it the first time. The falls is off the road, requiring a five-minute hike down a rough trail, where the roar of the water beckons you to continue. The falls tumble over a resistant layer of limestone, dropping 120 m (394 ft.) to the Snake Indian River.

General location: This trail is north of Jasper, beyond the end of Celestine Lake Road.

Elevation change: The trail begins at 1,243 m (4,080 ft.) and climbs to crest at 1,524 m (5,000 ft.), before dropping toward the falls.

Season: Much of this trail is open and sunny, but you must still wait until early June to ride. It stays open until mid-October.

Services: All services are available in Jasper.

Hazards: Although the trail follows good fire road, some of the downhills have drainage channels cut across them. These could cause some handlebar launches if the rider picks up too much speed. The ford at Shalebanks Campground will be fast and cold in early spring. Later in the season the water level drops low enough that you can cross with a few rock-to-rock jumps. Be sure to explore around the falls, but be aware that the cliff is sheer and slippery. No railings mean that you must be extra cautious.

Rescue index: This wilderness trail attracts long-distance hikers and a fair number of mountain bikers. You'll pass Shalebanks Campground at km 18.27 (mi. 10.95), where you can often find helpful campers. Just beyond the falls, another campground may offer help.

Land status: Jasper National Park, Parks Canada.

Maps: The 1:50,000 scale topographic maps for this trail are 83 E/01 Snaring River and 83 E/08 Rock Lake. The final section of trail is not indicated on Gem Trek's "Jasper and Maligne Lake" map. In addition, Parks Canada has produced a large-scale topographic map of Jasper. Some simple trail maps put out by the park are poor for visualizing actual features.

Finding the trail: From Jasper, head east along Highway 16 to the signed junction for Snaring River Campground. Follow this gravel road 29.4 km (18.23 mi.) to the trailhead. The road is access-controlled at km 14.8 (mi. 9.2). From this point on, the road is restricted to one-way traffic; the allowed direction for traffic is changed according to a schedule. You can check with the information centre in Jasper to find out the schedule before heading to the trail. Some books indicate that the trailhead is at the Celestine Lake parking lot; however, the road is closed 5.28 km (3.2 mi.) before this point. Begin riding at the gated parking lot.

Sources of additional information: Information for contacting Jasper National Park is listed in the introduction to this section.

RIDE 70 · Snake Indian Falls

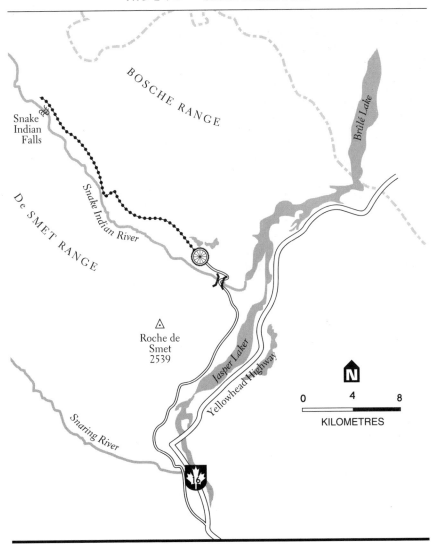

Notes on the trail: Starting at the trailhead, at an elevation of 1,243 m (4,080 ft.), follow the good gravel road downhill to a bridged crossing at km 0.5 (mi. 0.3). The trail begins climbing after the bridge, and, at km 1.2 (mi. 0.72) the views begin to open to the southwest. The climbing levels out temporarily at km 2.78 (mi. 1.7), where the trail enters an aspen forest. The views open up again at km 3.8 (mi. 2.3). You'll reach the Celestine Lake parking lot at km 5.28 (mi. 3.2). Other books list this as the trailhead; however, this stretch of road is no longer open.

At km 8.19 (mi. 4.9) the trail climbs gently to 1,524 m (5,000 ft.) and then takes on a rolling character. At km 16.5 (mi. 9.9) the views open up as you descend a

Snake Indian Falls is easy to miss, but once found, it's spectacular.

rocky section. Be cautious of a washout on the descent. At km 18.27 (mi. 10.95), you'll pass Shalebanks Campground. This site is followed by a river ford. In August I was able to move from rock to rock and stay dry. Earlier in the season it will be a knee-deep crossing. Shortly after the crossing, the trail passes a wooden gate left open to visitors, and the road follows the Snake Indian River. A steady descent at km 21.3 (mi. 12.78) has six different drainage channels cut across it. Be cautious, as they could easily catapult an unwary rider into the stratosphere.

The falls are easy to miss. The sign is a small brown marker at the bottom of a depression in the road. It's at km 25.0 (mi. 15.0). If you reach the Seldom Inn Campground, you've gone 1.5 km (0.9 mi.) too far. From the marker, the falls are a 100-m walk down a narrow trail to the viewing point.

YOHO NATIONAL PARK

Yoho National Park lies to the west of its much more famous neighbour, Banff National Park. Located in British Columbia, and bordering the Continental Divide, it is equally as spectacular as Banff and Jasper National Parks, yet it is much less well known. With the Trans Canada Highway (Highway 1) cutting it in half, its trails and roads radiate out of this main artery.

The beauty of the park is reflected in its name, a Cree Indian term that loosely translates as "wow!" Nestled within this 1,310-square-kilometre (507-square-mile) park, the town of Field acts as the primary service centre. While the town site is very small, it does offer basic amenities, including a few restaurants. Its residents are primarily employed by the railroad and the park service.

Heading west from Banff, the Trans Canada Highway enters British Columbia and Yoho National Park at the summit of the Kicking Horse Pass. This sharp summit formed one of the major obstacles to the building of the Canadian Pacific Railway (CPR). When surveyors descended the Kicking Horse Pass, they traveled on a 38-cm (15-in.) ledge, carved into the cliff 243 m (800 ft.) above the foaming waters of the Kicking Horse River. Many of these surveyors were so terrified that they would close their eyes, holding onto their horses tails for guidance. Into this vertical landscape a railway was to be built. When completed, the gradient of the tracks as they dropped from the pass toward the valley floor was an astounding 4.5%. Simply stated, with a five-car train, the front car would be 5 m (15 ft.) lower than the caboose. This death drop derailed many trains and killed numerous railroaders over the years. Finally, in 1909, the challenge of the Big Hill, as this drop became known, was solved with the opening of the Spiral Tunnels. These two tunnels, totaling approximately 1883 m (6,176 ft.), cross over themselves and essentially double the length of track required to drop down the pass. This in turn, reduces the gradient to an acceptable 2.2%. Today, one can watch some of our lengthy trains coming and going simultaneously. As the tail end continues to enter the upper portal, the front end emerges beneath itself, having made a complete loop prior to emerging.

With the hammering of the last spike of the Canadian Pacific Railway in 1885, the CPR turned its attention to ridership. The steep grades in the mountains made it difficult to pull the heavy dining cars, so the railroad began to build hotels along the main line. The first of these hotels was built near the present town of Field. Mount Stephen House began as a dining hall adjacent to the Field train station. It was quickly expanded to include overnight accommodations and was followed by hotels at Roger's Pass and Banff. While Mount

Stephen House no longer survives, the Banff Springs Hotel has become the flagship of the Canadian Pacific Hotel chain. The beauty of the mountain landscape surrounding Mount Stephen House led the government to establish Mount Stephen Reserve on October 10, 1886, one year after the establishment of Canada's first national park at Banff. In 1901, the park boundaries were expanded and the park was renamed Yoho National Park.

Highlights of the park include Emerald Lake and the world-famous Burgess Shales. Discovered in 1909, this fossil bed has provided some of the most important fossils of the middle Cambrian period (approximately 515-n-525 million years ago). Unique conditions resulted in unusually high levels of preservation of both hard- and soft-bodied animals. Generally, fossils only record the hard parts of animals, leaving paleontologists to guess about soft tissues.

The Yoho Valley winds north from the Trans Canada Highway toward Yoho Glacier and Takakkaw Falls. The falls were named by William Cornilius Van Horne, president of the CPR, after a Cree word meaning "it is magnificent." The waterfall thunders 380 m (1,249 ft.) down the mountain as runoff from the Daly Glacier feeds it during the summer months.

Mountain bikers have been severely limited in their access to trails within Yoho National Park. The trails are old fire roads, now closed to vehicles. The grades are wide and smooth, with periodic views of the surrounding peaks. Their present status is somewhat tenuous as rumours of increased closures abound. Be sure to check with the information centre in Field for current status on the trail network.

For more information, contact:

Yoho National Park Visitor Centre
P.O. Box 99
Field, British Columbia
V0A-1G0
(250) 343-6783; (250) 343-6012 (fax)
yoho_info@pch.gc.ca

RIDE 71 · Ottertail Road

AT A GLANCE

Length/configuration: 30.2-km (18.12-mi.) out-and-back.

Aerobic difficulty: Moderate, with a gradual climb of 320 m (1,050 ft.).

Technical difficulty: Generally easy, but numerous downed trees may lie across the trail.

Scenery: Periodic views of the Ottertail Range to the south and Mount Owen to the north. Near the terminus, the towering peak of Mount Goodsir rolls into view.

BC

Special comments: Keep your eyes open for delicate calypso orchids and the bird's-eye primrose during May and early June.

This wilderness trail follows the Ottertail River 15.1 km (9.06 mi.) from the Trans Canada Highway to its junction with McArthur Creek. At this point, you must retrace your steps to the trailhead for a total distance of 30.2 km (18.12 mi.). On your right, the craggy peaks of the Ottertail Range—and farther along, Fulmen Mountain—dominate the open views. To the left, Mount Owen's horn-like summit stands defiantly above the valley. The trail follows an excellent fire road and offers a wide, smooth track. The terminus at the McArthur Creek junction leaves you in a wonderful location for some extended exploring on foot. Views of Goodsir Mountain and a pristine alpine location make this a place worth revisiting.

General location: Yoho National Park, west of Field, British Columbia.

Elevation change: The trail climbs gradually from the trailhead at approximately 1,160 m (3,805 ft.) to a maximum elevation of 1,480 m (4,854 ft.).

Season: This ride is open by late May and should stay clear until late September.

Services: Maps and groceries are available in the town of Field. Lake Louise, approximately 30 km (about 18 mi.) east, has a small outdoor store where limited bike supplies are available.

Hazards: In early season, this trail is notorious for downed trees. When I rode it in mid-May, I had to negotiate 173 trees that blocked the trail—in both directions. Depending on the park, trail crews may or may not have cleared most of the trees. Also, a large avalanche slope at the 9.9-km (5.94-mi.) mark can offer an early season obstacle. It is usually passable, but it can be a slippery process. It is best to wait until late May or early June. Make sure to check with the information centre in Field as to trail conditions. The trail also passes through excellent grizzly habitat, so keep your eyes open.

Rescue index: This trail is not heavily traveled, but you're never more than 12 km (7.2 mi.) or so from the Trans Canada Highway. Assistance is always available on the road. The town of Field is 8.2 km (5.0 mi.)to the east, and emergency services can be contacted at the Information Centre. If the centre is closed, phone (604) 343-6324 to contact a park warden. For RCMP emergency, dial 0 and ask for "Zenith 50,000."

Land status: Yoho National Park, Parks Canada.

Maps: The 1:50,000 scale topographic maps for this trail are 82 N/7 Golden and 82 N/8 Lake Louise. Gem Trek produces a superior map, also at 1:50,000 scale, entitled "Lake Louise and Yoho."

Finding the trail: Drive west from the town of Field 8.2 km (5.0 mi.) to a parking lot immediately beyond the bridge that crosses the Ottertail River. The wide fire road leaves from this parking lot.

Sources of additional information: You can contact Yoho National Park by calling (250) 343-6783.

RIDE 71 · Ottertail Road

Notes on the trail: From the trailhead, at elevation 1,146 m (3,760 ft.) a single-track leads up the valley, quickly widening to a smooth double-track. The largely lodgepole pine forest is rimmed with an understorey of buffaloberry, a favourite of grizzlies in late summer and fall. The trail climbs above the valley, providing unobstructed views of the Ottertail Range and Mount Hurd with its prevalent avalanche slopes. Over the course of the first 2.0 km (1.2 mi.), the trail climbs 65 m (220 ft.). The first great view comes at km 2.8 (1.7 mi.) when the trail crosses a steep cut-bank above the Ottertail River and offers a clear view of the Ottertail Range to the south. Beneath you, the glacial deposits along the cut-bank have

Susan Cameron enjoys a view of the Ottertail Range while rolling along the Ottertail Road.

been eroded into rocky columns known as hoodoos. The trail begins to drop from a high point of 1,420 m (4,660 ft.) at km 6.0 (3.5 mi.) down to cross Float Creek as it enters the Ottertail River. Hikers exploring the route toward Goodsir Pass beyond the terminus of the mountain bike route may use a campsite located here.

The trail climbs the lower slopes of Mount Duchesnay after crossing Float Creek and switches back several times at the 7-km (4.2-mi.) mark. Shortly after crossing a steep side-cut at km 9.4 (5.6 mi.), the trail intersects a major winter avalanche path. The snow thunders down from the slopes of Mount Owen high above, and it may leave a hefty deposit at this point. Early in the season, you may have to scale a 5-m (15-ft.) pile of dirty snow in order to continue along the trail on the opposite side. The forest closes off the views during the next stretch until km 14.5 (8.7 mi.), where views open to the south and west. Just before crossing a bridge over McArthur Creek, a signed junction to the left indicates the trail toward McArthur Pass (15.1 km/9 mi.). The trails are closed to bikes beyond this junction, so you must return along the same route. Make sure to wander a short way farther along the trail to enjoy a wonderful panorama before heading back.

RIDE 72 · Kicking Horse Fire Road

AT A GLANCE

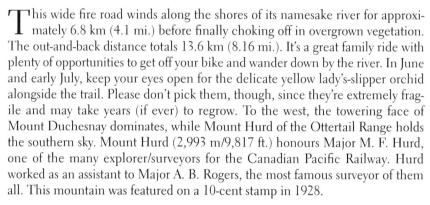

Length/configuration: 13.6-km (8.16-mi.) out-and-back.

Aerobic difficulty: Very easy.

Technical difficulty: The trail begins on a wide fire road, but as you pass the 5.0-km (3.0-mi.) mark, it begins to deteriorate, with the trail closing in on the ride.

Scenery: Clear views toward Mount Duchesnay to the west and Mount Hurd of the Ottertail Range to the south.

Special comments: This trail can be linked with the climb toward the Otterhead Fire Road to extend the riding.

This wide fire road winds along the shores of its namesake river for approximately 6.8 km (4.1 mi.) before finally choking off in overgrown vegetation. The out-and-back distance totals 13.6 km (8.16 mi.). It's a great family ride with plenty of opportunities to get off your bike and wander down by the river. In June and early July, keep your eyes open for the delicate yellow lady's-slipper orchid alongside the trail. Please don't pick them, though, since they're extremely fragile and may take years (if ever) to regrow. To the west, the towering face of Mount Duchesnay dominates, while Mount Hurd of the Ottertail Range holds the southern sky. Mount Hurd (2,993 m/9,817 ft.) honours Major M. F. Hurd, one of the many explorer/surveyors for the Canadian Pacific Railway. Hurd worked as an assistant to Major A. B. Rogers, the most famous surveyor of them all. This mountain was featured on a 10-cent stamp in 1928.

General location: Yoho National Park, just off the Emerald Lake Road.

Elevation change: Negligible.

Season: This is a good early season ride since it gets good exposure to the sun and quickly clears of snow. It should be rideable by mid-May, but check with the Information Centre in Field to be sure.

Services: Groceries and trail information are available in the town of Field. Lake Louise, approximately 30 km (18 mi.) distant, provides a few more options, but for bike repairs you'll need to travel to either Banff to the east or Golden to the west.

Hazards: This trail follows a wide, smooth fire road. Shortly after crossing the Otterhead River, a sagging culvert provides potential for a wipeout if you hit it going too fast. Also, as the trail closes in, the willows have a tendency to grab your handlebars.

Rescue index: The trailhead picnic area often has people relaxing by the river, and help may be available here. If the area is quiet, continue to the Natural

RIDE 72 · Kicking Horse Fire Road
RIDE 73 · Otterhead Fire Road

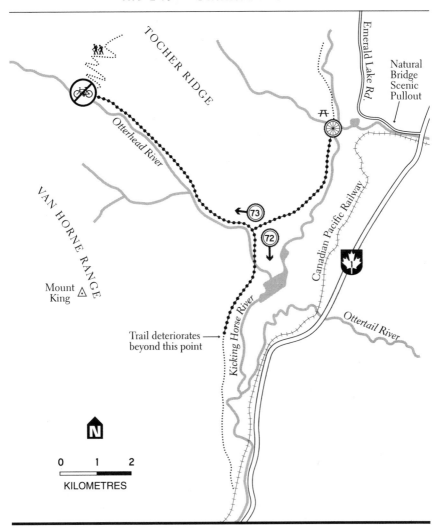

Bridge Day Use Area. Here, you will have either options for assistance or a chance to flag down a vehicle along the road to Emerald Lake. Park wardens are available at (604) 343-6324. To contact the RCMP, dial 0 and ask the operator for "Zenith 50,000." No cellular signal will be available.

Land status: Yoho National Park, Parks Canada.

Maps: The 1:50,000 series topographic map for this trail is 82 N/7 Golden. Map Town produces a superior map (also 1:50,000 scale) called "Lake Louise and Yoho" that offers more up-to-date trail information.

Finding the trail: The trail is accessed via Emerald Lake Road, 2.5 km (1.5 mi.) west of the town of Field. At the signed pulloff for the Natural Bridge, follow the gravel road that branches from the viewing point parking lot for 1.8 km (1.1 mi.) to its terminus at the trailhead. From the trailhead, a wide fire road offers an obvious attraction; however, this is the Amiskwi River Trail. The Kicking Horse Fire Road begins as a narrow single-track heading into the woods to the left of the trailhead.

Sources of additional information: You can contact Yoho National Park by calling (250) 343-6783.

Notes on the trail: Despite the subtle character of the trailhead, the fire road quickly widens to become double-track. The trail drops slightly through the woods until km 1.9 (1.14 mi.) when the views open up slightly. The Kicking Horse River is to your left, and the impressive slopes of the Ottertail Range rise above it. The end of Tocher Ridge is to your right. Soon the lodgepole pine forest gives way to an old-growth forest of spruce riddled with deadfall. The trail crosses a small creek at km 3.3 (mi. 2) and at elevation 1,158 m (3,800 ft.). The signed junction with the Otterhead Fire road is reached at km 4.2 (mi. 2.5). Turn left toward the now-distant sound of the Kicking Horse River.

The trail joins the Otterhead River and crosses it on a good-quality bridge at km 5.0 (3 mi.). After the bridge, the trail rapidly narrows and closes off as the forest begins to reclaim this old fire access route. An old culvert a short distance beyond the bridge has begun to sag, creating a potentially fast dismount if you hit it with too much speed. The views begin to open up to the left after this point, but the trail also begins to rapidly close in on you. The willows may grab your handlebars as you try to push your way through. The Ottertail Range, Mount Duchesnay, and Mount Owen dominate the eastern skyline as you look toward the Ottertail River Valley. After a rocky outcrop, the trail rapidly deteriorates until km 6.8 (4.1 mi.) where the river has cut a gouge across the trail. This is a good point to turn around. Return on the same trail, reaching your vehicle at km 13.6 (8.16 mi.).

RIDE 73 · Otterhead Fire Road

AT A GLANCE

Length/configuration: 21.6-km (12.96-mi.) out-and-back.

Aerobic difficulty: The trail climbs steadily, but gradually, for 275 m (902 ft.); it's just under 11 km (6.6 mi.).

Technical difficulty: Wide and smooth throughout its length.

BC

Scenery: Some great views are available toward Tocher Ridge, up and to the right, as well as Mounts King and Deville of the Van Horne Range to the left.

Special comments: Watch for yellow lady's-slippers in late June and early July.

The best reason to take this 21.6-km (12.96-mi.) out-and-back is for the quick access it provides to the 7.0-km (4.2-mi.) hiking trail to Tocher Ridge Lookout. From the summit, the views stretch in all directions: to the north, the glacier-capped peaks of the Presidents Range; to the south, the intricately carved peaks of the Van Horne Range. The ride itself is more limiting. Beginning along the wide gravel of the Kicking Hose Fire Road, you'll see some views of the Ottertail Range across the valley. Once you leave the wide channel of the Kicking Horse behind, you head northwest and follow the winding Otterhead River.

This wide fire road has periodic views as you climb of the glaciated slopes of Mounts Deville and King of the Van Horne Range. Farther along, you get a view of Tocher Ridge, high and to the right. On the return trip your views stretch to the opposite side of the valley and the towering slopes of Mount Duchesnay.

General location: Yoho National Park, British Columbia.

Elevation change: From the trailhead at 1,225 m (4,018 ft.), the trail climbs gradually to the Tocher Ridge junction at approximately 1,500 m (4,920 ft.).

Season: Save this trail for late May when the snow will be off its higher portions. This absence of snow also opens up the option of a day hike to the summit of Tocher Ridge.

Services: Groceries and trail information are available in the town of Field. Lake Louise, approximately 30 km (18 mi.) distant, provides a few more options, but for bike repairs you'll need to travel to either Banff to the east or Golden to the west.

Hazards: Most of the trail is wide fire road with few dangers. However, a sudden metre-deep drop in the trail at the 5.2-km (3.12-mi.) mark can easily send an unprepared rider over the handlebars.

Rescue index: The trailhead picnic area often has people relaxing by the river, and help may be obtained here. If the area is quiet, continue to the Natural Bridge Day Use Area. It will have options for assistance, or you can flag down a vehicle along the road to Emerald Lake. Park wardens are available at (604) 343-6324. To contact the RCMP, dial 0 and ask the operator for "Zenith 50,000." No cellular signal will be available.

Land status: Yoho National Park, Parks Canada.

Maps: The 1:50,000 series topographic map for this trail is 82 N/7 Golden. Map Town produces a superior map called "Lake Louise and Yoho" that, while also 1:50,000 scale, offers more up-to-date trail information; however, the western end of the ride is not included on this map. Also, see trail map on page 233.

Finding the trail: The trail is accessed via Emerald Lake Road, 2.5 km (1.5 mi.) west of the town of Field. At the signed pulloff for the Natural Bridge, follow the gravel road that branches from the viewpoint parking lot for 1.8 km (1.1 mi.) to its terminus at the trailhead. From the trailhead, a wide fire road offers an obvious attraction. However, this is the Amiskwi River Trail. The Otterhead Fire Road begins by following the Kicking Horse Fire Road. This route is visible as a narrow single-track heading into the woods to the left of the trailhead.

Sources of additional information: You can contact Yoho National Park by calling (250) 343-6783.

Park your bike at the terminus of the Otterhead Fire Road and hike to the abandoned fire lookout atop Tocher Ridge.

Notes on the trail: Despite the subtle character of the trailhead, the fire road quickly widens to become double-track. The trail drops slightly through the woods until km 1.9 (1.14 mi.) when the views open slightly. The Kicking Horse River is to your left, and the impressive slopes of the Ottertail Range rise above it. The end of Tocher Ridge is to your right. Soon, the lodgepole pine forest gives way to an old-growth forest of spruce riddled with deadfall. The trail crosses a small creek at km 3.3 (mi. 2), at elevation 1,158 m (3,800 ft.). The signed junction with the Otterhead Fire Road is reached at km 4.2 (mi. 2.5). Turn right onto this wide fire road.

The trail climbs gradually as it joins the Otterhead River off to the left. Ride across a small runoff channel and continue climbing as the trail winds away from the river. After the climbing becomes more gradual at km 5.0 (3.0 mi.), a sudden metre-deep gouge in the trail at 5.2 km (3.12 mi.) can easily send an unprepared rider over the handlebars. Soon the river comes back into view as the trail passes a brownish shale bank on the right. The climbing becomes steeper as the trail cuts across the lower slopes of Tocher Ridge. The climbing levels out slightly at km 6.7 (4.02 mi.), and the first views toward Tocher Ridge can be seen. Meet the junction with the Tocher Ridge Lookout Trail at km 10.8 (6.48 mi.). From here, a steep hiking trail climbs above the valley to the summit of Tocher Ridge. After the hike, mount your saddle and ride back to your car at the 21.6-km (12.96-mi.) point.

GOLDEN AREA RIDES

Nestled between the towering Rocky Mountains to the east and the rolling Purcell Mountains, the town of Golden is becoming a popular site for fat-tire enthusiasts. This thriving community has been built on a foundation of forestry and tourism.

Located at the confluence of the Kicking Horse and Columbia Rivers, the area was first visited by David Thompson in 1807. The area remained quiet until railroad crews arrived on the scene in the early 1880s. Major A. B. Rogers chose the site as the location for a camp, and later a railway siding. First known as the Cache, the name was changed to Golden City to compete against another siding near Banff with the name Silver City. In time, the name was shortened to simply Golden. As the railroad crews moved on, a few stayed behind to build homes.

With the completion of the railroad, Swiss guides were imported to escort guests on their forays into the high country. The railroad built the guides a Swiss-style village in Golden, and tourism boomed. The guides spent their summers working out of the Chateau Lake Louise and Glacier House. In all the years that the Swiss guides worked for the Canadian Pacific Railway, they did not have a single climbing fatality.

Along with the tourism imported by the railway, the residents of Golden also benefited from the surrounding forests. Today, the forest industry is still the heart and soul of this thriving community, accounting for 70 percent of the area's income.

South of Golden, the Columbia River flows along the Columbia Valley Wetlands, home to 180 species of birds and some 37 species of mammals. Each year in May, Golden celebrates the abundance of this area with the Golden Mountain Festival of Birds and Bears.

As riding in the Golden area has become more organized, local riders, as well as bike shops like Summit Cycle, have been working to map and sign the many trail systems. Be sure to stop by Summit Cycle at 1007-11th Avenue South or phone them at (250) 344-6600 for more information on local rides.

RIDE 74 · Moose Creek Road

AT A GLANCE

Length/configuration: 17.06-km (10.24-mi.) out-and-back.

Aerobic difficulty: The trail rolls for 4.82 km (2.89 mi.) before beginning a relentless climb. Continuing beyond this point will require strong legs and lungs.

BC

Technical difficulty: The road is wide and smooth for its entire length.

Scenery: The more you climb, the better the views. The glacier-capped peak of Mount Goodsir is the highlight, but this wild valley has some fabulous lush avalanche slopes and great views toward the mountains of the Vermillion Range.

Special comments: This trail is remote and wild. Keep your eyes open for bears that are taking advantage of the regrowth within the clear-cut.

If you want to leave civilization behind, but still stick to wide, smooth trails, then Moose Creek Road is perfect for you. It is a 17.06-km (10.24-mi.) out-and-back, that climbs moderately for 4.82 km (2.89 mi.) and then takes a decidedly uphill trend. You'll discover great views of the peaks of the Vermillion Range, including the granddaddy, Mount Goodsir (3,562 m/11,683 ft.). Dr. James Hector of the Palliser expedition named this glacier-capped peak in 1858 after John Goodsir (1814–67), his former professor of anatomy.

The lower slopes of the Vermillion Range have some lush avalanche slopes, which, along with the new growth occurring in the clear-cuts, makes for excellent bear habitat. I saw a black bear while riding this trail, so you'll want to keep your eyes open for Master Bruin while in the area.

General location: West of Yoho National Park.

Elevation change: From the trailhead at 1,350 m (4,428 ft.), the trail climbs to an eventual elevation of 1,760 m (5,5773 ft.). Most of this upward stretch is within the final 3.71 km (2.23 mi.).

Season: Late May to late September.

Services: All services are available in the town of Golden, but Golden is approximately 30 minutes west of the beginning of Beaverfoot Road. You'll need to be self-reliant on this ride.

Hazards: The trail is wide and smooth. But with the regrowth within the clear-cut, in addition to ample avalanche slopes on the opposite side of the valley, do watch for bears.

Rescue index: While this trail is wide and smooth, the area is exceedingly wild. You will probably be alone on the trail, so you must be ready to take care of yourself. Be sure to bring a well-equipped repair kit.

RIDE 74 · Moose Creek Road

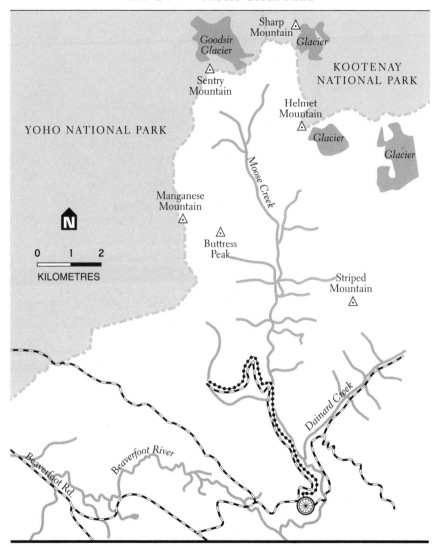

Land status: British Columbia Forest Service.

Maps: The NTS Series 1:50,000 map for this trail is 82 N/01 Mount Goodsir.

Finding the trail: Beaverfoot Road forks off the Trans Canada Highway (Highway 1), just west the western boundary of Yoho National Park. Follow this wide gravel stretch for 24.7 km (14.8 mi.) until the road forks with Kootenay Road. Stay to the left at this junction and continue for an additional 4.7 km (2.82 mi.) where a narrow gravel road again forks to the left. You may see a sign indicating Ice River at this junction. Follow this road for 2.8 km (1.7 mi.), where you'll meet a fork in the road. Park near this fork. Moose Creek Road is the left fork.

The wide gravel of the Moose Creek Road takes you high above the Beaverfoot Valley.

Sources of additional information: I was unable to find additional sources of information.

Notes on the trail: This former logging access road is wide and smooth. After rolling for 0.44 km (0.26 mi.), the road bends to the right and begins climbing. The road winds to the left at km 1.02 (0.61 mi.) and begins to level out. The break is short-lived, however, since the climbing resumes at km 1.57 (0.94 mi.). You begin passing a clear-cut to your left at km 1.93 (1.16 mi.), after which the trail takes a brief downhill gradient before leveling out. The trail drops to cross a small creek at km 4.28 (2.57 mi.) and soon forks, with a spur trail dropping to the right to cross a bridge over Moose Creek. Stay to the left at this junction. The trail makes a sharp left switchback at km 4.82 (2.89 mi.), at which time the climbing starts in earnest. Despite a rough trail continuing straight, be sure to turn left on this switchback.

After winding back to the right, the trail makes a final switchback left at km 6.2 (3.72 mi.). The climbing continues, and the views expand with each metre climbed. Stay right at a fork in the road at km 7.78 (4.67 mi.), then go left again at a junction at km 8.12 (4.87 mi.). You'll meet a closed metal gate at km 8.53 (5.12 mi.). Beyond this gate, the road makes a few more switchbacks before dead-ending in the clear-cut. This is a good turnaround point. Retrace your route and return to your vehicle at km 17.06 (10.24 mi.).

RIDE 75 · Glenogle Creek

AT A GLANCE

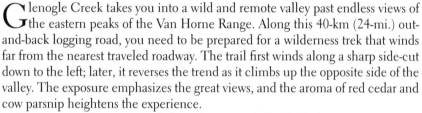

Length/configuration: 40.0-km (24.0-mi.) out-and-back, making it 20.0 km (12.0 mi.) in both directions.

Aerobic difficulty: With steep climbs in both directions, this trail requires a high level of fitness.

Technical difficulty: The road is wide, but it does pass some fairly exposed slopes. You must be comfortable with crossing steep side-cuts.

Scenery: Fabulous. This road parallels the Van Horne Range to the east and passes through a very remote, picturesque valley.

Special comments: This amazing road travels through a magical valley.

Glenogle Creek takes you into a wild and remote valley past endless views of the eastern peaks of the Van Horne Range. Along this 40-km (24-mi.) out-and-back logging road, you need to be prepared for a wilderness trek that winds far from the nearest traveled roadway. The trail first winds along a sharp side-cut down to the left; later, it reverses the trend as it climbs up the opposite side of the valley. The exposure emphasizes the great views, and the aroma of red cedar and cow parsnip heightens the experience.

This is one of those rare trails that takes you uphill in both directions. The work is well rewarded as you roll along the base of the Van Horne Range and make your way toward Spike Peak at the head of the valley. The Van Horne Range pays tribute to William Cornelius Van Horne, general manager of the Canadian Pacific Railway during its construction, without whom the line may never have been completed. One writer described Van Horne's assuming control of the railway in 1882: "Van Horne took the CPR in his hands like a giant whip, cracked it once to announce his presence, cracked it again to loose the sloth and corruption, and cracked it a third time simply because the first two had felt so good."

General location: East of Golden, British Columbia.

Elevation change: The trail is one of the few that travel uphill in both directions. From the trailhead, drop 105 m (344 ft.) to the first bridge over Glenogle Creek. Immediately begin climbing 465 m (1,525 ft.) to a maximum elevation of 1,600 m (5,248 ft.). Drop another 160 m (525 ft.) to the second bridge and climb back a final 60 m (197 ft.) to the end of the trail. Turn around and start all over.

Season: Late May to late September.

Services: All services are available in the town of Golden.

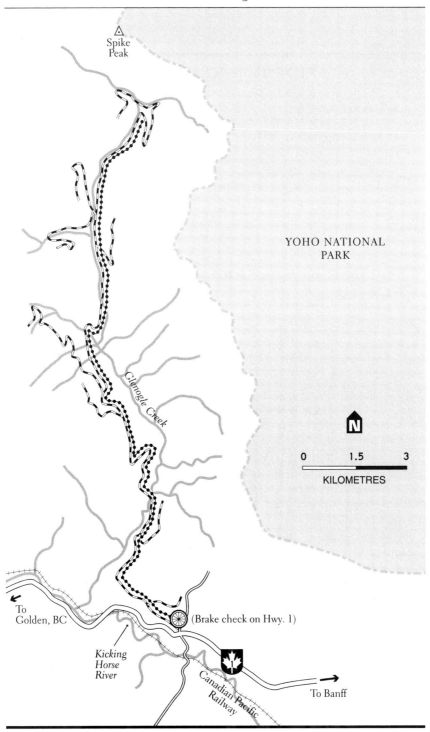

Spike Peak

YOHO NATIONAL PARK

N

0   1.5   3
KILOMETRES

Glenogle Creek

To
Golden, BC

(Brake check on Hwy. 1)

Kicking
Horse
River

Canadian Pacific
Railway

To Banff

Hazards: This is a wilderness ride, which means that you must assume all responsibilities. Have well-stocked repair and first-aid kits, and be aware that bears may be in the area.

Rescue index: You'll need to return to the trailhead to find assistance. This is wild country with no cellular signal.

Land status: Province of British Columbia Crown Land.

Maps: The NTS Series 1:50,000 map for this trail is 82 N/07 Golden.

Finding the trail: From the town of Golden, head east on the Trans Canada Highway for 17.2 km (10.3 mi.). On your left will be a pull-off for trucks to check their brakes before the steep descent to Golden. Turn left into this pull-off, and on the far side, a gravel road takes an offshoot. This is the trail.

Sources of additional information: Visit Summit Cycle at 1007 11th Avenue South in Golden, or phone (250) 344-6600.

Notes on the trail: The good gravel of Glenogle Creek Road immediately leaves the busy Trans Canada Highway (Highway 1) behind, trading it for a level, wide gravel logging road. At km 1.5 (0.9 mi.), a sign indicates that the route has been altered to promote drainage. At this junction, an older road drops down to the left—do not take it. Stay straight on the good-quality gravel. Ignore another spur road branching to the right at km 1.95 (1.17 mi.), and at km 2.4 (1.44 mi.), the trail begins a sharp descent. This hill drops 110 m (361 ft.) over 2.4 km (1.44 mi.) to a bridge over Glenogle Creek. During the descent, stay left as an old road forks off to the right at km 3.9 (2.34 mi.). After the bridge crossing, the trend changes to uphill, making a sharp switchback to the left at km 6.9 (4.14 mi.), followed by a matching turn to the right at 7.8 km (4.68 mi.). With each turn, the climbing continues. Stay to the left at a rough fork at km 9.2 (5.52 mi.). Pass a large clear-cut on the left at km 10.7 (6.42 mi.). Beyond this section, old roads branch off to the left at km 11.0 (6.6 mi.) and 11.9 (7.14 mi.)—stay straight on the main road at each junction. After switchbacking to the right at km 12.5 (7.5 mi.), you cross the second bridge over Glenogle Creek at km 13.95 (8.37 mi.). Beyond this crossing, the trail climbs gradually toward another clear-cut at km 15.8 (9.48 mi.). On the margin of the clear-cut, you'll see evidence of a forest fire. At km 16.2 (9.72 mi.), a stream flows across the road's surface. While still passable, the route may erode even more with time. Cross the final bridge, rickety with age, and stay right at a rough junction. The road ends in a clear-cut at km 20.0 (12.0 mi.). Retrace your route, arriving at the trailhead at km 40.0 (24.0 mi.).

RIDE 76 · Canyon Creek Canyon

AT A GLANCE

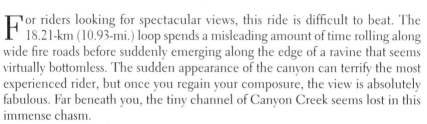

Length/configuration: 18.21-km (10.93-mi.) loop.

Aerobic difficulty: Moderate, with a few steep uphills.

Technical difficulty: The trail is only an intermediate-level ride, but the exposure on it has the potential to terrify.

Scenery: Wow! The view along the canyon edge must be seen to be appreciated.

Special comments: If you're not comfortable riding along the edge of a sheer cliff, save this ride until you are!

For riders looking for spectacular views, this ride is difficult to beat. The 18.21-km (10.93-mi.) loop spends a misleading amount of time rolling along wide fire roads before suddenly emerging along the edge of a ravine that seems virtually bottomless. The sudden appearance of the canyon can terrify the most experienced rider, but once you regain your composure, the view is absolutely fabulous. Far beneath you, the tiny channel of Canyon Creek seems lost in this immense chasm.

The trail winds along the sheer drop of Canyon Creek Canyon for more than 2.0 km (1.2 mi.) before dropping down an expert single-track back to your car.

General location: Adjacent to Nicholsen, British Columbia.

Elevation change: The trail climbs gradually from the trailhead at 825 m (2,706 ft.) to a maximum elevation of 1,185 m (3,887 ft.) at km 12.33 (7.4 mi.). The remainder of the ride is downhill.

Season: May to October.

Services: All services are available in the communities of Nicholsen and Golden.

Hazards: While most of the trail is wide and smooth, once you join the canyon you'll be riding smack against a sheer cliff with no margin for error. Beyond these challenges, you'll have to face only a few sharp switchbacks and one quick drop down a river gully.

Rescue index: Much of this route is within cellular range, but you may not meet other riders en route.

Land status: A combination of private land and British Columbia Forest Service land.

Maps: The NTS Series 1:50,000 maps for this trail are 82 N/07 Golden and 82 N/02 McMurdo.

Finding the trail: From Golden, take Highway 95 south to the community of Nicholsen. Turn right onto Nicholsen Road, then right again onto Canyon

Watch your step
as you ride the rim
of Canyon Creek
Canyon. Few rides
offer the combination
of great views and
exposure found
on this ride.

Creek Road. Cross the narrow bridge over the Columbia River and continue along Canyon Creek Road for an additional 1.73 km (1.04 mi.). As Canyon Creek Road makes a 90-degree left turn, stay straight and park near the point at which the road is blocked to vehicles.

Sources of additional information: Visit Summit Cycle at 1007 11th Avenue South, in Golden, or phone (250) 344-6600.

Notes on the trail: From the trailhead, travel toward the creek and follow the wide double-track that climbs gradually to the northwest. Almost immediately, as you pass a high embankment on your left, you'll see the bottom of the expert descent from the Canyon Creek Canyon Trail. Stay straight on the wide track, and at km 0.73 (0.5 mi.) stay straight at a trail junction. Dropping down to this point from the left is the beginner descent from the Canyon Creek Canyon Trail. Continue to climb on this wide double-track until approximately 2.43 km (1.46 mi.), where you'll come out on the access road to Sander Lake Campground. Turn left at this point and begin rolling along the marshy shoreline of Sander Lake. The road winds to the right at km 2.81 (1.69 mi.), leaving the lake behind. You'll meet a three-way junction at km 3.01 (1.81 mi.). To your left is the wide double-track of Tower Road, which provides access to a communications tower and some of the trails of the Moonraker Network. To the right is a long driveway. You want to stay on the middle road, then left when the road forks again at km 3.36 (2.02 mi.). Do not take the road on the right—not only is it a private driveway but a very fast and very mean dog lives there. The road to the left is marked "No Trespassing" and is gated with thick wire. Mountain bikers have been given permission to roll along this road, but only if we continue to respect the landowner's property. Please stay on the main road.

Beyond the gate is a wide, smooth gravel road. Several rough forks veer off from this road, but the ride remains on the main path to the right at each of them. At km 6.57 (3.94 mi.), you'll begin to join the deep channel of Cedar Creek. Follow the road as it winds around to the left and brings you to a junction with a road heading to the southwest (left). This is the road to Cedar Lake—do not take it. Stay straight. Almost immediately, you'll have another chance to turn left. A sign on a post at the intersection reads "Moonraker Trails." Take this left turn and begin climbing. You will pass two of the Moonraker Trails: first, North Star; later, Cedar Snag. Each of these trails forks off to the left, but you should stay on the main road.

You'll meet an important junction at km 9.0 (5.4 mi.). Stay left at this junction, then right at a second junction that you'll immediately reach. A sign indicates Canyon Creek. The trail now traverses a recent clear-cut and passes an old trapper's cabin to your right at km 9.47 (5.68 mi.). As you climb beyond the cabin, the trail becomes rougher. Stay left at another major junction at km 10.68 (6.41 mi.) and join an even rougher double-track. This section drains very poorly, and along some sections you may get wet feet. At km 12.49 (7.49 mi.), you'll meet a stretch that makes it difficult to stay dry. On the right is a rough bypass; it takes you through some dense devil's club, however. Rejoin the trail at km 12.64 (7.58 mi.) and enjoy a much drier ride from this point on.

The trail starts a steady descent now, and you'll meet another junction at km 13.01 (7.81 mi.). A single-track forks off to the right and is marked by a small red plaque nailed to a tree. Do not take that trail; instead stay to the left. Keep your eyes open for another junction at km 13.46 (8.08 mi.). You'll see a green panel with a white arrow pointing toward a single-track that forks to the left. Take this fork and be prepared for a shock. The single-track climbs briefly and then spits you out right on the edge of the canyon. This spot is extremely dangerous since the drop is more than 100 m (328 ft.) straight down. Once you regain your composure, the trail traverses the cliff on a smooth single-track.

Leave the cliff briefly at km 13.68 (8.31 mi.) and head down several sharp switchbacks. After crossing a small creek, you'll climb the opposite side and rejoin the canyon at km 14.72 (8.83 mi.). As you continue to drop, you'll leave the cliff and meet a "Slow" sign at km 15.22 (9.13 mi.). Heed this marker since just beyond it you'll find yourself back on the edge of the ravine. Before long, you'll pass the remains of an old cabin on your left, and the single-track will continue to widen. At km 15.77 (9.46 mi.), the trail traverses a side-cut, with a wooded ravine down to the right.

Beyond this point, you'll see another "Slow" sign. Pay attention since just beyond this marker you emerge into a short, gravel gully that drops to a small creek. Cross a small stream and pass two of the Moonraker Trails on your left

RIDE 76 · Canyon Creek Canyon
RIDE 77 · Moonraker Trail System

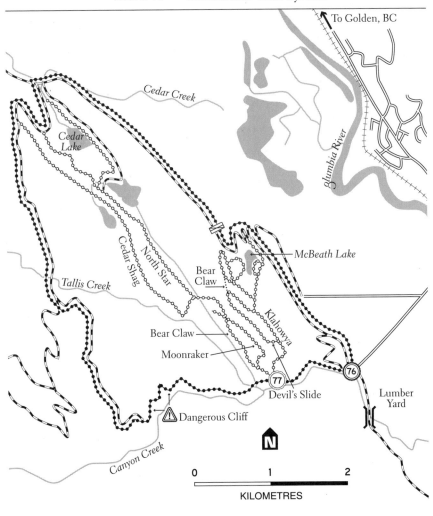

To Golden, BC

Cedar Creek

Cedar Lake

Columbia River

McBeath Lake

Cedar Shag

North Star

Bear Claw

Tallis Creek

Klahowya

Bear Claw

Moonraker

77

76

Devil's Slide

Lumber Yard

⚠ Dangerous Cliff

N

Canyon Creek

0   1   2

KILOMETRES

(Moonraker and Klahowya Trails). Beyond these, a hiking trail forks to the left at km 16.87 (10.12 mi.), and at km 16.9 (10.14 mi.), you'll meet another **Y** intersection. The junction is marked with a tall stump decorated with old bike tubes. To the right is an expert descent back to the trailhead. This stretch heads straight down the fall line and offers some great technical challenges. Less adventurous riders can turn left and continue on the wide double-track, which will bring you to a junction with the trail that started this ride. Turn right and return to your vehicle at km 18.21 (10.93 mi.).

RIDE 77 · Moonraker Trail System

AT A GLANCE

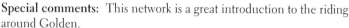

Length/configuration: Variable, with lengths of a few kilometres to 10.0 km (6.0 mi.) or more.

Aerobic difficulty: Variable, generally moderate.

Technical difficulty: Variable, generally beginner to intermediate.

Scenery: The trail is mostly in the trees, with periodic views of the surrounding peaks of the Purcell Range to the west.

Special comments: This network is a great introduction to the riding around Golden.

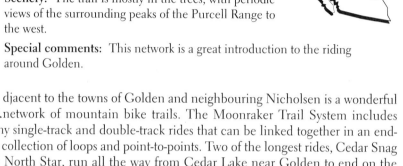

BC

A djacent to the towns of Golden and neighbouring Nicholsen is a wonderful network of mountain bike trails. The Moonraker Trail System includes many single-track and double-track rides that can be linked together in an endless collection of loops and point-to-points. Two of the longest rides, Cedar Snag and North Star, run all the way from Cedar Lake near Golden to end on the Canyon Creek Canyon trail at Nicholsen. The bulk of the network lies toward the south, also adjacent to Nicholsen. Access for this southern section of the trail system is at the Sander Lake Campground. From this marshy pond, you can jump right into the main part of the network.

General location: Adjacent to the towns of Golden and Nicholsen, British Columbia.

Elevation change: The trails have limited changes in elevation, but depending on the route chosen, changes of approximately 200 m (656 ft.) are possible.

Season: May to October.

Services: All services are available in Nicholsen and Golden.

Hazards: Most of these rides are rated intermediate, and they follow wide trails. You'll encounter some natural hazards, such as roots and rutted sections, and you should be prepared for muddy sections.

Rescue index: Much of this route is within cellular range, but you may not meet other riders en route.

Land status: A combination of private land and British Columbia Forest Service land.

Maps: The NTS Series 1:50,000 maps for this trail are 82 N/07 Golden and 82 N/02 McMurdo. You can pick up a free map at Summit Cycle or at the B.C. Forest Service office in Golden. Also, see trail map on page 247.

Finding the trail: The principal access point for this network is in the community of Nicholsen. From Golden, take Highway 95 south to Nicholsen. Turn right onto

Nicholsen Road, then right again onto Canyon Creek Road. Cross the narrow bridge over the Columbia River and continue along Canyon Creek Road for an additional 1.73 km (1.04 mi.). As Canyon Creek Road makes a 90-degree left turn, stay straight and park near the point at which the road is blocked to vehicles. You can follow the wide double-track as it continues beyond the road end. This stretch quickly makes a sharp switchback to the left near the bottom of Canyon Creek Canyon. As you climb, the route provides many access points to the Moonraker Trails. You can also follow the main Canyon Creek Canyon Trail. Its trail description indicates many access points with the Moonraker system.

Sources of additional information: Visit Summit Cycle at 1007 11th Avenue South, in Golden, or phone (250) 344-6600.

Notes on the trail: The Moonraker system is a tight network of trails that defies individual description.

RIDE 78 · Mount Seven Summit Road

AT A GLANCE

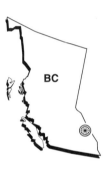

Length/configuration: 22.3-km (13.38-mi.) out-and-back.

Aerobic difficulty: The ride follows an unrelenting uphill gradient, climbing 1,095 m (3,592 ft.) before reaching the summit.

Technical difficulty: The climb is very steep and challenging, followed by a steep descent back to the trailhead.

Scenery: From the summit, you have the Columbia Valley spread out at your feet as you look down toward the Rocky Mountain Trench.

Special comments: If you're lucky, you may be treated to the sight of hang gliders and paragliders launching from this wind-blasted summit.

U p, up, and away! Mount Seven is the only way to fly. This trail is the best-known ride in the Golden area, and for good reason. It climbs unstintingly for 11.15 km (6.69 mi.), rising 1,095 m (3,592 ft.) over this distance. Your lungs will scream and your camelback may run dry, but keep on climbing. The trail winds to an outlier of Mount Seven that attracts paragliders and hang gliders from all over the world. Once you've rested, turn your tire downhill and scream your way back to the trailhead at km 22.3 (13.38 mi.).

From the summit, you look down on the Rocky Mountain Trench and the lazy course of the Columbia River Valley. The Rocky Mountain Trench marks the eastern boundary of the Rocky Mountains and the beginning of the Purcells to the west of this huge depression. On the summit, local hang-gliding pilots have placed a photograph showing various landing sites for people launching themselves from the summit platform. As you watch them silently float away on

RIDE 78 · Mount Seven Summit Road

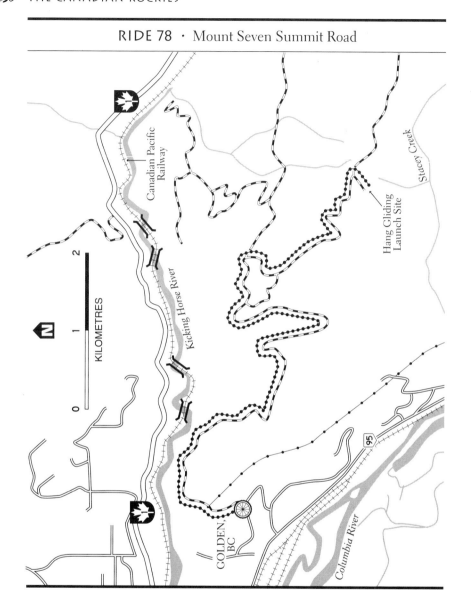

canvas wings, you'll think to yourself—what a waste. They're going to miss all the fun on the downhill!

General location: Above the town of Golden, British Columbia.

Elevation change: The trail climbs steadily from the trailhead at 840 m (2,755 ft.) to the hang-gliding platform at 1,935 m (6,347 ft.). Total elevation gain is 1,095 m (3,592 ft.)—ouch!

Season: Because of the high elevation of this ride, wait until early June before riding, and expect it to be snowbound by mid-September.

Paragliders take a shortcut off the summit of Mount Seven Summit Road.

Services: All services are available in Golden.

Hazards: Keep in mind that this four-wheel-drive route is popular, so watch out for vehicles.

Rescue index: This is a popular route for cyclists and four-wheel-drives. You may be able to get help en route, but you may need to return toward Golden if no one else is on the trail.

Land status: British Columbia Forest Service.

Maps: The NTS Series 1:50,000 map for this trail is 82 N/07 Golden.

Finding the trail: As you approach Golden, take the Highway 95 junction and follow this route for approximately 6.2 km (3.72 mi.) until you reach 9th Street. Turn left onto 9th and then right onto 14th Avenue South, which is signed Selkirk Hill and eventually Spruce Drive. Begin climbing the paved hill and continue on the pavement until you see a prominent road off to the left signed "North Ridge Mount 7." Park near this point and begin riding.

Sources of additional information: Visit Summit Cycle at 1007 11th Avenue South, in Golden, or phone (250) 344-6600.

Notes on the trail: As you begin climbing the wide gravel of the Mount 7 Road, stay straight when a rough single-track branches off at km 1.0 (0.6 mi.). The first section of this ride passes fences and private property on either side, leaving populated areas behind at a sharp left switchback at km 2.7 (1.62 mi.). The trend continues uphill to a right switchback at km 3.9 (2.34 mi.), then another to the left at 4.95 km (2.97 mi.). After this second switchback, the gradient, which has been unrelenting to this point, moderates for a brief stretch. The views begin to open toward Golden at km 6.3 (3.78 mi.). Just beyond this point, a rough road drops down to the right—stay straight on the main road. Stay right at a junction at km 7.5 (4.5 mi.) as the Mount 7 Road makes a sharp switchback to the right. The road going straight eventually peters out in a clear-cut.

Beyond this junction the route gets rougher as it begins the final ascent toward the summit. Stay on the wide, four-wheel-drive route, taking the left fork as a rough trail continues at km 8.75 (5.25 mi.). Stay right at the final junction at km 10.95 (6.57 mi.) as you pass the Mount 7 North Ridge Forest Service recreation site. Finally, emerge at the summit at km 11.15 (6.69 mi.). The view spread out at your feet will be reward enough for all your hard work. Retrace your route, arriving at the trailhead at km 22.3 (13.38 mi.)

RIDE 79 · Gorman Creek

AT A GLANCE

Length/configuration: 35.4-km (21.24-mi.) out-and-back with a 6-km (3.6-mi.) out-and-back hiking option at the far end.

Aerobic difficulty: The ride has a stiff elevation gain of 1,025 m (3,362 ft.).

Technical difficulty: The road is wide and smooth for its full length.

BC

Scenery: As you begin to reach the higher points on this trail, you enter a wild valley with some lush growth along avalanche slopes.

Special comments: This road can be busy with vehicles on weekends. Save it for a weekday.

This wide logging road takes you high onto the eastern edge of the Purcell Mountains toward Gorman Lake, a tiny glacial tarn. The 35.4-km (21.24-mi.) out-and-back circuit winds from the manicured greens of the Golden Golf and Country Club, high into a remote wilderness valley. The route provides some great views of the Dogtooth Range of the Purcells and the lush growth along some of its many avalanche slopes. As you roll along one section, the road cuts across a steep side-cut with a sheer drop to a lush valley on your right. The combination of flourishing avalanche slope and regenerating clear-cuts makes for some ideal grizzly habitat. I was lucky enough while on this trail to see one bear from a distance, so keep your eyes open. Don't forget to pack along an extra water bottle for the climb.

General location: Adjacent to Golden, British Columbia.

Elevation change: The road climbs steadily from 820 m (2,690 ft.) to 1,845 m (6,052 ft.), for a total climb of 1,025 m (3,362 ft.).

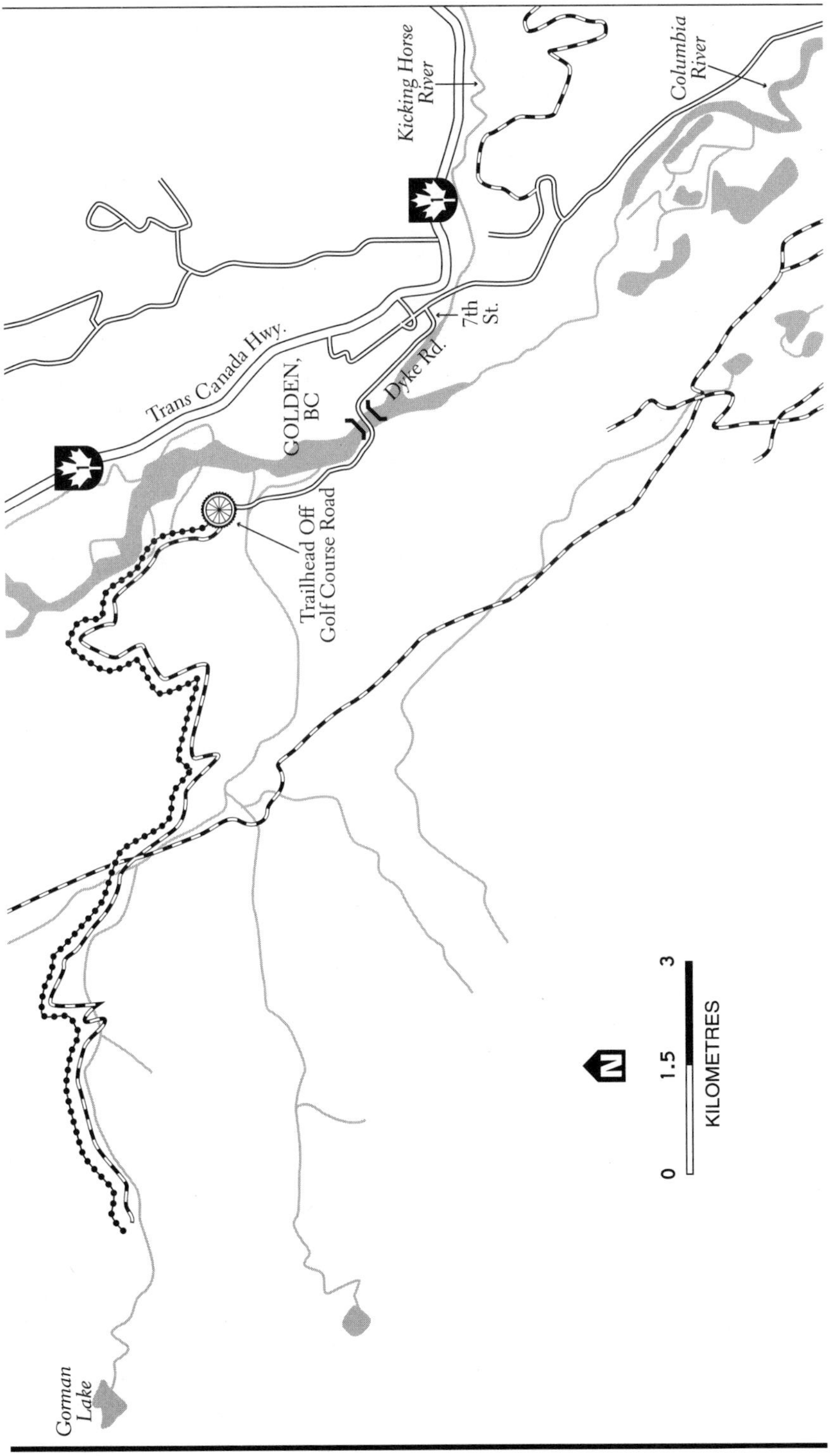

Kicking Horse River

Columbia River

7th St.

Trans Canada Hwy.

GOLDEN, BC

Dyke Rd.

Trailhead Off Golf Course Road

N

0   1.5   3
KILOMETRES

Gorman Lake

The glacier-scoured landscape above Gorman Creek makes for great grizzly habitat.

Season: Mid-May to mid-September.

Services: All services are available in the town of Golden.

Hazards: While the road is wide and smooth, it does take you far from civilization. Be prepared.

Rescue index: While this is a popular road, with plenty of vehicles on weekends, you may not see many people during the week. Be prepared to return to Golden for assistance. You may also get a cellular signal for much of the route, but it will fade out as you go farther up into the valley.

Land status: British Columbia Forest Service.

Maps: The NTS Series 1:50,000 maps for this trail are 82 N/06 Blaeberry and 82 N/07 Golden.

Finding the trail: Within the town of Golden, take the exit for Highway 95. This road winds around to join 10th Avenue. Turn right at the first intersection onto 7th Street. Follow this road as it winds around to parallel the Columbia River. Stay on the pavement as it crosses the river on a narrow bridge. Stay right on the pavement, as the Dogtooth Canyon Forest Service Road branches to the left. After crossing a small bridge, you'll begin to parallel the Golden Golf and Country Club. Just beyond the bridge, a gravel road goes to the left. This is the trailhead. Park near this junction and begin the wide, dusty climb to Gorman Lake.

Sources of additional information: Visit Summit Cycle at 1007 11th Avenue South, in Golden, or phone (250) 344-6600.

Notes on the trail: This road is easy to follow, and the gravel is wide and smooth for its entire length. At km 3.6 (2.16 mi.), a rough road continues straight, while Gorman Lake Road switchbacks to the left. Stay right at another junction with a rough road at km 4.5 (2.7 mi.). After a short downhill at km 7.8 (4.68 mi.), the route forks with a rough road dropping down to the left. Stay to the right on the good gravel. Stay straight at the major junction at km 10.0 (6.0 mi.) and grind as the climbing steepens at km 12.2 (7.32 mi.). The trail levels out as you meet a junction at km 12.7 (7.32 mi.). Following the sign for Gorman Lake, stay to the left. After crossing a bridge over Gorman Creek at km 13.2 (7.92 mi.), the road makes three sharp switchbacks with the views opening up as you round the third switch. As you traverse a sharp drop down to your right, you'll join a clear-cut up to your left. At km 15.4 (9.24 mi.), the road makes a sharp switchback to the left, but you want to stay straight on the rougher road. The main road ends at km 17.7 (10.62 mi.). From here, a rough hiking trail continues for the final 3.0 km (1.8 mi.) to Gorman Lake. Retrace your route and return to your car at km 35.4 (21.24 mi.).

RIDE 80 · Hospital Creek

AT A GLANCE

Length/configuration: 21.6-km (12.96-mi.) out-and-back.

Aerobic difficulty: The climb is steady, but it is spread out over 10.8 km (6.48 mi.), giving the full ride a moderate rating.

Technical difficulty: The road is generally wide and smooth for its full length.

Scenery: The trail winds through some formerly logged areas, with good views of Moberly Peak and the surrounding ranges of the Rockies. On the way back, you can look across the Rocky Mountain Trench toward the mountains of the Purcell Range.

Special comments: This is logging road for its entire length, which may relegate it to a lower spot on your riding priority list.

Hospital Creek Road climbs from the area above Golden, British Columbia, high up into the western slopes of the Canadian Rockies. Along this 21.6-km (12.96-mi.) out-and-back, you get many views of the surrounding peaks and pass some lush growth along avalanche slopes. Along the way, you traverse many recent clear-cuts that show varying amounts of regrowth. The views are pleasant,

RIDE 80 · Hospital Creek

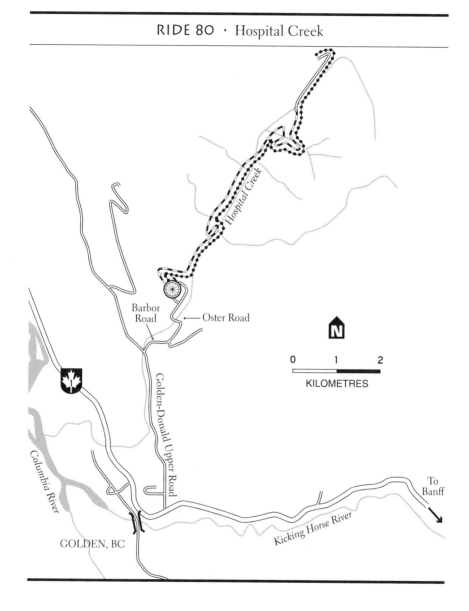

with the ride out focusing on Moberly Peak to the west and the lower slopes of the Rockies to the north and east. Once you turn your bike downhill, you get good views of the Dogtooth Range of the Purcell Mountains on the opposite side of the valley.

The ride has many unmarked junctions, so use the notes on the trail and keep track of your progress. Along the way, enjoy the feeling of elevation and the periodic views of the surrounding mountains.

General location: Adjacent to Golden, British Columbia.

The author takes a break on the Hospital Creek trail.

Elevation change: From the trailhead, the trail has a steady uphill trend. It rises 800 m (2,624 ft.) from the trailhead at 1,060 m (3,477 ft.) to its terminus at 1,860 m (6,101 ft.).

Season: Mid-May to mid-September.

Services: All services are available in the town of Golden.

Hazards: While the road is wide and smooth, it does take you far from populated areas. Be prepared. The lush growth on avalanche slopes, along with the regrowth associated with recent clear-cuts, also makes for great bear habitat. Keep your eyes open.

Rescue index: While four-wheel-drives may appear along this route, you'll likely be on your own. Also, keep in mind that cellular service will quickly diminish as you head up this valley.

Land status: British Columbia Forest Service.

Maps: The NTS Series 1:50,000 map for this trail is 82 N/07 Golden.

Finding the trail: From Golden, head east on the Trans Canada Highway (Highway 1). As you climb the steep hill out of Golden, turn left onto the Golden–Donald Upper Road. Follow this winding road for 3.9 km (2.34 mi.), then turn right onto Barbor Road. Turn right onto Oster Road after an additional 0.7 km (0.42 mi.). After crossing a bridge over Hospital Creek, the road becomes gravel. Turn left 0.5 km (0.3 mi.) after the bridge. At this junction, two green Canada Post community mailboxes can be used as a marker. As you wind around this road, two roads go to the left after 0.4 km (0.24 mi.). The first is a private driveway, the second is the trailhead. To the right of this junction is a long wooden fence made of two logs forming **X** supports, with more long logs placed across these supports. Turn left up this gravel road and find a place to park. Continue riding from this point.

Sources of additional information: Visit Summit Cycle at 1007 11th Avenue South, in Golden, or phone (250) 344-6600.

Notes on the trail: The trail follows a narrow four-wheel-drive road that begins by heading west, away from Oster Road. Stay straight as a rough road comes in from the right at km 0.5 (0.3 mi.). As the road makes a sharp right beyond this junction, you'll see a sign saying "Woodlot No. 1588." Beyond this point, another sign indicaties Hospital Creek Road. Begin climbing a short hill and roll along the gravel. Since the road has been decommissioned, many gouges have been left where culverts were removed. Make a sharp switchback to the left at km 1.9 (1.14 mi.), followed by a quick switch right. The road makes another hard left switchback at km 2.8 (1.68 mi.) and counters to the right at 3.2 km (1.92 mi.). Cross a bridge over Hospital Creek at km 5.6 (3.36 mi.). As the road makes a sharp switchback at km 6.59 (3.95 mi.), stay right and climb around this turn, ignoring a rough road that continues straight at this point. Several switchbacks occur in succession over the next stretch. The road forks at km 7.88 (4.73 mi.), with one road making a sharp switchback up into the clear-cut. Ignore this road and stay on the rougher road to the left. You'll need to cross a short washout before the road improves again.

As you climb, ignore another switchback climbing to the right at km 8.78 (5.27 mi.), once again opting for the lower left-hand fork. Beyond this junction, the trail follows a rough debris flow for a short distance as the sound of the river begins to keep you company. After the trail smooths out again, you'll cross a bridge over Hospital Creek at km 9.39 (5.63 mi.). The final ascent begins as the road continues to climb before finally ending in an old clear-cut at km 10.8 (6.48 mi.). Retrace your route and return to your vehicle at km 21.6 (12.96 mi.).

RIDE 81 · Blaeberry River

AT A GLANCE

Length/configuration: 29.8-km (17.88-mi.) out-and-back.

Aerobic difficulty: The trail climbs sharply for the final 5 km (3 mi.) and requires a good level of fitness.

Technical difficulty: The trail is wide and smooth.

Scenery: Views defy description. To the west, the Cairnes Glacier, part of the Freshfield Icefield, sends meltwater down the face of Fisher Peak, creating a beautiful waterfall.

Special comments: While this ride stays on gravel roads, it offers a fabulous panoramic view.

The Blaeberry River Road mixes wide gravel roads with some breathtaking views along its 29.8 km (17.88-mi.) out-and-back route. It begins by winding along the lush slopes at the base of Fisher Peak, where the constant meltwaters of the Freshfield Icefield have soaked its slopes and created an amazingly lush landscape. As you cross the river and begin climbing, the views quickly expand. At first you notice the lush avalanche slopes on Fisher Peak, along with the ribbonlike waterfall that cascades along its face. As you climb even higher, the Freshfield Icefield becomes clearly visible along the western horizon. While you roll your way through this rugged landscape, it's hard to imagine that the Banff–Jasper Highway winds just over the peaks of the eastern skyline. This major tourist route shuttles millions of visitors each year—yet here, the mountains are silent and the views virtually untouched.

General location: North of Golden, British Columbia.

Elevation change: From the trailhead at 1,100 m (3,608 ft.), the trail climbs 580 m (1,902 ft.) to reach a maximum elevation of 1,680 m (5,510 ft.). Most climbing occurs within the final 5.0 km (3.0 mi.), during which time it climbs 420 m (1,378 ft.).

Season: Mid-June to early October.

Services: All services are available in the town of Golden.

Hazards: The trail is wide and smooth, but it goes through some wild country. Be prepared for its wilderness character.

Rescue index: While this road provides access to a trail to Mistaya Lodge, it is nonetheless a quiet route with only occassional vehicles. Be prepared to backtrack toward Golden should you need assistance. Generally, in the summer months someone will be staying at Mummery Creek Recreation Area. Also, no cellular signal is available in this remote valley.

Land status: British Columbia Forest Service.

Maps: The NTS 1:50,000 Series topographic map for this trail is 82 N/10 Blaeberry River. Also, see trail map on page 263.

Finding the trail: From Golden, head east on the Trans Canada Highway (Highway 1). As you climb the steep hill out of Golden, turn left at km 1.7 (1.02 mi.) onto the Golden–Donald Upper Road. Stay on this wide road until you meet a junction with Moberly School Road at km 14.1 (8.46 mi.). Turn right onto this gravel road and stay straight as the Oberg–Johnson Road joins it at km 16.2 (9.72 mi.). Soon after this junction, turn right onto Blaeberry Road. Stay to the left as the road forks at km 23.5 (14.1 mi.), then cross over the Blaeberry River on a wide bridge. Follow the wide gravel of Blaeberry Road until you meet Mummery Creek Recreation Area at km 55.3 (32.88 mi.). Park here and continue on your bike.

Sources of additional information: Visit Summit Cycle at 1007 11th Avenue South, in Golden, or phone (250) 344-6600. If you liked this valley, you may also want to contact Mistaya Lodge (located at the head of the Wildcat River

The Blaeberry River Valley rolls through glacier-surrounded wilderness.

drainage) at Box 809, Golden, B.C., V0A 1H0 They may be reached by phone or fax at (250) 344-6689).

Notes on the trail: From the Mummery Creek Recreation Area, follow the wide gravel of Blaeberry Road north. The road is wide and smooth. Stay right as a rough road forks to the left at km 0.2 (0.12 mi.). At km 0.5 (0.3 mi.), stay left as the road forks with a bridge visible off to the right. A rough road labeled "Mummery Glacier Trail" forks to the left at km 0.9 (0.54 mi.). Stay right on the main road at this junction. Pass a cable swing built for water-flow studies at km 2.1 (1.26 mi.). At km 2.8 (1.68 mi.), the road forks, with another bridge visible to the right. Do not cross the bridge. That road would take you to Collie Creek and Ensign Creek Rides. Stay left on the main road.

The river begins to encroach on the road at km 4.0 (2.4 mi.), and then the road bounces up a loose debris slope. The views become increasingly impressive as you continue a gradual climb. Two small streams flow across the road at km 6.85 (4.11 mi.), but the flow is only axle deep and easily rideable. The trees along the next stretch lean over the road, creating a virtual tunnel of poplars.

The road continues rolling along the base of Fisher Peak until km 10.0 (6.0 mi.) where the trailhead to Howse Pass forks to the left. Stay right as the road begins to wind to the east and climbs. You'll cross the Blaeberry River almost immediately, then start a sharp climb. With the rise in elevation, the views become more and more impressive. At approximately 11.7 km (7.02 mi.), the trail makes a sharp right switchback and leaves the drainage of Wildcat Creek behind. The trail finally ends at km 14.9 (8.94 mi.). Retrace your route to return to Mummery Creek Recreation Area at km 29.8 (17.88 mi.).

RIDE 82 · Collie Creek

AT A GLANCE

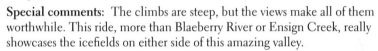

Length/configuration: 32.4-km (19.44-mi.) out-and-back.

Aerobic difficulty: The steep climb of 700 m (2,296 ft.) on this trail requires a strong set of lungs.

Technical difficulty: The trail is wide and smooth for its entire length.

Scenery: The views toward Fisher Peak and the Freshfield Icefield are balanced with some equally great views toward the icy-blue expanse of the Wapta Icefield and the Waputik Range to the southeast.

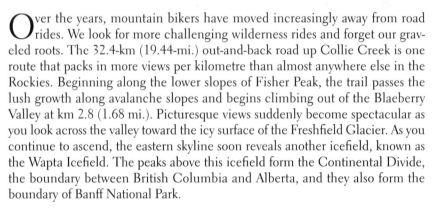

Special comments: The climbs are steep, but the views make all of them worthwhile. This ride, more than Blaeberry River or Ensign Creek, really showcases the icefields on either side of this amazing valley.

Over the years, mountain bikers have moved increasingly away from road rides. We look for more challenging wilderness rides and forget our graveled roots. The 32.4-km (19.44-mi.) out-and-back road up Collie Creek is one route that packs in more views per kilometre than almost anywhere else in the Rockies. Beginning along the lower slopes of Fisher Peak, the trail passes the lush growth along avalanche slopes and begins climbing out of the Blaeberry Valley at km 2.8 (1.68 mi.). Picturesque views suddenly become spectacular as you look across the valley toward the icy surface of the Freshfield Glacier. As you continue to ascend, the eastern skyline soon reveals another icefield, known as the Wapta Icefield. The peaks above this icefield form the Continental Divide, the boundary between British Columbia and Alberta, and they also form the boundary of Banff National Park.

General location: North of Golden, British Columbia.

Elevation change: From the trailhead at 1,100 m (3,608 ft.), the trail climbs 700 m (2,296 ft.) to reach a maximum elevation of 1,800 m (5,904 ft.).

Season: Mid-June to early October.

Services: All services are available in the town of Golden.

Hazards: The trail is wide and smooth, but it goes through some wild country. Be prepared for its wilderness character.

Rescue index: This is a quiet route with only occassional vehicles. Be prepared to backtrack toward Golden should you need assistance. Generally, in the summer months, someone will be staying at Mummery Creek Recreation Area. Also, no cellular signal can reach this remote valley.

Land status: British Columbia Forest Service.

Maps: The NTS 1:50,000 Series topographic map for this trail is 82 N/10 Blaeberry River. Also, see trail map on page 263.

The wide gravel of the Collie Creek trail winds amidst a backdrop of glaciers and sheer mountain faces.

Finding the trail: From Golden, head east on the Trans Canada Highway (Highway 1). As you climb the steep hill out of Golden, turn left at km 1.7 (1.02 mi.) onto the Golden–Donald Upper Road. Stay on this wide road until you meet a junction with Moberly School Road at km 14.1 (8.46 mi.). Turn right onto this gravel road and stay straight as the Oberg–Johnson Road joins it at km 16.2 (9.72 mi.). Soon after this junction, turn right onto Blaeberry Road. Stay to the left as the road forks at km 23.5 (14.1 mi.) and cross over Blaeberry River on a wide bridge. Follow the wide gravel of Blaeberry Road until you meet Mummery Creek Recreation Area at km 55.3 (32.88 mi.). Park here and continue on your bike.

Sources of additional information: Visit Summit Cycle at 1007 11th Avenue South, in Golden, or phone (250) 344-6600.

Notes on the trail: From the Mummery Creek Recreation Area, follow the wide gravel of Blaeberry Road north. The road is wide and smooth. Stay right as a rough road forks to the left at km 0.2 (0.12 mi.). At km 0.5 (0.3 mi.), stay left as the road forks with a bridge visible off to the right. A rough road labeled "Mummery Glacier Trail" forks to the left at km 0.9 (0.54 mi.). Stay right on the main road at this junction. Pass a cable swing built for water flow studies at km 2.1 (1.26 mi.). At km 2.8 (1.68 mi.), the road forks with another bridge visible to the right. Turn right and cross this bridge.

The climbing begins immediately as you leave the valley of the Blaeberry River behind. The climbing moderates for a few minutes at km 3.9 (2.34 mi.), and you'll cross a bridge over Ensign Creek at km 4.25 (2.55 mi.). The climbing, which resumes as the trail starts a series of seven switchbacks at km 4.9 (2.94 mi.), moderates at the end of this series of switchbacks at km 7.8 (4.68 mi.).

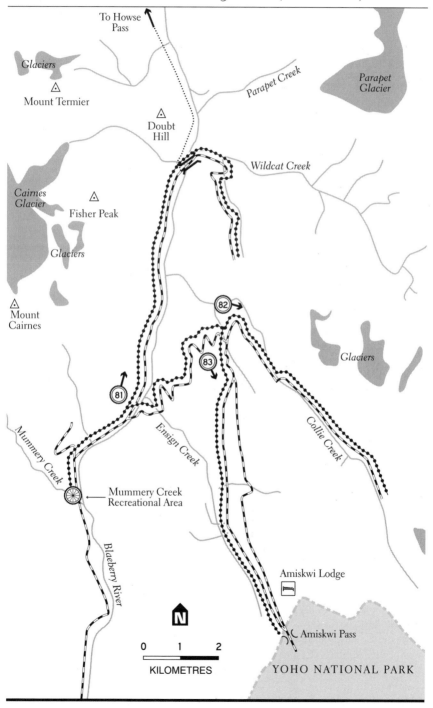

To Howse Pass

Glaciers

⚠ Mount Termier

Parapet Creek

Parapet Glacier

⚠ Doubt Hill

Wildcat Creek

Cairnes Glacier

⚠ Fisher Peak

Glaciers

⚠ Mount Cairnes

82 →

Glaciers

83 →

81 ↑

Mummery Creek

Ensign Creek

Collie Creek

Mummery Creek Recreational Area

Blaeberry River

Amiskwi Lodge

N

0 1 2
KILOMETRES

⟨ Amiskwi Pass

YOHO NATIONAL PARK

The road is now wide and smooth, with many runoff channels. Enjoy the break because you'll begin your next series of switchbacks at km 8.8 (4.68 mi.). After the fourth switchback, the road forks at km 10.4 (6.24 mi.). This is the junction of Collie Creek and Ensign Creek Roads. For this ride, stay left at this junction. Beyond this junction, the road will make a sharp left-and-right switch as the road hugs the edge of the cliff. Soon the trail winds to the southeast, and the views toward the Wapta Icefield open up. The next stretch has numerous washouts that remain passable. Cross a bridge over Collie Creek at km 13.7 (8.22 mi.). Stay right at a final fork at km 15.85 (9.51 mi.). The ride ends at km 16.2 (9.72 mi.) where a bridge over Collie Creek has washed away, leaving a channel too deep to ford safely. Retrace your route and meet your vehicle at km 32.4 (19.44 mi.).

RIDE 83 · Ensign Creek (Amiskwi Pass)

AT A GLANCE

Length/configuration: 39-km (23.4-mi.) out-and-back.

Aerobic difficulty: This steep trail climbs 880 m (2,886 ft.) to the summit of Amiskwi Pass. Save it for later in the season when you've had some time to build up your lung capacity.

Technical difficulty: The ride is wide and smooth, with the exception of the final 1.2 km (0.72 mi.) from the road terminus to the summit of Amiskwi Pass.

Scenery: The views to the west showcase the Freshfield Icefield and the lush growth along the slopes of Fisher Peak.

Special comments: Keep in mind that while you can link this trail with the Amiskwi Valley Trail in Yoho National Park, the route from this point is not open to cycling, so you'll have to push your bike for approximately 6 km (3 mi.) from the end of the Amiskwi Road to the pass. If rumours prove true, a larger section of the Amiskwi River Trail soon may be closed to bikes, making this option unavailable.

This ride, like the others in this area, mixes a great combination of elevation and scenery along its 39-km (23.4-mi.) out-and-back route. From the valley bottom, the views quickly focus on the majesty of the Freshfield Icefield and the lush growth along the steep avalanche slopes of Fisher Peak. As you continue to climb, the views continue to expand. As the trail becomes contained within the Ensign Creek drainage, you'll discover some excellent views of the Waputik Range. This mountain range forms the Continental Divide and the boundary with Banff National Park. Hidden from view along this route are the many glaciers of the Wapta Icefield that lie at the base of these immense mountains.

From the parking area forming the trailhead for continuing to Amiskwi Pass, another trail branches off. This one climbs to the rustic Amiskwi Lodge, a great place to extend your stay in the area for a more thorough exploration.

General location: North of Golden, British Columbia.

Elevation change: From the trailhead at 1,100 m (3,608 ft.), the road climbs 880 m (2,886 ft.) to crest Amiskwi Pass at approximately 1,980 m (6,494 ft.).

Season: Mid-June to early October.

Services: All services are available in the town of Golden.

Hazards: The trail is wide and smooth, but it traverses some wild country. Be prepared for the ride's wilderness character. Also, don't leave your bike unattended for long. Porcupines in the area have been known to munch on the rubber tires of mountain bikes.

Rescue index: While this road provides access to Amiskwi Pass and Amiskwi Lodge, it is still a quiet route with few vehicles. If you need assistance, be prepared to backtrack toward Golden. Generally, in the summer months, someone will be staying at Mummery Creek Recreation Area. Also, no cellular signal reaches this remote valley.

Land status: British Columbia Forest Service.

Maps: The NTS 1:50,000 Series topographic map for this trail is 82 N/10 Blaeberry River.

Finding the trail: From Golden, head east on the Trans Canada Highway (Highway 1). As you climb the steep hill out of Golden, turn left at km 1.7 (1.02 mi.) onto the Golden–Donald Upper Road. Stay on this wide road until you meet a junction with Moberly School Road at km 14.1 (8.46 mi.). Turn right onto this gravel road, and stay straight as the Oberg–Johnson Road joins it at km 16.2 (9.72 mi.). Soon after this junction, turn right onto Blaeberry Road. Stay to the left as the road forks at km 23.5 (14.1 mi.) and cross over the Blaeberry River on a wide bridge. Follow the wide gravel of Blaeberry Road until you meet Mummery Creek Recreation Area at km 55.3 (32.88 mi.). Park here and continue on your bike.

Sources of additional information: Visit Summit Cycle at 1007 11th Avenue South in Golden, or phone (250) 344-6600. If you want more information on Amiskwi Lodge, call the lodge directly at (403) 678-1800.

Notes on the trail: From the Mummery Creek Recreation Area, follow the wide gravel of Blaeberry Road north. The road is wide and smooth. Stay right as a rough road forks to the left at km 0.2 (0.12 mi.). At km 0.5 (0.3 mi.), stay left as the road forks with a bridge visible off to the right. A rough road labeled "Mummery Glacier Trail" forks to the left at km 0.9 (0.54 mi.). Stay right on the main road at this junction. Pass a cable swing built for studying water flow at km 2.1 (1.26 mi.). At km 2.8 (1.68 mi.), the road forks, with another bridge visible to the right. Turn right and cross this bridge.

The climbing begins immediately, leaving the valley of the Blaeberry River behind. The climbing moderates for a few minutes at km 3.9 (2.34 mi.), and you'll cross a bridge over Ensign Creek at km 4.25 (2.55 mi.). The climbing, which recurs as the trail begins a series of seven switchbacks at km 4.9 (2.94 mi.), again moderates at the end of this series of switchbacks at km 7.8 (4.68 mi.).

The road is now wide and smooth, with numerous runoff channels. Enjoy the break because you'll begin your next series of switchbacks at km 8.8 (4.68 mi.). After the fourth switchback, the road forks at km 10.4 (6.24 mi.). This is the junction of Collie Creek and Ensign Creek Roads. Take the right fork.

The switchbacks soon continue, and the climbing stays steady until you crest the final switchback at approximately 13.8 km (8.28 mi.). This route will take you past an old clear-cut on your left with lots of old, burned stumps. Enjoy a little downhill roll at km 14.7 (8.82 mi.). The main ride ends at a parking lot at km 18.3 (10.98 mi.) used as a staging area for hikers heading to Amiskwi Lodge and Amiskwi Pass. Determined riders can continue on the bumpy single-track to reach Amiskwi Pass at approximately 19.5 km (11.7 mi.). Retrace your route back to your car at km 39 (23.4 mi.).

KOOTENAY–INVERMERE RIDES

Kootenay National Park borders Banff National Park on the east and Yoho National Park to the north. Of the four mountain national parks, it tends to be the forgotten one. Kootenay National Park is not located on the main tourism routes that see vehicles traversing Banff and Yoho National Parks along the Trans Canada Highway (Highway 1), or crossing Banff and Jasper National Parks on the world famous Icefields Parkway (Highway 93 North). To locate Kootenay, you need to abandon these routes and head south at Castle Mountain Junction on the Trans Canada Highway. Taking this exit brings you into a wonderful world where tour buses are few and the wilderness still seems wild.

This road took many years to develop. Dr. James Hector of the Palliser expedition recommended a road over the Vermillion Pass as early as 1860. It was one of the most easily traversed of the mountain passes and seemed much more logical for a road than other locales—especially the infamous Kicking Horse Pass. In 1905, an Invermere businessman, Randolph Bruce, resurrected the idea. He believed that the orchards of Invermere could be turned into a success if only a road could connect with the lucrative markets on the other side of the Continental Divide.

Construction began in 1911, but it faced sterner obstacles than the towering peaks and the torrential rivers. After building just 37 km (22 mi.), money ran out, and even worse, the First World War erupted in Europe. After the war, Bruce approached the Canadian government with an idea. If the government would complete the road, the province of British Columbia would give it 8 km (5 mi.) on either side of the road for a national park. The deal was struck in 1919, and the highway was finally opened in 1922. Ironically, poor climate proved an insurmountable challenge to the orchards, and Bruce never managed to ship fruit over the road he had spearheaded. Instead, Kootenay National Park has become an integral part of the Canadian National Park system, bringing a different type of prosperity to the communities of Radium, Invermere, and Windermere at the southern end of this ribbon of pavement.

Today, tourism plays a major role in the economic well-being of this mountain valley. Every weekend, thousands of travelers head toward cottages on the shores of Windermere Lake. In the winter, helicopter skiers head toward the mountain mecca of Panorama Ski Resort. Mountain biking is finding a new genesis in this mountain outpost. As riders rediscover this area, the trail systems are improving and opportunities increasing.

Contact Information: Kootenay National Park, (250) 347-9615. You may also want to contact Columbia Cycle and Motorsports, 375 Laurier Street in Invermere at (250) 342-6164 or Rob's Bicycle Works, #3 Rear 505 7th Avenue, also in Invermere, at (250) 342-7231. In an emergency, the Kootenay Warden Service can be contacted at (403) 762-4506. RCMP Emergency is (800) 642-3800.

RIDE 84 · West Kootenay Fire Road

AT A GLANCE

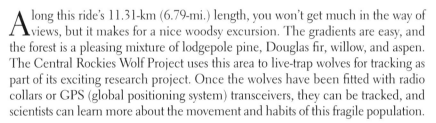

Length/configuration: 11.31-km (6.79-mi.) point-to-point or make a 19.86-km (11.92-mi.) loop using Highway 93.

Aerobic difficulty: This trail has only 100 m (328 ft.) of elevation gain, making for an easy ride.

Technical difficulty: With the exception of a few rutted sections and some overgrown foliage, this ride is very easy.

Scenery: The trail remains in the trees with few open vistas.

Special comments: Since this route clears of snow by mid-May, its pleasant woodland roll makes for a nice early season ride.

A long this ride's 11.31-km (6.79-mi.) length, you won't get much in the way of views, but it makes for a nice woodsy excursion. The gradients are easy, and the forest is a pleasing mixture of lodgepole pine, Douglas fir, willow, and aspen. The Central Rockies Wolf Project uses this area to live-trap wolves for tracking as part of its exciting research project. Once the wolves have been fitted with radio collars or GPS (global positioning system) transceivers, they can be tracked, and scientists can learn more about the movement and habits of this fragile population.

General location: Kootenay National Park.

Elevation change: From the trailhead at 1,204 m (3,950 ft.), the trail climbs gradually to a maximum of 1,304 m (4,277 ft.) before descending toward Crook's Meadow Group Campground at 1,169 m (3,834 ft.).

Season: Mid-May to mid-October.

Services: No services are available nearby. You'll need to either continue south to Radium and Invermere or return north to Banff.

Hazards: The trail has a few loose sections with minor rutting problems. There is one rideable ford, but the willows beginning to encroach on the trail make for a wet ride if their leaves are damp from rain or dew.

Rescue index: The trail begins at the Kootenay Crossing Warden Station, which is a good place to look for assistance. If nobody is there, you can always flag down vehicles along Highway 93. No cellular signal is available here.

Land status: Kootenay National Park, Parks Canada.

RIDE 84 · West Kootenay Fire Road

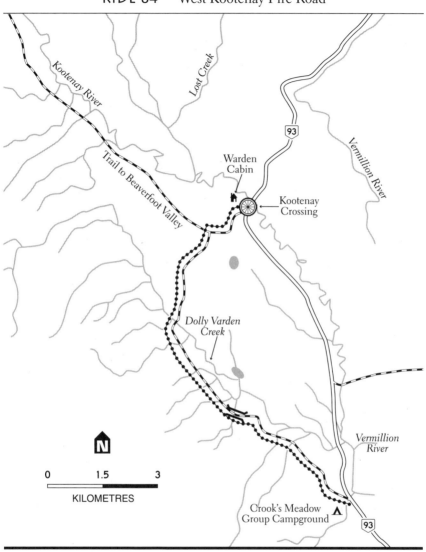

Maps: The NTS 1:50,000 Series topographic map for this trail is 82 K/16 Spilli-macheen.

Finding the trail: From the Trans Canada Highway (Highway 1), head south on Highway 93 for 61.7 km (37.1 mi.), then turn right into the Kootenay Crossing Warden Station. Drive beyond the building, where you'll find a trailhead for West Kootenay Fire Road.

Sources of additional information: Phone Kootenay National Park at (250) 347-9615.

You may get wet feet on the West Kootenay Fire Road.

Notes on the trail: The ride begins on a slightly overgrown double-track rolling through a forest of lodgepole pine. Pass a trail sign and soon begin a gradual climb. Crest this short climb at km 0.54 (0.32 mi.) and meet a trail junction at km 0.89 (0.53 mi.). Stay to the left at this junction (the trail to the right heads to the Beaverfoot Valley). The trail begins climbing again at km 1.19 (0.71 mi.), and the grade continues until km 2.15 (1.29 mi.), where you pass a small marshy meadow off to the left. At km 2.74 (1.64 mi.), the trail begins to descend toward a high-quality bridge over Dolly Varden Creek at 3.66 km (2.14 mi.). Beyond the bridge, stay left at the trailhead for Luxor Pass. Soon, the trail becomes slightly overgrown as willows reclaim the trail. Ride through a 2-m-wide, axle-deep ford at 6.96 km (4.18 mi.) and continue rolling through willows that are encroaching on the trail. You'll see a hitching post for horses on the left at km 9.05 (5.43 mi.), and at km 9.8 (5.88 mi.) a sign indicates that this area is used to trap wolves for the Central Rockies Wolf Project. You meet Crook's Meadow Group Campground at km 10.85 (6.51 mi.). As you approach the campground, take the road to the right, which will bring you past a locked gate to meet Highway 93 at km 11.31 (6.79 mi.). Turn left, kick into high gear and head north on the pavement. Return to the trailhead at km 19.86 (11.92 mi.).

RIDE 85 · Paradise Mines

AT A GLANCE

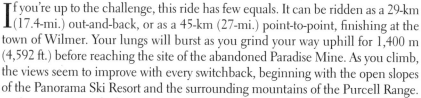

Length/configuration: Either 29-km (17.4-mi.) out-and-back, or as a 45-km (27-mi.) point-to-point back to the town of Wilmer.

Aerobic difficulty: Extreme! The trail climbs 1,400 m (4,592 ft.) before cresting the summit on the slopes of Watch Peak.

Technical difficulty: The trail follows a wide road for its entire distance.

Scenery: Magic! Beginning with views to the slopes of Panorama Ski Resort, the views expand with the climb. As you reach the summit, vistas stretch to Mount Assiniboine to the northwest and the Rockies to the east.

Special comments: If you've got the legs, this is just the ride to test them.

If you're up to the challenge, this ride has few equals. It can be ridden as a 29-km (17.4-mi.) out-and-back, or as a 45-km (27-mi.) point-to-point, finishing at the town of Wilmer. Your lungs will burst as you grind your way uphill for 1,400 m (4,592 ft.) before reaching the site of the abandoned Paradise Mine. As you climb, the views seem to improve with every switchback, beginning with the open slopes of the Panorama Ski Resort and the surrounding mountains of the Purcell Range.

As you approach the mine site, take the time to explore this bit of history before climbing the last section of road to the pass. As you roll north toward the drainage of Bruce Creek, the views roll to the northwest toward the Rockies, and on clear days you can see all the way to Mount Assiniboine, the Matterhorn of the Canadian Rockies.

You have the option of returning along the same route, or if you've left a vehicle in the town of Wilmer, drop down onto the old road along Bruce Creek and scream your way downhill all the way to Wilmer at approximately km 45 (27 mi.).

General location: West of Invermere, British Columbia.

Elevation change: The ride climbs an unrelenting 1,400 m (4,592 ft.) before finally cresting the summit of the pass.

Season: The elevation of this ride limits it to early June until early September.

Services: All services are available in the town of Invermere.

Hazards: This is wild country, so be prepared for mechanical (if not physical) breakdowns. The track is generally wide, but expect some exposed areas en route. Also, bring an extra water bottle and some food as the climb will burn off more than a cheeseburger or two.

Rescue index: In an emergency, you can return to either the Toby Creek Adventures office at the trailhead or find help at the Panorama Ski Resort, just

RIDE 85 · Paradise Mines

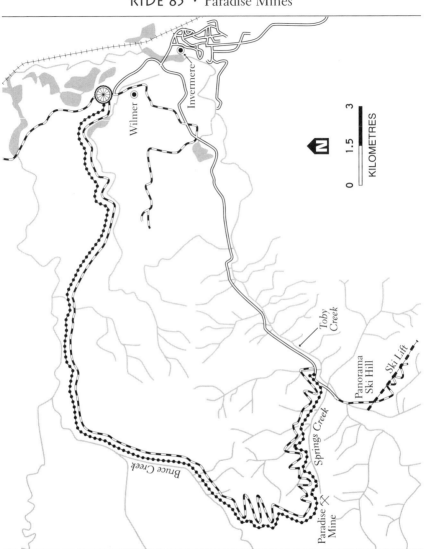

1.5 km (0.9 mi.) farther up the road. From the summit, you may also get some cellular signal to call for assistance. This trail is popular, and you may run into ATVs or four-wheel-drives along the route.

Land status: British Columbia Forest Service.

Maps: The NTS Series 1:50,000 maps for this trail are 82 K/08 Toby Creek and 82 K/09 Radium Hot Springs. The entire route is shown on the 1:100,000 scale Invermere and Columbia Valley map, which is available in most gas stations and sports shops in the area, or you can get it by contacting Dave's Book Bar, Box 2190, Invermere, B.C., V0A-1K0; (250) 342-6511.

Finding the trail: In the town of Invermere, turn west onto the signed road for Panorama/Wilmer. Stay left at the junction at km 2.0 (1.2 mi.) and follow signs for Panorama. Follow this winding road until the 18.2-km (10.92-mi.) point, where you'll see the log cabin headquarters of Toby Creek Adventures on your right. Just beyond this cabin is a vehicle pull-off on the left. The trail begins just slightly farther in an opening in the fence to the right of a Columbia Rafting Adventures sign. While private property signs are posted, bikes are allowed on this route. Toby Creek Adventures has the sole licence for ATVs on the trail.

Sources of additional information: Drop by Columbia Cycle and Motorsports, 375 Laurier Street in Invermere, or phone (250) 342-6164; you can also visit Rob's Bicycle Works, #3 Rear 505 7th Avenue, also in Invermere, or phone (250) 342-7231.

Notes on the trail: From the trailhead, be prepared to point your tire uphill and suck it up. For the first 12.5 km (7.5 mi.), the climb is relentless, during which you'll experience some serious feelings of exposure as you traverse the side-cuts along the steep second half of this trail. Pass the mine buildings and take some time to explore the mine relics before continuing the climb toward the pass. After you crest the summit, the trend is downhill for the rest of the day. The road along Bruce Creek winds its way downhill all the way to the town of Wilmer at approximately km 44.5 (26.7 mi.).

WATERTON LAKES NATIONAL PARK

The area of Waterton Lakes National Park was used for generations by the ancestors of the Kootenay Indians. They knew it as *Omok-sikimi*, which translates as "beautiful waters." The name is equally appropriate today, as the emerald waters of these glacially fed lakes grab the eyes and steal the heart.

The first white men to see the lakes were two fur traders, LeBlanc and LaGasse. They had been sent by David Thompson in 1800 to teach the Kootenay Indians how to prepare furs for market. The next visit was more than 50 years later, when, in 1858, Thomas Blakiston of the Palliser Expedition passed through the area and named the highest peak after himself. He also caught sight of the lakes and immediately renamed them Waterton Lakes after an English naturalist, Charles Waterton.

Seven years later, in 1865, John James "Kootenai" Brown arrived on the scene. Educated at Eton and Oxford, he had an inordinate love of beautiful women, which resulted in his retirement from the imperial army. He also loved gold and followed the yellow metal through the gold fields of San Francisco, the Caribou, and North Saskatchewan. At one point, while working as a dispatch rider for the U.S. Army, he was captured and almost killed by Sitting Bull. Later, he became a buffalo hunter. When buffalo became scarce, he hunted wolves. Eventually, Brown returned to the Waterton Lakes area to set up a whiskey shack to trade the poison to local Indians. This stint was followed by a stay in a U.S. jail while he awaited trial on a charge of murder. After he was found not guilty, he returned permanently to the Waterton Lakes area, becoming its first settler.

A local rancher, F. W. Godsal, also enamoured with the beauty of the place, requested that the area be set aside, and, in 1895, 140 square kilometres (54 square miles) were preserved and called the Kootenay Lakes Forest Reserve. Brown became the reserve's first game warden. In 1911 the area's status was upgraded to that of a park, but it was reduced to 35 square kilometres (13.5 square miles). At the same time, its name was changed to Waterton Lakes Park.

In 1914 the park was again enlarged, this time to 1,095 square kilometres (423 square miles). A town site began to form around the lakes, and that same year Kootenai Brown retired. Two years later, he died and was buried on the shores of Waterton Lakes.

In 1936, at the urging of Rotary clubs in Montana and Alberta, Waterton Lakes in Alberta and Glacier National Park in Montana were designated as the

Waterton–Glacier International Peace Park. The boundaries were changed one more time in 1955, reducing the park to today's 525 square kilometres (202.8 square miles).

Mountain biking in the park is restricted to certain trails, some of which are described in this section. Make sure you check with the park information office to find out about changes. As is the case with most parks, mountain biking trails can change with little notice.

For more information:

Waterton Lakes National Park
Waterton Park, Alberta
T0K-2M0
(403) 859-2262

RIDE 86 · Crandell Mountain Circuit

AT A GLANCE

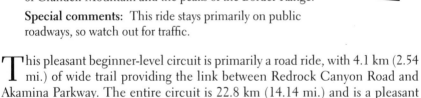

Length/configuration: 22.8-km (14.14-mi.) loop.

Aerobic difficulty: Moderate climb up a public roadway, before the trail takes a downhill trend for the rest of the ride.

Technical difficulty: Easy.

Scenery: The open nature of this ride offers expansive views of Crandell Mountain and the peaks of the Border Range.

Special comments: This ride stays primarily on public roadways, so watch out for traffic.

This pleasant beginner-level circuit is primarily a road ride, with 4.1 km (2.54 mi.) of wide trail providing the link between Redrock Canyon Road and Akamina Parkway. The entire circuit is 22.8 km (14.14 mi.) and is a pleasant sunny-day activity.

Following the main park road, parts of Redrock Canyon Road, and the Akamina Parkway, the route is linked by a trail passing the shores of Crandell Lake.

The ride circumnavigates Crandell Mountain (2,378 m/7,801 ft. in elevation), formerly known as Black Bear Mountain. Its present name commemorates Edward Henry Crandell, a Calgarian who was involved in an ill-fated attempt to strike it rich with oil in the area. Kootenai Brown, an early settler, had used oil from numerous seepages in the area to dress wounds and to coat the flanks of horses to ward off black flies. Brown was not interested in the mountain's commercial value, but before long the secret leaked out. Wells dug as early as 1901 were failures, but oil-seekers kept trying. Finally, in September 1902, the first oil well in western Canada came in at a depth of only 311 m (1,020 ft.). The oil boom never really developed, and the wells that were drilled never became large producers. They did, however, lend a hand in the development of a town site in this remote area of the province.

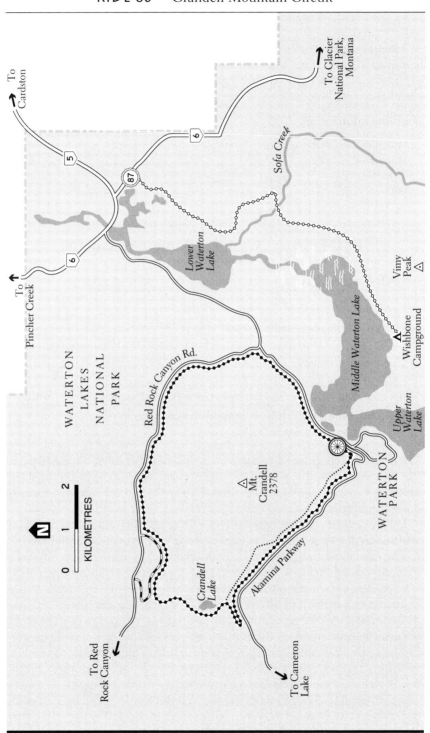

General location: The trail is in Waterton Lakes National Park in southern Alberta.

Elevation change: From the town site, at an elevation of 1,279 m (4,196 ft.), the trail climbs gradually as it rolls up Redrock Canyon Road, maxing out at the low pass beyond Crandell Lake at 1,585 m (5,200 ft.).

Season: This trail is passable from early June to late September.

Services: All services are available in Waterton Park.

Hazards: Few hazards will confront you on this well-maintained route. However, the paved roads tend to have very narrow shoulders, so you'll need to be cautious of vehicles sharing the road.

Rescue index: You're never more than 3 km (1.9 mi.) from a road, so you'll rarely have difficulty attracting attention.

Land status: Waterton Lakes National Park.

Maps: The 1:50,000 scale topographic map for this trail is 82 H/4 Waterton Lakes; however, the Parks Canada map, Waterton Lakes National Park, provides better and more up-to-date information.

Finding the trail: From Waterton Park, the trail begins on the main road leaving town.

Sources of additional information: Information for Waterton Lakes National Park is listed in the introduction to this section.

Notes on the trail: From the town site, follow the main park access road out of town toward the park entrance. At the turnoff to Redrock Canyon at km 3.2 (mi. 2.0), turn left and follow this road. At km 10.1 (mi. 6.26), turn left into the Crandell Mountain Campground. Following the road through the campground, you'll find access to the Crandell Trail. Follow this wide former fire road past Crandell Lake at km 13.5 (mi. 8.37). Beyond the lake it climbs to 1,585 m (5,200 ft.). Stay on the trail as it drops toward the Akamina Parkway. Turn right at a prominent fork near the pass and join the road at km 16.0 (mi. 9.9). Follow this wide road back to town at km 22.8 (mi. 14.14).

RIDE 87 · Wishbone Trail

AT A GLANCE

Length/configuration: 22.0-km (13.6-mi.) out-and-back.

Aerobic difficulty: Easy.

Technical difficulty: Moderate, with the trail deteriorating toward its south end.

Scenery: The ride parallels the shoreline of Middle Waterton Lake, with endless views toward Crandell Mountain across the lake and the cliffs of Vimy Peak high to your left.

Special comments: This trail can be linked with the Crypt Lake Hiking Trail.

This easy 22.0-km (13.6-mi.) out-and-back provides an opportunity to ride the length of Middle Waterton Lake before ending at Wishbone Campground at km 11.0 (mi. 6.8). The trail varies between overgrown fire road, grassy paths, and bad washouts, but it is passable all the way.

The views are spectacular as the ride crosses some wide, marshy meadows. To the south, Vimy Peak provides a sheer rock barrier. To the west, the imposing slopes of Crandell Mountain stand 2,378 m (7,801 ft.). As the trail passes the junction to Vimy Ridge (which commemorates Canada's greatest victory during World War I) and begins traversing the lower slopes of Vimy Peak, the condition deteriorates until it becomes barely passable. Most riders will prefer to turn around at this point, but the trail is passable all the way to Wishbone Campground.

To make a full day of it, arrange for the shuttle boat from the town site to drop you at Wishbone Campground; don't forget your bike. Hike to Crypt Lake and return along the mountain bike trail. Along the 8.7-km (5.4-mi.) Crypt Lake Trail, you'll see roaring waterfalls, crawl through a tunnel, and finish at a beautiful alpine gem of a lake. The opposite end of Crypt Lake lies in Montana.

General location: The trail is in Waterton Lakes National Park in southern Alberta.

Elevation change: The trail begins at 1,290 m (4,232 ft.) and climbs to a maximum of 1,365 m (4,478 ft.).

Season: This trail is at its best from early June to mid-September. Avoid riding too early in the season, as the ford over Sofa Creek can be very challenging in high water.

Services: All services are available in Waterton Park.

Hazards: This trail travels along the lower slopes of Vimy Peak and is highly susceptible to damage from spring runoff. The floods of 1995 apparently caused extensive damage, so much so that riding is not recommended beyond the Vimy Ridge junction. It is passable, but extreme caution is necessary. As the trail passes through some excellent grizzly bear habitat, you need to be vigilant for Master Bruin. Make lots of noise and keep your eyes and ears open.

Rescue index: This trail begins as a popular hiking route and gradually becomes a fairly remote wilderness ride. Its popularity is high between the trailhead and the Vimy Ridge Trail junction. Beyond this point, the trail deteriorates and is not heavily traveled. The Wishbone Campground is popular, and help may be available there.

Land status: Waterton Lakes National Park.

Maps: The 1:50,000 scale topographic map for this trail is 82 H/4 Waterton Lakes. However, the Parks Canada map, Waterton Lakes National Park, provides more up-to-date information.

Finding the trail: From Waterton Park, follow the park access road past the gates to the junction with Highway 6. Head south for 0.7 km (0.43 mi.). Just before the highway passes a large gate, a parking lot is on your left. The trail is visible on the opposite side of the highway.

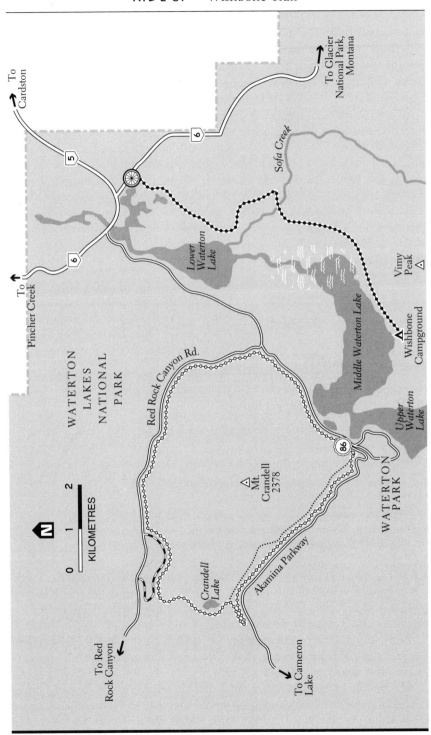

Sources of additional information: Information for Waterton Lakes National Park is listed in the introduction to this section.

Notes on the trail: The trail begins on a wide, overgrown double-track with lush growth all around. At km 0.52 (mi. 0.3), the trail makes the first of numerous bridged creek crossings, opening up at km 0.78 (mi. 0.5) with some striking views. The route varies between sparse aspen forest and open, marshy trail. At many points the grass almost obscures the path, but it is easy to follow.

At km 5.2 (mi. 3.2) Sofa Creek makes its way down to the trail, necessitating a ford. Beyond the Vimy Ridge junction at approximately km 7.0 (mi. 4.34), the trail deteriorates in quality as it traverses the lower slopes of Vimy Peak. During the floods of 1995, much of the trail was washed out, and, for most cyclists this is a good point to turn around. For hard-core riders, you'll find yourself pushing through numerous washouts before the trail improves as it approaches the campground. Some riders take the boat from Waterton Park town site to the campground and ride back to the road. This is an option. If you've succeeded in riding all the way to Wishbone Campground, make sure you give yourself enough time to hike one of the most spectacular trails in the mountains—the Crypt Lake Trail.

RIDE 88 · Snowshoe Trail

AT A GLANCE

Length/configuration: 18.12-km (11.23-mi.) out-and-back.

Aerobic difficulty: Easy.

Technical difficulty: The wide trail is easy, but has numerous rocky washouts.

Scenery: Many open views of Mount Glendowan, Newman Peak, and Avion Ridge to the north and Anderson Peak to the south.

Special comments: An extended ride can be made by pushing your bike over Avion Ridge and dropping down to the valley of the South Castle River. This requires a distant pickup, though, and an explorer's spirit.

This 18.12-km (11.23-mi.) out-and-back, beginner-level trail starts at the hugely popular Red Rock Canyon Day Use Area. It quickly leaves the crowds behind along a wide fire road. The road has many washouts due to the floods of 1995, so be careful as you negotiate these obstacles.

With bear grass along the margins, the trail follows the base of Mount Glendowan to the right and Anderson Peak to the left. To the south, Hawk Mountain's glacial bowl, or cirque, stands out sharply.

The trail shows the iron-rich red rock that has made this area famous. Shortly beyond the trailhead, views open up toward the bowl on Newman Peak above Goat Lake. As you travel below Avion Ridge, the lower slopes become a

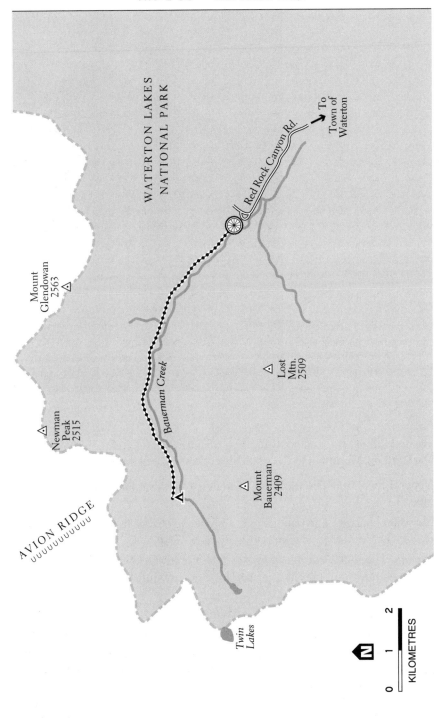

Snowshoe Trail involves numerous river fords, making it better suited for later in the season. As the water levels drop, it becomes a pleasant wide-track trail, providing access to remote hiking country.

wonderland of cow parsnip as the trail traverses a long avalanche slope. The bowl on Lost Mountain to the south also offers a wonderful photo opportunity.

General location: The trail is in Waterton Lakes National Park in southern Alberta.

Elevation change: The trail has only a moderate change in elevation. It begins at 1,500 m (4,921 ft.) and climbs to 1,730 m (5,675 ft.).

Season: This trail is rideable from early June to early October. Due to some river fords, you may want to wait until late June or early July for the water levels to drop.

Services: All services are available in Waterton Park.

Hazards: The trail was once an easy fire road, but the road was badly eroded during the floods of 1995. At least a dozen washouts, some extensive, mar the route. All washouts are passable, but they require moderate speed and quick reflexes when you're coming downhill. This trail traverses an avalanche slope at km 6.94 (mi. 4.3) that forms excellent grizzly habitat. The loud stream nearby means that the bears may not be able to hear your approach. This is a good time to make some noise.

Rescue index: Since the trail begins at the popular Red Rock Canyon Day Use parking lot, help is readily available. The trail is a popular hike, as well as a pleasant ride, so you can usually find help along the route. At the trail's terminus, a warden's station may be staffed by someone who can help. The campground at this location may also provide options for assistance.

Land status: Waterton Lakes National Park.

Maps: The 1:50,000 scale topographic map for this trail is 82 G/1 Sage Creek. However, the Parks Canada map, Waterton Lakes National Park, is a better trail guide.

Finding the trail: Follow the Crandell Mountain Road 14.8 km (9.2 mi.) to its terminus at Red Rock Canyon. Cross the bridge. The trail continues westward down the valley.

Sources of additional information: Information for contacting Waterton Lakes National Park is listed in the introduction to this section.

Notes on the trail: From the trailhead at a bridge over Red Rock Canyon, the trail immediately leaves the popular day-use area. The trail has a wide track for its entire length, with numerous washouts from the floods of 1995, all of which may be repaired in the future.

The trail climbs gradually as you follow Bauerman Creek until km 1.29 (mi. 0.8), where views open up toward Newman Peak to the northwest. The first ford is at km 3.5 (mi. 2.17). I was able to keep my feet dry by heading upstream to a narrow point in the river. At km 4.83 (mi. 3.0), the trail to Goat Lake heads off to the right. This offers the option of a half-day hike to a beautiful alpine lake.

Beyond this junction, the trail follows the impressive lower cliffs of Avion Ridge. A bridged crossing at km 6.2 (mi. 3.8) takes you over the creek. The trail begins traversing an avalanche slope at km 6.94 (mi. 4.3). A short, steep hill at km 7.8 (mi. 4.8) slows things down to a low-gear grind for a short distance. The campground at km 9.06 (mi. 5.62) marks the end of the cycle trail. From here, you can hike to Twin Lakes and Sage Pass or to Lost Lake, 1.8 km (1.12 mi.) to the northwest.

SOUTHERN ROCKIES

Alberta's southern pass, the Crowsnest, provides a wonderful combination of history, recreation, and landscape. When the Canadian Pacific Railway (CPR) completed its southern main line through the valley in 1898, settlers were not far behind. Beneath the mountain faces, a hidden bonanza of black diamonds—coal—was waiting to be cultivated. Before long, towns like Bellevue, Blairmore, Coleman, Frank, and Hillcrest burst from the landscape. The valley blossomed amid the smoke and noise of the coal mines.

Coal mining is dangerous work. Every miner knew the potential for disaster was always around the corner. A cave-in might crush a worker as he tried to place timbers. An explosion of firedamp could kill dozens of miners within seconds. For many others, the slow death caused by years of inhaling coal dust would see them gradually waste away.

One quiet night in 1903, while the night-shift workers were in the mine at Frank, something went very wrong. It wasn't an explosion, but something much worse. Suddenly, 90 million tons of rock came down the side of Turtle Mountain and trapped all the miners inside the mine; all the ventilation shafts had been sealed. The river had been dammed and was rapidly filling the mine from the entrance upward. Making their way to the upper levels, the miners tried to push their way out through a vent shaft. Finally, as they stumbled into the morning light, they saw the extent of the disaster. Although they had survived, the slide had covered the town below the mine. Many of their families had been killed.

Officially, 68 people died. We will never know the exact count, because most of the bodies are still buried beneath the rubble. Few would have expected the miners to return, but return they did. Before long, people moved back to those parts of town not destroyed, and the mine reopened. It closed briefly in 1913, but soon reopened again and operated until a terrible explosion closed it permanently in 1917.

Just down the road, Hillcrest also learned the dangers of coal mining. On June 19, 1914, a huge explosion of firedamp ripped through the mine and snuffed out the lives of 189 men. Up to that time, the mine had been the safest in the valley. On June 21, 1914, following a moving ceremony, 150 of the dead were buried in a mass grave. The remainder were interred in family plots in the valley and elsewhere. The explosion left 130 widows and 400 fatherless children in its wake, yet, once again, life went on. The mine reopened and operated until 1939.

Over the years, families grew up and the coal industry died. Today, all that remains are the scars left behind and the old mine buildings. The Bellevue Mine now offers tours, replacing the active mining that built this small town. It opened in 1903 and didn't close until 1957.

The largest coal producer of the valley, Coleman Collieries, survived longer than all its neighbours and closed in 1983. The old coking ovens are still visible at the south end of town.

The mines may have closed, but the pass is beginning to replace the coal with something equally valuable—tourism. Although the growth in tourism has been slow, it continues to build momentum. Facilities like the Frank Slide Interpretive Centre and the Leitch Collieries help move the pace along. The Frank Slide Interpretive Centre is a large museum that details coal mining history and the rock slide that made the pass famous. Leitch Collieries, once a thriving mine, is now a self-guided interpretive site describing that mine's history.

The Flathead Range of mountains stretches to the south of the pass, marking the boundary between Alberta and British Columbia. Farther south, the West Castle Ski Area forms the entrance to numerous other exploration possibilities. What makes this area unique is the combination of exploration and logging roads that cross the landscape, providing endless opportunities for travel.

Exploration is the operative term. Most of these trails have no signs and are riddled with spur trails and unmarked junctions. Finding your way can be nearly impossible without a clear trail description. This is one area where good topographic maps and a good trail guide are essential.

For more information contact:

Alberta Forest Service
Bow-Crow Forest, Blairmore Ranger Station
11901 19th Avenue, P.O. Box 540
Blairmore, Alberta
T0K-0K0
(403) 562-7307

RIDE 89 · Lille Coal Mine Trail

AT A GLANCE

Length/configuration: 12.8-km (7.7-mi.) out-and-back.

Aerobic difficulty: Easy.

Technical difficulty: Two major fords mark this otherwise easy ride.

Scenery: Few open views, but you'll see some very interesting mining artifacts.

Special comments: Be sure to respect the private land at the west end of the ride.

This pleasant 12.8-km (7.7-mi.) out-and-back, beginner-level trail takes you to the remains of a turn-of-the-century coal mine and traverses some picturesque rolling terrain. The wide double-track includes two major fords caused by the floods of 1995, which washed out bridges. In past years you could ride a long loop, but portions of the loop have been closed by private landowners. Please respect their wishes.

The Lille mine was opened in 1901 by West Canadian Collieries, but, with a drop in demand for coal, it closed in 1913. With little elevation gain, the trail is perfect for riders looking for an afternoon of exploration.

Beginning along a back road adjacent to the Frank Slide Interpretive Centre, this route follows Gold Creek toward the distant slopes of Grassy Mountain. As you look at the slopes, the area's once plentiful coal is evident in the scar left behind by open-pit mining on Grassy Mountain. The mining here was much more recent, occurring in the early 1950s.

General location: The trail is located in the Crowsnest Pass, near the Frank Slide Interpretive Centre, which is found along Highway 3.

Elevation change: This trail exhibits little change in elevation.

Season: With its low elevation, the trail is clear of snow by early May; however, because of two major river fords, the trail is better left for mid- to late July. It remains rideable until mid-October.

Services: All services are available in nearby Blairmore and Coleman.

Hazards: The trail crosses Gold Creek in three places. Two of these fords are knee deep. The floods of 1995 took out bridges over the stream and necessitated the fords. The area is also used by free-ranging cattle, so the possibility of collision is always present. Be cautious along some of the downhill runs.

Rescue index: This trail begins only 1.6 km (0.96 mi.) from the Frank Slide Interpretive Centre access road's junction with Highway 3. You can always flag down a vehicle on this highway or find assistance at the Frank Slide Centre (during operating hours). The trail is often used by dirt bikers, fishermen, and cyclists, so you can often find help en route.

Land status: The trail lies within the province of Alberta; however, the area seems to be a mixed jumble of private and Crown land.

Maps: The best map for this trail appears on page 287. The main topographic map for the area is 82 G/9 Blairmore; this trail, however, is not indicated on it.

Finding the trail: Follow the signs to the Frank Slide Interpretive Centre. Take the exit to the facility, but 1.2 km (0.7 mi.) along this winding access road you'll see a gravel road branching off to the left. Take it. You'll cross a cattle guard and follow the gravel for 1.6 km (0.96 mi.) to the top of a long uphill. Shortly after you pass a gas pipeline, you'll see a good gravel road heading off to the left.

Sources of additional information: The best option for additional information is the Forest Ranger Station in Blairmore at (403) 562-7307. The Frank Slide Information Centre also provides information on the coal mining history of the area.

RIDE 89 · Lille Coal Mine Trail

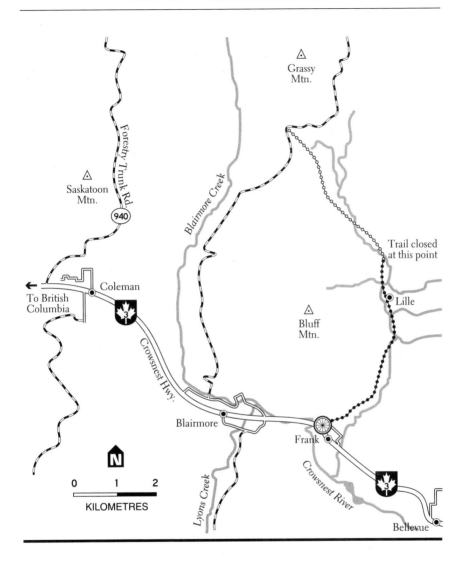

Notes on the trail: From the start, this trail is in excellent condition. It is a wide four-wheel-drive road that descends over its first several kilometres. As it winds through the woods, the trail passes through a parkland environment made up largely of aspen with some sections of lodgepole pine. At km 2.1 (mi. 1.26), a gated road to the left bears an old, barely readable sign: "Sorry, No Personal Cheques Cashed." Its origin is a mystery, as no buildings stand nearby. Stay on the main trail at all gated junctions along the route. At the 3.0-km (1.8-mi.) mark, the trail intersects with a large power line and follows it for a short distance.

Dropping from the last junction, the trail meets Gold Creek where—after crossing a rickety bridge followed by a shallow, rideable crossing—you'll meet the main river. At km 3.55 (mi. 2.13), you'll need to ford the river. The ford is approximately 6 m (20 ft.) across and knee deep during low water. After the ford, climb until the 4.0-km (2.4-mi.) mark where the trail leaves the power line. At km 4.8 (mi. 2.9) the river has removed another bridge, necessitating another knee-deep, 6-m (20-ft.) ford. Beyond this ford is some inconspicuous evidence of the former town of Lille. A small stone foundation is visible to the right, and some scattered debris can be found in the woods. After another shallow ford, the foundation of a building is visible to the left. It may be the remains of the coking ovens, but it's difficult to tell from the minimal remains left today. To the north, the view of Grassy Mountain opens up; you'll be able to see the open-pit scars left behind by mines that operated on its slopes. The trail is blocked at the 6.4-km (3.84-mi.) mark by a closed gate indicating that trespassers will be prosecuted. Before this gate was erected, it was possible to continue all the way to the Blairmore Creek Road and make a loop with the Lille Trail. Unfortunately, the only option now is to return along the same route.

RIDE 90 · Hastings Ridge Rider

AT A GLANCE

Length/configuration: 21.76-km (13.1-mi.) loop.

Aerobic difficulty: Steep climb of 609 m (1,998 ft.) to crest Hastings Ridge.

Technical difficulty: This trail has some route-finding difficulties along with some challenging washouts.

Scenery: Great views of the many peaks of the Flathead Range.

Special comments: Be sure to bring along a good topographic map.

This arduous trail provides spectacular views of the peaks surrounding the Crowsnest Pass. With an altitude gain of approximately 600 m (2,000 ft.), it climbs a high pass between Hastings Ridge and Hillcrest Mountain. The views from this pass are spectacular, with the impressive faces of the Flathead Range dominating the western skyline. From the pass, the trail drops to either Lyons Creek or Drum Creek roads.

The trail forms a loop of approximately 20 km (12 mi.) via Drum Creek and 40 km (24 mi.) along Lyons Creek. During the floods of 1995 the Drum Creek route was badly damaged.

The trail is a route finder's dream. Don't even think of riding it without a topographic map and a compass. Like many trails in the Crowsnest area, it is often a jumble of unmarked junctions and alternate trails. But the rewards are worth the confusion, and this trail is highly recommended.

RIDE 90 · Hastings Ridge Rider

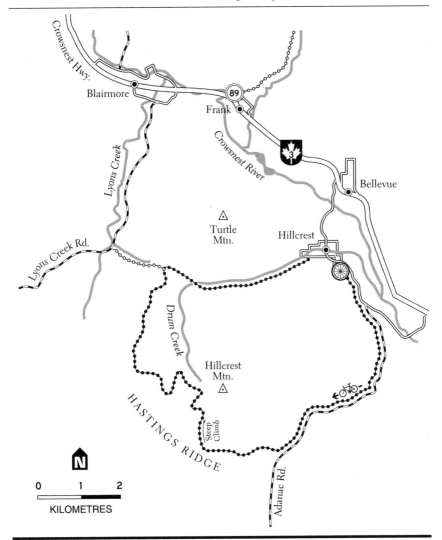

General location: The trail is located in the Crowsnest Pass along Highway 3 within the community of Hillcrest.

Elevation change: Climbing from an elevation of 1,292 m (4,240 ft.), it crests the pass at 1,901 m (6,240 ft.). It begins at the valley bottom and climbs steadily toward the pass. After following the crest of the pass, it drops steeply to Lyons Creek Road.

Season: Due to the heavy snowfall in the mountains, this trail is rideable from mid-June to mid-October.

Services: All services are available in Blairmore or Coleman.

Hazards: The most obvious hazard along this trail is the possibility of getting lost. Make sure you have a good topographic map and a compass. In addition, during the climb toward the pass, the trail traverses a steep slope, so caution is advised. From the pass, the drop to Lyons Creek Road is steep and treacherous—especially after the floods of 1995.

Rescue index: This trail is seldom ridden. I met nobody else when I was out, and, with some of the flood damage from 1995, it may need a few years to heal before it sees more traffic. Expect to be on your own until you rejoin the road in Hillcrest.

Land status: The trail lies within the Bow-Crow Forest, a preserve along the eastern slopes of the Rocky Mountains operated by the province.

Maps: The topographic map for this trail is 82 G/9 Blairmore, but it is somewhat outdated.

Finding the trail: The trailhead is located in Hillcrest in the Crowsnest Pass. Entering the community from Highway 3, follow the main road as it travels through the residential area. At the end of the main street, the road turns left and eventually meets with the beginning of Adanac Road. The junction is actually the intersection of 12th Avenue and 232 Street.

Sources of additional information: Information is available at the Frank Slide Interpretive Centre in Frank at (403) 562-7388 or at the Blairmore Forest Ranger Station at (403) 562-7307.

Notes on the trail: From the trailhead, travel 1.5 km (0.9 mi.) along a paved track until you meet the junction for Lynx Creek Recreation Area. Turn right onto this good gravel road as it climbs steadily toward the junction with the Hastings Ridge Trail. Watch for heavy trucks, as Shell Oil is doing exploration in the area. On weekends, you'll encounter a lot of camper traffic. During the winter this road is used by snowmobiles and is unmaintained for vehicles. At km 2.7 (mi. 1.6), a spur road leaves to the right; stay straight at this junction. At km 4.13 (mi. 2.5), an old exploration road forks to the right; ignore it.

At the 7.0-km (4.2-mi.) mark, look for a trail heading off to the right. It may be difficult to spot because the junction was badly damaged by flooding during the spring of 1995. If you watch carefully, you will also notice that the stream crosses the road at this point. Just after starting the trail, it makes a sharp right-hand turn and becomes a good double-track that soon begins a gradual climb.

At km 7.9 (mi. 4.75), a trail heads up the slope to the right; stay on the main trail. At this point, the forest is a mixture of lodgepole pine and balsam poplar, with an understory of thimbleberry, bergamot, northern bedstraw, and daisy. The climb becomes more interesting at km 8.42 (mi. 5.1), where it moves onto an open slope and traverses the lower slopes of Hillcrest Mountain. The views gradually improve as you climb toward the ridge top. By the 9.44-km (5.7-mi.) mark, the trail becomes a soft, grassy track crossing an avalanche slope alive with cow parsnip and false hellebore. The forest is primarily trembling aspen.

You'll reach the pass at km 12.0 (mi. 7.2). From there, the ridge ride is spectacular. The trail becomes a wide single-track as you approach the pass, a change from the narrower trail during some of the climbing. As you ride the pass, you'll spend some time traversing a steep slope that drops off to the left.

At km 15.25 (mi. 9.15), the view to the north extends all the way to Blairmore. The trail begins to drop as the ridge begins to give way, and the trail heads gradually toward the valley. At km 17.1 (mi. 10.26), you'll meet the junction with the Drum Creek/Lyons Creek access trail. This wide single-track offers the options of a short loop back to Hillcrest by turning right, or you can extend the ride down a steep trail to Lyons Creek Road and Blairmore. As of this writing, the Drum Creek option was in dangerous condition, so check with local sources before attempting this route.

After turning right to drop to Drum Creek, the trail quickly loses elevation. Near the bottom of the long downhill, some of the trail has been damaged by the floods of 1995. You will definitely get wet as you cross the creek several times. Just before Hillcrest, the trail passes the remains of an old mine site, now closed. You'll reach Hillcrest at km 21.76 (mi. 13.1).

RIDE 91 · Ironstone Lookout

AT A GLANCE

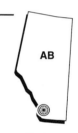

Length/configuration: 26.42-km (15.85-mi.) loop.

Aerobic difficulty: Difficult 841-m (2,760-ft.) ascent.

Technical difficulty: A wide and easy former fire road.

Scenery: To the west, the peaks of the Flathead Range form the Continental Divide and the boundary between Alberta and British Columbia.

Special comments: Pack along an extra water bottle for this steep climb.

Don't miss this climb to the crest of Willoughby Ridge, where the Ironstone Lookout perches atop one of the best views in the area. The ride to the lookout is 13.21 km (7.9 mi.) one-way. It can be negotiated by riders of all technical abilities, but it requires excellent aerobic capacity for the steep 841-m (2,760-ft.) ascent to the summit. The trail follows York Creek Road for five kilometres before branching off from the creek and beginning the steep climb to the lookout.

The trail forms an out-and-back that begins on a secondary road and finishes with a steep climb to the ridge summit. The fire lookout is private property, so please respect the lookout's privacy and stay well away from the building.

General location: The trail begins in the community of Coleman in the Crowsnest Pass.

Elevation change: This trail begins at 1,268 m (4,160 ft.) and climbs to the fire lookout at 2,057 m (6,749 ft.). The total change in elevation is 841 m (2,760 ft.).

RIDE 91 · Ironstone Lookout

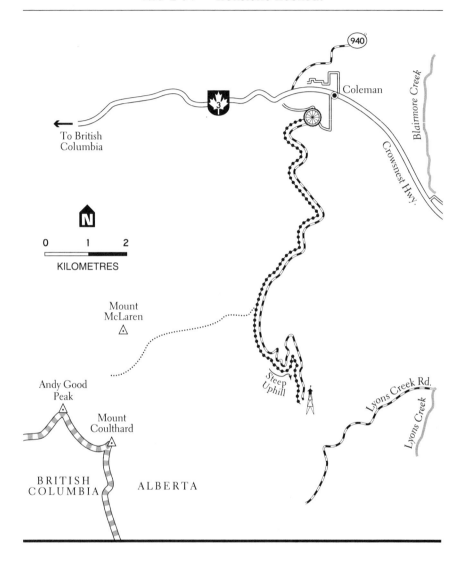

Season: Like most trails in the Rockies, this one is rideable from mid-June to mid-October.

Services: All services are available in Coleman and Blairmore.

Hazards: The trail follows good road and double-track for most of the route; however, one steep section was badly washed out during the floods of 1995. It is still passable, but it has deeply rutted sections that are difficult to ride uphill and are perfect for handlebar flips on the way down. Due to the high elevation of this trail, another hazard is lightning. As you approach the lookout, you'll be openly exposed. If the weather begins to change, descend without delay.

Rescue index: This trail begins and ends in Coleman, where help can always be found. At the terminus, the lookout has a two-way radio and can call for help as well. Along the route, you may see riders trudging their way up or screaming their way down. It's not a busy trail, so keep an eye on your odometre for the return distance to Coleman. Since it is steeply uphill all the way to the lookout, it will generally be easier, even if farther, to return to Coleman.

Land status: The trail falls within the Bow-Crow Forest, controlled by the Alberta Forest Service.

Maps: The trail is split between two topographic maps. You can get away with purchasing only 82 G/10 Crowsnest, but a bit of the gravel road is on 82 G/9 Blairmore.

Finding the trail: Enter east Coleman, make the first left, and cross the tracks. Follow the road and make a left on 83rd Street. Cross the bridge and turn right on 13th Avenue. Follow this route until it becomes York Creek Road. Park at the edge of town and begin riding on the gravel road.

Sources of additional information: One of the best sources of information is the Forest Ranger Station in Blairmore at (403) 562-7307. The forest rangers are very helpful in providing information about current trail conditions and hazards.

Notes on the trail: Beginning at an elevation of 1,268 m (4,160 ft.), the trail starts to climb right away. It is a wide gravel road. During the first kilometre (0.6 mi.), the road switches back to provide excellent views toward Coleman. At km 1.5 (mi. 0.9), the road enters the Bow-Crow Forest. At a fork in the road at km 2.1 (mi. 1.25), stay straight. At km 4.7 (mi. 2.82) and an elevation of 1,426 m (4,680 ft.), the trail crosses York Creek on a good bridge. The road turns sharply to the left at km 6.03 (mi. 3.62), and the trail goes straight, leaving the road behind. Turn left at km 8.06 (mi. 4.84) and left again at km 8.82 (mi. 5.29). Just beyond the junction, a gate blocks the trail, limiting access to hikers and mountain bikers. At km 9.24 (mi. 5.55), portions of the road have been washed out by heavy runoff in the spring of 1995. You'll need to push your bike through this stretch. Beyond this point, the road is rideable again. By km 10.25 (mi. 6.15), the elevation has risen to 1,847 m (6,060 ft.). The views open up shortly after this point as the trail begins to traverse the ridge for a short distance. At km 12.36 (mi. 7.4), the trail joins a power line for the final assault up to the lookout. The lookout is at km 13.21 (mi. 7.9) and an elevation of 2,057 m (6,749 ft.).

RIDE 92 · Racehorse Pass–Deadman's Pass

AT A GLANCE

Length/configuration: 38.5-km (23.9-mi.) loop.

Aerobic difficulty: Moderate, with a steep 499-m (1,637-ft.) climb to crest Racehorse Pass.

AB

Technical difficulty: The descent from Racehorse Pass to the Alexandra River Valley can be very steep and challenging. This is an expert-level wilderness ride.

Scenery: Passing Mount Ward to the south, this ride offers open views of the peaks of the High Rock Range.

Special comments: This is one of very few mountain bike rides to cross mountain passes on the Continental Divide twice in one circuit.

This long, remote wilderness loop crosses two mountain passes, with a little orienteering thrown in. The total distance for the loop is 38.5 km (23.9 mi.). The country is remote and the trails difficult to find, but the rewards are well worth the challenge. This route is suitable for advanced cyclists only. Make sure that you have good topographic maps, local snowmobile maps (for junction signs), and a compass.

The trail begins with a climb through a former clear-cut along a route designed for the exploration of oil and gas. The biggest challenge is finding the proper trailhead. The trail quickly climbs out of the valley bottom and trends toward the summit of the pass, where many years ago a ledge was blasted out of the rock to facilitate exploration. From the pass, the downhill is unrelenting. Unfortunately, during the floods of 1995, many sections of the trail vanished. I ended up carrying my bike through a jumble of large rocks for about 45 minutes. Once you reach the valley bottom, it's a relatively easy ride along Alexander River Road, a four-wheel-drive route that varies in quality, to the junction with Deadman's Pass. The route up to this pass is relatively easy, but—be forewarned—it lacks the long downhill reward of most passes due to its low elevation. With a few route-finding problems, you'll follow the trail makes its way back to Atlas Haul Road.

General location: This loop begins and ends on the Atlas Haul Road a few kilometres west of Coleman in the Crowsnest Pass.

Elevation change: The trailhead is at 1,585 m (5,200 ft.). It climbs to 1,731 m (5,680 ft.) before heading off the road and onto the trail. You'll meet Racehorse Pass at 2,084 m (6,840 ft.) before dropping to the Alexander River Valley at 1,377 m (4,520 ft.). The trail climbs again to Deadman's Pass at 1,609 m (5,280 ft.).

Season: Racehorse Pass tends to hold snow late into the season, so wait until mid-July before attempting this route. In addition, the ford of Alexander Creek at the base of the pass is only safe during the low water of late summer. It should remain rideable until mid-September.

Services: All services are available in Coleman and Blairmore.

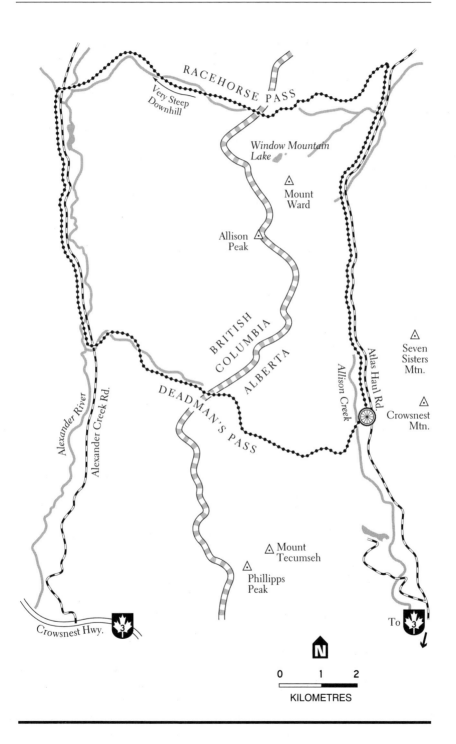

Hazards: This is a truly remote trail, with sections where the trail is difficult to find. It requires good map skills, as it is easy to get off the route; with the extensive jumble of cut-blocks in this area, you need to be confident in your route-finding skills. The biggest difficulty on this route lies in finding it and then, once found, staying on it. The steep drop off Racehorse Pass makes riding impossible and secure footing difficult. Also, where the river has destroyed the trail, it's a difficult, rocky portage for almost 45 minutes to the junction with Alexander Road.

The route includes a ford of the Alexander River on the British Columbia side, which can be hazardous early in the season. The remote nature of this trail creates excellent grizzly habitat. I followed fresh tracks all along Alexander River Road. Keep your eyes open and make lots of noise.

Rescue index: You're completely on your own for this one. Once you head out, you'll see few travelers. The route to the summit of Racehorse Pass carries the occasional hiker and cyclist, but it is usually quiet. From the summit down to Alexander River Road, you will travel through wilderness and are unlikely to see a soul. Along the four-wheel-drive route, you'll see a few cabins that may have some inhabitants, but the road is generally serene. As you approach Deadman's Pass, the amount of horse activity increases, so these riders may be able to offer assistance. At either end lies Atlas Haul Road.

Land status: Alberta Forest Service.

Maps: The 1:50,000 scale topographic maps for this trail are 82 G/10 Crowsnest and 82 G/15 Tornado Mountain. Also, try to obtain a copy of the Allison–Chinook winter snowmobile map; it will help you find your way through the tangle of cut-lines to the correct trailhead.

Finding the trail: Head west from Coleman a few kilometres to Allison Lake Road. Head north on the road and, after 2.8 km (1.6 mi.), take the right-hand fork along the quality gravel road. This is Atlas Haul Road. Watch for mileposts—white numbered signs on some of the trees. These will help you find the trailheads. At the 5.0-km (3.1-mi.) point, you'll pass the staging area for winter snowmobiling. Shortly after mile marker 3, at 8.0 km (4.96 mi.), you'll see a sign on the left for "Western Adventures." Park here, since this is where Deadman's Pass returns.

Sources of additional information: The address for the Alberta Forest Service is listed in the introduction to this section.

Notes on the trail: Ride your bike north on Atlas Haul Road, climbing in elevation from 1,585 to 1,731 m (5,200 to 5,680 ft.). At km 11.4 (mi. 6.8) you'll see mile marker 10 to the right and a good gravel road climbing to the left. Take this road, which, after a short climb, switches back to the left, climbing over a forested shoulder before heading toward the pass. By the 14.0-km (8.4-mi.) point, the views toward the pass open up as the trail has climbed above the forested valley. To the south, Mount Ward dominates the skyline with its steeply bedded slopes of limestone. At km 14.6 (mi. 8.75), the trail crosses a scree slope and begins to traverse the narrow ledge toward the pass. This ledge was blasted out of the mountain many years ago during oil and gas exploration. You'll reach the pass at km 16.0 (mi. 9.6) and an elevation of 2,084 m (6,840 ft.).

The pass drops quickly to the west. The forest on the British Columbia side of the Continental Divide is lush, making for difficult bushwhacking if you stray off the trail. As you drop, the trail is periodically washed out, necessitating short pushes. At km 20.65 (mi. 12.39), the trail has been obliterated by the floods of 1995; however, if you look closely, you'll see the trail climbing up the opposite side. This is easy to miss, leading you to head down the jumble of rocks. At km 20.77 (mi. 12.5), the trail forks, leaving you with a choice to make. The faint left trail will take you directly toward the valley bottom and cut significant distance off the ride. But be forewarned, much of this trail is overgrown, which necessitates a steep downhill push/slide followed by a stretch where it has been completely destroyed. This destruction forces you to push and carry your bike for about 45 minutes down to the junction with the Alexander River. This is the option I chose when describing this trail.

At km 23.5 (mi. 14.1) you'll meet the Alexander River, where a ford is necessary. Later in the season, this ford is easy, and, on the other side, the trail reappears. As other trails join in the valley, stay on the main trail as it heads south until km 30.0 (mi. 18.0), where the trail to Deadman's Pass leaves to the left just after a bridge crossing. This prominent trail is quite difficult to miss. The climb toward the pass reaches a fork at km 31.6 (mi. 19.0); take the right-hand branch. It follows the lower approach to the pass and makes for a more pleasant climb to the summit. At km 34.53 (mi. 20.7) you'll reach the pass at 1,609 m (5,280 ft.). The pass is treed, but it does open up a few times to provide views of the surrounding slopes. There are no views of the surrounding valleys.

At km 38.44 (mi. 23.1) you'll meet a junction where you need to follow the left fork. The sign indicates that this route takes you to the road. After another kilometre, another junction marked by the letter "H" beckons you to the left. After a final bridged crossing, head right, passing a marker with the letter "G," and within a few hundred metres you'll arrive at the trailhead.

RIDE 93 · Sunkist Ridge

AT A GLANCE

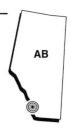

Length/configuration: 33-km (19.8-mi.) out-and-back.

Aerobic difficulty: A steep climb of 780 m (2,560 ft.).

Technical difficulty: This is an expert ride that requires strong route-finding skills.

Scenery: After passing a tiny alpine tarn, the trail climbs to the summit of the pass with open views to Sunkist Mountain in British Columbia as well as to Lys Ridge and West Castle to the north.

Special comments: Advanced wilderness riders can continue down the south side of the pass, making a loop with Commerce Creek and Middle Kootenay Pass.

This 16.5-km (9.9-mi.) out-and-back is for adventurous, expert riders only. With a total length of 33.0 km (19.8 mi.) and an elevation gain of 780 m (2,560 ft.), this trail will test the strongest riders.

It begins at the West Castle Ski Area and follows the river of the same name. The area is alive with snowshoe hares and coyotes, so keep your eyes open. It is also a good area for grizzly bears; therefore, make some noise as you continue on. As you ride beneath towering Barnaby Ridge to the east and Rainy Ridge to the west, the trail crosses numerous washouts from the floods of 1995. The scenery in this area is spectacular, and the valley is narrow. It feels like a box canyon, but the pass, although it may not seem like it at times, does exist.

The pass is windy and exposed. The trail climbs onto a shoulder of Sunkist Ridge as it approaches the pass, and beneath you a tiny lake feeds the West Castle River. As you approach the pass area, the trail traverses some stands of subalpine larch amid the desolate scree that makes up most of the pass area. The last 0.5 km (0.3 mi.) is a traverse across steep scree.

From the pass, the views into British Columbia and the continuation of Sunkist Ridge make this an area worth exploring. You'll have many options for off-trail hikes from this point, and a lengthy ridge walk is possible.

General location: The trail is located west of Pincher Creek, Alberta, at the West Castle Ski Area.

Elevation change: The trail begins at 1,390 m (4,560 ft.) and climbs to the summit at 2,170 m (7,120 ft.). Much of the elevation gain is during the last 2.0 km (1.2 mi.).

Season: With the many fords on this trail, it's best to wait until the spring runoff has dropped. From early August to late September the trail is passable. Be cautious of early snows if you wait until the end of the season.

Services: All services are available in the community of Pincher Creek, but basic supplies can be purchased in Beaver Mines or Burmis en route.

Hazards: This trail travels through a landscape that has been dissected many times by four-wheel-drive roads and logging access routes. It is very easy to get off the main trail and end up backtracking. I ended up adding an extra 4.5 km (2.7 mi.) as a result of taking several incorrect turns the first time I traveled the route.

The river fords are regular and have the potential to be dangerous during spring runoff. Wait until August before attempting this trail. By August, the river level drops and fords are more manageable.

On the pass, the winds are very high and the area extremely exposed. It is difficult to see weather patterns moving in from the west until you crest the summit. Be cautious of any significant changes.

Finally, the numerous washouts along the trail can be hazardous if you pick up speed on the descent. Take it slow!

Rescue index: This trail alternates between popular four-wheel-drive routes and total, utter wilderness. For the first 13.44 km (8.1 mi.) the route is clearly defined and traveled by various vehicles, cyclists, horseback riders, and hikers. Beyond this point, the trail at times is almost obscured and you'll see little evidence of

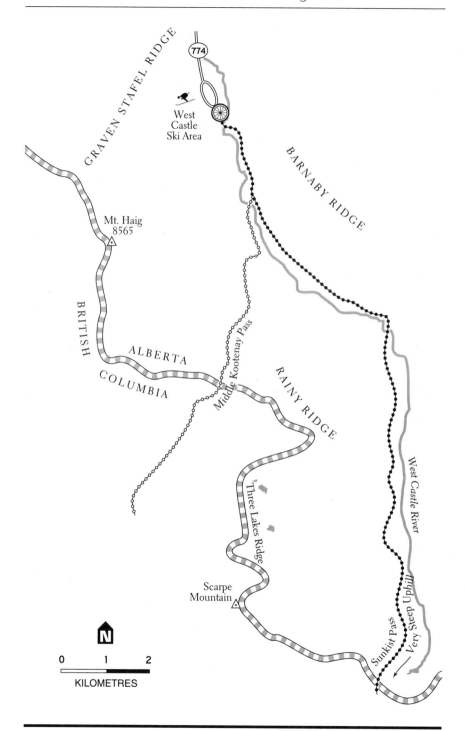

774

GRAVEN STAFEL RIDGE

West
Castle
Ski Area

BARNABY RIDGE

Mt. Haig
8565

BRITISH

ALBERTA

COLUMBIA

Middle Kootenay Pass

RAINY RIDGE

West Castle River

Three Lakes Ridge

Scarpe
Mountain

Sunkist Pass

Very Steep Uphill

N

0   1   2

KILOMETRES

people. At the trailhead at the West Castle Ski Area, you'll find numerous recreational trailers where you can find assistance.

Land status: Alberta Forest Service.

Maps: The 1:50,000 scale topographic maps for this trail are 82 G/1 Sage Creek and 82 G/8 Beaver Mines.

Finding the trail: The trailhead is easy to find by heading south from Burmis, in the Crowsnest Pass, on Highway 507 and then following the signs to the West Castle Ski Area. At the West Castle parking lot, you'll see a gate on the far left side. Park near this point and follow the road to the right on the far side of the gate. This is the start of the trail.

Sources of additional information: Information for contacting the Alberta Forest Service is listed in the introduction to this section.

Notes on the trail: From the trailhead, follow the good four-wheel-drive road. Almost immediately you'll come to the West Castle River where a bridge has dropped from almost being washed away during the floods. It was still hanging on when I rode the trail, so I managed to cross, but its prospects for survival were poor. Expect to ford here.

At km 0.31 (mi. 0.2) take the left fork at the trail junction and another left at km 2.71 (mi. 1.6). After turning, the trail begins to climb on a narrow gravel road. For several kilometres the trail traverses the base of Barnaby Ridge. Because of the floods of 1995, several small runoff channels cause washouts on the trail as they cross its gradient. At km 6.72 (mi. 4.0) the trail opens up to cross some wide avalanche slopes.

You'll come to a bridged crossing at km 7.67 (mi. 4.6). At the fork in the trail at km 7.84 (mi. 4.7) stay right on the main route. Trend left at another junction at km 10.47 (mi. 6.3). After a short distance, the trail crosses West Castle River at a tenuously crossable bridge. The bridge will not likely survive another flood season, so expect another ford there.

Take the right fork at km 11.9 (mi. 7.14) and again at km 12.5 (mi. 7.5). Another ford is necessary at km 13.44 (mi. 8.1). After crossing the river, avoid the temptation to go right; instead, continue straight. You'll find a narrow trail; stay on this route. Over the next several kilometres, the trail will become quite narrow and will require a push up the steep ascent toward the pass. The push begins at km 14.54 (mi. 8.7). From the start of the push, the trail stays almost unrelentingly uphill all the way to the pass at km 16.5 (mi. 9.9). From the pass, turn back and return on the same trail.

RIDE 94 · McGillivray Creek

AT A GLANCE

Length/configuration: 21.56-km (12.94-mi.) out-and-back.

Aerobic difficulty: Moderate climbing throughout its length.

Technical difficulty: The biggest challenge along this ride are the large mudholes from endless four-wheel-drives chewing dual ruts along its soft path. You'll also face several shallow fords on this ride.

Scenery: The lower section of the trail provides some great views of Crowsnest Mountain, but once you head up the four-wheel-drive route, the trail stays in the trees.

Special comments: From the far end of the road, the potential exists for you to make a hike up an outlier of Seven Sisters Mountain.

This trail begins with an urban character, passing through a rural landscape beneath the towering face of Crowsnest Mountain. Once you pass the McGillivray Flats Snowmobile Staging Area, the trail's character changes to become a wide four-wheel-drive route heading up the valley of McGillivray Creek. Distances will vary with your perseverance level, but an average would be around 21.5 km (12.9 mi.). With the increase in distance traveled, the condition of the trail becomes wetter and wetter. You need to be prepared for wet feet on this ride, and be sure to take it only in dry weather. Once you reach the upper end of the valley, the road deteriorates and a rough track climbs up toward an outlier of Seven Sisters Mountain. For most riders, this will be a hike, but the views open up as you gain this final bit of elevation.

General location: Near the town of Crowsnest Pass, Alberta.

Elevation change: The trail climbs gradually from the trailhead at 1,366 m (4,480 ft.) to a maximum elevation of 1,700 m (5,576 ft.), for a total climb of 334 m (1,096 ft.).

Season: Save it for dry weather.

Services: May to October.

Hazards: The trail has a few shallow fords along with many mudholes. Save this ride for very dry conditions.

Rescue index: The random camping area often accommodates ATV users, and help can be accessed here. You may also meet ATVs and four-wheel-drives as you make your way up the valley. In a worst-case scenario, simply return to the trailhead in the town of Coleman, where assistance will be easy to find.

Land status: Alberta Forest Service.

Maps: The 1:50,000 scale topographic map for this trail is 82 G/10 Crowsnest.

Finding the trail: In the town of Coleman, head west along Highway 3, and

RIDE 94 · McGillivray Creek

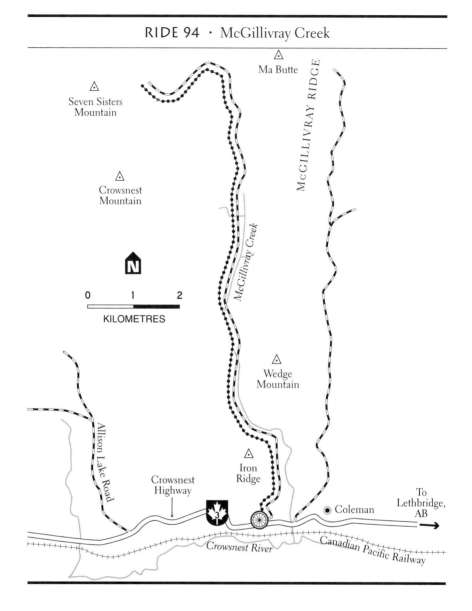

turn right onto 23 Avenue, an upgraded wide gravel road that may be oiled. The road is 1.5 km (0.9 mi.) west of the exit for the Coleman Town Centre.

Sources of additional information: The address for the Alberta Forest Service is listed in the introduction to this section.

Notes on the trail: Begin by climbing up this winding road, passing the Ragged Ass Ranch at km 1.4 (0.84 mi.). After a cattle guard, the road is paved for a few metres before returning to gravel. By km 3.1 (1.86 mi.), the road has begun to roll through pleasant ranchland beneath Crowsnest Mountain. Enter the forest reserve at km 3.4 (2.04 mi.), then pass several power lines. This area is popular

McGillivray Creek trail makes for a wet roll, but provides numerous options for scrambling to an outlying ridge on Seven Sisters Mountain.

with ATVs, and many trails cross this area. Stay to the right as you pass a sign indicating a gun range on the road to your left and enter McGillivray Flats Snowmobile Staging Area. Ride past the random camping area, and at km 5.3 (3.18 mi.) you'll pass the McGillivray Creek Youth Camp entrance on your left. Stay to the right and the road quickly deteriorates into a single-lane four-wheel-drive route.

Many muddy ruts occur along the road, which brings you to a rideable ford at km 5.84 (3.5 mi.). Beyond the ford, there are several more muddy washouts at km 6.23 (3.74 mi.), followed by a moderate uphill section. As the river approaches the right side of the trail at 6.96 km (4.18 mi.), there is a rocky and mucky section. This trail remains wet for much of its remaining course, bringing you to a boggy pool at km 8.14 (4.88 mi.). It is rideable but axle deep and about 5 m wide. After negotiating another rideable tire-wetter at km 8.47 (5.08 mi.), you'll need to negotiate a large mudhole at km 8.62 (5.17 mi.), followed by a ford of the creek at km 8.76 (5.26 mi.). You may be able to jump from rock to rock at this ford, but you will most likely have to get wet. You might as well simply accept wet feet, because you have a calf-deep ford at km 8.91 (5.35 mi.). The next section stays quite wet, and at a ford at km 9.3 (5.58 mi.) someone has placed three pine logs to make a slippery bridge. Beyond this ford, you pass the remains of an old cabin at km 9.52 (5.71 mi.). A fork to the left provides a bypass around another wet section at km 9.82 (5.89 mi.), but it also has several large mudholes along its length. Rejoin the main trail at km 10.09, and by km 10.78 (6.47 mi.) the trail begins to deteriorate, which makes this spot a good place to turn around. Return to your vehicle at km 21.56 (12.94 mi.).

RIDE 95 · Ptolemy Pass

AT A GLANCE

Length/configuration: 11.19-km (6.71-mi.) point-to-point. A 24.8-km (14.88-mi.) loop option is available by linking this ride with Michel Creek Road and Tent Mountain Pass.

AB

Aerobic difficulty: The trail climbs 266 m (872 ft.) over 6.43 km (3.86 mi.), making for a moderate challenge.

Technical difficulty: Some sharp drops, as well as many large mudholes, make for an intermediate rating.

Scenery: The views from the pass extend both east and west, spanning the Continental Divide.

Special comments: Be sure to have a good map and compass.

Bikers in the Canadian Rockies suffer from a definite shortage of mountain passes that allow mountain bike access. Either such passes have been closed to fat-tire travel, or they're simply too rugged and difficult to be used. Ptolemy Pass, with its 11.19-km (6.71-mi.) point-to-point, provides easy access to a mountain pass on the Continental Divide. Loop options are available with Tent Mountain Pass to make a 24.8-km (14.88-mi.) loop.

The trail stays within the trees, following the winding course of East Crowsnest Creek, until you gain elevation as you approach the pass. Climbing, you enter a world where wildflowers like grass-of-parnassus, spiraea, hedysarum, lupine and paintbrush thrive. By km 3.0 (mi. 1.8), you begin to get good views of the hornlike summit of Mount Ptolemy (2,815 m/9,234 ft.). From a distance, it resembles a sleeping figure with arms crossed, and so was named Ptolemy by A. O. Wheeler. As you roll over the actual summit, the road drops into the drainage of Andy Good Creek. This large watershed honours Andrew Good, who was once the proprietor of the Crows Nest Hotel. You can't help but notice the terraced slopes of a pyramid-shaped mountain in the distance, all part of the Corbin Mine. The trail ends along the wide gravel of Michel Creek Road.

General location: Southwest of Coleman, Alberta.

Elevation change: The trail climbs steadily from the trailhead at approximately 1,450 m (4,756 ft.) to the summit of Ptolemy Pass at 1,716 m (5,628 ft.), before reversing the trend and descending to the junction with Michel Creek Road at 1,475 m (4,838 ft.).

Season: June through September.

Services: All services are available in the communities of the Crowsnest Pass.

The winding
Ptolemy Pass trail
climbs to a panoramic
summit on the
Continental Divide.

Hazards: The trial has many natural challenges, including some steep descents and many large mudholes. At km 7.89 (4.73 mi.), a culvert has been removed from the road, creating the potential for an ejection if you hit it going too fast.

Rescue index: This is a wilderness trail, on which you may not encounter anyone. Be prepared, therefore, to take care of yourself. Also keep in mind that there will not likely be any cellular service.

Land status: Alberta and British Columbia Forest Service.

Maps: The 1:50,000 scale topographic map for this trail is 82 G/10 Crowsnest.

Finding the trail: From the town of Coleman, head west on Highway 3 toward the British Columbia border. You'll pass Continental Lime's Summit Plant at km 10.6 (6.36 mi.). Just beyond this point, at km 11.2 (6.72 mi.), a gravel road forks off to the left. Turn left on this road, and pass a sign indicating "Private Road, Use at Your Own Risk." Follow this road for km 4.5 (2.7 mi.), staying left as the road forks at km 4.4 (2.64 mi.). The trail to Ptolemy Pass heads off to the left. It is easy to find, since a metal gate will block the road ahead. The trail to the left has a metal post marked with an orange rectangle bearing a black silhouette of a snowmobile.

Sources of additional information: The address for the Alberta Forest Service is listed in the introduction to this section.

RIDE 95 · Ptolemy Pass
RIDE 96 · Tent Mountain Pass

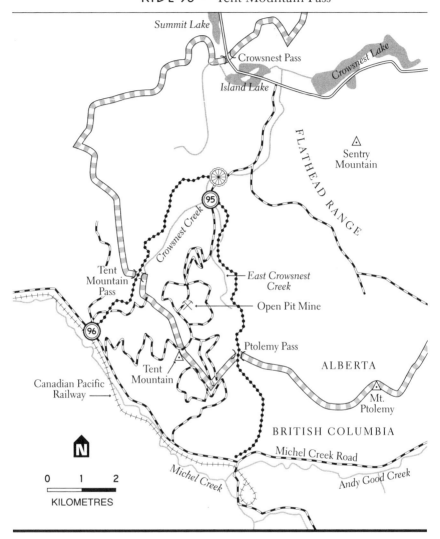

Notes on the trail: Soon after you begin the ride, you'll soon pass a sign on the left that says "Corbin" as you begin to follow the channel of East Crowsnest Creek on your left. After the sign, the trail takes on a rougher character, gradually climbing uphill and cresting a small summit at km 1.5 (0.9 mi.). This brings you to a small, axle-deep ford, after which the trend becomes uphill again. As you climb, the views begin to open toward Mount Ptolemy and the Continental Divide. After the trail levels out at km 2.82 (1.69 mi.), stay to the left as the trail forks at km 2.9 (1.74 mi.). The trail resumes climbing until km 3.49 (2.09 mi.), when it begins a gradual descent to the southwest, heading back toward East

Crowsnest Creek. After the route drops steadily to an informal junction at km 4.34 (2.6 mi.), a rough trail at this point winds to the right, but the main trail stays straight (left) and quickly meets a four-way junction at 4.36 km (2.62 mi.). Go left and begin climbing to circumnavigate a small, marshy pond. The climb breaks at km 5.2 (3.12 mi.) as the trail follows a short descent with a moderately level stretch. After winding away from the pass briefly, the route winds to the south again at km 5.69 (3.41 mi.). Use of this trail by four-wheel-drive vehicles has left plenty of mudholes to be negotiated, but most of them can be bypassed on one side or the other. Stay left (straight) at a trail junction at km 5.81 (3.49 mi.) marked by some flagging tape. This stretch brings you up the pass at km 6.43 (3.86 mi.) and 1,716 m (5,628 ft.). You'll know when you meet the pass, because the drop on the British Columbia side is sharp and sudden.

As you descend the south side of the pass, you'll encounter many large mudholes at km 6.86 (4.12 mi.), beyond which the descent continues to a potential hazard at km 7.89 (4.73 mi.). A culvert has been removed from the road, leaving a deep gouge that could easily send a rapidly approaching cyclist over the handlebars—watch for it! As you keep dropping, you'll go through two large mudholes before dropping down sharply to another muddy spot at km 7.89 (4.73 mi.). Be careful; this soft-bottomed mudhole will suck up your front tire and stop you instantly. This is the theme of the next stretch: downhill while dodging mudholes. A rideable ford at km 8.64 (5.18 mi.) is followed by a short uphill. The route quickly reclaims its downhill trend until it reaches another rideable ford at km 9.27 (5.56 mi.). Climb again after this ford, pass two large mudholes, and get your first views of Michel Creek Road. At km 10.39 (6.23 mi.), turn right as the trail emerges on a wide, private road. Join Michel Creek Road at km 11.19 (6.71 mi.). If you want to make a loop with Tent Mountain Pass, turn right and follow Michel Creek Road north for 6 km (3.6 mi.) to the junction with Tent Mountain Road and then follow the description for Tent Mountain Pass.

RIDE 96 · Tent Mountain Pass

AT A GLANCE

Length/configuration: 7.64-km (4.58-mi.) point-to-point. A 24.8-km (14.88-mi.) loop option is available by linking this ride with Ptolemy Pass and Michel Creek Road.

Aerobic difficulty: Moderate, with only 125 m (410 ft.) of elevation gain.

Technical difficulty: Other than some minor rutting and route-finding challenges, this is an easy ride.

Scenery: The ride passes two small mountain ponds and provides some excellent views toward Sentry Mountain and the Flathead Range to the east.

Special comments: This mountain pass is easily accessible for riding, but it includes some route-finding challenges.

This is one of the most moderate mountain passes accessible by mountain bike. While it's not lengthy—only 7.64-km (4.58-mi.) point-to-point—an excellent 24.8-km (14.88-mi.) loop can be made by linking it with Ptolemy Pass and the Michel Creek Road. The ride is smooth and easy, rolling along over a carpet of needles, past a small, marshy pond, and finally cresting the summit of the Continental Divide. Once you're on the Alberta side, the views open toward the sharp summit of Sentry Mountain, part of the Flathead Range. You also roll past a small mountain lake, before finally entering a large clear-cut. The wide logging access roads will guide you the remainder of the distance back to the trailhead.

General location: Southwest of the town of Coleman, Alberta.

Elevation change: From Michel Creek Road at 1,400 m (4,592 ft.), the trail climbs gradually to the summit of Tent Mountain Pass at 1,525 m (5,002 ft.). The trail drops off the pass to the north trailhead on Tent Mountain Mine Access Road at 1,450 m (4,756 ft.).

Season: June through September.

Services: All services are available in the communities of the Crowsnest Pass.

Hazards: The trail has many natural challenges, including some steep descents and large mudholes. With the lack of signage, and the trail's lack of use, route finding is another challenge. Be sure to bring along a good map and compass.

Rescue index: On this wilderness trail you may not encounter anyone else, so be prepared to take care of yourself. Keep in mind that cellular service is unlikely.

Land status: Alberta and British Columbia Forest Service.

Maps: The 1:50,000 scale topographic map for this trail is 82 G/10 Crowsnest.

Finding the trail: From Coleman, head west into British Columbia for approximately 9 km (5.4 mi.), then go south on Michel Creek Road. Follow this wide road for 15.5 km (9.3 mi.), to the junction with Tent Mountain Road on the left. A large sign at the junction indicates that the area is closed to the public due to environmental concerns. You'll also see a yellow marker "89." This is the trailhead.

Sources of additional information: The address for the Alberta Forest Service is listed in the introduction to this section.

Notes on the trail: From the trailhead, follow the wide gravel of Tent Mountain Road, staying straight as a wide road forks to the left at km 0.29 (0.17 mi.). Stay left as another road branches to the right at km 0.34 (0.2 mi.) and begin climbing as the road ascends sharply. Soon after passing Marker "90" at km 1.18 (0.71 mi.), look for a slash pile on the left. Essentially, as the road climbs, an extremely faint trail forks off to the left near this pile of slash at km 1.33 (0.8 mi.). I spent much of the day riding dead-end after dead-end looking for this ride. Absolutely nothing marks the trail. While you climb on the wide logging road, an extremely faint trail forks to the left. It is easy to miss, so make sure you've got an odometer in hand so that you can find it. For those of you with GPS sensors and topo maps,

As you descend the east side of Tent Mountain Pass, the quiet ride widens to become a busy logging road. This is your sign that the trailhead is nearing.

the junction is at Grid Reference 634926. Once you actually find the junction, the hard part is done.

The grassy single-track leaves the logging road, making two rolling dips before dropping sharply to cross a tributary of Michel Creek on a narrow bridge at km 1.7 (1.02 mi.). The crossing is easily rideable, and the climb up the other side is a very loose, steep climb/push. Once up this short grind, the climbing moderates as the trail begins rolling along a wide, carpeted single-track. As you pass a small pond to the right at km 2.3 (1.38 mi.), the trail slowly climbs toward the pass. Stay right at a T intersection at km 2.7 (1.62 mi.) and follow a red arrow with white letters indicating "Inn." Another sign, coming from the opposite direction says, "Managed Forest 27. Private Property. Access at your own risk." These signs are on the south side of the pass. Beyond the pass, the trail descends and the peaks to the east side of the pass roll into view. The descent is quick and loose. At km 3.05 (1.83 mi.), a small hole in the centre of the trail can grab your front tire and send you airborne. There is a small pond off to your right as you descend at km 3.37 (2.02 mi.). As you approach the pond, the trail climbs above the left shoreline, topping out at km 3.71 (2.23 mi.).

After the climbing levels off, stay straight on the old roads that join in from the left at km 4.03 (2.42 mi.) and again at km 4.34 (2.6 mi.). Pass another sign for the "Inn" at km 4.61 (2.77 mi.), and meet civilization as you enter a recent clear-cut at km 4.95 (2.97 mi.). As you enter the jumble of tracks running through this logging area, stay on the upper road, which is also the most major of the logging roads. Stay straight at a four-way junction at km 5.94 (3.56 mi.) and stick with this main road as other roads join in from the left at km 6.41 (3.85 mi.) and the right at km 6.62 (3.97 mi.). Stay to the right as the road makes a sharp right turn at km 7.3 (4.38 mi.); ignore a road that enters from the left. As you cross a bridge at km 7.47 (4.48 mi.), the trailhead comes into view. Meet the lime plant access road at km 7.64 (4.58 mi.). If you have done this as a loop with Ptolemy Pass, you will be at km 24.8 (14.88 mi.).

RIDE 97 · South Drywood Creek

AT A GLANCE

Length/configuration: 12.16-km (7.3-mi.) out-and-back.

Aerobic difficulty: The trail climbs very sharply from the trailhead to Bovin Lake.

AB

Technical difficulty: The trail is wide, with few physical challenges.

Scenery: Great views of the arid slopes up to the right.

Special comments: This ride reminds one of an old western movie, rolling along a narrow box canyon with a high ridge to the top.

Some rides evoke long-past memories, and this 12.16-km (7.3-mi.) out-and-back doesn't disappoint. Riding up this 6.08-km (3.65-mi.) box canyon reminds me of a western movie, with a line of Blackfoot warriors on white horses lining the top of the ridge. Along with the imagined magic of this ride, its physical beauty excels. Following Bovin Creek toward its source on Bovin Lake takes you past a pleasant waterfall as the runoff begins its long journey to the ocean. While the water flows to your left, the landscape to your right is somewhat parched. The sun-baked slopes of this valley support a diversity of wildflowers that have adapted to live on its arid slopes. Some of these floral residents include stonecrop, lupine, cinquefoil, bedstraw, aster, sticky geranium, yellow columbine, and spiraea. The valley ends at a tiny tarn, Bovin Lake. You may encounter fishermen trying to catch some of the brook trout that make this lake home. A spur option heads over Victoria Ridge drops down into the valley of the South Castle River. This would make for an extended ride, though most cyclists ride this route as an out-and-back.

General location: Southwest of Pincher Creek, Alberta.

Elevation change: From the trailhead at 1,630 m (5,346 ft.), the trail climbs steadily to its terminus at Bovin Lake at 2,075 m (6,806 ft.), for a total elevation gain of 445 m (1,460 ft.).

Season: June to September.

Services: All services are available in the town of Pincher Creek.

RIDE 97 · South Drywood Creek

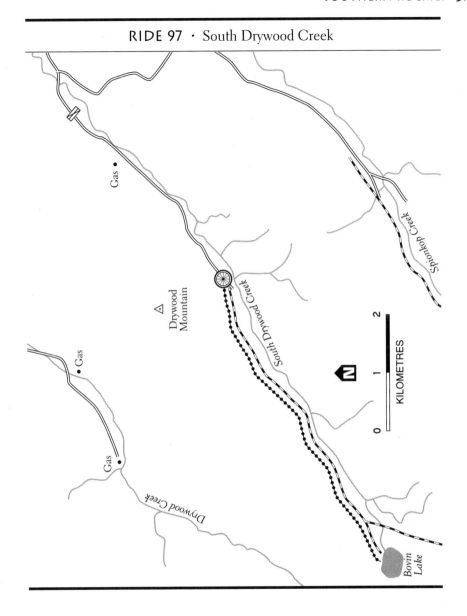

Hazards: The trail is wide and smooth, with few dangers beyond the ordinary.

Rescue index: Along the ride, you'll need to rely on other users, perhaps the owners of the ATVs parked at the trailhead. A cell signal is unlikely along the ride, but soon after arriving back at the trailhead and driving east, you should be back in the land of the wired.

Land status: Alberta Forest Service.

Maps: The NTS 1:50,000 Series topographic maps for this ride are 82 G/01 Sage Creek and 82 G/08 Beaver Mines.

The arid valley of South Drywood Creek is contrasted by the pleasant stream that bubbles along parallel to the trail.

Finding the trail: From Pincher Creek, head south on Highway 6 for 33.5 km (20.1 mi.) and turn right onto Spread Eagle Road. Follow this road past numerous side roads, and turn right at a T intersection at km 8.3 (4.98 mi.). Follow this road as it crosses numerous cattle guards, finally meeting South Drywood Road after km 8.6 (5.2 mi.). Turn left onto South Drywood Road, and after 1 km (0.6 mi.), pass a gate and a trail sign. The sign indicates that the trail is open to recreational vehicles from June 15 until September 1. Continue driving beyond this gate. South Drywood Road passes numerous gas wells, ending at a large metal shed some 4.1 km (2.5 mi.) after the gate. As the road winds to the left to approach the shed, a rough road continues straight. This is the trail.

Sources of additional information: I was unable to find any additional sources of information for this trail.

Notes on the trail: The trail begins rolling along a wide four-wheel-drive route as it winds up the valley of South Drywood Creek. While four-wheel-drive vehicles can make their way up this valley, the culverts have been removed, which will stop all but the most determined drivers. You may still meet the odd dirt bike or quad-track vehicle as it climbs to Bovin Lake. The trail passes a small waterfall on your left as you crest a steep uphill, at km 2.86 (1.72 mi.). The trail continues to climb steeply, crossing a small stream at km 4.19 (2.51 mi.). By km 4.67 (2.8 mi.), the high ridge to your right begins to fade as the climbing gradually moderates. The trail meets a sharp gully at km 5.27 (3.16 mi.). This gully will stop OHVs at this point, but cyclists can simply make a detour to the left over several downed logs. Beyond the gully, a cut-line branches to the south (left) to head toward Bovin Pass. As you begin to approach the sheer rock face ahead of you, the trail narrows to a single-track before arriving at the lakeshore at km 6.08 (3.65 mi.). Retrace your path, returning to the trailhead at km 12.16 (7.3 mi.).

RIDE 98 · South Castle River

AT A GLANCE

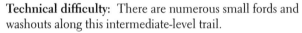

Length/configuration: Variable with a maximum out-and-back distance of approximately 62 km (37.2 mi.).

Aerobic difficulty: The trail climbs very gradually, making for an easy climb.

Technical difficulty: There are numerous small fords and washouts along this intermediate-level trail.

Scenery: The views of the peaks of the Border Range are spectacular, and they become more frequent as you head farther up the valley.

Special comments: This is a wilderness ride, so be prepared for self-rescue. Be sure to bring maps, a good repair kit, and extra food and water.

Looking for a wild ride? The valley of the South Castle River may just be what you need. This remote logging road extends 31.0 km (18.6 mi.) up this valley, finally ending at the base of the Continental Divide. An out-and-back, its total distance can be as lengthy as 62.0 km (37.2 mi.) by the time you return to your vehicle. Before you head out, make sure you're prepared for a long trip into a remote mountain valley. The actual length of this ride varies, as most riders do not follow the trail all the way to its terminus. You can vary the length as your mood desires.

The views are grand, although somewhat enclosed by trees. Rolling beneath the peaks of the Border Range, you begin by rounding the high slopes of Whistler Mountain on your left, then trending southeast toward Windsor Ridge and Castle Peak. To the west, Lys Ridge and West Castle dominate. As Windsor Ridge seems to fade away, the valley opens up somewhat, with Mount Matkin to the south, indicating that the trail will soon need to wind eastward. With this change in direction, and with Sage Mountain appearing to the southeast, you rejoin Windsor Ridge on your left. The route you're on passes a rough trail that climbs to a pass on Victoria Ridge at km 25.7 km (15.42 mi.). This route provides access to South Drywood Creek. Stay right and follow the valley as the trail finally winds south to end beneath the Continental Divide. The summit ridge to the south marks the boundary with British Columbia, while the height of Avion Ridge to the southeast marks the north boundary of Waterton Lakes National Park.

General location: South of the Crowsnest Pass.

Elevation change: From the trailhead, the road climbs gradually from 1,433 m (4,700 ft.) to its terminus at 1,780 m (5,838 ft.). The total climb is 347 m (1,138 ft.).

Season: June to September.

Services: All services are available in the town of Pincher Creek.

Hazards: The trail is wide and smooth, with few dangers of note.

Rescue index: Along the ride, you'll need to rely on other users—perhaps ATV and four-wheel-drive owners bouncing their way up this valley. There will not be any cell signal along the ride.

Land status: Alberta Forest Service.

Maps: The NTS 1:50,000 Series topographic maps for this ride are 82 G/01 Sage Creek and 82 G/08 Beaver Mines.

Finding the trail: From the Crowsnest Pass, head south on Highway 507. You can also head west on Highway 507 from the town of Pincher Creek. In either case, you'll go south at the junction with Highway 774 to the community of Beaver Mines. After 15.0 km (9.0 mi.), turn left onto a gravel road and follow signs for Beaver Mines Lake. Follow the gravel for 3.8 km (2.3 mi.), then turn right onto an unsigned gravel road. You can park along this route, or continue to 0.6 km (0.36 mi.), where the road forks. The trail along South Castle River crosses the bridge at this point and continues up the valley. Some riders prefer to drive the first 7.0 km (4.2 mi.) to save their energy for the less urban sections of trail.

Sources of additional information: I was unable to find any additional sources of information about this ride.

Notes on the trail: From the junction with the road to Beaver Mines Lake, roll along the gravel of this South Castle River access road for 0.6 km (0.36 mi.) and stay straight as the road forks. Cross a bridge and begin to bounce your way up this wild valley. Numerous snowmobile trails fork to the left and right along this road, but you should stay on the main trail. Cross a cattle guard at km 4.5 (2.7 mi.). At km 5.7 (3.42 mi.), a rough trail forks to the right and heads up the valley of Grizzly Creek. This trail, once a good mountain bike trail, was destroyed in the floods of 1995. Today, it is primarily the domain of horseback riders. Stay straight on the good gravel and pass a random campsite on the right at km 7.15 (4.29 mi.). At km 7.7 (4.62 mi.), the road becomes much rougher as the trail bounces up a washout. The first washout ends at km 7.9 (4.74 mi.), and along the next section culverts have been removed, leaving deep depressions in the road. The trail continues to vary between wide road and rough four-wheel-drive track for most of its length.

At km 12.0 (7.2 mi.), a deep washout will stop most four-wheel-drive vehicles, but not mountain bikes and four-tracks. The trail begins climbing after the washout, then levels out at km 13.1 (7.86 mi.). Stay left as a rough road forks to the right at km 14.66 (8.79 mi.); next meet a calf-deep ford at 14.8 km (8.88 mi.). Another crossing is necessary soon after at km 15.17 (9.1 mi.). As you approach this crossing, the road appears to fork. Stay left here. The road then seems to

RIDE 98 · South Castle River

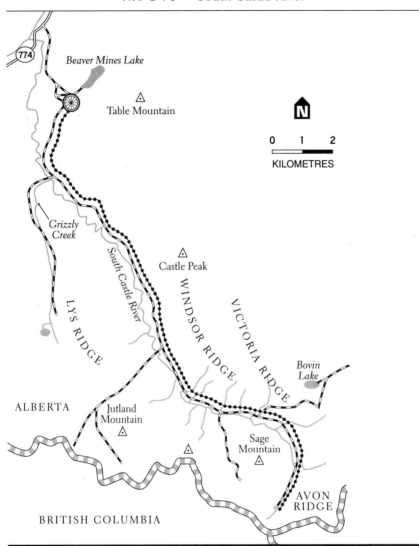

wash out, but a narrow trail on the left will take you over a rickety bridge. This trail is marked with a snowmobile sign.

At km 16.87 (10.12 mi.), several old bridges are lying beside the road as the trail bypasses to the left to cross a dry channel. An old fence crosses the trail at km 17.28 (10.37 mi.). It's composed of log tripods with horizontal posts, along with a bit of barbed wire. It's easily passable. Stay straight as a rough road joins from the right at km 17.54 (10.52 mi.); again, remain on the same course, as a major trail, marked with an orange diamond, forks to the right at km 17.88 (10.73 mi.). This route heads up the drainage of Scarpe Creek. The trail forks again at km

At what appears to be a river ford, a narrow spur offers a bridged crossing of the South Castle River.

18.59 (11.15 mi.), with a sharp hill, marked by an orange diamond, climbing to the left. Take this trail and continue to roll up the valley. While both roads eventually rejoin, the upper trail avoids numerous river crossings. Pass the junction with Font Creek at approximately km 23.7 (14.22 mi.), then another junction at approximately km 25.7 (15.42 mi.). To the left, a rough trail climbs toward a pass on Victoria Ridge, leading toward Bovin Lake and South Drywood Creek. Stay right at this junction and continue to roll toward the peaks of the Continental Divide. The trail gradually deteriorates, ending beneath the cliffs of the Continental Divide at approximately km 31 (18.6 mi.). Retrace your route, returning to the vehicle at km 62.0 (37.2 mi.).

RIDE 99 · Fernie Alpine Resort

AT A GLANCE

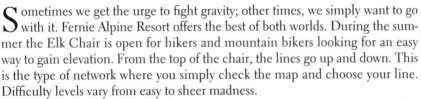

BC

Length/configuration: Variable.

Aerobic difficulty: If you use the chairlift, the challenges are minimal, but some riders may choose to use the many access roads to gain free elevation.

Technical difficulty: Easy to extremely difficult.

Scenery: Great views across the valley toward Castle Mountain.

Special comments: This is a great place to play, allowing for some virtually unlimited downhill mileage.

Sometimes we get the urge to fight gravity; other times, we simply want to go with it. Fernie Alpine Resort offers the best of both worlds. During the summer the Elk Chair is open for hikers and mountain bikers looking for an easy way to gain elevation. From the top of the chair, the lines go up and down. This is the type of network where you simply check the map and choose your line. Difficulty levels vary from easy to sheer madness.

If you want a guided trip on the mountain, Fernie Alpine Resort offers free mountain bike tours at noon on Saturdays. Call for availability.

General location: Near the town of Fernie.

Elevation change: The base of the hill is approximately 1,000 m (3,280 ft.), with lines maxing out at 1,690 m (5,543 ft.).

Season: June to early October.

Services: All services are available in Fernie.

Hazards: The hazards vary, but they may include sharp drops, natural obstacles, and just about anything else imaginable, depending on the route you choose.

Rescue index: Even if no other riders are out, you need only make your way to the base, where you can easily get help during operating hours.

Land status: Private land.

Maps: The NTS 1:50,000 Series topographic map for this ride is 82 G/11 Fernie, but the best map is *Fernie Trail Guide*, produced by Savage and Huxley Marketing, 2 Boardman Road, P.O. Box 2025, Fernie, B.C. V0B-1M0.

Finding the trail: From Fernie, head south on Highway 3 and follow signs to Fernie Alpine Resort.

Sources of additional information: Contact Fernie Alpine Resort at (250) 423-4655 or by mail at Fernie Alpine Resort, Ski Area Road, Fernie, B.C., V0B-1M1.

Notes on the trail: From the top of the Elk Quad you can drop straight down the absolutely extreme line of Kodiak Karnage, or you can roll along the wide

RIDE 99 · Fernie Alpine Resort

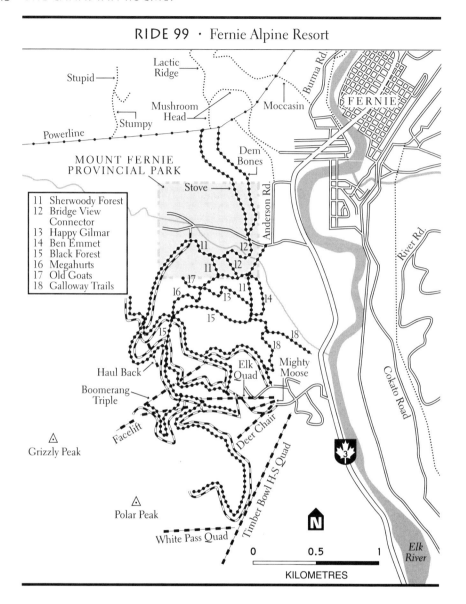

gravel of Boomerang toward another expert line down the Black Forest. More sedate riders may choose the intermediate line of Megahurts. These are only a few of the many options available, so be sure to check the current trail map.

RIDE 100 · Coal Creek Trails

AT A GLANCE

Length/configuration: Variable, up to 6.0 km (3.6 mi.) or more.

Aerobic difficulty: Some of the uphills are steep, but in general the network is of moderate aerobic challenge.

Technical difficulty: The trails range from easy to extreme. Be sure to stick to trails within your ability range.

Scenery: The trails are primarily in the trees, but the higher lines do offer some good views west toward Fernie Mountain.

Special comments: Climb, drop, rock and roll . . . this network offers a bit of everything.

This diverse network, located immediately to the west of the town of Fernie, offers a great diversity of intermediate and expert rides. Access to the main road is off Coal Creek Road, bringing you into the heart of the network. The rides can be linked together in a multitude of ways. The upper trails, like the Bear Chutes (37), climb high above the valley and offer great views to the west to Fernie and Proctor Mountains. Another high line runs south of Coal Creek and climbs up Roots (28) and Extension (29)—and steeply up Hyperextension (30). Riders looking for tricks and technical challenges will want to incorporate Kids Stuff (43), Splitting Bears (36), and Little Chainring Big Trouble (44). This network has loads of challenges accompanied by lots of moderate single-track. Make sure you have a good map. Since the trails change over time, check in with local bike shops for the current scoop.

General location: Fernie, British Columbia.

Elevation change: Variable.

Season: June to September.

Services: All services are available in the town of Fernie.

Hazards: Depending on the route you choose, expect sharp drops, man-made and natural obstacles, and variable conditions.

Rescue index: If you can't find help from other riders on the network, simply head back toward town, where plenty of help is available. If you have a cell signal, you can contact police at (250) 423-4321 or an ambulance at (800) 461-9911.

Land status: British Columbia Forest Service.

Maps: The NTS 1:50,000 Series topographic maps for this network are 82 G/11 Fernie, 82 G/06 Elko, and a bit of 82 G/10 Crowsnest. The best map, *Fernie Trail Guide,* has been produced by Savage and Huxley Marketing, 2 Boardman Road, P.O. Box 2025, Fernie, B.C. V0B-1M0.

RIDE 100 · Coal Creek Trails

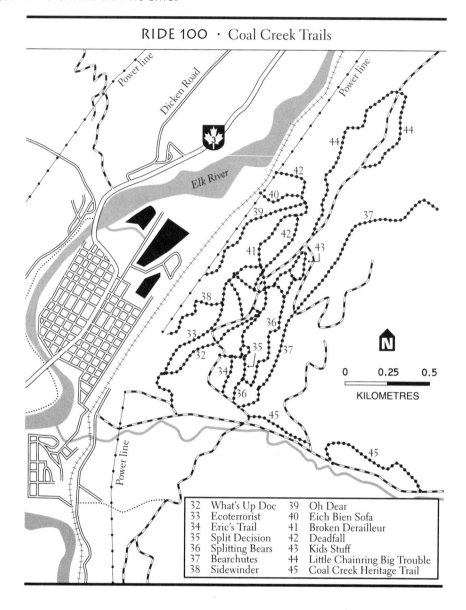

32	What's Up Doc	39	Oh Dear
33	Ecoterrorist	40	Eich Bien Sofa
34	Eric's Trail	41	Broken Derailleur
35	Split Decision	42	Deadfall
36	Splitting Bears	43	Kids Stuff
37	Bearchutes	44	Little Chainring Big Trouble
38	Sidewinder	45	Coal Creek Heritage Trail

Finding the trail: There are numerous access points for this network, but the main ones are along Coal Creek Road. In Fernie, head south on 5th Street and follow it until it ends at a T intersection with Park Avenue. Turn right onto Park Avenue, then left on 4th Street to cross the railway tracks. Over the tracks, head right on Pine Avenue, then left on Coal Creek Road. There are numerous access points along Coal Creek Road, but one of the main ones is the parking lot where River Road and Ridgemont Road cross Coal Creek Road, approximately 2.5 km (1.5 mi.) along Coal Creek Road. From this parking lot, trail options radiate out in both directions.

Sources of additional information: Contact the Fernie Information Centre at (250) 423-2811 or drop into Fernie Sports at 1191 7th Avenue, Fernie. You can reach Fernie Sports at (250) 423-3611.

Notes on the trail: It is difficult to describe this network. So many lines are possible that a particular route is difficult to single out. The introductory paragraph provides a few options, but the real secret is to grab a map, head out, and explore. Since the network is contained by the power line and railroad tracks on the west, simply make your way downhill to these features when you're ready to depart.

RIDE 101 · Hartley Pass

AT A GLANCE

Length/configuration: 17.72-km (10.63-mi.) out-and-back.

Aerobic difficulty: The trail climbs a steady 405 m (1,328 ft.) over 8.86 km (5.32 mi.).

Technical difficulty: It follows a wide road for its entire length.

Scenery: Some great views of Three Sisters and Mount Hosmer, and Hartley Lake is worth a quick side trip.

Special comments: Avoid weekends when this route can be busy with vehicles.

This is a great ride for those days when you simply want to get out and burn off some steam. The total distance for this out-and-back is 17.72 km (10.63 mi.). The climbing is steady, with few breaks, but as you gain elevation the views open up toward Three Sisters Mountain to the west and Mount Hosmer to the east. Along the way, a short side trip to Hartley Lake offers a pleasant diversion. Popular with fishermen, this tiny lake attracts many vehicles to this narrow road, so avoid this ride on busy weekends. From the pass, the return route is fast and furious.

General location: Fernie, British Columbia.

Elevation change: The trail climbs steadily from the trailhead at approximately 1,070 m (3,510 ft.) and to the pass at approximately 1,475 m (4,838 ft.).

Season: June to September.

Services: All services are available in the town of Fernie.

Hazards: Few hazards are found along this wide road. Be sure to share the road with vehicles.

Rescue index: If you can't find help from other riders or vehicles along this route, head back toward town, where plenty of help is available. If you have a cell signal, you can contact police at (250) 423-4321 or an ambulance at (800) 461-9911.

RIDE 101 · Hartley Pass

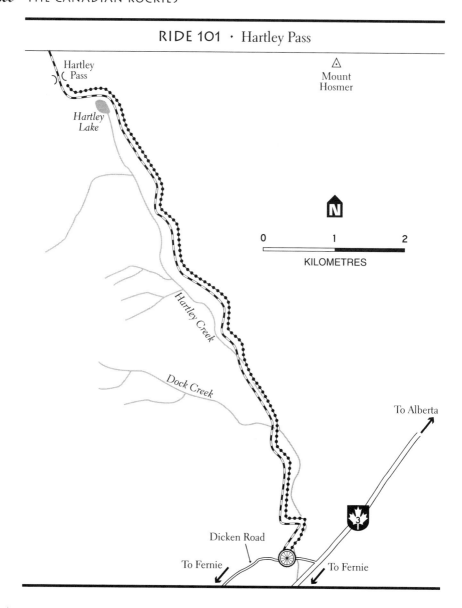

Land status: British Columbia Forest Service along with some private land.

Maps: The NTS 1:50,000 Series topographic map for this ride is 82 G/11 Fernie.

Finding the trail: As you approach Fernie, turn right at the Information Centre on Highway 3. Turn right again immediately onto Dicken Road. Follow this road for 3.7 km (2.22 mi.) and turn right onto Hartley Lake Road. This is the trailhead.

Sources of additional information: Contact the Fernie Information Centre at (250) 423-2811 or drop into Fernie Sports at 1191 7th Avenue, Fernie. You can reach Fernie Sports at (250) 423-3611.

Hartley Lake makes a pleasant diversion on the long climb toward Hartley Pass.

Notes on the trail: The trail begins climbing right away, staying right at a fork in the road at km 1.3 (0.78 mi.). The road crosses a bridge over Hartley Creek at km 3.7 (2.22 mi.), shortly before it reaches a passable washout at km 4.0 (2.4 mi.). The climbing then steepens until km 5.2 (3.12 mi.). Enjoy the level section, because the climbing begins again soon enough. As you roll along, there is a steep drop down to your left. The Mount Hosmer hiking trail heads off to the right at km 7.2 (4.32 mi.), while the main trail stays to the left. At km 8.2 (4.92 mi.), you get your first views of Hartley Lake down to your left; beyond this point, the road down to the lake forks to the left. You reach the actual pass at km 8.86 (5.32 mi.), after which the road begins to drop. Retrace your route, returning to the trailhead at km 17.72 (10.63 mi.).

RIDE 102 · Morrissey Ridge

AT A GLANCE

Length/configuration: 19.2-km (11.52-mi.) out-and-back.

Aerobic difficulty: Moderate challenge, with an elevation gain of 712 m (2,335 ft.) over 9.6 km (5.76 mi.).

Technical difficulty: The trail is wide, but route finding can be a challenge.

Scenery: Great views toward the valley of Coal Creek.

Special comments: Be sure to bring a good map.

Morrissey Ridge rises high above the Fernie Elk Basin, with the Elk River Valley and the Lizard Range to the west. This 19.2-km (11.52-mi.) out-and-back climbs from Coal Creek Road to a pair of communication towers on the top of the ridge. Beginning in the valley of Coal Creek, the road rises quickly, crossing a sharp side-cut with a steep drop to the right toward a tributary of Coal Creek. Numerous small waterfalls dot this creek and tumble their way toward Coal Creek—and eventually the Pacific Ocean. Farther along, the trail branches several times, allowing for many exploratory routes. While most of these routes are not shown on topographic maps, you can wander widely on this pleasant upland. The primary reason for heading up Morrissey Ridge, though, has to do with heading toward the communications towers on its western edge. To achieve this vantage point, carefully follow the directions in this trail description. When you are ready, retrace your path back towards the trailhead.

General location: Fernie, British Columbia.

Elevation change: The trail rises from the trailhead at 1,430 m (4,690 ft.) to the communications towers at 2,142 m (7,027 ft.).

Season: June to September.

Services: All services are available in the town of Fernie.

Hazards: While this is a wide route, it has numerous unmarked junctions, so be sure you have a good map and pay attention to the various junctions. The route on the NTS map, however, bears no resemblance to reality, so use the map in this book as a good example of current logging roads and junctions.

Rescue index: This route is quiet, so you may have to return toward Fernie for help. If you have a cell signal, you can contact police at (250) 423-4321 or an ambulance at (800) 461-9911.

Land status: British Columbia Forest Service.

Maps: The NTS 1:50,000 Series topographic map for this ride is 82 G/07 Flathead Ridge.

Finding the trail: In Fernie, follow Coal Creek Road, staying right at a fork at

RIDE 102 · Morrissey Ridge

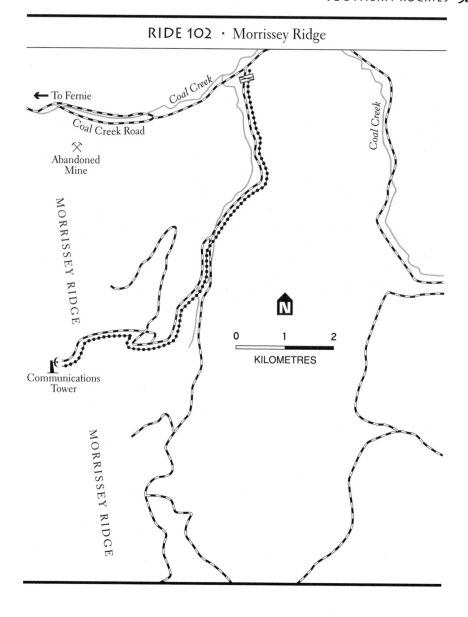

km 5.4 (3.24 mi.). Follow this wide gravel route, staying straight when roads fork to the right at km 7.7 (4.62 mi.). The junction is marked by two garages on the left, as a road heads to the right at a T intersection. A sign indicates Matheson Creek Road, while another sign says: "Microwave Station 8 km." Follow this wide road past a yellow gate.

Sources of additional information: Contact the Fernie Information Centre at (250) 423-2811 or drop into Fernie Sports at 1191 7th Avenue, Fernie. You can reach Fernie Sports at (250) 423-3611.

Notes on the trail: This wide road begins by traversing the deep valley of Coal Creek to the right. After km 1.4 (0.66 mi.), the road gets a bit rougher, but it still maintains its wide, rideable surface. The climbing is steady along this section, bringing you to a junction at km 3.9 (2.34 mi.). Stay right and almost immediately cross a bridge. By km 5.1 (3.06 mi.) the climbing moderates. Stay left as a road climbs sharply to the right; follow the road you're on as it makes a sharp switchback to the right at km 7.1 (4.26 mi.). Another rough road forks off to the left at km 7.46 (4.48 mi.). It is not marked in any way, so keep your eye out for it. The road ahead continues to serve as an active logging route. Take this left turn and begin the final climb toward the communications tower on Morrissey Ridge. Meet the towers at approximately km 9.6 (5.76 mi.). Retrace your route, finishing at km 19.2 (11.52 mi.).

CYPRESS HILLS PROVINCIAL PARK

Although not located in the Rockies, the Cypress Hills provide a little bit of the mountains nestled within the plains. In the extreme southeastern corner of Alberta, Cypress Hills Provincial Park is as unique in its landscape as in its history. Only one-fourth of this 2,590-square-kilometre (1,000-square-mile) area lies within Alberta, but development in this corridor provides excellent mountain biking opportunities.

The park contains a system of short but enjoyable trails. However, the trails need increased maintenance. Several are rapidly deteriorating, and their bridges are rotting. On the bright side, this park's unique landscape and remote character make it a wonderful place to explore.

Basic supplies are available locally. For repairs and biking supplies before heading to the park, you'll want to check in Medicine Hat, the nearest large centre. All the necessary services are available there. From this major centre, head south on Highway 41 for 65 km (40 mi.) to the town of Elkwater and Cypress Hills Provincial Park. Elkwater takes its name from the Blackfoot word *Ponokiokwe*, meaning "many deer congregating at the lake."

The Cypress Hills, as a highland amid endless plains, have the ability to attract inclement weather. As weather patterns climb to crest the hills, they cool down and drop their moisture as rain. The resulting wet weather is both a blessing and a curse. It allows for lush forest growth, but it can also mean muddy trails. The mountain biker should be prepared for sudden storms and should always carry rain gear.

What's so unique about the Cypress Hills? Their claim to fame is their status as a nunatak—a high point of land that remained unglaciated during the last Ice Age. With a maximum altitude of 1,466 m (4,810 ft.), they stand more than 600 m (2,000 ft.) above the surrounding prairies. During the last Ice Age the ice covered everything below 1,372 m (4,500 ft.). The highest points of the Cypress Hills rose above the ice like rocky islands. The remainder disappeared beneath the icy ocean.

Long before the glaciers appeared, this area was composed of a jumble of coarse gravel cemented together to form a rock called conglomerate. The Cypress Hills are an erosional remnant, towering high above the surrounding plains. Once more extensive than they are today, the majority of the deposit eroded away millions of years ago. Today, only the Cypress Hills remain.

Plant life here is incredibly diverse. With the park's upland character and increased precipitation, it supports a plethora of plant species. Many of the plants are more commonly found in the mountains, which are more than 320 km (200 mi.) to the west. This anomaly suggests that most of Alberta was forested in the period following glaciation. When the climate warmed, the plains traded in their forests for sparser grassland. The forests in the mountains—and in the Cypress Hills—maintained their forest cover, although separated by 200 mi. More than 669 different plants have been identified within the park.

The park also supports a diversity of wildlife. Fossils of 40-million-year-old mammals have been found in the area's rock layers. Over 40 different ancestral mammals have been unearthed, including several species of primitive rhinoceros—right here in Alberta! Just over 100 years ago, the area boasted grizzly bears, bison, and pronghorn. Today, the bison and the bears are gone, but the pronghorn remain. They are often seen on the grasslands in the south end of the park. Although raccoons are rare in the province, the park also supports a population of them, along with the ever-hungry porcupine—keep anything with sweat on it away from their sharp choppers. Porcupines seem to love the salt in sweat, and more than one pair of shoes or packstraps have formed a tasty meal for these critters. Other animals found in the park include mule, white-tailed deer, mink, Nuttall's cottontail, and snowshoe hare.

For bird-watchers, at least 207 different varieties of birds have been recorded in the park. Most breed in the uplands, some merely pass through, and others stick it out and remain through the cold winters. Some especially interesting representatives are the Audubon and MacGillivray's warblers and the Oregon junco; all of these are normally mountain residents. Trumpeter swans, back from the brink of extinction, also form a welcome sight within the park. And double-crested cormorants breed on an island in the middle of Cypress Lake. On my first night camping in the park, I was awakened at sunrise by an awful racket. As I looked out the entrance of my tent, I noticed a wild turkey circling my campsite. The bird kept me awake for about an hour until a family of ravens moved in to take over. Wild turkeys are around, but they're not often seen; keep your eyes and ears open.

The area's human history is equally diverse. For generations, the park was known by a variety of names. For the Blackfoot, the area was *Katewius Netumoo*, or "the Pine Hills." To the Crees, it was *Mun-a-tuh-gow*, or "the beautiful uplands." It took the coming of the white man to provide this site's the modern name. Fur trader Peter Fidler arrived in the early 1800s, and his French voyageurs called the site *Montagnes de Cyprès*, or "Cypress Hills." In reality, no cypress are in the Cypress Hills. These traders mistook lodgepole pine trees for cypress.

By the 1860s, Metis, displaced by increased settlement farther east, began to use the hills as a winter site. In 1872, a small band of Cree and Metis traveled south across the border and stole some horses from a group of American fur traders. The Americans came north and, in retaliation, massacred 30 Assiniboine Indians at Battle River on the Saskatchewan side of the hills. The slaughtered Indians, however, had no connection with the original raiding party. The Battle River Massacre hastened the formation of the Northwest Mounted Police, who arrived on the plains in 1874. The Cypress Hills then became a meeting place and a place of refuge. Even the mighty Sitting Bull, fresh from his victory over the 7th Cavalry at Little Bighorn, fled north and arrived in the hills in 1876. He spent several years in this area, protected from the Americans by the Canadian Mounties.

As time went on and more settlers arrived, the Indians were moved to reserves, and the land became prime ranching country. Some early ranches raised more than 25,000 head of cattle. Ranching is still one of the principal industries in the area, and you will encounter cattle while riding in the area.

For more information, contact:

Cypress Hills Provincial Park
P.O. Box 12
Elkwater, Alberta
T0J-1C0
(403) 893-3777

For campsite reservations, contact:

GRF Management
(403) 893-3782

RIDE 103 · Spruce Coulee Trail

AT A GLANCE

Length/configuration: 22.4-km (13.4-mi.) beginner loop.

Aerobic difficulty: Easy.

Technical difficulty: You'll encounter technical, rooted sections, along with a rough section of corduroy.

Scenery: Spruce Coulee Reservoir is a pretty upland pond.

Special comments: Don't forget to bring along a fishing rod.

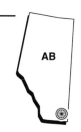

This pleasant 22.4-km (13.4-mi.) beginner loop includes 8.0 km (4.8 mi.) of trail riding, followed by a pleasant road route back to the trailhead. It's the longest trail in Cypress Hills Provincial Park and gives you a chance to see a little of the park's quieter areas. When I rode it, I saw no one else on the trail until I arrived at Spruce Coulee Reservoir, where a family was camping in one of the tent sites provided there.

The trail offers a combination of deep forest riding and pleasant road pedaling through ranch country. From the trailhead in a grassy meadow, the trail climbs over a small height with an eye-pleasing growth of wildflowers before it descends several times through some wet terrain. Keep your eyes open for moose as you travel through these wet areas. The combination of dry up-slope conditions with marshy lowlands makes this trail unique.

From the reservoir, a pleasant road ride returns you to the trailhead at km 22.4 (mi. 13.4).

General location: This trail is located just west of the town of Elkwater off Highway 41.

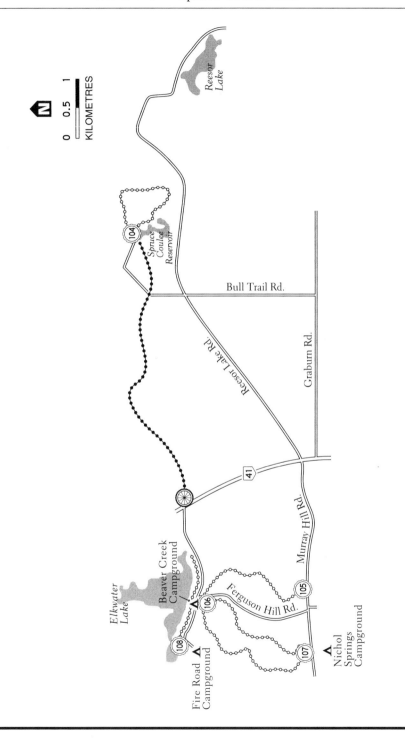

Elevation change: The trail exhibits little change in elevation. It begins at approximately 1,250 m (4,100 ft.) and rises 122 m (400 ft.) to Spruce Coulee Reservoir at 1,371 m (4,500 ft.).

Season: The trail dries up by early June and stays rideable into late September or early October.

Services: All services are available in Medicine Hat, 63 km (39 mi.) to the north. In Elkwater, basic camping supplies are available, along with an automobile service centre.

Hazards: Parts of the trail have a fine clay surface. Clay has a tendency to hold water and provide an almost frictionless surface. When I rode the trail, a downed aspen blocked the trail, so I had to dismount and climb over the deadfall. With a lack of regular maintenance, this could be a common danger. I found evidence of a porcupine at km 3.45 (mi. 2.1). It had badly chewed a plywood sign. Porcupines can make short work of gear left out—especially if it has sweat (full of yummy salt) on it. At certain points on the trail (some wet, rooted sections), the trail tends to grab the front wheel, possibly catapulting you out of the saddle. Be cautious. This trail is complicated by several unrideable corduroy bridges.

Rescue index: This trail crosses Bull Trail Road, where vehicles may be flagged down. If you don't see any traffic, head north toward the Spruce Coulee Campground, where campers or fishermen can often lend a hand.

Land status: The trail is within a provincial park and is managed by Alberta Environmental Protection.

Maps: Cypress Hills Provincial Park produces a trail map with simplified trail information and a local trail map. It is available at the Park Information Centre or by contacting the park at the address listed in the introduction to this section.

Finding the trail: Spruce Coulee trailhead is in a grass parking lot just south of the rodeo grounds. From Elkwater, head slightly south on Highway 41. Beyond the rodeo grounds, you'll see a sign that says, "No services for some distance," and another sign that indicates a trailhead to the left. Pull into the grassy parking lot; the trail is up the hill.

Sources of additional information: The Cypress Hills Provincial Park address is listed in the introduction to this section.

Notes on the trail: The trail begins with a short uphill. The soil is slippery when wet. At km 0.15 (mi. 0.1), you pass a marshy area where the aspen have been flooded out. Shortly after, at km 0.52 (mi. 0.31), you pass a fence, which may be closed. You pass another fence at km 0.8 (mi. 0.48), after which the trail follows the fence for a short distance. At km 1.0 (mi. 0.6), stay straight at a junction with the Highline Trail and follow a long uphill to km 1.36 (mi. 0.82). At km 1.5 (mi. 0.9), you meet another winter trail junction; go straight. Shortly after this junction, the trail becomes swampy for a short distance before climbing back above the valley bottom.

At km 2.38 (mi. 1.42), you pass a sign indicating a steep, winding downhill. Depending on weather conditions, the descent varies between muddy and dry single-track. At the base of the hill, at km 2.71 (mi. 1.63), the trail tends to get very muddy and rooty. Before long, it drops down into a marshy area and then rises up again. A bridge crossing at km 3.24 (mi. 1.94) shows that the park is starting to reduce impact on the trail system, but they still have a long way to go. At km 3.45 (mi. 2.07), ignore the porcupine-chewed "End of Trail" sign. This is a winter sign; in spring, summer, and autumn, the trail does continue.

After this sign, the quality of the trail improves, becoming a smooth single-track on a bed of pine needles. A short uphill at km 3.84 (mi. 2.3) is followed by a short, roller-coaster downhill. At km 4.53 (mi. 2.72), you'll meet another barbed-wire fence. Beyond the fence, a short climb to a grassy knoll at km 4.88 (mi. 2.93) gives you a panoramic view before you descend back into an aspen forest. By km 5.0 (mi. 3.0) the trail begins to deteriorate again, with muddy stretches. Be wary; it's easy to hit a root and flip over the handlebars. The trail is very technical along this stretch and will likely require some pushing. At km 5.4 (mi. 3.24), you pass a small corduroy bridge; I felt more comfortable pushing around it. A short climb is followed by a descent into a muddy slog. Two bridges bypass some of the mud, followed by another corduroy bridge. Go around the corduroy. After this wet stretch, the trail becomes rideable again.

At km 7.26 (mi. 4.36), the trail passes a fence and crosses Bull Trail Road. On the other side of the road, the trail continues through deep grass along an embankment that rises above some marshland. Soon the trail passes another barbed-wire fence with a V-shaped gate to allow passage. It's a tight squeeze, but a mountain bike fits around the corner. This is another stretch with poor drainage, a few hills, and two more corduroy bridges. At km 8.0 (mi. 4.8), the trail passes the first junction with the Lakeside Trail. Stay straight and at km 8.11 (mi. 4.9) you'll enter Spruce Coulee Campground.

From Spruce Coulee you can take the Streamside Trail and add to the final length of this loop an extra 5.39 km (3.23 mi.). To return to the starting point from Spruce Coulee Campground, follow Bull Trail Road as it leaves the reservoir. The road climbs from the lake to km 9.23 (mi. 5.53), where it levels off. At km 9.41 (mi. 5.64), the route passes a gravel road. Stay on the paved road to the left of the junction. After more climbing, the road passes the point where the trail originally crossed on its way to the campground. The pavement gives way to gravel at km 10.77 (mi. 6.46), but it intersects with Reesor Lake Road at km 13.16 (mi. 7.9). Turn right on this paved roadway. Follow Reesor Lake Road to its junction with Highway 41 at km 17.38 (mi. 10.43). Turn right on the highway and enjoy a final 5.0-km (3.0-mi.) downhill run to the trailhead.

RIDE 104 · Streamside Trail

AT A GLANCE

Length/configuration: 5.39-km (3.23-mi.) loop.

Aerobic difficulty: Easy, with little change in elevation.

Technical difficulty: Moderate, with muddy, rooted sections.

Scenery: This trail winds around the north and east shores of Spruce Coulee Reservoir.

Special comments: This trail can be linked with the Spruce Coulee Trail to make an extended 27.79-km (16.67-mi.) out-and-back.

AB

This 5.39-km (3.23-mi.) loop is perfect for advanced beginner riders looking for technical challenges. Highlights include wonderful views of Spruce Coulee Reservoir, along with views of several old beaver dams. Waterfowl are often on the lake, and the rolling terrain is wonderfully scenic. One grassy stretch provides prairie-riding at its best, and even the poorer stretches pass through some interesting wetlands.

The lake is a popular place for fishermen, and, more often than not, you'll see a few floating in inner tubes around the lake. Keep your eyes open for some of the plentiful bird life as you ride through varied terrain. The meadows are awash in wildflowers during July and August, and even the wetlands have wildflowers, such as water smartweed, blooming.

General location: The trail is just east of Elkwater at the northeast end of Bull Trail Road.

Elevation change: Beginning at the lakeshore, at approximately 1,372 m (4,500 ft.), the trail climbs about 30 m (100 ft.) to its high point on the grassy meadow before descending back to lake level.

Season: The trail is rideable from June to early October.

Services: All services are available in Medicine Hat, 63 km (39 mi.) to the north. In Elkwater, basic camping supplies are available, along with an automobile service centre.

Hazards: This trail has some wet, rooty stretches that are a natural for handlebar leaps. Several bridges are in poor condition and should be crossed only with extreme caution. Also, for some reason, beyond the lake a few signposts have been made of sharp, barbed metal—don't ride too close to them.

Rescue index: This trail begins and ends at Spruce Coulee Campground. If you don't have a vehicle at the trailhead, someone at the campground may be able to get you to town, where you can get further assistance. While riding along the reservoir, you may meet hikers or fishermen, but the rest of the trail, although short, is not heavily traveled.

Land status: The trail is within a provincial park and is managed by Alberta Environmental Protection.

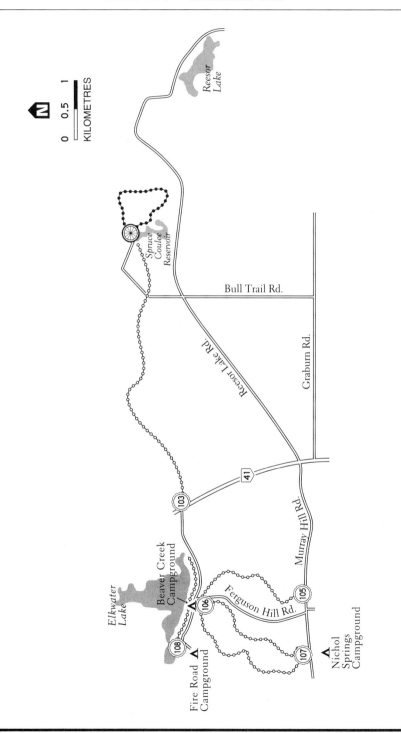

Maps: Cypress Hills Provincial Park produces a trail map that provides simplified trail information. It is available at the Park Information Centre or by contacting the park at the address listed in the introduction to this section.

Finding the trail: From Elkwater, head south on Highway 41 to its junction with Reesor Lake Road. Turn left, then left again, at Bull Trail Road. Follow the road to the Spruce Coulee Reservoir. The trail crosses the dam and climbs above the lake on the far side.

Sources of additional information: The Cypress Hills Provincial Park address is listed in the introduction to this section.

Notes on the trail: Beginning at the campground, cross the reservoir and begin climbing the hillside on the opposite side. At first a wide double-track, the trail provides pleasing views of the reservoir below. The first kilometre (0.6 mi.) takes you toward the far end of the reservoir, past a marshy inlet at the southeast end. The trail then follows the stream that flows into the lake, however, the trail doesn't cross it right away—it's tempting to cross, but follow the water source. At km 1.22 (mi. 0.73), the trail turns right and bypasses the stream. This brief jog is followed by a short uphill push. The trail now becomes a narrow single-track. At km 1.9 (mi. 1.15), the trail passes the beaver dam responsible for some of the surrounding wetland and continues on good, grassy track. When crossing the dam area, be aware that the bridge has fallen apart and use caution when crossing the rickety remains.

From the bridge, or what remains of it, the trail climbs a grassy hillside where there is a slight rutting problem. The route then heads into an aspen forest for a stretch of pleasant, rolling terrain. After a technical descent back toward the beaver dam, the trail crosses a simple bridge made of two logs sliced in half lengthwise. After the bridge, the trail becomes technical, but still pleasant. By km 3.6 (mi. 2.16), the trail turns back on itself, and a short, steep push ensues. Some old steps, long since disintegrated, make the pushing more difficult. Ironically, now that the trail is at its worst, an excellent bridge appears at km 4.0 (mi. 2.4), followed by another at km 4.24 (mi. 2.5). With the newfound confidence that you've gained in the crossings, a bridge at km 4.57 (mi. 2.74) seems rideable, but avoid the temptation. I tried it, and it collapsed under me, so I ended up pushing over it. The trail continues to deteriorate. Although it is a pleasant ride, this trail is in need of heavy repair and maintenance. Km 5.39 (mi. 3.23) brings you back onto the road near the campsite.

RIDE 105 · Mitchell Trail

AT A GLANCE

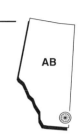

Length/configuration: 2.73-km (1.64-mi.) point-to-point, or make a 7.05-km (4.23-mi.) loop, using Ferguson Hill Road.

Aerobic difficulty: Easy.

Technical difficulty: The trail has a tendency to hold water and can become a rough runoff channel during rain storms.

Scenery: The trail remains in the trees.

Special comments: This ride can be linked with other Cypress Hills trails to extend its length and duration.

This expert-level trail can be cycled as a point-to-point or as a 7.05-km (4.23-mi.) loop, using Ferguson Hill Road. It is a great trail for riders who like a challenging downhill ride with a touch of danger thrown in. The trail drops steadily and steeply, and it includes some sections badly washed out from the floods of 1995.

Partway down the hill, there is a nice view of Elkwater Lake in the distance; the trail then passes through a pleasant mix of aspen and lodgepole pine. Don't spend too much time looking around, though, as you'll need all your concentration for the technical sections. Strap on your helmet and have fun.

General location: Mitchell Trail lies south of Elkwater Lake and east of Ferguson Hill Road.

Elevation change: From the town of Elkwater, at 1,219 m (4,000 ft.), the climb is along Ferguson Hill Road, with an ascent of 213 m (700 ft.) in 3.39 km (2.0 mi.).

Season: The trail is rideable from June to early October.

Services: All services are available in Medicine Hat, 63 km (39 mi.) to the north. In Elkwater, basic camping supplies are available, along with an automobile service centre.

Hazards: This trail tends to become a runoff channel in wet weather. When I rode it, it was literally a stream. The steep stretches are rocky and badly eroded, with sharp corners. I recommend walking these stretches.

Rescue index: This steep trail runs between Elkwater Campground and Murray Hill Road. It's easy to find assistance at the campground. If Murray Hill Road has little traffic, descend Ferguson Hill.

Land status: The trail is within a provincial park and is managed by Alberta Environmental Protection.

Maps: Cypress Hills Provincial Park produces a trail map that provides simplified trail information. It is available at the Park Information Centre or by contacting the park at the address listed in the introduction to this section.

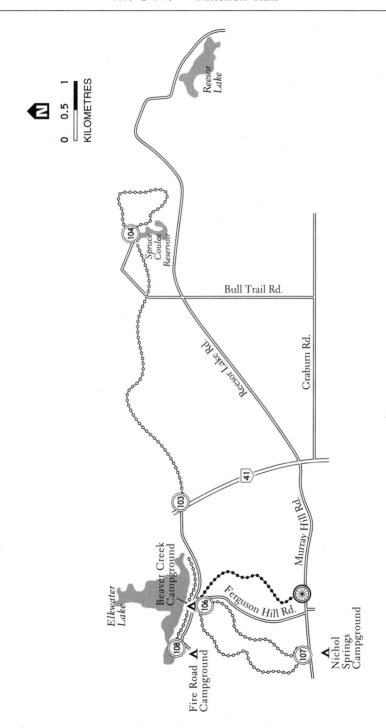

Finding the trail: The trail is easy to find. Ferguson Hill Road climbs from the main park access road. As you climb the road, you will want to keep your eyes open on the left for the access route to the Mitchell Trail. If you miss this access point, another means of access is found along Murray Hill Road.

Sources of additional information: The Cypress Hills Provincial Park address is listed in the introduction to this section.

Notes on the trail: Follow Ferguson Hill Road uphill for 3.39 km (2.0 mi.) to the signed junction for Mitchell Trail. Head left at this junction and left again at km 4.32 (mi. 2.6). At km 4.9 (mi. 2.9), a log bridge on the trail can be bypassed. The trail is a high-quality single-track, and at km 5.2 (mi. 3.1) it passes two bridges in succession. At km 6.7 (mi. 4.0), it drops steeply, which may require some walking due to a sharp corner at the bottom. The trail also has a tendency to become a runoff channel during heavy rainfall, so it can be dangerous when wet. Take a left turn at the junction at km 6.5 (mi. 3.9). The trail levels out at the campground at km 7.05 (mi. 4.23).

RIDE 106 · Beaver Creek–Nichol Springs Campground Trail

AT A GLANCE

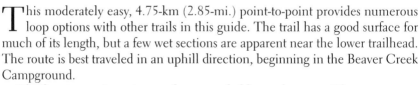

Length/configuration: 4.75-km (2.85-mi.) point-to-point.

Aerobic difficulty: Moderate 213-m (700-ft.) climb.

Technical difficulty: The trail is wide and smooth. However, one of the bridges was damaged, and numerous trees had fallen across the trail.

Scenery: The trail stays in the trees.

Special comments: This trail can be linked with Horseshoe Canyon to make a great 10.25-km (6.15-mi.) loop.

This moderately easy, 4.75-km (2.85-mi.) point-to-point provides numerous loop options with other trails in this guide. The trail has a good surface for much of its length, but a few wet sections are apparent near the lower trailhead. The route is best traveled in an uphill direction, beginning in the Beaver Creek Campground.

The forest cover is a mixture of aspen and old-growth spruce. The spruce trees are covered with a stringlike lichen known as old man's beard. The trail also takes you past some beaver ponds that provide a great opportunity to see this industrious animal, along with other wetland residents.

General location: The trail lies south of Elkwater Lake and west of Ferguson Hill Road.

Elevation change: From the campground, at 1,219 m (4,000 ft.), the trail rises 213 m (700 ft.).

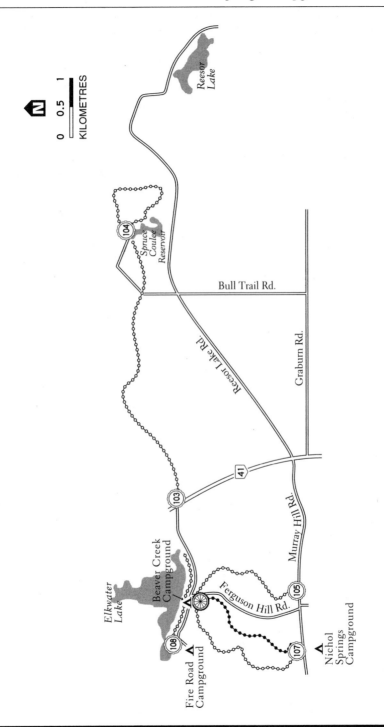

Season: The trail is rideable from June to early October.

Services: All services are available in Medicine Hat, 63 km (39 mi.) to the north. In Elkwater, basic camping supplies are available, along with an automobile service centre.

Hazards: Hazards are limited. One of the bridges has experienced some erosion on one side, leaving it tenuously attached to the bank. It will likely get worse over time if not repaired. Several trees were also down along the trail, so keep your eyes open for obstacles. Since the trail progresses steadily uphill, you won't have many opportunities to pick up speed, so the trail allows plenty of time to avoid obstacles.

Rescue index: This popular trail sees a lot of walking traffic, since it provides a link between Nichol Springs and Beaver Creek campgrounds. You should have no problem finding help should the need arise.

Land status: The trail is within a provincial park and is managed by Alberta Environmental Protection.

Maps: Cypress Hills Provincial Park produces a trail map that provides simplified trail information. It is available at the Park Information Centre or by contacting the park at the address listed in the introduction to this section.

Finding the trail: The trailhead is in the Beaver Creek Campground, just beyond the town of Elkwater. It begins on the main campground road and continues beyond the road's end.

Sources of additional information: The Cypress Hills Provincial Park address is listed in the introduction to this section.

Notes on the trail: The trail begins as a potentially muddy single-track. At km 0.42 (mi. 0.25), a sign indicates that this trail is also known as the Nichol Springs Campground Trail. A short loop option takes off to the right. Stay straight. At km 0.55 (mi. 0.33), the trail dries up and becomes a pleasant single-track. The trail rises above a small beaver pond at km 0.79 (mi. 0.47); after this point, you'll notice evidence of where beavers have chewed on some of the trees. The trail then becomes a tricky, rooty, but rideable climb. Keep your speed up to make it over the roots. At km 1.39 (mi. 0.83), the trail crosses two bridges made of 4-by-6-inch planks. Shortly after the bridges, you'll encounter the first potential push of the trail. If you hit it with a bit of speed, it is rideable.

You'll cross another wooden bridge at km 1.97 (mi. 1.2) as the trail passes through an old-growth spruce forest. You'll cross more bridges at km 2.29 (mi. 1.37), 2.39 (mi. 1.43), and 2.66 (mi. 1.6). Shortly after the last bridge, the trail was obstructed by two downed trees, making for a tight squeeze to get my bike through. This debris may have been cleared, as this is a main trail. Next, the trail crosses a meadow at km 3.13 (mi. 1.9), branches numerous times, and then joins up again at the opposite side of the meadow. It doesn't matter which branch you take since they all seem to join up again. The trail after the meadow, in wet weather, requires a short, mucky push, followed by a good bridge at km 3.61 (mi. 2.2). Another steep uphill stretch at km 3.9 (mi. 2.34) may require pushing in wet weather. The hill also has some deep rutting, which makes riding difficult. From the top of the hills, the trail widens. A gate at km 4.39 (mi. 2.6) takes you past a barbed-wire fence to the Nichol Springs Campground. Continue on, and at km 4.75 (mi. 2.85) you have the option of returning via the access road or turning right and taking the Horseshoe Canyon Trail to create a loop.

RIDE 107 · Horseshoe Canyon Trail

AT A GLANCE

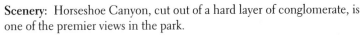

Length/configuration: 5.67-km (3.42-mi.) point-to-point or make a 10.25-km (6.15-mi.) loop with Beaver Creek Trail.

Aerobic difficulty: If done in the recommended downhill direction, this trail is rated easy.

Technical difficulty: Watch for a barbed-wire fence after the main canyon viewpoint, and be sure to keep your speed under control.

Scenery: Horseshoe Canyon, cut out of a hard layer of conglomerate, is one of the premier views in the park.

Special comments: A great location for flowers like lupine and locoweed.

If you ride only one trail in the Cypress Hills, make this the one. It's an easy point-to-point that can be linked with the Beaver Creek Trail to make a 10.25-km (6.15-mi.) loop.

You'll reach the canyon viewpoint almost immediately, and the view is spectacular. Here the resistant conglomerate that makes up the heights of the Cypress Hills has been eroded, forming a steep drop with views all the way to Elkwater Lake.

As you ride through the high country of the Cypress Hills, wildflowers are everywhere. The blue of lupine and the yellow of the locoweed predominate, but an endless variety awaits the curious rider who takes the time to look.

General location: The trail lies south of Elkwater Lake and west of Ferguson Hill Road.

Elevation change: The trail begins at approximately 1,430 m (4,700 ft.) and drops to Beaver Creek Campground at 1,219 m (4,000 ft.).

Season: The trail is rideable from June to early October.

Services: All services are available in Medicine Hat, 63 km (39 mi.) to the north. In Elkwater, basic camping supplies are available, along with an automobile service centre.

Hazards: Shortly after the canyon viewpoint, you'll need to lift your bike over a barbed-wire fence, as the V-shaped gate is too narrow to push a bike through. Be cautious of the sharp barbs.

Other than this minor hazard, the trail is primarily downhill, so it is natural to pick up speed, especially since most of the downhill is wide double-track. Beware of hidden obstacles and mule deer along this trail.

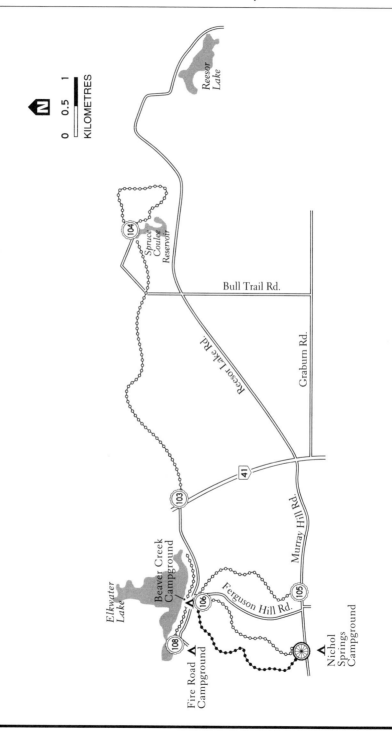

Reesor Lake

KILOMETRES

0   0.5   1

Spruce Coulee Reservoir

104

Bull Trail Rd.

Reesor Lake Rd.

Graburn Rd.

41

103

Murray Hill Rd.

Beaver Creek Campground

Elkwater Lake

Ferguson Hill Rd.

106

105

108

Fire Road Campground

Nichol Springs Campground

Rescue index: This trail takes you to one of the best viewpoints in the park, so it sees a lot of hiking traffic. If you encounter no other hikers or bikers, you'll most likely find assistance at the campgrounds at either end of the trail.

Land status: The trail is within a provincial park and is managed by Alberta Environmental Protection.

Maps: Cypress Hills Provincial Park produces a trail map that provides simplified trail information. It is available at the Park Information Centre or by contacting the park at the address listed in the introduction to this section.

Finding the trail: Follow Ferguson Hill Road to its junction with Murray Hill Road and turn right. The trailhead is in the Nichol Springs Campground.

Sources of additional information: The Cypress Hills Provincial Park address is listed in the introduction to this section.

Notes on the trail: From the Nichol Springs Campground, follow the 1-km (0.6-mi.) access trail that takes you to Horseshoe Canyon Trail. Along this route, at km 0.26 (mi. 0.15), the trail levels off into a wide single-track. Follow the signs at an intersection at km 1.12 (mi. 0.7). The trail heads across a wide, open, grassy knoll. At km 1.3 (mi. 0.78), you arrive at Horseshoe Canyon. From here, you'll need to lift your bike over a barbed-wire fence, as the V-shaped gate is too narrow to squeeze a bike through. At km 1.43 (mi. 0.9), the trail continues across a field of lupine and locoweed. The trail beyond the fence is double-track, an old road followed by a wonderful downhill run until km 3.43 (mi. 2.06). The downhill temporarily ends with the trail climbing a knoll to km 4.32 (mi. 2.6). From the knoll, it's downhill all the way to the junction at km 5.08 (mi. 3.05). A sign there indicates the Firerock Trail access to the left; go straight. The trail ends in the campground at km 5.67 (mi. 3.42).

RIDE 108 · Shoreline Trail

AT A GLANCE

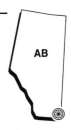

Length/configuration: 4-km (2.4-mi.) out-and-back.

Aerobic difficulty: Easy.

Technical difficulty: Easy along this flat, paved track.

Scenery: The trail traverses Elkwater Lake, with lots of potential photo sites.

Special comments: Bring along your binoculars and your bird book.

AB

This ride is flat, paved, and pleasant. It varies in length depending on the stretch you choose to ride. Generally, it averages approximately 4.0 km (2.4 mi.) as an out-and-back. Following the lake shore past numerous marshy bays, the route is alive with birds, and it provides excellent views across Elkwater Lake.

General location: This trail lies along the shores of Elkwater Lake in the town of Elkwater.

Elevation change: Virtually none.

Season: The trail is rideable from early May to mid-October.

Services: All services are available in Medicine Hat, 63 km (39 mi.) to the north. In Elkwater, basic camping supplies are available, along with an automobile service centre.

Hazards: Riders are the main hazard on this trail. Since this trail is a pedestrian walkway, you need to be courteous to people on foot.

Rescue index: Since this very urban trail parallels the main park road, assistance is available along its entire length.

Land status: The trail is within a provincial park and is managed by Alberta Environmental Protection.

Maps: Cypress Hills Provincial Park produces a trail map that provides simplified trail information. It is available at the Park Information Centre or by contacting the park at the address listed in the introduction to this section.

Finding the trail: Drive to the town of Elkwater. As you approach the lake, you'll see numerous access points to the shoreline trail. The main boat launch provides an ideal place to park.

Sources of additional information: The Cypress Hills Provincial Park address is listed in the introduction to this section.

Notes on the trail: This trail needs to provide little information along the route, as it is all paved with boardwalks over marshy sections. It also has several access points. I began at the boat launch and headed west.

From the launch, the trail follows a nice boardwalk as it goes through a wetland along the shoreline. At km 0.61 (mi. 0.37), the boardwalk ends, but the pavement continues. To your left, some of the homes of Elkwater are visible, and the lake is to your right. The homes end soon, and the trail becomes slightly more rustic. You pass some public washrooms at km 1.18 (mi. 0.71), followed by more boardwalks. For a short while, the trail leaves the road and stays close to the lake. The trail ends at Firerock Campground at km 1.98 (mi. 1.2).

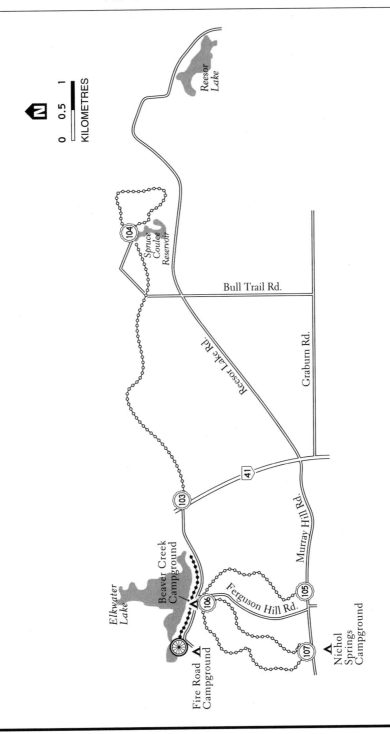

APPENDIX: METRIC CONVERSION

Though many of Canada's metric signs and measures include handy conversions for the visiting Yank, it's not something you want to count on—especially out on the trail, where missing a turn can cost you hours of backtracking.

All measurements in this book include both metric and standard values, but just in case, here's a few general conversion tips, plus some examples.

Kilometres and Miles

1 kilometre = 0.62 mile (or about two-thirds of a mile). To convert kilometres to miles, you can approximate by multiplying total kilometres by 0.6. To go back the other way and get kilometres, multiply total miles by 1.6.

Kilometres	Miles
1	0.62
2	1.24
5	3.1
10	6.2
15	9.3
20	12.4

Metres, Yards, and Feet
1 metre = 1.09 yards = 3.28 feet.

Metres	Yards	Feet
1	1.09	3.28
10	10.9	32.8
100	109	328
500	546	1,640
1,000 (1 km)	1,093	3,280

Temperature: Celsius and Fahrenheit

This is the tricky one. Strictly speaking, degrees Celsius = (degrees Fahrenheit minus 32) multiplied by 5/9. However, unless you have a slide rule in your brain, don't stake your comfort level on your math skills. Below is a handy chart that will let the nonmetrically inclined figure out Celsius weather forecasts.

°Celsius	°Fahrenheit
40	104
35	95
30	86
25	77
20	68
15	59
10	50
5	41
0 (freezing)	32 (freezing)

GLOSSARY

This short list of terms does not contain all the words used by mountain bike enthusiasts when discussing their sport. But it should serve as an introduction to the lingo you'll hear on the trails.

ATB	all-terrain bike; this, like "fat-tire bike," is another name for a mountain bike
ATV	all-terrain vehicle; this usually refers to the loud, fume-spewing three- or four-wheeled motorized vehicles you will not enjoy meeting on the trail—except, of course, if you crash and have to hitch a ride out on one
blaze	a mark on a tree made by chipping away a piece of the bark, usually done to designate a trail; such trails are sometimes described as "blazed"
blind corner	a curve in the road or trail that conceals bikers, hikers, equestrians, and other traffic
blowdown	see "windfall"
bollard	a post (or series of posts) set vertically into the ground which allow pedestrians or cyclists to pass but keep vehicles from entering (wooden bollards are also commonly used to sign intersections)
braided	a braided trail condition results when people attempt to travel around a wet area; networks of interlaced trails can result and are a maintenance headache for trail crews
buffed	used to describe a very smooth trail
Carsonite sign	a small, thin, and flexible fiberglass signpost used to mark roads and trails (often dark brown in color)

catching air	taking a jump in such a way that both wheels of the bike are off the ground at the same time
cattle guard	a grate of parallel steel bars or pipes set at ground level and suspended over a ditch; cows can't cross them (their little feet slip through the openings between the pipes), but pedestrians and vehicles can pass over cattle guards with little difficulty
clean	while this may describe what you and your bike won't be after following many trails, the term is most often used as a verb to denote the action of pedaling a tough section of trail successfully
combination	this type of route may combine two or more configurations; for example, a point-to-point route may integrate a scenic loop or an out-and-back spur midway through the ride; likewise, an out-and-back may have a loop at its farthest point (this configuration looks like a cherry with a stem attached; the stem is the out-and-back, the fruit is the terminus loop); or a loop route may have multiple out-and-back spurs and/or loops to the side; distance for a combination route is for the total distance to complete the ride
cupped	a concave trail; higher on the sides than in the middle; often caused by motorcycles
dab	touching the ground with a foot or hand
deadfall	a tangled mass of fallen trees or branches
decomposed granite	an excellent, fine- to medium-grain, trail and road surface; typically used in native surface road and trail applications (not trucked in); results from the weathering of granite
diversion ditch	a usually narrow, shallow ditch dug across or around a trail; funneling the water in this manner keeps it from destroying the trail
double-track	the dual tracks made by a jeep or other vehicle, with grass, weeds, or rocks between; mountain bikers can ride in either of the tracks, but you will find that whichever one you choose, no matter how many times you change back and forth, the other track will appear to offer smoother travel
dugway	a steep, unpaved, switchbacked descent
endo	flipping end over end
feathering	using a light touch on the brake lever, hitting it lightly many times rather than very hard or locking the brake

four-wheel-drive	this refers to any vehicle with drive-wheel capability on all four wheels (a jeep, for instance, has four-wheel drive as compared with a two-wheel-drive passenger car), or to a rough road or trail that requires four-wheel-drive capability (or a one-wheel-drive mountain bike!) to negotiate it
game trail	the usually narrow trail made by deer, elk, or other game
gated	everyone knows what a gate is, and how many variations exist upon this theme; well, if a trail is described as "gated" it simply has a gate across it; don't forget that the rule is if you find a gate closed, close it behind you; if you find one open, leave it that way
Giardia	shorthand for *Giardia lamblia*, and known as the "backpacker's bane" until we mountain bikers expropriated it; this is a waterborne parasite that begins its life cycle when swallowed, and one to four weeks later has its host (you) bloated, vomiting, shivering with chills, and living in the bathroom; the disease can be avoided by "treating" (purifying) the water you acquire along the trail (see "Hitting the Trail" in the Introduction)
gnarly	a term thankfully used less and less these days, it refers to tough trails
graded	refers to a dirt road that has been smoothed out by the use of a wide blade on earth-moving equipment; "blading" gets rid of the teeth-chattering, much-cursed washboards found on so many dirt roads after heavy vehicle use
hammer	to ride very hard
hammerhead	one who rides hard and fast
hardpack	a trail in which the dirt surface is packed down hard; such trails make for good and fast riding, and very painful landings; bikers most often use "hardpack" as both a noun and adjective, and "hard-packed" as an adjective only (the grammar lesson will help you when diagramming sentences in camp)
hike-a-bike	what you do when the road or trail becomes too steep or rough to remain in the saddle
jeep road, jeep trail	a rough road or trail passable only with four-wheel-drive capability (or a horse or mountain bike)
kamikaze	while this once referred primarily to those Japanese fliers who quaffed a glass of sake, then flew off as human bombs

in suicide missions against U.S. naval vessels, it has more recently been applied to the idiot mountain bikers who, far less honorably, scream down hiking trails, endangering the physical and mental safety of the walking, biking, and equestrian traffic they meet; deck guns were necessary to stop the Japanese kamikaze pilots, but a bike pump or walking staff in the spokes is sufficient for the current-day kamikazes who threaten to get us all kicked off the trails

loop	this route configuration is characterized by riding from the designated trailhead to a distant point, then returning to the trailhead via a different route (or simply continuing on the same in a circle route) without doubling back; you always move forward across new terrain but return to the starting point when finished; distance is for the entire loop from the trailhead back to trailhead
multi-purpose	a designation of land which is open to many uses; mountain biking is allowed
off-camber	a trail that slopes in the opposite direction than one would prefer for safety's sake; for example, on a side-cut trail the slope is away from the hill—the inside of the trail is higher, so it helps you fall downhill if your balance isn't perfect
ORV/OHV	a motorized off-road vehicle (off-highway vehicle)
out-and-back	a ride where you will return on the same trail you pedaled out; while this might sound far more boring than a loop route, many trails look very different when pedaled in the opposite direction
pack stock	horses, mules, llamas, etc., carrying provisions along trails
point-to-point	a vehicle shuttle (or similar assistance) is required for this type of route, which is ridden from the designated trailhead to a distant location, or endpoint, where the route ends; total distance is for the one-way trip from the trailhead to endpoint
portage	to carry your bike on your person
pummy	soil with high pumice content produced by volcanic activity in the Pacific Northwest and elsewhere; light in consistency and easily pedaled; trails with such soil often become thick with dust
quads	bikers use this term to refer both to the extensor muscle in the front of the thigh (which is separated into four parts) and to maps; the expression "Nice quads!" refers always to

the former, however, except in those instances when the speaker is an engineer

runoff rainwater or snowmelt

scree an accumulation of loose stones or rocky debris lying on a slope or at the base of a hill or cliff

side-cut trail a trail cut on the side of a hill

signed a "signed" trail has signs in place of blazes

single-track a single, narrow path through grass or brush or over rocky terrain, often created by deer, elk, or backpackers; single-track riding is some of the best fun around

skid road the path created when loggers drag trees through the forest with heavy equipment

slickrock the rock-hard, compacted sandstone that is great to ride and even prettier to look at; you'll appreciate it even more if you think of it as a petrified sand dune or seabed (which it is), and if the rider before you hasn't left tire marks (from unnecessary skidding) or granola bar wrappers behind

snowmelt runoff produced by the melting of snow

snowpack unmelted snow accumulated over weeks or months of winter—or over years—in high-mountain terrain

spur a road or trail that intersects the main trail you're following

squid one who skids

stair-step climb a climb punctuated by a series of level or near-level sections

switchback a zigzagging road or trail designed to assist in traversing steep terrain; mountain bikers should not skid through switchbacks

talus the rocky debris at the base of a cliff, or a slope formed by an accumulation of this rocky debris

tank trap a steep-sided ditch (or series of ditches) used to block access to a road or trail; often used in conjunction with high mounds of excavated material

technical terrain that is difficult to ride due not to its grade (steepness) but to its obstacles—rocks, roots, logs, ledges, loose soil . . .

topo short for topographical map, the kind that shows both linear distance and elevation gain and loss; "topo" is pronounced with both vowels long

trashed	a trail that has been destroyed (same term used no matter what has destroyed it . . . cattle, horses, or even mountain bikers riding when the ground was too wet)
two-track	see "double-track"
two-wheel-drive	this refers to any vehicle with drive-wheel capability on only two wheels (a passenger car, for instance, has two-wheel drive); a two-wheel-drive road is a road or trail easily traveled by an ordinary car
waterbar	an earth, rock, or wooden structure that funnels water off trails to reduce erosion
washboarded	a road that is surfaced with many ridges spaced closely together, like the ripples on a washboard; these make for very rough riding, and even worse driving in a car or jeep
whoop-de-doo	closely spaced dips or undulations in a trail; these are often encountered in areas traveled heavily by ORVs
wilderness area	land that is officially set aside by the government to remain natural—pure, pristine, and untrammeled by any vehicle, including mountain bikes
windchill	a reference to the wind's cooling effect upon exposed flesh; for example, if the temperature is minus 12 degrees Celsius and the wind is blowing at 32 kilometres per hour, the windchill (that is, the actual temperature to which your skin reacts) is minus 36 degrees; if you are riding in wet conditions things are even worse, for the windchill would then be minus 59 degrees!
windfall	anything (trees, limbs, brush, fellow bikers . . .) blown down by the wind

INDEX

Ward Cameron has worked as a naturalist and information officer throughout the Canadian Rockies. For many years he has brought the natural and human history of the Rockies to life through a combination of speaking programs, interpretive and tour guide service, writing, and photography. This is the second of three books he has authored. His first book, A Kananaskis SuperGuide, provides an overall look at the Kananaskis, an area described in detail in this book. His third book, A Natural History of the Canadian Rockies, is scheduled for release in the spring of 2000.

Mountain biking is a way of life in the Rockies. As a photographer, Ward uses his mountain bike to cover significant distances in a single day. Mountain biking also provides a wonderful way to see a bit of the vast wilderness that makes up the Rockies. This book is a natural extension of Ward's enjoyment of this rapidly growing sport.